Unresolved Grief

This book is dedicated to Joy

Unresolved Grief

A practical, multicultural approach for
health professionals

John C. Gunzburg

CHAPMAN & HALL
London · Glasgow · New York · Tokyo · Melbourne · Madras

Published by Chapman & Hall, 2–6 Boundary Row, London SE1 8HN

Chapman & Hall, 2–6 Boundary Row, London SE1 8HN, UK

Blackie Academic & Professional, Wester Cleddens Road, Bishopbriggs, Glasgow G64 2NZ, UK

Chapman & Hall Inc., 29 West 35th Street, New York NY10001, USA

Chapman & Hall Japan, Thomson Publishing Japan, Hirakawacho Nemoto Building, 6F, 1-7-11 Hirakawa-cho, Chiyoda-ku, Tokyo 102, Japan

Chapman & Hall Australia, Thomas Nelson Australia, 102 Dodds Street, South Melbourne, Victoria 3205, Australia

Chapman & Hall India, R. Seshadri, 32 Second Main Road, CIT East, Madras 600 035, India

Distributed in the USA and Canada by Singular Publishing Group Inc., 4284 41st Street, San Diego, California 92105

First edition 1993

© 1993 John C. Gunzburg

Typeset in Palatino by Best-set Typesetter Ltd., Hong Kong
Printed in Great Britain by the University Press, Cambridge

ISBN 0 412 49080 3   1 56593 198 X (USA)

A catalogue record for this book is available from the British Library

Library of Congress Cataloging-in-Publication data
Gunzburg, John C.
    Unreserved grief : a practical, multicultural approach for health professionals / John C. Gunzburg.—1st ed.
        p.   cm.
    Includes index.
    ISBN 0-412-49080-3 (alk. paper)
    1. Grief therapy—Case studies.   I. Title.
    [DNLM: 1. Grief—case studies.   2. Counseling—case studies.   BF
575.G7   G977u   1993]
RC455.4.L67G86   1993
155.9′37—dc20
DNLM/DLC
for Library of Congress   93-6912
                                                                        CIP

Contents

'The out-of-focus, the ugly, is very much a part of life, and an honest artist must work both the ugly and the beautiful.'

Felix Werder: More than music,
Council of Adult Education, Melbourne, 1991

Foreword

I was sixteen when my father died. He suffered from Alzheimer's disease and had spent the last six months of his life in a mental hospital, during which time I didn't see him. On the morning of my father's funeral the family doctor offered me a valium tablet to 'help me cope'.

Valium tablets were not likely to help me, or the other members of my family, to cope. What we needed was a family doctor like Dr John Gunzburg, someone who understood the importance of grief, someone whose methods of helping were psychological rather than pharmaceutical, someone who knew about families.

John Gunzburg was for sixteen years a family doctor in the state of Victoria, Australia. Such was his interest in how his patients struggled to resolve their difficulties that he trained as a psychotherapist and family therapist and now practises in this capacity full time. *Unresolved Grief* is his second book. In it he presents a compelling series of case studies, the stories of how he and his clients have worked together to resolve their problems. He convincingly demonstrates how unresolved grief is a major theme in the lives of people who seek the help of doctors, counsellors and therapists. As Dr Gunzburg says, grief is not confined to that which follows loss through death, as in my own case, but every kind of loss. Such losses include: loss of relationships through separation and divorce; the loss of nurturing during childhood, often compounded with betrayal through abuse; the loss, through disability or chemical abuse, of the person we once were, or whom we hoped to become. Grief, too, may be expressed in a variety of ways, notably, anger, denial, depression and emptiness.

In this handbook, John Gunzburg presents an eminently practical approach to working with unresolved grief. His approach is fundamentally client-centred – his concern is to understand how clients are feeling and thinking about their problems and the context in which those problems arose. Dr Gunzburg shows how, if they are already relating their problems to an underlying loss, their views can be affirmed, their strengths highlighted, and ways found to enable them to express their feelings. If, on the other hand, they are set on the path of blaming themselves or others, he demonstrates how to 'deconstruct' their view and how to offer other ways of seeing the problem. Changes in their perceptions are affirmed, leading to the expression of unresolved grief. John Gunzburg then describes how client and therapist can work together to reconstruct a more liberating context for the client's life.

John Gunzburg shines through this book as a warm and caring man, sensitive to the various forms of disempowerment and gender bias in society, and as a highly creative therapist. For example, in helping a student of literature to understand the oppressive nature of her relationships with men, he offers her a re-scripting of the *Taming of the Shrew*. However, what is even more impressive are his demonstrations of how to release the creativity of clients, through drawing, writing and conversation. Thus, he encourages a woman, burnt up with anger, to draw her former, abusing lover and to devise ten curses to call down on him. He invites an art director to script a conversation between his 'passion' and his 'control'. He suggests to a woman from an orthodox religious background that she write a letter to the God who has not been hearing her prayers; on seeing it, her husband does likewise, bringing them closer together than before. The drawings, letters and conversations are reprinted here. They are a wonderful illustration of the results of empowering clients to bring and use their own creative resources in therapy.

John Gunzburg is a clear and engaging writer and an excellent teacher. He is careful to draw out the lessons from the case examples and to summarize the argument as he goes along. He offers questions to consider and helpful exercises to do at the end of each chapter. I am sure that therapists will find *Unresolved Grief* a liberating and empowering book as well as an engrossing one.

John Carpenter
Editor, *Journal of Family Therapy*
University of Kent at Canterbury, England
April, 1993

Preface

This book takes up the theme of unresolved grief originally introduced in the *Family Counselling Casebook* (Gunzburg, J., McGraw-Hill, Sydney, 1991, Chapter 24). After an introduction as to why the topic of unresolved grief is so significant within our society, the first counselling interview is examined in some detail and then the process of therapy during the 2nd–10th sessions is explored. Next, the emotions so often related to unresolved grief are considered and ways of expressing them are outlined. Some of the contexts in which unresolved grief arises are then presented, and finally, options and directions for the future, after grief has been resolved, are considered. Throughout this text there is a rich description of casework with individuals, couples and families from a variety of backgrounds, and many examples are given as to how therapist and clients utilize their creative resources, working together to resolve grief.

John Gunzburg

Acknowledgements

My thanks go to the many clients who gave permission for their stories to be told. Their names, and sometimes their ages and the places where events occurred, have been changed in an effort to preserve confidentiality. If by chance, readers recognize any identity in this book, I would ask them to respect privacy and esteem the courage and goodwill of those persons who have contributed their tales so that others may learn from their lives.

I am grateful to Rabbi Yaacov Barber, Zena Burgess, Ron Findlay, Joy Gunzburg, Barbara Knothe, David Ingamells, David Lancaster, Nada Miocevic, Steven Smith, and Elizabeth Ward for their conversations and friendship during the course of this writing.

I am also grateful to McGraw-Hill for permission to reprint Case 2A: 'a time to be sad' from my previous book, *The Family Counselling Casebook* (pp 152–3, McGraw-Hill, Sydney, 1991).

Finally, to my family, who have waited patiently, and sometimes frustratedly, while I completed this venture: I love you all!

PART ONE
Introduction and Overview

'Give sorrow words, the grief that does not speak,
Whispers the o'er-fraught heart, and bids it break.'
William Shakespeare, *Macbeth*, Act 4, Sc 3,
lines 209–210, 1606

Why a book on unresolved grief?

1

This volume is to be regarded as arising out of my first book, the *Family Counselling Casebook* (1991). That work was written with the aim of presenting a variety of ideas which would enable readers to imagine ways of expanding their own therapeutic practice, and of combining those ideas in creative ways to achieve new outcomes. It proposed the concept that, as therapy progressed, various themes with which clients were struggling would arise and demand to be addressed. It expressed the hope that readers would tune into those therapeutic themes and that the flow of themes throughout the whole text would parallel the process of therapy. There was a reflection also on the notion that some of the themes raised, i.e. unresolved grief, ethics, the creation of useful therapeutic anecdotes etc., demanded much more attention than there was space to give them at the time, and that, if a future opportunity arose, the author would focus on them in greater detail elsewhere. That is the *raison d'être* of this text: to further develop a major theme, that of unresolved grief (or 'soul ache' as one of my colleagues terms it), and to explore more fully the ways it may be tackled therapeutically.

But why select 'unresolved grief' as a primary theme? An incident that occurred after a final-year medical examination, in the late 1960s, comes to mind. One of the questions on the paper had requested a clinical description of and the treatment for malaria. The students were outraged; none had thought to study this topic. 'Imagine setting a question on a subject of so little relevance to Australian medicine in a final examination!', they criticized. 'Oh, really?', responded the professor responsible for the question. 'Only 20 million of our neighbours are infected with it.'

The *Family Counselling Casebook* expressed the idea that 'our society has been described as one in which material gains, status, power plays, technological advances, work programmes, possessions, property, and the quest for fame and immortality are predominant. Often, within such a world view, our emotions can be denied and swept aside as irrelevant to 'the good life'. One such emotion that is frequently kept out of sight is 'grief', yet the occasions to grieve within our lives are plentiful: decrease in good health, or death; loss of employment; missed opportunities in personal advancement; divorce; intimate friends moving to another territory; even the passage through transitional life stages (such as youth left behind us, children leaving home, retirement) can all be cause for sorrow, reflection and letting go. Rarely do we learn formally about grieving, and many of our patients come to us practitioners to learn for the first time that their experience of 'depression', stagnation and impotence may in fact be grief, triggered by an event, or the anniversary of an event.'

More recently, I decided to list the percentage values of the 81 case studies presented in the *Family Counselling Casebook* which included those family situations that might lead to unresolved grief. These figures are illustrated in Table 1.1. No claim is made that these percentages reflect the incidence of such situations in the general community. They would certainly be influenced by my own personal bias, my own particular style and interest in therapy, and the area in which I practice – Elwood (and formerly, Mitcham). They do, however, indicate that a significant number of families in attendance at a primary care practice have encountered a variety of troubles after which grieving might be appropriate. The figures suggest that, like malaria, unresolved grief might be a condition that is prevalent, and little thought about, within the general community.

On reading these lines, and perusing Table 1.1, I recall that it is February, 1991. The United Nations Forces, which include citizens of the United States of America, Britain, France, Italy, Egypt, Syria, Saudi

Table 1.1 Family situations that may lead to unresolved grief

Family situation	%
Physical abuse	33
Divorce/separation	30
Chemical abuse	21
Physical illness	20
Remarried/blended families	16
Incest	15
Affairs	14
Death	11
Fostering/adoption	6
Change in vocation	5
Past involvement in a war zone	2
Catastrophic loss	1

Arabia, the United Arab Emirates, Belgium, Netherlands, Canada, Australia, and numerous others, are currently in conflict with Iraq, battling for influence over Kuwait. The populations of the world are staggering within the grip of an economic recession that rivals the Great Depression of the 1930s. Marital breakdown in the western world is said to have reached epidemic levels . . . almost one in two marriages is expected to result in divorce, with the separation rate for remarriage being slightly higher. With the emphasis throughout the 1980s shifting from rewarding intimacies and family life towards the accumulation of material assets, a significant number of children appear to be leaving home to live on the streets, and more and more of our senior citizens seem to be retiring into a lifestyle of poverty and despair.

All these events might be cause for reflection: how much more grief, unresolved or otherwise, will be experienced in the next generation as a result of war, our financial woes and the struggles of families trying to cope with the vicissitudes of the 1990s? The observations of *Family Counselling Casebook*, repeated above, appear as relevant today as when they were formulated in 1987. A composition on 'unresolved grief – soul ache' at this time seems appropriate!

SUMMARY

During Chapter 1 we considered:

1. *Unresolved Grief* has been written as a sequel to the *Family Counselling Casebook*. Whereas the first book was written to introduce a number of therapeutic themes and emphasize eclecticism in therapeutic practice, the second one has been prepared to explore in greater depth one major theme of the first.
2. Situations leading to unresolved grief are frequent within our society, and unresolved grief is often ill-attended to by community members.
3. There is a likelihood that, with the advent of situations such as the Gulf war and economic recession, the number of people experiencing unresolved grief will be increased in the future.

POINTS FOR REFLECTION

1. Consider the following questions: What situations, if any, have occurred in your life that required grieving? How did you cope with them? Do you know of any intimates or friends who experienced loss and grieving? How did they manage? Did they cope in a way that was different from your way of dealing with grief in a similar

situation? Would their way of coping with grief be of use to you in the future?

REFERENCE

Gunzburg, J.C. (1991) *Family Counselling Casebook*, McGraw-Hill, Sydney.

The language of therapy

2

This chapter considers a means whereby we can structure the language of our therapeutic conversation, so that we are more able to understand our clients (and perhaps, as importantly, encourage them to understand more clearly what they are trying to communicate to us).

Considerable debate currently exists as to what exactly are the effectors of change during successful therapy. As Towns and Seymour (1990) write: 'Psychotherapy outcome research to date has suggested that all forms of psychotherapy are equivalent despite the content of the therapy (Stiles, Shapiro and Elliot, 1986). That is, despite different interventions there is no apparent difference in therapeutic outcome between the main schools of psychotherapy. While behavioural researchers have queried this conclusion on methodological grounds (Kazdin, 1980), other researchers have wondered whether these findings might indicate that all successful therapies are operating on an equivalent meta-level. That is, are there certain therapist factors, such as empathy, warmth and understanding (Truax and Carkhuff, 1965), certain client factors, such as self-efficacy (Bandura, 1977), or certain interactional factors associated with the ability of the therapist to come to an understanding with the client about goals (Sachs, 1983), which when addressed appropriately produce favourable therapeutic outcomes irrespective of the therapist's theoretical basis.'

If it proves correct that all successful therapies are operating at an equivalent meta-level (many decades may pass before we have gathered definitive empirical evidence for this), then perhaps our principal task as therapeutic practitioners is to ensure the quality of the therapeutic conversation, rather than to focus on any specific therapeutic technique, school or theory.

The *Family Counselling Casebook* presented a concept that considered the quality of dialogue during the therapeutic encounter (Gunzburg, 1991). The suggestion was that our clients entered therapy to learn about themselves at different levels. They desired to:

1. define exactly what their problems are (the descriptive level of learning);
2. become more familiar with the context in which their problems arose, or were currently occurring (the contextual level of learning);
3. achieve a resolution of their problems, and expand their world view, utilizing their own choices and resources (the experiential level of learning).

At the experiential level of learning, a nourishing environment was considered to be created, involving warmth, empathy, clear yet permeable boundaries, a definite sense of self, and a genuine liking for people. In such an atmosphere, clients were regarded as exploring, growing, changing and healing. They could learn to cease being overly preoccupied with their own problems, and interact within a wider social community. Learning at this level was considered to be mutual, although practitioners of therapy were held to be responsible for all changes made as being in their clients' best interest, i.e. maintaining clients' safety, dignity, independence and autonomy, enabling them to contest the various abuses they might be facing in their lives, and increasing their flexibility of choice. Therapists would have to be open to their own learning processes during the therapeutic encounter. Some of the ways that therapists could best foster experiential learning were thought to be: offering insight (Freud, 1960), enabling self-actualization (Maslow, 1968) and expression of the 'true self' (Laing, 1965), encouraging congruency and accurate expression of feelings (Rogers, 1975), engaging in an intimate dialogue where values could be defined and dilemmas discussed (Friedman, 1960), and the use of reframing (Watzlawick, 1974). Humour and a playful imagination, as well as serious contemplation and the knowledge of a number of therapeutic models, where considered essential.

Unresolved Grief further develops this concept that the quality of the therapeutic conversation can be enhanced if these three basic levels of learning are incorporated within it.

1. There is initially a descriptive level of discussion during which therapists and their clients together explore and define the emotions with which the latter are struggling. (Therapists who find themselves battling with the same feelings in their personal lives may need to focus on their own dilemmas within their own supervision, peer interchange and therapy, so that their own personal agenda does not impinge on those of their clients.) Questions during the descriptive discussion are usually open-ended and non-specific, and geared to elicit information as to how clients are experiencing their problems:

What is happening in your life at the moment?
What has brought you along to therapy?
How can I be of help to you?

2. There is next a contextual level of discussion within which practitioners and their clients endeavour to understand the ground against which the troublesome emotions evolved, and the current situation that maintains their existence. Questions at this level are usually more specific in seeking the details surrounding the problem:

When was the first time that you noticed this problem?
When did you learn to respond like this?
Who else is involved in this?

3. Finally, there is an experiential level of discussion during which clients seek a resolution of their emotional struggles while experiencing trust, safety, autonomy, adequate boundaries, appropriate closeness–distance between therapist and client, cooperation, development of mutuality and reflection. During this phase, clients are encouraged to search for those resources that are available to them and the ethical options that exist to promote future change, growth and healing:

Have you ever handled this situation in a different manner?
Do you know of anyone who has tackled the problem differently?
Would you speak about it with him/her?
What are your strengths, talents, spiritual resources?

The following case study illustrates how these levels of discussion (and learning) can be used within therapeutic practice.

——————— . . . ———————

CASE STUDY

Case 2A   . . . a time to be sad . . .
Stuart, 15, had 'created problems' for his parents and two sisters over the past several months. During that time, he had started missing school (he would set out for school in the mornings, as usual, but would not arrive there) and had packed his bags and run away from home to a friend's place for the night at least four times during this period. The whole family now sat in my room, with Stuart appearing quiet, morose and withdrawn. When queried further as to exactly when Stuart had first indicated his distress, his parents Ross, 42, and Greta, 41, replied that he had been an outgoing and likeable lad until

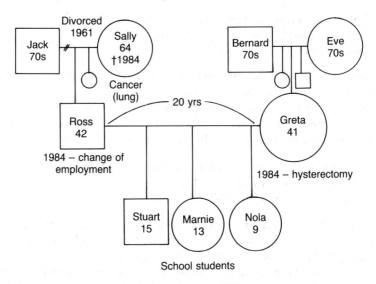

Fig. 2.1 Family commenced therapy in May 1988.

about four years ago, when he had become moody and had begun to throw tantrums. Up until the current date, Stuart would have violent fights with his sisters Marnie, 13, and Nola, 9, if he did not get his way.

Many events had happened during that year, when Stuart's behaviour had changed for the worse. Ross had moved to new employment and his mother had died of lung cancer following a lengthy hospitalization. Greta reported that she and Ross had considered separating about that time, but had worked together to resolve their problems, which centred on a lack of emotional support for each other within the marriage. Greta had undergone a hysterectomy for a non-malignant condition, and at this time the family home had also been destroyed and the family members' lives threatened in the Ash Wednesday bushfires. It had indeed been 'the year of living dangerously'!

I told the family that I admired their enormous display of strength in surviving this period of turmoil, and asked Stuart about his relationship with his late grandmother. Stuart, moist-eyed, replied that he was very close to his grandmother and refused to speak further on the subject. We spoke about the other distressing occurrences around that time, but the grandmother's death seemed to be the one that had created most impact. I asked Ross and Stuart to go out together, before our next meeting, to a restaurant and to discuss what the elderly lady's death had meant to them, and what it was about her that they had missed.

At the subsequent session a week later, the family attended without Stuart. His parents said that he was now attending school regularly, without any absences during the week, but he had said that he would not go to the restaurant with Ross if they were going to discuss his grandmother. He also wasn't going to see 'that doctor' who kept asking him questions about his grandmother! I praised Stuart's perception. Grief is a very private matter, and I had obviously been too hasty in expecting Stuart to cope with it during our initial session. I told Greta and Ross that I believed that Stuart had assessed more ably than I that it was too early to broach upon this issue, and asked them to pass on my message to Stuart. I would be happy to see the whole family at a future date if necessary. In the meantime, the family had worked very hard to overcome their troubles and I asked Marnie and Nola to plan a fun activity to give everyone a treat.

One month later, the entire family attended. Stuart presented himself at this session as a rather cheeky and easygoing teenager. There had been no missing of school, much less family infighting, and we discussed various issues appropriate to Stuart's development: adequate pocket money, rules about privacy, and the question of siblings entering each other's rooms. I touched on one further point: Ross's parents had divorced when he had been 15. I commented that this was Stuart's current age. Ross may have missed out on a number of activities during adolescence because of the divorce. Would he and Stuart get together (perhaps another restaurant?) and share how 'teenagehood 1988' compared with the 1961 version?

· · ·

DISCUSSION

Descriptive level

1st session Stuart is described as the 'family problem'. He is playing truant and also has become irritable, throwing tantrums and arguing violently with his sisters. His emotions are reflected in his quiet, morose, withdrawn demeanour.

2nd session Stuart does not attend therapy with the rest of the family. However, his parents report that he is attending school regularly, without any days missed.

3rd session Stuart's behaviour has changed into a much happier and outgoing mood, there has been no further truancy, and the fights between the siblings have decreased markedly, indicating that a favourable change has occurred.

Contextual level

1st session As mentioned above, the family enters therapy regarding Stuart as the cause of their woes. It is extremely common in western cultures for clients to view their struggles in a 'linear' or 'blaming' context. The philosophy underlying this context is that there is one underlying reason to a problem, for which there is one sole cure. The problem is being created by something or someone, and if only the specific cause can be uncovered, a solution will become readily apparent. Our clients often regard therapists as the experts who will discover the cause of their pain and provide the cure. One of our initial tasks, then, as therapists is to indicate that we are facilitators rather than experts. Our job is to divert our clients' energies from searching for an underlying treatable cause towards trying to view the context of the problem from a different angle. We can do this by:

1. affirming the client's efforts in trying to cope with the difficulty;
2. emphasizing a different context which might be influencing the problem, and the family members' interactions.

There are a number of contexts within which Stuart's altered behaviour might be viewed:

1. the insecurities surrounding the father's change of vocation;
2. unresolved grief, related to the grandmother's death;
3. anxieties due to the mother and father's underlying marital conflict;
4. dislocation and unsafety, relating to the loss of home and threat to life due to the bushfire disaster;
5. the mother's hospitalization and surgery;
6. the behaviour might be regarded within a developmental context, i.e. an expression of Stuart's progress through adolescence.

First, the family is admired for their survival skills and cohesive strengths over the duration of their strife. Our clients come to us usually having experienced many months, even years, of negative feelings towards themselves and each other. They have often forgotten many of the rewarding aspects of their lives, and the therapist's affirming of one of their qualities can create remarkable initial impact: 'Hey', they may think, 'someone has noticed something that is going well, or something that we are doing well'.

Next, we enter a conversation about the various troubled areas in their lives. The one which brings the most powerful response seems to be the grandmother's death, and a grieving task is arranged: Stuart and his father are to go out and share their memories about her.

2nd session Stuart refuses to attend and sends me a clear communication that, although unresolved grief may well have been the context for his changed behaviour, I had been too eager in trying to get him to work on it.

At this stage, a conversation within a developmental context is thought to be most useful. Greta and Ross's parenting skills are praised, particularly the fact that they have raised Stuart to achieve a degree of autonomy in making his decisions. He definitely knows better than I when and how to grieve (note how this statement de-emphasizes my expertise as the problem-solver!). They have succeeded in raising a teenager who knows the value of privacy. I express my pleasure that Stuart has attended school regularly, even if only for a week. It indicates his willingness to change and help things improve. The parents are admired for the hard work that they are putting into their family and, considering the tough times that they had endured and the general business of raising a family of adolescents, there did not seem to have been much time for family enjoyment. The sisters are asked if they would be the 'agents for family fun' and plan a leisure activity, and Stuart is nominated as the most appropriate person to decide if the family needed to return for a further session. (This part of the conversation is designed to involve, and give status to, Stuart's sisters. They may have been on the periphery of family action for much of the time since the family focus shifted on to their brother's struggles. It also aims to further boost Stuart's esteem as the family expert on 'grieving in privacy'.)

Experiential level

Many experiential changes have already been touched upon in the section on context. It may well be that, as the context of conversation changes as therapy proceeds, so do clients notice a change in the way they are experiencing the problem.

1st session Clients often enter therapy experiencing a great deal of failure and 'badness' about themselves. Greta and Ross, although they blame Stuart for their troubles, also express their opinion of themselves as 'flawed parents': 'It is pretty rough, doctor', they say, 'having to come to a counsellor for this sort of thing. We should be able to sort it out for ourselves'. Stuart's communications are largely monosyllabic, and his sisters say that 'It is hopeless. Nothing is going to change'. In this first session, it is essential that a sense of interest, concern, potency and optimism be injected: that, with mutual goodwill, we can all learn to understand each other. It is necessary to give encouragement and a sense of reliability, a 'readiness to be there for them', so that they can converse safely, 'speaking the unspeakable', in the search for their own resources and solutions.

At this stage, the family's basic strengths are affirmed and a general description of the problem is obtained. Some of the contexts in which the problem may have arisen are explored, and a task is planned to obtain further information as to the impact of the grandmother's death.

2nd session When Stuart does not attend, he signals that I had moved too rapidly into the area of grief. It is important now to help Greta and Ross avoid experiencing further feelings of inadequacy that they cannot even bring their rebellious son to therapy, and conversation is directed towards developmental issues: the fact that Greta and Ross are raising Stuart as a perceptive lad who values privacy in which to experience his emotions. He has attended school regularly since we last met, indicating that he can indeed alter his behaviour. Marnie and Nola are also asked if they would plan some family entertainment, emphasizing their importance to the family group as a whole.

3rd session There are major changes within the family. Stuart's mood is happier, he is more communicative, there has been no truancy, and there is much decreased fighting between Stuart, Marnie and Nola. At this stage, a further conversation is pursued within the developmental context, covering the issues of pocket money and privacy in the siblings' bedrooms. Finally, Ross and Stuart are encouraged to have a discussion about adolescence past and present. Ross's parents had divorced during his own teenage years; perhaps father and son can share their adolescent experiences and indirectly complete any grieving that needs to be finished?

SUMMARY

In Chapter 2, we considered:

1. that the effectors of change during therapy are by no means certain, and that the quality of the therapeutic conversation appears important (i.e. empathy, warmth, understanding in therapists, self-efficacy in clients, the ability of therapists and clients to achieve an understanding about the future goals and direction of therapy);
2. that the descriptive, contextual and experiential levels of learning, and discussion, may provide a basis for improving the quality of the therapeutic conversation;
3. how the descriptive, contextual and experiential levels of discussion may apply in an actual case situation.

POINTS FOR REFLECTION

1. What are some of the questions that you might ask of your clients to obtain
   (a) a clear description of the problem?

(b) information about the contexts in which the problem may be regarded to have evolved?

(c) information as to what resources are available to clients to enable them to seek problem resolution?

2. Consider a recent case study, and think about how you engaged your clients at descriptive, contextual and experiential levels of conversation.

REFERENCES

Bandura, A. (1977) Self-efficacy: towards a unifying theory of behavioural change. *Psychological Review*, **84**, 191–215.

Freud, S. (1960) *A General Introduction to Psychoanalysis*, Washington Square Press, New York.

Friedman, M. (1960) *Martin Buber: The Life of Dialogue*, Harper & Row, New York.

Gunzburg, J.C. (1991) *Family Counselling Casebook*, McGraw-Hill, Sydney.

Kazdin, A.E. (1980) *Research Design in Clinical Psychology*, Harper & Row, New York.

Laing, R. (1965) *The Divided Self*, Penguin, New York.

Maslow, A. (1968) *Towards a Psychology of Being*, Van Nostrand Reinhold, Princeton, New Jersey.

Rogers, C. (1975) *Client-Centred Therapy*, Constable, London.

Sachs, J.S. (1983) Negative factors in brief psychotherapy: an empirical assessment. *Journal of Consulting and Clinical Psychology*, **51**, 557–564.

Stiles, W.B., Shapiro, D.A. and Elliott, R. (1986) Are all psychotherapies equivalent? *American Psychologist*, **41**, 65–180.

Towns, A. and Seymour, F. (1990) What about the family in family therapy research? *Australian and New Zealand Journal of Family Therapy*, **11**, (4), 222–228.

Truax, C.B. and Carkhuff, R.R. (1965) Experimental manipulation of therapeutic conditions. *Journal of Consulting Psychology*, **29**, 119–124.

Watzlawick, P., Weakland, J.H. and Fisch, R. (1974) *Change: Principles of Problem Formation and Problem Resolution*, Norton, New York.

PART TWO
Defining the Problem

'To see a world in a grain of sand
And heaven in a wild flower,
Hold infinity in the palm of your hand
And eternity in an hour.'
   William Blake, *Auguries of Innocence*.

The first interview 3

This chapter examines the elements of the first interview, and how we can converse with our clients to get a sense of their experiential 'world' within the initial therapeutic hour.

THE REFERRAL

'Hi, I am John', I start. 'How do you come to be here?', or, 'How did you get to hear of me?'

Knowing the client's source of referral can give clues to a number of important factors as to the issues that they are bringing with them into therapy.

1. If they were referred by a family member or friend, ask yourself: Do the issues that these clients bring reflect the interactions within their family or social group? Are clients acting as 'agents' for their family or wider intimate network?
2. If referred by your colleagues, question yourself: What sort of therapy do your colleagues anticipate that you will offer these particular clients? Does the referral indicate a problem area within the relationship between the client and their referee? Does their referral reflect a specific dislike by the referring colleague?
3. If referred by a disciplinary authority (police, law court, school board), caution yourself: Are these clients attending therapy to avoid punishment? Are they coming to please the authorities, yet ultimately wish to retain the status quo?
4. When attendance is due to self-referral, think: Do these persons *believe* that they need therapy, or *do* they need therapy?
5. If the client has sought your skills previously, wonder: Is this a new situation that they present, or continuation of a former one?

There are many reasons why people seek therapy, and it is essential for therapists to contemplate 'where they are coming from'.

INTRODUCING YOURSELF

I continue: 'I started out working for 16 years in a general medical practice partnership . . . delivering babies, doing anaesthetics, even performing the occasional tonsillectomy in the early days . . . and became interested as to how problems formed within families and how people tried to sort out their problems. Eventually, I trained as a family therapist and psychotherapist, and moved full-time into this area, and enjoy thinking about resolving people's struggles in a non-pharmaceutical way'.

By introducing yourself in a friendly, open manner, you are offering your client some information about your values and world view:

1. Although you have had some training in the field, you may not want to be categorized as a specialist, or expert healer!
2. You indicate that you are willing to make a definite commitment, involving negotiation, sharing and cooperation with others, to a long-term venture, and learn the various aspects and facets of it.
3. You can show that you value change in direction, the developing of self-needs, taking risks, imagination, innovation, optimism and hope, and working within a different environment to achieve new goals.

Almost inevitably, I am asked by clients: What is the difference between a psychiatrist, a psychologist and a psychotherapist? I reply that a psychiatrist can be regarded as a doctor who is trained to recognize disturbances of mental functioning as illnesses, and treat them, often using medication. A psychologist can be regarded as a non-medical practitioner who is trained to recognize disturbances of mental functioning as imbalances of perception and behaviour, and treat them using behavioural programmes. Psychiatrists and psychologists can undergo further training to become therapists, as can general practitioners, social workers, lay and pastoral counsellors, and anyone in the helping professions. Indeed, clients would be prudent to inquire very carefully as to the training of their therapists, from whatever background these practitioners may come, before proceeding with therapy. Psychotherapists and family therapists are trained to recognize and treat disturbances of behaviour as messages, arising within a given context, at a certain stage in development. Family therapists usually recognize the family and, more recently, the wider sociopolitical scene, as the context for problem formation, whereas psychotherapists denote different areas of human functioning, e.g. the 'unconscious', as the context for problem formation. Many therapists take an eclectic view (Gunzburg, 1991), learning a number of therapeutic models such as family therapy (Minuchin, 1974), psychodynamic therapy (Malan, 1979) or feminist therapy (Walters, 1988), and using them to mould their therapy according to their clients' needs, rather than trying to fit all clients into one therapeutic model. By talking together, both therapist and client can clarify the latter's messages, which often prove to be questions that the clients are trying to ask of themselves. They can both come to understand better the context in which these questions arose, and search for more useful questions to the problems that the client is attempting to address. Psychotherapy and family therapy might well be described as the search for better questions to the solution of problems, rather than the provision, by the expert therapist, of absolutely correct answers. I take pains to emphasize that these definitions of psychiatrist, psychologist and psychotherapist are my own, and reflect my own general-practice bias; other therapists would have quite different views. Note also that I offer these definitions to clients in language that is appropriate to their understanding, education, etc.

DRAWING A GENOGRAM

I continue my contribution to the conversation: 'Because I think in terms of families, I would like to build up a picture of what your family is like, find out who is in it and who is important to you, and then move on to the problems that bring you here'.

This sort of statement can be offered whether it is an individual, a couple or family who are present. A genogram drawn at this stage of the proceedings will often reveal the significant information that is required, within a few minutes.

———————————— . . . ————————————

CASE STUDY

Case 3A   Back to the future
Michael, 36, commenced his first therapy session by saying that he was 'depressed'. He complained of loss of energy, lack of motivation and an inability to concentrate at work. Although he spoke slowly in a listless voice, and sat with shoulders slumped, Michael presented himself as a man skilled in logic and analysis, with even a flair for the occasional humorous quip. Normally, he said, he was an excellent worker, able to adhere to necessary time schedules. Now, he had experienced lethargy and a sense of emptiness for about four weeks.

As I drew the genogram shown in Fig. 3.1, I noted that the current date was at the beginning of August, 1983. We had been chatting quite matter-of-factly during the construction of the genogram, and on its completion, I lowered my voice, and commented softly: 'August seems to have been an important month in your life, Michael. Do you think that there are any leftovers from an August in the past?'

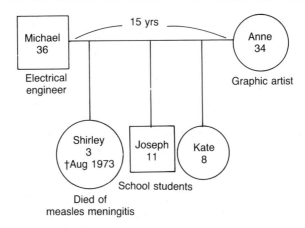

Fig. 3.1 Michael commenced therapy in August 1983.

Michael appeared to enter a different conscious state. 'She is lying there in front of me', he exclaimed in distress. 'She is dead. I should be able to do something. I should have prevented this!'

We continued to converse as though we were living in the time of August 1973, and Michael expressed his feelings of impotence and incompetence that his daughter should have died from so humble a disease as measles. Over the next 30 minutes, we shared the disappointments that can occur within an unpredictable and sometimes harsh life – those insecure and 'bloody' moments of reality. (I had lost a much-beloved uncle, who had died of melanoma in his early 40s, when I was a teenager. I did not share this fact openly with Michael . . . it is important not to intrude feelings of our own that are triggered off during the therapeutic process on to our clients as they tell us their story, but I was certainly able to appreciate his experience of grieving.) As we talked, Michael gradually came back to the future; back to 1983, calmer, easier, both of us watery-eyed. At a further session, one month later, Michael confirmed his continued ease, rediscovered zest and renewed application to his vocation.

———————————   . . .   ———————————

DISCUSSION

Descriptive level

Michael's dull voice, stooped shoulders, and the words he uses: 'loss of energy, lethargy, no motivation, unable to concentrate and emptiness' describe well his internal experience of depression.

Contextual level

The genogram indicates Shirley's death on a date close to that of Michael's mood change and attendance at therapy. Using a fairly simple hypnotic technique – lowering my voice and offering the suggestion that Michael's feelings might be related to the anniversary of his daughter's death (Edelstein, 1981), I encourage Michael to enter a trance state and 'travel' back to the event.

Experiential level

Within the trance state, Michael is able to re-experience the moment and express his feelings of helplessness, and his guilt that he could not prevent the tragedy. As he tells his story, we are able to explore together our experiences of sadness at our respective losses. We both end the session with grief turned to the mellow warmth of mutually shared comfort.

A genogram may be the tool that helps clients to connect very rapidly the various pieces of their lives about which they need to know, but more often 'open-ended' questions are needed to proceed. Open-ended questions aim to encourage the client's free verbal description about an event ('What happened then? Would you tell me more about that?'), whereas 'closed' questions narrow the focus of conversation on to a topic in the search for specific answers ('Do you work outside the home? How often has he missed school?').

After discussing a client's referral sources and introducing oneself, some questions that might encourage further conversation are: 'What is happening with you? How might I be of help to you? What has brought you here today? How could things be different for you?'.

Where there are initial pauses, I often comment: 'Sometimes it is difficult to start. It takes quite a deal of courage to come along to therapy; just coming along is often half the problem solved'. Humour often serves to break the ice: 'I guess you have come along to help your life be better. I never had someone say to me: "Dr Gunzburg, I want you to help me make my life worse", or "Show me the second best way to be happy!"'.

Where there is an overflow of words from the client, sometimes incomprehensible, a useful response can be: 'I can hear that you are eager to have me understand what is troubling you. Let us take it a little easier. I am going to be here for the next 20 years. I do not guarantee my presence beyond that period of time'.

With these queries and statements, clients can be offered safety, comfort and a genuine interest in their situation, without being pushed too hard for information. They can be given the opportunity to tell their story at their own pace. If clients have grown within families of origin in which they were unable to develop trust in the adult world, i.e. families in which an adult violated them as children, a task can be set to enable them to describe their current struggles: 'Would you write a few lines (or draw a picture, or compose a poem or song) for the next session, describing what it is like for you at the moment?'.

· · ·

CASE STUDY

Case 3B   The farmer's wife
The 1st session Hilary, 27, a farmer's wife, who attended our first session of therapy on her own, told me that she had grown to young

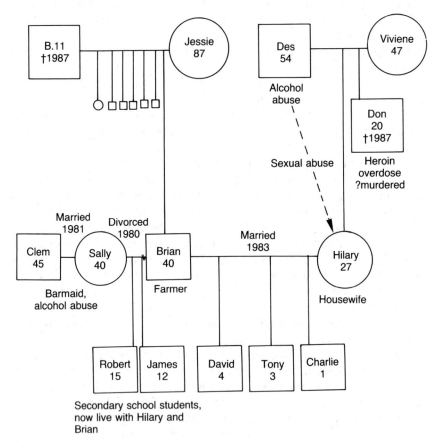

Fig. 3.2 Hilary commenced therapy in October 1989.

adulthood within a family for whom she had had little reason to develop trust. Her father, Jim, 54, an abuser of alcohol, who had been diagnosed medically as 'paranoid' and who had a past gaol record for violence, had beaten both Hilary and her mother Fay, 47, and had sexually abused both Hilary and her brother Don over many years during their childhood and early adolescence. Don had been a heroin addict and dealer who had died of a heroin overdose in 1987, although Hilary asserted that some police evidence suggested that he may have been murdered by his criminal associates. When she was 14, Hilary said, she had been raped by a 24-year-old neighbour, who had been brought to trial and released without punishment. Hilary had been married to Brian, 40, for six years. She described him as 'a good man' who ran the farm effectively and was 'really good' at doing all the chores, but who was withdrawn and quiet, talking to her hardly at all, and showing her little sign of affection. Their sexual relationship was almost inactive, and though Brian often muttered to her that he would like to have a 'more normal' marriage, Hilary said he had never 'forced' himself upon her. Hilary and Brian lived with their three children, David, 4, Tony, 3, and Charlie, 1, and the two sons from Brian's previous marriage, Robert, 15, and James, 12. Hilary had become disheartened, unable to cope with the routines of everyday life, although she said that she had continued to survive 'day by day', and showed no signs of ceasing her domestic and farm work.

Hilary's responses to me during this first session were largely monosyllabic, and I had to strive hard to build up a picture of her experience. She certainly had no immediate reason to feel safe with me. I asked Hilary if she would write a few words to describe how she was feeling. Even though Hilary brought her description to the second session of therapy, I present it here because it arose so readily out of our first meeting.

Hilary wrote:

'When I feel depressed –
I am marooned on an island after being shipwrecked. There is no-one else on the island and it is a lonely desperate place with little vegetation or wildlife.
I send up smoke signals trying to attract passing ships but they don't stop. I assume my S.O.S. signals are not noticed by them. However, I persist.
The frustration I experience plus the let-down feelings as yet again I am left here all alone, is indescribable.
Perhaps I will never leave this place, no matter how hard I try to attract the attention of passing ships and perhaps I will remain

here on this God forsaken island until the end of my life which seems so inconsequential.

It is then that I feel so depressed – the utter hopelessness of it all!'

— — — · · · — —

DISCUSSION

Hilary's description uses the metaphor of a deserted island to communicate very clearly her experience of depression: her sense of isolation, her signals for help, her frustration at being ignored, her determination to persist in making contact, her despair that nothing will change, and her feelings that her life will remain insignificant, and that she will never escape from her island.

Note that in the cases of both Michael and Hilary a clear description of the underlying emotions being experienced was reached within one or two sessions of therapy. More often it takes several sessions, months even, to fully comprehend the struggles of our clients. Sometimes, however, it is simply not possible to engage clients within the therapeutic process from the outset.

— — — · · · — —

CASE STUDY

Case 3C   The fury!

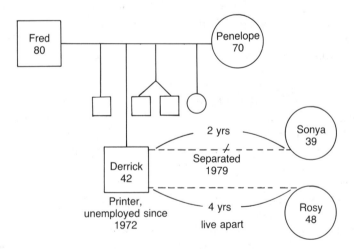

Fig. 3.3 Derrick commenced therapy in October 1989.

Derrick, 42, arrived at my counselling room agitated and brimming over with fury. Before I could utter a word of greeting, Derrick declared: 'I wish more of them had been killed . . . I hate Americans!'. The devastating San Francisco earthquake of 1989 had occurred two days previously, with about 150 casualties. I was too dumbfounded to reply, but Derrick proceeded with his next pronouncement anyway. 'I wish I was dead!', he growled. 'I wish that I could look down on my relatives at my grave and witness their sorrow. They all deserve that!'

I did not have the fortitude to voice my immediate thoughts: that perhaps Derrick, if dead, would not be looking down on his relatives, he would be looking up at them, and that perhaps they might not be anguished at his passing, they might be dancing on his grave!

I started to gather some details of Derrick's past. He had been diagnosed as having a 'schizo-affective' disorder many years ago, for which he was taking medication. There had been several losses in his life. A printer by trade, he had suffered a moderately severe hearing deficit due to the noise of the machinery, and because of this and his emotional instability he had remained unemployed for 15 years. A much-loved pet dachshund, Heidi, had died several years earlier, and more recently, a relationship with a girlfriend had also ended. Derrick said that he had attended three years of weekly psychotherapy from 1985, but it had done him 'no good', and, in fact, everyone within his social network – relatives, medical attendants, his current girlfriend – were all to be blamed for his present discomforts. We met for two more sessions, but I could not influence Derrick's perspective that everyone else was responsible for his struggles. I thought: 'I had better be careful, I could easily prove to be yet another available target for his anger'.

Two days after our third encounter, Derrick telephoned me and, without greeting, immediately began to tell me of a confrontation he had endured that morning with a door-to-door salesman. I cautioned Derrick that I usually spoke to clients between sessions only in the most acute emergencies.

'Do you mean I have to put up with the upset that this fellow has caused me until I see you again?', Derrick snorted. 'That is the usual idea of therapy', I replied, 'to think about events that happen between sessions, and then to bring your thoughts with you for discussion'.

Derrick did not return for any further therapy with me.

--- . . . ---

DISCUSSION

Derrick appears to be interested in entering a conversation with me, not to view his problems from a different angle or contemplate his losses, but rather to use me as a vent for his rage. I find that in such situations, delineating boundaries (when and where I am willing to speak with clients) produces an outcome that is satisfactory for us both.

Towards the end of the first session, a contract can be made: 'Let us meet for another ten sessions. It usually takes about that time for both of us to find out what we are dealing with, if we have become comfortable with each other, and if we can trust each other. Many people say to me after that period, "You are a nice fellow, John, but I have got better things to do with my time". Ten sessions seems to have been enough time to sort out what they brought into therapy. Others say, "Yes, ten sessions has been good, but I am intrigued. I want to know more about myself". These people might continue for eight months to a year. Lastly, I have some people from what I call very primitive families . . . those who have experienced incest or physical violence, and come from families where alcohol and drug abuse in parents were the problem . . . who may require years of therapy. But I do not do really long-term therapy, you know, the sort that Woody Allen has received . . . he has been 25 years plus in therapy, I believe, and says that he writes and directs brilliant films out of it!'

At this stage also, especially where clients have grown within families of origin in which physical and sexual abuses occurred, I make a clear statement on my attitudes against such abuses, taking pains to delineate clear boundaries.

'Your story resembles something out of a concentration camp', I may say, 'but I want you to know that there are some things that we are not going to do in here. We are not going to damage each other, or each other's property, we are not going to have sex, we are not going to call each other abusive names. What we are going to do is to have a conversation that will help you to experience our relationship as something quite different from some of those you have experienced in the past, and that will enable you to view your struggles in a different light'.

Where physical and sexual abuse is occurring within the current family, I ask perpetrators to cease their abuse and make a commitment of non-abuse. I comment that, in my experience, abuse has never served members of families well, and that I am unwilling to participate in therapy while one person is abusing another. When the abuse continues, I see my role as facilitating abused people towards a place of refuge and safety. With an agreement to cease the abuse, I give a guarantee to use all of my skills and energies in enabling perpetrators to maintain their commitment of non-abuse, in protecting and empowering the abused, and in helping family members find another way of relating.

Finally, clients can be reminded that they are expected to attend sessions which they have booked, or to give at least 48 hours' notice of cancellation, to pay their accounts, and to be as honest as possible with the stories that they tell.

By offering these statements to clients, we can share some of our expectancies of the therapeutic process with them: that the length of therapy varies with the client's needs; that responsibility in attendance and payment of fees is expected; and that honesty and integrity during the therapeutic conversation are valued.

SUMMARY

In Chapter 3 we considered elements of the first interview:

1. the importance of exploring the referral source of our clients;
2. introducing oneself in a way that offers clients safety and comfort, and that helps to define something of the therapist's view of therapy;
3. the value of drawing a genogram early, and the case of Michael, with whom drawing a genogram led to an immediate defining of his unresolved grief, and its rapid resolution;
4. the use of open-ended questions to enable clients to describe their internal experience of the problem;
5. the setting of tasks to encourage a description of the client's internal experience of the problem, and the case of Hilary, whose written words provided an eloquent and accurate description of her depression;
6. that defining the problem may take one, a few or many sessions of therapy, as in the case of Derrick, who appeared interested in a relationship that was not therapy!;
7. clarifying some rules of therapy.

POINTS FOR REFLECTION

1. Plan an introduction of yourself that you believe will allow your clients to feel safe with you. What will you tell them about your ideas regarding therapy?
2. Practise drawing some genograms on clients who are currently in therapy with you. Do the genograms clarify any information about your clients which you both need to know to progress in therapy?
3. Formulate some open-ended questions which will facilitate your clients' descriptions of their internal experience.
4. Contemplate writing a short essay, or drawing a picture, or composing a poem to describe one of your current internal experiences (it can be a happy one! these tasks need not only be applied to problems).

Do you have a clearer understanding of your experience on completing the task?
5. Reflect on a few rules that you believe will increase the efficacy of your therapy.

REFERENCES

Edelstein, G. (1981) *Trauma, Trance and Transformation*, Brunner-Mazel, New York.
Gunzburg, J.C. (1991) *Family Counselling Casebook*, McGraw-Hill, Sydney.
Malan, D. (1979) *Individual Psychotherapy and the Science of Psychodynamics*, Butterworths, London.
Minuchin, S. (1974) *Families and Family Therapy*, Tavistock Publications, London.
Walters, M. *et al.* (1988) *The Invisible Web*, Guilford, New York.

The second to tenth sessions

4

This chapter examines the issues that need to be addressed during the first three months of therapy. One has already been covered in some detail in Chapter 3: obtaining a clear description of the problem from the client. Another was alluded to in Chapter 2: that clients frequently enter therapy regarding the formation of their problems within a linear or 'blaming' context. It is necessary to explore the blaming context at this point, because the therapist must know how to counter this quite painful and limiting world view.

There are a number of elements of the blaming context which appear constant, whether it be individuals, couples or families who seek help.

1. Clients regard their problems as being attributable to one sole cause and resolvable by one effective cure or approach.
2. Clients usually put their faith in the care of an outside expert, whose all-knowing wisdom – and often magical interventions – will provide a healing for their troubles.
3. Clients often use 'blaming' language. There can be self-blame: 'I should have done/known better'; 'How could I have been so stupid?'; 'I never do anything right!' This language serves to lower the speaker's self-esteem, and avoids responsibility in searching for ways to affirm themselves, rather than discount themselves. There can be blame of others: 'He is a disgrace to us all'; 'You have got to make her see reason, doctor'; 'They are incorrigible! We can't do anything with them'. Such language creates feelings of inadequacy in the speaker, lowers the self-esteem of the blamed, and usually enables the speaker to avoid responsibility in acknowledging his/her contribution to the problem under discussion. There can be blame of people past: 'Mum was a real brute!'; 'My father never was there for me'; 'My elder brother always got the better deal'. This sort of talk enables the speaker to avoid coping with her/his current struggles, and shifts the responsibility for present discomfort to some ancestral

villain. There can also be blame of people within the wider social network: 'The Gulf war is part of a Zionist–American–Anglo–Franco–Latin conspiracy'; 'The Antipodean Freethinker's Party is ruining this country'; 'The school-teachers should stop mucking around, and teach my kid properly'. This language gives a sense that the speaker's struggles are influenced by sinister dark forces outside themselves and beyond the scope of personal resources, so that the speaker can avoid responsibility for tackling their problems directly.

Within the 'blaming' context, a number of negative experiences are common.

1. There can be expressions of unease, insecurity and a disinclination to trust the goodwill of others: 'Who gives a damn?'; 'People always let you down'; 'Husbands are all the same... let them get their dirty socks into your washing machine, and they all turn out to be bastards!'.

2. Clients often speak with a sense of shame that they have not found the resources to cope with their struggles. There may be decreased autonomy, clients having run out of energy to try to proceed further: 'I am tired. I am so worn out. I cannot be bothered with this nonsense any more'.

3. There may be a lack of new ideas; the self-defeating patterns have been present for such a long time that personal resources and initiative have decreased. Clients may express guilt that they have come to this situation of 'not knowing what to do': 'We are a pretty normal family. We should know what to do. We should have cracked this nut by now! What on earth do we do?'

4. There may be feelings of inferiority: 'All those other families... the Brady Bunch, Bill Cosby, the Simpsons... they have all the answers... they know what to do. We are hopeless!'

5. Clients may describe a loss of personal family identity: 'Where are we going? What has happened to us? What are we doing? We are lost!'

6. Clients may feel isolated and experience a lack of intimate connection with each other. When they do spend time apart, they may not know how to refresh themselves when they get together again: 'He never speaks to me. She ignores me completely. When we go out together, we have nothing to talk about'.

7. There may be stagnation, a 'stuckness' that paralyses clients in their search to generate solutions: 'We are trapped! Things will never change between us. We just keep on arguing and it gets us nowhere'.

8. Clients may despair, on reflection: 'We have always been like this! It has never been any other way! We have never been able to agree on

a single damn thing!' (A useful response to a sentence such as this last one is to ask each person who has attended the therapy session if he/she agrees as to the validity of the statement just made.)

Our task then, as therapists, is to counter these negative experiences which are often communicated to us so passionately by our clients. We can do this by:

1. offering an environment which engenders comfort, safety and trust; some ways of offering these qualities, e.g. the manner in which we introduce ourselves and reveal a portion of our world view to clients, were considered in Chapter 3;
2. affirming clients' strengths, resources and efforts in attempting to resolve their problems thus far;
3. exploring new or forgotten resources; setting tasks, and encouraging more positive ways of regarding the problem;
4. sharing family experiences common to humanity: the struggles of our clients are not unique, and anecdotes are often useful to connect their dilemmas with those of the general community;
5. discussing how 'things can be different', and rearranging the family structure;
6. encouraging initiative and autonomy, and exploring the closeness–distance of intimacy within the therapeutic relationship;
7. exploring what to give to future generations;
8. reflection: 'What is happening now that is better for you?'

--- · · · ---

AFFIRMING STRENGTHS

CASE STUDY

Case 3B   The farmer's wife (continued)
The 2nd session After Hilary had read me out her description of her 'desert island', I affirmed her courage and determination in seeking a rewarding family life. She had experienced some quite horrible events with men during her youth, yet she had chosen to pursue family life with Brian, a man who respected her and was dutiful and loving towards her. I admired her persistance too, that although her energy levels were low she proceeded with her tasks steadily, if slowly. However, I told Hilary that I was troubled that she may have been cast, in her original family, in the role of 'family cleaner-upper for men', trying to contain some of her father's 'emotional garbage' (and perhaps also some of Don's, as he had been very reliant on her for

support during his brief life), and I was concerned that this pattern did not repeat itself within her current family. I asked Hilary if she would bring Brian to the next session to discuss the situation further. Hilary replied that she was sure that he would come.

DISCUSSION

After praising those characteristics which have enabled Hilary to survive an exceedingly difficult passage to adulthood, I consider the role for which she seems to have well been trained in her family or origin: that of 'garbage-collector of distasteful emotions, expressed by men, within the family'. It is this training which may now be interfering with her experiencing a more rewarding relationship with Brian, a more respectful man, who appears to hold his emotions within, rather than dumping them on others.

EXPLORING RESOURCES

CASE STUDY

Case 4A   My funny valentine
Noah, 27, formerly a delicatessen assistant and now unemployed, had requested therapy to help him resolve his relationship with Tali, 23, a research officer. They had known each other for some 18 months. Many aspects of their relationship appealed to Noah: their affection for each other, their wonderful physical encounters, and the fun they had socializing. However, some disagreeable, and increasingly frequent, arguments were creeping into their friendship, and they had become disillusioned about their future. Noah was an intense, well-educated young man, who said he was dedicated to the search for Truth. Now, he was filled with recriminations that, as a man experienced in the ways of many women, he should have been able to sort Tali out. As we talked, it became apparent to me that Noah had sought female company more to bolster his own sense of self, and self-esteem, rather than to foster a mutually satisfying relationship. He had a tendency to plan strategies regarding his friendships, controlling them rather than allowing them to develop a life of their own. Noah also described episodes of 'emptiness' for which he needed the distraction of female company. 'I cannot remember an occasion when I ever felt comfortable

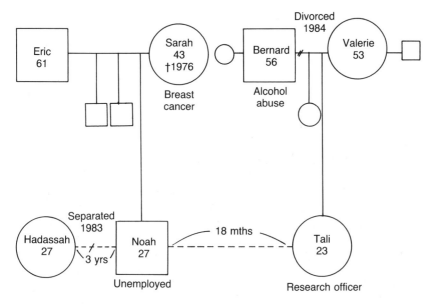

Fig. 4.1 Noah commenced therapy in November 1990.

on my own', said Noah. We discussed the loneliness that he had experienced after his mother's death, and his need to 'be in charge' of his deeper friendships to prevent future rejections. After all, his mother *had* left him when he was 14! I suggested that, perhaps underneath it all, Noah knew that he had to do some growing on his own, rather than within an intimate relationship, and perhaps it was this that prevented him making a more permanent commitment to Tali. Tali had also been attending a therapist for some time and had declined an invitation to come for a joint session with Noah. Surely, she too was interested in searching for her own truth. Her father had been a physically violent, alcohol-abusing man during her formative years. Perhaps they both realized that they were bringing agendas into their relationship that were much too powerful for any intimacy to bear, and that had to be addressed elsewhere.

Our conversation appeared to have an impact on Noah. He told me, after five weekly sessions of therapy, that he and Tali had decided to separate, but that he was now obsessed with thoughts about her. 'I cannot get her out of my mind', he said. 'I even sent her an unsigned Valentine's Day card yesterday. I don't know why I did that. It was a stupid thing to have done! Perhaps I really want to have Tali back?' 'Perhaps you really want to let Tali go', I responded, and quoted a line by Blaise Pascal: "The heart has its reasons which reason does not know" (Oxford Dictionary of Quotations, 1979). 'Perhaps sending the card was a letting-go exercise; it was your way of saying goodbye. It validated the love that you feel for Tali. The love is real, and being genuine, is something that you can let slip into the past. You can grieve its loss, and eventually let the good memories nourish you in the future, when your grieving is done. It was kind of you not to have signed the card. You were able to let Tali know that she is indeed loved, without raising any false hopes for the future. Would you compose a few lines that you might have written on the card, and bring your message to our next session?'

Noah wrote that, although he missed Tali's warmth and effervescence, he was now more aware that they had different paths to follow. He had accepted that they would not be travelling the same journey together. Though regretful, he was taking good care of himself, renewing some former acquaintances, and taking life more quietly as a whole.

Noah's obsessive thoughts disappeared after two further sessions. He is currently self-employed in the computer software industry, enjoys a number of leisure activities, has a variety of social contacts, but no friendship that he would nominate as a major one.

——————————— · · · ———————————

DISCUSSION

Noah comes to therapy well-versed in the dynamics of the blaming context: life needs to be controlled to prevent rejections; relationships are to be viewed in terms of winning or losing; one should continually develop expertise and skills to always achieve one's goals; and there are right and wrong ways of behaving within friendships. Noah is handling life within a well-structured intellectual context. Our conversation touches on a number of ideas that seem to be new to Noah: how the 'emptiness' left after his mother's death might be influencing his choice of intimate partner; that reason is not the only mechanism by which we resolve problems; and that the Valentine's card might be symbolic of a letting-go stage of Noah's growth, rather than a foolish lapse of rationality. Noah's letter to Tali indicates that he has started to express the softer emotions of grief. By the completion of ten therapy sessions, the intellectual blaming context within which Noah has sought to tackle his relationship struggles appears to have been exchanged for one in which problems are resolved via a more sensitive expression of feelings.

· · ·

SHARING EXPERIENCES

CASE STUDY

Case 4B   The burden

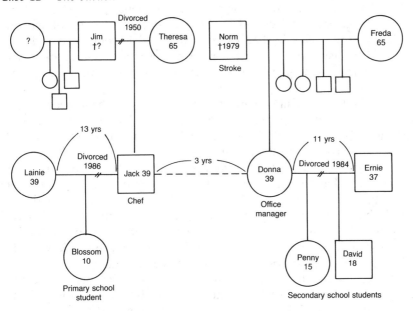

Fig. 4.2 Jack and Donna commenced therapy in February 1991.

Jack, 39, a chef, and Donna, 39, an office manager, said that they had been experiencing stress for many months and were now at the point of separation. Donna blamed Jack for his constant lack of energy and inability to offer her practical and emotional support. She felt cheated. Jack had been such a docile and friendly guy since they had first met, several years previously, but it had all disappeared within weeks after they had commenced living together under the same roof. Their life together had become a chore, with little leisure or fun, and almost no affection or physical intimacy. Jack complained that Donna nagged him continually and he felt that he had to walk away from her and keep his distance, to protect his sanity. He claimed that Donna had never made any real attempt to understand his personal problems. All throughout his life, Jack said, he had carried a huge internal affliction. He could not remember a time when he had ever been free of this feeling, and rather than try to comprehend and nurture him, Donna had forever demanded his participation in family life. Now, Jack felt that he was about to crumple into a heap.

As we talked, I learned more about this couple's past. There had been a great deal of loss. Jack's father had left his family when Jack was three months old and, for as long as Jack could remember, his mother had repeatedly targeted him as the reason for the marital split. Donna's father had died of a stroke several years previously, and she said that her first marriage had ended in divorce because of her ex-husband's violent nature. Jack said that his first marriage had concluded in divorce for similar reasons as the strains on his current relationship: the ex-wife had described Jack as 'a hopeless man who would never do anything' for her.

We talked for a while about how difficult it must have been for Jack to have carried the responsibility for his father's departure. I commented that he must have indeed been a powerful and influential three-month-old son to have driven his father away!

'Your story, Jack', I said, 'reminds me of the tale of Sysiphus, the Greek mythological character who was condemned to push a large rock up a hill for eternity. Any cessation of the momentum up the hill would have resulted in Sysiphus being crushed as the rock rolled back onto him. It seems, Donna, that Jack has got tired of shoving the load on his own, and he has enlisted your help to push the rock with him. Clever, huh? . . . and you feel that you have been conned!'

'Yeah', commented Donna, 'all men are bastards; just let them get their socks into your washing-machine, and they soon show you their true colours!' We all burst into gentle laughter at this point.

I asked Jack and Donna if they would do some tasks to see if their relationship could be different. Would Jack write a brief essay describing his 'Sysiphus' rock'? Would the two of them remember back to the time they were courting, in 1988, and think about what they had hoped for at the beginning of their acquaintance; how could 'together-ness' in 1991 be achieved? And would they prepare a special meal together, and while eating it, occasionally feed one another a tasty morsel?

At the subsequent session, one week later, Jack commented that the best way to describe his 'Sysiphus' rock' was like an enormous emptiness, a huge black hole that sucked everything into it. 'So', I queried, 'would any rage that you felt because Mum blamed you for Dad leaving be stuck inside you, and not be able to get out? and would any affection that you felt for your intimates also be trapped in there?' Jack nodded in agreement.

They had both made and eaten a delicious meal, but when it came to feeding each other, Jack said that he couldn't, and Donna said that she wouldn't! Finally, Donna said that she had received a shock when Jack had responded with a burst of verbal, though not violent, anger during a moment when he had felt unsupported.

——————————————   . . .   ——————————————

DISCUSSION

After a violent first marriage, Donna appears to have chosen Jack because of his seemingly calm and stable temperament. However, Jack's quiescence belies an internal space from which no feelings could escape.

A number of interventions are made to facilitate emotional release:

1. The story of Sysiphus is told, and makes overt Jack's cunning ploy in obtaining Donna's aid to help him move his burden forward.
2. Jack is encouraged to describe his personal 'Sysiphus' rock'.
3. This couple is stimulated to explore other ways of nourishing their relationship, i.e. contemplating courting; 'feeding' each other.
4. When Jack describes his 'emptiness' at a subsequent session, it is linked to his mother's past blaming, and he is offered the metaphor of a black hole, which prevented the expression of the appropriate emotions, i.e. anger and affection.

These tasks yield some important information by the next session. Jack is not able to write about his 'Sysiphus' rock', being content to present a simple, verbal description instead. Whereas Jack really does not know how to feed Donna, she is too angry to feed him. However, some change does occur, in that Jack shows his anger towards Donna during a disagreement, much to her surprise. This information directs the next few sessions of therapy towards

1. improving Jack's communication skills and further expression of his grief, so that he assumes responsibility for the unpleasant aspects of his emotional world, without co-opting Donna's support in doing so;
2. continuing to encourage a cooperative dialogue within Jack and Donna's relationship, supporting each other as they continue to talk of their losses;
3. offering negotiating skills;
4. commencing some physical intimacy, e.g. massage, cuddles, hugs, without necessarily proceeding to sex;
5. considering a regular 'togetherness' routine, (say) one evening or afternoon per week devoted to shared activities.

REARRANGING STRUCTURES

―――――――――   · · ·   ―――――――――

CASE STUDY

Case 3B   The farmer's wife (continued)
The 3rd session At this, our third weekly session, at which both Hilary and Brian attended, I asked Hilary: 'What is it specifically that troubles you about your relationship with Brian?'

'It is just that he will not do anything', she replied. 'I ask him to tell Robert and James to keep quiet when they are screaming at each other, and he will not. I ask him to get Robert and James to help me around the house, and he does not. They are his sons! I have said that I will take care of them because their mother will not have anything to do with them, but Brian just does not support me. He lets me do all the policework!

And I want him to be more affectionate to me. I love cuddles and being held, but whenever we do, Brian always wants to go further. He never forces himself on me, and he looks after himself whenever he wishes to go 'all the way'. He says he has never been unfaithful to me, and I believe him. I know he's disappointed when I do say no to him. I'd like more hugs, but I would also like to learn to be a 'real' wife to him.'

We discussed for a while Hilary's past violations. Brian expressed his anger at those men who had preceded him, abusing Hilary, and ruining whatever chances they had of a happy marriage. He appeared genuinely sensitive and concerned about his wife's struggles within the sexual area.

'But Hilary is pretty upset about the demands your boys make on her too', I commented. 'It is common, in remarried families, for family members to assume that the new woman will fit nicely into the 'mothering' role, and that the new family will work just like the older traditional models. I wonder if the two of you would sit down, for a couple of hours each week, and talk about how Hilary could support *you*, Brian, in the parenting of *your* boys? You would be responsible for disciplining Robert and James, and Hilary would be your wise adviser.'

They both warmed to this idea. In fact, they had few disagreements in the parenting of their three biological children, and both worked mutually in this area.

'I wonder if you would also do a trade in the physical aspect of your marriage?', I continued. 'Brian, would you make sure that there is plenty of cuddling time for Hilary, as she says she enjoys this way of being together with you. Hilary could guide you as to how much is enough. Perhaps you could even give Hilary a massage, and she could let you know which areas of her body feel the safest for her to be massaged? And Hilary, would you be prepared sometimes to 'be with' Brian when he does pleasure himself? Brian does understand and respect your dislike of coupling, and is prepared to take responsibility for his own sexual needs. Perhaps, Hilary, you could gently stroke Brian's face or shoulders, and share in his pleasure this way?'

I suggested that it might be important for me to see Brian, Robert and James for a joint session, to gather information as to how father and sons viewed the situation, an arrangement to which Hilary emphatically agreed. She was happy to have someone else check out these pro-blematic men! In the meantime, I said that I would like to see Hilary on her own, for ten sessions, to explore how she might be a 'real' wife to Brian. I would then see them together again.

--- . . . ---

DISCUSSION

The restructuring of this family consists of:

1. changing roles: rather than Hilary adopting the traditional 'mothering' role for all family dependents, she is given the status of 'valued consultant' to Brian, who is to adopt responsibility for Robert and James' welfare;
2. the institution of weekly meetings to confront problems, rather than avoiding them;
3. the introduction of a routine which involves a 'trade' relating to this couple's emotional and physical needs. They are to explore cooperative ways of being together in a difficult situation.
4. arranging an appointment for Brian, Robert and James to shift the responsibility for the 'boys' bad behaviour' from Hilary to the three individuals involved.

--- . . . ---

ENCOURAGING AUTONOMY . . .

CASE STUDY

Case 3B   The farmer's wife (continued)
The 4th and 5th sessions During the next two sessions of her individual therapy, Hilary vented her feelings regarding her difficulties in trusting men, her general lack of safety in all social relationships, her residual

sense of shame and helplessness at the violations that had occurred, and her relief that she had found, in Brian, a partner who had indicated a measure of responsibility and reliability towards her. Hilary also expressed concern over a physical complaint that had bothered Brian for a lengthy period of time. He had a large swelling in his right groin,

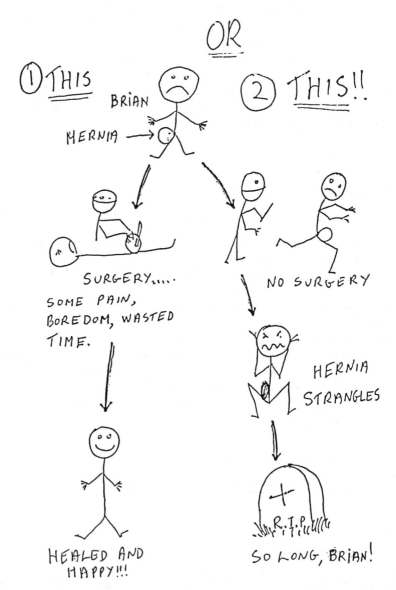

Fig. 4.3 John's drawing for Brian.

which had been diagnosed as a hernia. Surgery had been advised, but Brian had refused to seek further attention for this. I affirmed Hilary's concern as reasonable; such hernias can eventually strangulate and cause very serious complications.

'Let's see if we can budge him', I said, and drew for Hilary the diagram represented in Fig. 4.3. Hilary took the illustration home and eventually showed it to Brian; within three months he had sought, and obtained, surgical correction for his condition!

· · ·

DISCUSSION

Hilary believes that, although she has expressed her genuine concern to Brian over his tardiness in obtaining appropriate treatment for a potentially serious ailment, she can have no further influence. She has to continue to live in fear because of her husband's hesitation. I share with Hilary an artistic resource that (fortunately!) creates impact. Hilary expresses her surprise that the drawing has done the trick, and we discuss how people often use creative resources to achieve their goals and increase their power in a given situation, whether it be facilitating competent therapy or being a more effective 'real' wife.

· · ·

CASE STUDY

Case 4C   Images
During most of her first therapy session, Rosa, 31, a magazine photographer, who had attended on her own, was in tears. Richard, 45, a world-renowned sculptor who specialized in legendary forms, had left their relationship of three years over the past weekend. The arguments between them, she said, had increased both in frequency and the ugliness of the words they used. I asked if Richard would be prepared to come to a joint session, and three weeks later they both attended.

Richard commenced the narrative by saying that there were many aspects of Rosa that he loved. She was the first intimate friend with whom he had felt 'alive, vibrant', but her barbs of late had been particularly cruel and hurtful, and he felt that separation was the only answer. Richard was in the process of organizing an exhibition of his work, and also trying to arrange the property settlement from his previous marriage. 'It is rather interesting', he commented dryly, 'that everyone believes that I am a wealthy man, whereas my talent has offered me quite modest means'. In particular, Richard claimed that

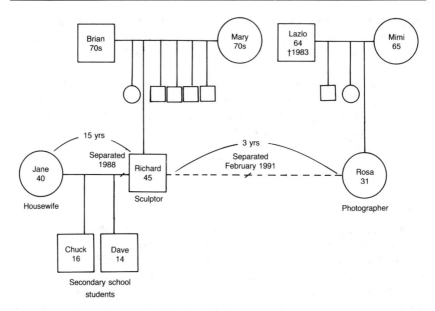

Fig. 4.4 Rosa commenced therapy in February 1991.

Rosa did not realize just how important achieving stability within his current life, resolving distress resulting from the past family split, and maintaining contact with his children were to him at this stage of his life.

Rosa continued the conversation by saying that although she was satisfied in her vocational life, she had begun to plan for her own family life, with the birth and raising of children, as well as continued advancement in her career. Rosa wanted to achieve these goals with Richard, but felt that she could not compete with Richard's fame. She felt that his talent would always take priority.

'And yet you both seem to have the skills that might make this into a wonderful relationship', I commented. 'Firstly, although there has obviously been a great deal of pain between the two of you, you seem to be treating each other, in this room, with a genuine respect and liking for each other. I get many people in here who are filled with hatred for one another, and express it freely. This does not seem to be the case with you two. Secondly, both of you appear to be at different stages of your development. You, Richard, are as if you are leaving midlife time, where you are 'closing off' some of the distressing experiences of that time and preparing for the second half of your life, whereas you, Rosa, might be described as entering midlife, exploring and 'opening up' to events that give you the best skills and information with which to further proceed.

As you were talking, I was thinking of the magazine editor who, on seeing a photograph of the Andromeda galaxy, exclaimed: "That is a great shot! Could we get a different angle on it?" Now, that is something you could do, Richard. You are a person who creates perceptive images of mythical reality. You could give us a uniquely different angle on the Andromeda galaxy. But when it comes to analytic detail, you, Rosa, are the one who is a perceptive observer of practical reality. Your skills can give us accurate information about the structure of the galaxy, spectrography and its chemical nature. That is a wonderful blend, mythology and practicality, the stuff of which great relationships are made!'

We continued to converse about their losses: Richard's first marriage, the death of Rosa's father, and how they might support each other in their grief. I shared some of my writings: for Richard, an essay on humour and satire (Gunzburg, 1991); for Rosa, an account of how the struggles within a triangular relationship were resolved creatively (Gunzburg, 1991) (Rosa feared that Richard's fame might prove a rival, taking him away from her).

'But perhaps you have the practical ability to help him give his fantasy substance, to consider the benefits in remaining close to you', I said. 'After all, he is only your average Australian genius'.

Three months later, during my daily constitutional, I met Rosa bouncing along the footpath. She gave me a huge smile 'Oh, he's living back again with me now', she said, 'and we are much better together. It is different. We still have our ups and downs, but we are managing so much better with it all'.

Five months later, the general practitioner who had referred Rosa told me that she was pregnant, and 18 months later, they introduced their new daughter to me.

------------------- · · · -------------------

DISCUSSION

Our discussion during therapy emphasized

1. the differing developmental stages of this couple, and the view that their arguments might be regarded as attempts to negotiate these periods of their lives;
2. that intimacies can work in a cooperative fashion; neither Richard nor Rosa had experienced this in the past;
3. how intimacies can form to utilize the different resources that each partner brings to the relationship, e.g. practicality/imagination;
4. the importance of respect and liking within relationships, as well as passion;

5. giving support to each other in their grief;
6. that Rosa need not be overawed by Richard's talent; her practical grasp on reality might be just the quality he needed to contemplate how better to keep his feet on the ground.

——————————— · · · ———————————

GIVING TO THE FUTURE

CASE STUDY

Case 3B   The farmer's wife (continued)

The 6th session During the sixth session, at which Brian, Robert and James attended, our conversation focused mainly on the boys' anger that their mother had never wanted custody of them. They rarely saw her, and when they did, they said that she seemed much more occupied and interested in her new family than in their presence. I commented that perhaps Robert's and James' mother saw them more as a reminder of her previous 'failure' in her first marriage, and hence worthy of rejection. 'It is enough to make you angry at women for the rest of your life!', I suggested. The boys vigorously nodded their assent.

We talked a bit about what they hoped for their lives, and if they thought that they would reach adulthood within their current family. Both seemed certain that Hilary and Dad would stand by them until they achieved their own independence.

'And yet you both really know how to make Hilary angry', I said. 'Robert seems to have learnt how to live better in this family. The stories that I hear from Hilary about how helpful he has become are encouraging. But you, James, you seem to have trouble fitting in. What could happen out of that? I hear that you are confident that Hilary and Dad will stick by you, but what would they do if you pushed them just that bit too far?'

There was no mention of violent beatings, or unfair detention to rooms, but the words 'boarding school, foster care and military college' as a final resort, entered our conversation. Finally, I suggested that part of James' struggle might be that he was finding greater difficulty than his elder brother in 'belonging' to this family, and gave them all a task to think of ways that they might be able to encourage James to be more a part of their group. They had all 'belonged' to their original family until Brian's marital split; how could Brian and Robert include James more within the activities and routines of their current family?

——————————— · · · ———————————

DISCUSSION

At this stage of therapy, our conversation includes

1. discussing Robert's and James' anger at their mother's rejection of them, and their feelings of helplessness that they have no say, either in the original decision to split, or how to be a part of their mother's new family;
2. exploring their insecurities: do they feel confident about reaching adulthood? Is it worthwhile to grow to adulthood, with all the struggles that they have already witnessed within their families? Is adulthood all hard work and sorrows, with little fun and few rewards?
3. pointing out to James that actions have consequences. Robert's improved cooperation is valued, but continued destructive actions on James' part may result in his being placed in another environment, where he will be encouraged to grow to adulthood by different methods.
4. wondering if James has problems 'belonging' to this current family, and encouraging the family to consider ways that will enhance his esteem, status and pride as a valued family member.

——————————— . . . ———————————

REFLECTION

CASE STUDY

Case 3B   The farmer's wife (continued)
The 14th session During the rest of her individual weekly therapy, Hilary continued to share the fears, doubts and anxieties that resulted from her previous violations.

'It is good to be able to come and talk', she said. 'I never thought that anyone would believe me how bad it was'.

When I saw Hilary and Brian together again, they said that their lives had improved. Robert was much more helpful, although James still gave a lot of cheek to Hilary. Their physical relationship had increased to the extent that they had coupled on one occasion (after complete abstinence since James' birth). Hilary said that she had gained no sexual pleasure from the actual act, but had enjoyed very much the holding and caressing. I commented that one of the most serious effects of sexual abuse of children by adults, and of rape, was the decrease in quality of the sexual experience in the survivors. However, I was absolutely delighted that Brian and Hilary were learning to find pleasure in what they were able to do together.

It was shortly after this session that Hilary gave Brian the drawing regarding his hernia, and that Brian sought surgery. We had a break from therapy for about six weeks.

The 15th–29th sessions Following Brian's surgery, I saw Hilary and Brian every two to three weeks. Our conversation concentrated mainly on:

1. improving the quality of their marriage; how they were negotiating, sharing, spending leisure time;
2. parenting issues as they arose;
3. discussing their hopes and plans for the future, and ways of achieving their goals.

The 30th session During our final session, Hilary expressed disappointment that she was still not a 'real' wife to Brian. Though they now enjoyed far more physical contact than previously, they still rarely coupled. I restated how incest and rape often left permanent limitations in sexual enjoyment for the survivor, and that sometimes, to be 'real' was to grieve over the losses experienced and to accept and live within the resulting limitations. Hilary and Brian had certainly worked hard in therapy on this aspect of their relationship, and in fact their dedication, courage and persistence had resulted in much greater expression of affection, with even the occasional intercourse. Moreover, Brian had no complaints of Hilary in this area, as he had at the commencement of therapy. All this was 'very real' progress to me, and I was admiring of it.

'He still does not bring me flowers', Hilary commented. We talked for a while about the changes that had occurred in the way Brian had expressed himself. We all agreed that Brian would probably always remain a quiet man, a follower rather than an initiator. However, they were spending more time together talking as a couple, and had even spent a week's holiday together (with the three youngest children, but nonetheless, a break from the farm routine). So Hilary had managed to convince Brian to tear himself away from the farm to which he was so committed. This would have been unthinkable previously. He simply would not have done it!

Robert's and James' behaviour, they said, had reached the level of 'normal teenage cheekiness', one which Hilary and Brian could well tolerate. The session where the boys had vented their anger at their mother seemed to have helped.

Therapy took a little under a year to complete, and as Table 4.1 illustrates, the major process of change was grounded well within the first ten sessions.

As therapists counter the experiences of the blaming context, the language of participants changes. The absoluteness of 'He must', 'You

Table 4.1 The processes of change within the first ten sessions of therapy

Session (frequency)	Clients attending	Focus of conversation
1 (weekly)	Hilary	Defining Hilary's problem, description of her 'desert island'
2 (weekly)	Hilary	Affirming Hilary's strengths; outlining her 'carer' role in her family of origin
3 (weekly)	Hilary and Brian	Restructuring family; Brian's responsibility for his sons; learning new ways to express and share physical affection
4–5 (weekly)	Hilary	Encouraging autonomy; discussion of Hilary's past violations, Brian's surgery
6 (weekly)	Brian, Robert and James	Mother's rejection of Robert and James, limitations, 'belonging'
7–13 (weekly)	Hilary	Further ventilation of Hilary's feelings re. past violations
14 (6 weeks' break)	Hilary and Brian	Reflection on progress to date
15–29 (fortnightly)	Hilary and Brian	Negotiating, parenting, future hopes
30	Hilary and Brian	Reflection on progress overall

should', 'We have to' phrases change to 'We tried this', or 'She is now doing that', or 'This is now happening'. There is a shift from viewing behaviours as part of a static problem, to being part of a process of development which all participants – therapists and clients – have a role in creating. This shift in perspective was partly explored in 'The farmer's wife', where Hilary and Brian's conversation changed from being an interchange between complainants into a mutually cooperative dialogue. Brian and Robert were also encouraged to help James 'belong' to the family, rather than continue to label him as the 'troublemaker'. Case 4D illustrates the shift further.

· · ·

CASE STUDY

Case 4D   The reprobate
The 1st session (family seen weekly) Rhonda, 39, a housewife, and her three offspring, Daphne, 14, Amos, 12, and Lara, 9, all attended the first therapy session. Rhonda claimed that she was at her 'wits' end' regarding Amos' behaviour. His grades at school had been steadily

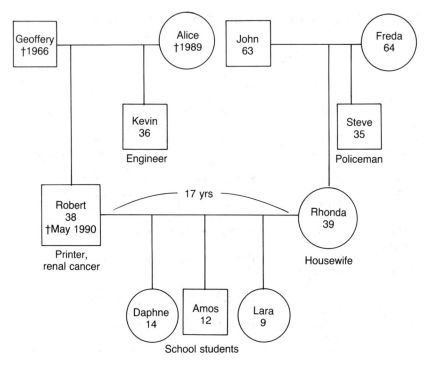

Fig. 4.5 Family commenced therapy in September 1990.

deteriorating during the second and third terms of the school year, and he had been suspended for the past two weeks for 'disrespectful and disruptive' behaviour in the classroom. Amos was also described as having been 'provocative and violent' towards his sisters for many weeks.

The most important event that had occurred within this family in recent times had been the death of husband/father Robert, 38, printer, from renal cancer, five months previously.

'He was alive and well for Xmas', Rhonda said, 'and dead five months later! Just like that!'

I asked each family member what it was that they remembered especially about Robert. Rhonda told of his dependability and caring, sensitive nature, although he had been easily aroused to anger and could be described as 'verbally violent'. He seemed to have had an extremely short fuse. Robert had always been determined that he was 'the boss' within the group, and Rhonda had been content to be his assistant. Now, she very much missed his leadership and strength, and felt quite lost without him. Daphne said that she had many good memories of Dad but was finding it difficult at present to recall them.

Lara stated that the best thing that she had liked about Dad was the numerous activities that they had shared together. She had especially liked Robert's ability to draw accurate pictures of the landscape. Amos was silent during much of the session.

I remarked that I was touched by the sensitivity of their stories of Robert. He was obviously a man who had been present in his family when alive. His death must have caused them enormous turmoil. I admired very much that, although Amos seemed to be signalling the whole family's distress, they appeared to be demonstrating a remarkable ability to stick together and not disintegrate during this crisis. I particularly admired them for their willingness to improve their family's lot and seek help through outside consultation. It takes courage to come and tell sensitive issues to someone who is largely a stranger.

We talked a little about the developmental stage the family had reached. I commented that it can be difficult for teenagers to lose a parent just when they need all the help that they can get to learn about the adult world. Daphne mentioned that Rhonda was always entering her bedroom, and we discussed the value of privacy for adolescents in thinking about where they were at, and where they were going.

Finally, I wondered if the family would do some tasks for the next session to enable me to gather more information as to how to help them. Would Daphne prepare a list of her good memories about Robert, and choose those she wanted to keep secret and those that she would reveal? Would Lara bring some of Robert's drawings to the next session? I asked Amos if he would do a sketch of the family as he saw them, and he grunted his assent. And I asked Rhonda if she would write herself a letter 'from Robert' advising her on how to cope in this difficult situation. *The 2nd session* The family all attended and told me that there had been much shedding of tears during the week by all members except Amos. Daphne read out to us her list of good memories of Robert. There was nothing that Daphne felt she could not share, and I thanked her for her generosity. Lara showed us Robert's drawing of two ducks. She liked them because they were alive and happy. 'Robert's letter' to Rhonda spoke of his pride in his family as to how they were coping, and his confidence that they would all pull through. Amos had done his drawing (Fig. 4.6) and I commented that with their frowns, sighs, unusual nose shapes and innovative hair fashions, musical voices and laughter, they appeared to be a family with a variety of emotions, with humour, individuality and wisdom. Daphne said that Mum had stopped coming into her room and she enjoyed her new-found sense of territory and Rhonda's respect.

Conversation turned to an incident that had happened at a family barbecue over the weekend, when Amos and his uncle, Steve, 35, a policeman, had become embroiled in a fight. Rhonda said that Steve,

Fig. 4.6 Amos's drawing.

her brother and a former street-fighter, tended to use his fists to resolve all arguments. Robert's brother, Kevin, 36, an engineer, was concerned about the fight and said that he wanted to help in Amos' welfare any way he could. I said that I was troubled over the appearance of physical action within the family and wondered if Steve, Rhonda and Kevin would attend a future joint session.

The 3rd session At this meeting, to which Steve, Rhonda and Kevin came, Kevin presented very much as a kind, warm, empathic negotiator, prepared to spend endless periods of time with Amos, promoting his development and growth. Steve proved to be a stocky, boxer-type of a man who declared that Amos was 'going down the tube', and that nothing would save him. 'I have seen it all happen before, doc', asserted Steve. 'A thrashing is the only language he will understand.' Steve was deeply disappointed that I was not a psychiatrist by training and did not have the proper authority to control the boy! In fact, Amos had confided in me the previous session that although he liked his Uncle Kevin, who always had an ear for him, Amos thought him a bit weak; he talked a lot, but did not really achieve anything. Uncle Steve, on the other hand, was much hated. Amos would listen to him and do as he said, only because he feared him. Amos avoided Steve like the plague and they saw each other perhaps twice yearly.

As we discussed the fight on the day of the barbecue, Rhonda said that Amos had begun throwing a tantrum for no obvious reason, and Steve had come in and clipped him one. The two had then started trading blows. Rhonda said that when Robert had been alive he had always been able to get Amos to snap out of it. She was becoming a bit frightened of Amos' temper. They seemed more and more to resemble Robert's outbursts. Amos was growing to quite a large stature, and Rhonda was concerned that he might eventually lash out at her and his sisters, and do some real damage.

We concluded the meeting with the agreement that when Rhonda needed a 'wise counsellor', she would contact Kevin for a chat, but if she ever felt that she or her daughters were in danger, she would 'call in the cavalry' and telephone Steve, a suggestion at which Steve grinned with relish. I secured an agreement with Steve that, if Rhonda did ask him for help, he would not include 'thrashing' in his discipline of Amos. I said that I would discuss our decision with Amos at our next session.

The 4th session With only Rhonda and Amos present, we got down to the very private business of Amos' rage. Rhonda stated that the family situation continued to settle and that Amos was much more cooperative, although he still threw the occasional tantrum. We talked for a while about these outbursts, and that when a parent dies, grief can sometimes make children of any age act out their anger in seemingly outrageous ways.

'Do you think that Amos is going mad?', I asked Rhonda suddenly. 'Yes, I do wonder about that at times', she replied. 'I guess that I can understand your concern', I continued. 'If Amos was going mad, you would want to help and protect him. You would want to watch him very carefully, perhaps even crowd him a little. But if his anger is part of his grief, just as you have begun to let Daphne enjoy the privacy of her room, perhaps you need to let Amos experience the privacy of his grief?'

I turned to Amos and discussed how, when some men became angry they could appear very intimidating and frightening to their friends, without even realizing it. Rhonda had said that Robert had at times appeared frightening and intimidating to those around him. Perhaps the same thing was happening to Amos, and he did not know it. Amos also appeared to have difficulty in deciding what sort of man he might be. Those men that he knew well seemed to have contradictions: would Amos be strong yet frightening, like Robert? tough yet hated, like Steve? kindly yet weak, like Kevin? I wondered how Amos would solve his dilemma in the future. Rhonda left the session looking a little puzzled, but the handshake that I received from Amos was one of the warmest that I can remember!

The 6th–7th sessions These sessions were requested by Rhonda for some individual conversation. Arising out of our last session with Amos, Rhonda had realized just how much she had put the children's needs in front of hers since Robert's death. In fact, she had been so concerned about their reactions, she had not made much time for her own grief. She had thought about my suggestion that Amos be left to grieve in privacy, and had felt herself becoming quite angry that she had denied herself the space to contemplate her own sorrow. We talked about her 'secondary role' to Robert during their marriage, and indeed, she had learnt well to defer to Robert, Steve, Kevin . . . it had been a strong family tradition that the men came first.

'Now', said Rhonda, 'I have an opportunity to show that women can be strong; we can have lives of our own. I think that this is important for Daphne and Lara'. 'For Amos too', I added.

The 8th session (one month after last session) Rhonda, Daphne, Amos and Lara came to tell me that Amos had not thrown a tantrum for the past month, and that he had gained a distinction in a recent mathematics test. Daphne and Lara said that they were less stressed and were having more fun, at home and with their friends. Rhonda described her own continuing changes as fulfilling. She was coming to enjoy being in control of her life, and somehow doubted that she would be needing either the services of Counsellor Kevin, or a charge from Cavalry Commander Steve!

· · ·

DISCUSSION

There are many occasions during the earlier sessions of therapy where the language of the blaming context is used. Rhonda terms Amos' behaviour as 'disrespectful, disruptive and provocative'. Steve thinks Amos is 'going down the tube', and that there is no hope for him; a thrashing seems to be the only appropriate response.

The influence of the blaming context is countered by:

1. Affirming this family's cohesive strengths in crisis and their determination to find a better way to cope.
2. Shifting the focus of conversation from Amos as a reprobate, on to his actions as an expression of grief. In doing this, family members are encouraged to utilize their creative resources and share how each of them is handling Robert's death. Their drawings and letters reveal underlying qualities of humour, individuality and wisdom.
3. Exploring how the family is dealing with developmental tasks at this 'adolescent' stage: privacy, negotiating, sharing, social contacts, leisure.
4. Rearranging family structures: Kevin and Steve are invited to a session, to discuss how they can be most useful in helping Rhonda and her teenagers.
5. Giving to the future: Rhonda is encouraged to consider the limitations of her previous role in deferring to male family members, and how she might take charge of her future pathway. At this stage, Rhonda is engaged in a cooperative male–female relationship, sharing skills, ideas, information and imagination, without dogmatism or direction. Amos' dilemma in growing towards adulthood is also highlighted. The male intimates in his life all appear to have contradictory characteristics within their personalities. How will he discover which ones to take with him into manhood, and which to leave behind?
6. Reflection: the family's conversation now contains descriptions of self-achievement and adequacy: Amos' cessation of tantrums and his academic success; Daphne's and Lara's easier emotional and social life; Rhonda's feelings of empowerment and hope for the future. The family is experienced, by all of us, as a pleasant place to be!

Therapy might thus be considered as proceeding from a blaming context, in which the family is stuck with past unresolved emotions, to a grieving context, in which the family expresses those past unresolved emotions, to a developmental context, in which the members explore how the family might grow and how events might be different in the future (Table 4.2).

Table 4.2 The process of therapy through blaming, grieving, and developmental contexts

Session	Context	Conversation
1	Blaming	Stagnation, blame, tantrums, violence, stress
2	Grieving	Becoming 'unstuck', expressing feelings, creative resources
3–8	Developmental	Future goals, new ways of relating, new ideas and options

TWO SPECIAL CONSIDERATIONS

1. It is important when a pause or impasse is reached during the first few sessions of therapy not to dismiss clients too easily and end therapy too soon. The therapeutic process may have reached a sensitive point at which they wish to explore a more painful area more thoroughly.

——————————— · · · ———————————

CASE STUDY

Case 4E   The designer
Justin, 45, a graphic designer, told me during the first three sessions of weekly therapy that he had suffered emotional mood swings for the

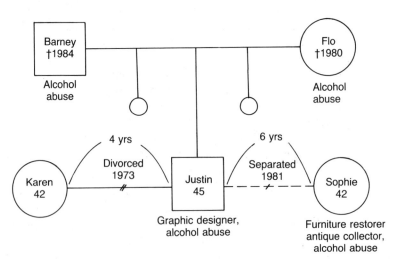

Fig. 4.7 Justin commenced therapy in February 1991.

past six years, and would like to find a way to stop them. He would experience quite steady periods when he had lots of energy and could work effectively, but then would sink into the depths of black despair and resort to whisky for solace. Justin said that he felt angry at how hard he had to work just to maintain his equilibrium during the good times, and wondered if he would ever find peace.

Justin described his early life as a battleground. 'Barney and Flo were always fighting', he said, 'and they both were heavy drinkers; you could probably call them alcoholics'. Justin described his father as a man unable to offer any emotional support and nourishment to anyone else in the family, and although he termed his mother a 'verbally abusive' person, he never had any doubts about her genuine love and interest in his welfare. Although Barney stuttered, Justin dated his own stammer from his bout of polio meningitis when he was six years old. Justin had been married for four years, and this had ended 18 years previously with his wife leaving him for another man. He had enjoyed a second relationship for six years with Sophie, 42, a furniture restorer and antique collector, and although they had separated ten years previously, they still kept company frequently. One current problem was that they both stimulated each other's patterns of alcohol abuse, and many evenings would be spent together lost in inebriation. Though Justin had received a strict Catholic training from 'the Brothers', which, he said, had engendered much guilt and fear of divine wrath within him, he still very much valued the warm spirituality of his religion and said that it remained an important element of his life. He had sought help through counselling on two occasions, but to no avail.

At the end of the third session I affirmed Justin's inner strength and resourcefulness. Despite a lengthy history of emotional deprivation and some distressing experiences, such as his fight with polio and his wife's rejection, he had managed to maintain employment, social intimacy and an interest in spirituality. I wondered where we could go, in therapy, from here. 'All my previous therapists have got stuck at this point', commented Justin disconsolately.

I asked Justin if he would write a brief description of his 'emotional territory' (Gunzburg, 1991), both during distressing times and during times of contentment.

At our fourth session, Justin described his emotional territory in terms of space: during his downswings, there was an overwhelming feeling of claustrophobia, a lack of space within which he experienced staccato rhythms, disjointedness and disharmony. Every effort seemed so hard within this cramped and jerky space! During the more comfortable times, Justin experienced an expanded space in which his life flowed calmly, with flexibility and ease. Justin continued to tell me of a particularly pleasant long weekend, just past, that he had spent with Sophie in the gently folded volcanic hills of western Victoria. The weekend had been largely drink-free, but for the final evening, when they had both become soused and had woken to the morning of a new working day with huge hangovers. Otherwise, the weekend had been spent in bushwalks, restaurants and quiet music and affection.

I complimented Justin that he seemed to have translated his desire for 'inner flowing space' into very real terms over the weekend, finding solitude and tranquillity with his companion in the rolling hills of the countryside. Perhaps the final evening's overindulgence was more a response to the ending of their holiday, a little 'grief reaction', rather than due to some internal sinister black mood. This latter view seemed readily acceptable to Justin.

At our fifth session, Justin said that his week had been easy and adequate. The current economic recession had slowed his business sales and he was having no problems in finding the energy needed in researching new markets. A favourite pet of 15 years, a cat named Ankh, had died and Justin showed me his final tribute to Ankh, a written description of a last moment shared together:

> 'One balmy autumn night, I waved the last swaggering guests farewell (they all tooted, despite the neighbours) and then was left with the weariness of the house, collecting the dirty crystal ashtrays and glasses, straightening the rugs . . . recollecting. Ankh in the lounge looked tired, standing in the middle of the room. She gave out a slight sigh, and stared up bewildered. 'You too', I said and smiled and moved the record stylus across to that slow haunting ballad and we danced. A dance of this and that, and other things, and Ankh looking so terribly beautiful as we turned and turned . . . and all in the soft mauve smoky light.'
>
> [Ankh passed away peacefully last night after a short illness. A small service was held at that little church on the hill and was attended by immediate family and a few close friends. She will be sadly missed].

--- . . . ---

DISCUSSION

After obtaining a clear description of Justin's struggles, and how he is coping, there is a momentary pause in therapy. Perhaps both Justin and I are hesitant in approaching his internal distress more closely. A creative resource is used to bridge the impasse. Justin writes of his inner turmoil, and of how life might be, and his images are accompanied by positive changes: Justin spends an enjoyable weekend in the country with Sophie, without over-reliance on alcohol. He reports that, although business sales are declining, he is finding the zest to seek new customers, and, when a beloved pet dies, Justin uses his ability to write yet again, to grieve and let go, rather than sink into a maudlin depression.

2. Do not be disheartened if clients 'disappear' after the first session of therapy. The passage of time is sometimes required before they feel able to proceed.

———————————————   · · ·   ———————————————

CASE STUDY

Case 4F   The librarian

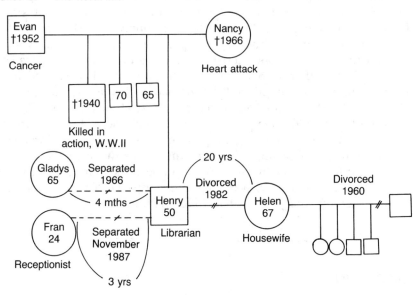

Fig. 4.8 Henry commenced therapy in April 1988.

Henry, 50, a librarian, arrived at his first session of therapy complaining of a sense of emptiness and lack of meaning in his life. He had experienced many losses over the years: his parents' death from illness when he was a youth; his brother's demise, killed in action during World War Two; and the dissolution of his 20-year marriage to Helen, 67, a housewife, six years previously. Henry said the marriage had 'died of boredom'. More recently, a three-year relationship with Fran, 24, a receptionist, had ended. Henry described Fran as a 'clinging, dependent' companion who had pressed him constantly to proceed towards marriage and children. Henry said that he had found himself more in the role of 'aged parent' to Fran, rather than mutual intimate, doing most of the housework and giving most of the emotional support. 'She swore that she would kill herself if I did not meet her wishes', said Henry. Eventually, Fran had left Henry for a younger partner. Henry stated that he still harboured feelings of guilt and low self-esteem in relation to an affair during the early years of his marriage.

I expressed by appreciation to Henry for his honesty and the clarity of information that he had given to me, in this our initial session. I remarked that there appeared to be many areas of loss for which he might be grieving, and we could examine some of these further in future sessions. We booked a second session for the following week.

Henry came to our second meeting three years and one month later! He said that after our first encounter his stress levels had greatly increased, and he had not felt capable of continuing at that stage. During the ensuing years, Henry had continued to work and develop his life on his own, without any deeper intimacies. This had worked well for him. He had come to realize that, out of all the events we had discussed, his affair with Gladys was the one that had created most impact. He particularly grieved that he had not made a choice to leave Helen at that time and commence a new relationship with Gladys, who, he felt, would have proved to be a much more suitable partner. In fact, he had met Gladys again quite recently. She was not interested in renewing a relationship with him, and it was this meeting that had made clear for him exactly which loss had been most important to him. He was coping well now, was planning a trip overseas, did not need further therapy, and just wanted 'to let me know'.

——————————— · · · ———————————

DISCUSSION

Henry presents in the first session with a large number of losses in his life. Talking about them proves too stressful, and it takes a lengthy period of time, plus a chance reunion with a former intimate, to enable him to understand what has been troubling him more clearly.

SUMMARY

In Chapter 4 we considered:

1. further elements of the blaming context;
2. ways of countering the blaming context;

3. the shift that occurs during therapy from the blaming context to other contexts that encourage expression of feelings and expansion of options;
4. the issues of pauses or impasses in therapy, and of clients leaving therapy unexpectedly.

POINTS FOR REFLECTION

1. Contemplate a conversation between yourself and your client within the blaming context. Have the client use as many words of blame, labels, accusations, discounting phrases as you can imagine, as they describe their problems to you.
2. Now consider a therapeutic strategy to counter the blaming context of your client. How would you
   (a) affirm their strengths?
   (b) explore their resources?
   (c) share their family experiences?
   (d) rearrange family structures?
   (e) encourage autonomy and intimacy?
   (f) discuss how the family can give to the future?
   (g) reflect with the family on their changes and successes?
3. Reflect on a conversation during a hypothetical last session. What language would you and your client use that might indicate a shift away from the blaming context?

REFERENCES

Oxford Dictionary of Quotations, 3rd edn. (ed. L. Brunschvicg). Oxford University Press, Oxford, p. 369: Blaise Pascal, Pensées.
Gunzburg, J. (1991) *Family Counselling Casebook*, McGraw-Hill, Sydney, pp. 155–9; 185–7; 239–40.

Anger 5

During the next four chapters consideration is given to the situation where a client's problem is defined as an emotional state, e.g. anger, denial or depression, rather than a behavioural or interactional problem such as tantrums, truancy or drunkenness.

In her ground-breaking work on death and dying, Elisabeth Kubler-Ross (1973) noted that loss was followed by a number of emotional states, which she organized into a sequence. As so often happens, a rigid, 'reified' theory arose out of her innovative ideas, and therapists were eager to encourage their clients to progress exactly according to this sequence of emotions, as if there was only one way to achieve resolution of grief. A more rewarding path can be to:

1. clarify which emotional state clients are experiencing (as always, countering any blaming or accusations that may occur);
2. encourage creative expression of the emotional state;
3. explore future directions along which clients might develop, or options that they may choose.

During these four chapters, I shall rely solely on case studies and discussion to convey the subtle nuances relating to the therapeutic process as each emotional state is being considered. Readers are encouraged to note the therapeutic process illustrated in each of the case studies:

1. At the descriptive level:
   (a) The description of the problem, including any attributed blame.
   (b) The definition of the problem as an emotion.
2. At the contextual level:
   (a) The context within which the problem has formed, i.e. separation, violence, deprivation. Naturally, in this book, the context in which the problem has formed will always involve unresolved grief.

(b) How the problem is addressed creatively and expressively, within the grieving context.
3. At the experiential level:
   (a) How the future is explored and charted autonomously by the client.

———————— · · · ————————

CASE STUDY

Case 5A   The little devil

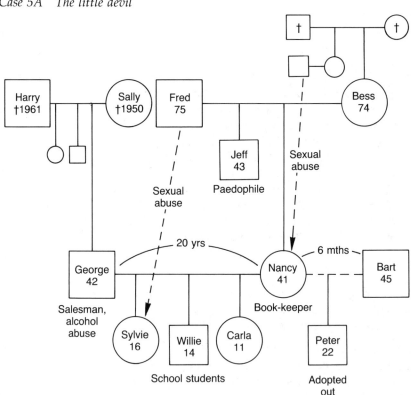

Fig. 5.1 Nancy commenced therapy in September 1990.

Nancy, 41, a book-keeper, had come to therapy on her own, stating that she was at the end of her tether since her husband George, 42, a salesman, had left the family home one month earlier. George, an abuser of alcohol for the duration of their marriage, had gone to a mountain retreat for rehabilitation. Three weeks later, he had announced that he had found God, that he had beaten the booze, and that he would not be returning home. Moreover, as he had just resigned from his job, there would not be any finances available for him to continue supporting his family. And yes, there were other 'people' in his life, although he had made no plans for future commitment.

The family climate since George's decision, Nancy said, could only be described as tempestuous. The mood of the three adolescents fluctuated from bouts of hours-long silences to episodes of fighting, kicking and screaming, with Nancy having to be referee. She was particularly frightened of Willie's temper, that he would do some real physical damage to either herself or one of his sisters. She herself felt furious at the unilateral nature of George's decision. Nancy believed that she had dutifully supported her husband throughout his drinking habit for many years, and now he was leaving for what he perceived as the good life, dumping all family responsibilities on to her shoulders. 'He's never been of any real use around the house', said Nancy, 'and he has spent little enough time with the children . . . but at least he did pay the bills reliably!'

The first five weekly sessions were spent with Nancy and her adolescents. All the old cherries of self-blame usually associated with one member of a family leaving, were trotted out. 'If only we had paid Dad a bit more attention, he would have stayed', claimed Sylvie. 'I feel so guilty', said Nancy. 'I feel like a rotten wife and mother. George has gone, and I cannot do anything with these three. If I had been able to put in more, things would have turned out better'. George had often reminded Nancy just how unsatisfactory a wife and mother she was! We explored these beliefs together: was George's behaviour – his drinking, his leaving – a response to theirs, or was he responsible for his own actions and choices? What 'unspeakable things' had they really done to drive him away? Was George behaving with goodwill towards his family; people do have the right to choose to leave the family at any given time, but was the way George was doing it respectful and sensitive to the needs of other family members?

Nancy, Sylvie and Carla decided that George, although having the right to leave, was being ill-mannered in his mode of departure. Willie, however, defended his father and asserted that 'Mum should have treated him better'. He wanted George to come back. The others did not want him to return. We moved on to a grieving task: the family were to look at some early photos and remember the good times. They were also to consider what information they needed to know to decide if the separation was a mistake or not. We discussed some ways the family might work more effectively in the new situation: negotiation of an adequate level of pocket money; establishing a dish-washing roster; Sylvie and Carla to discuss access arrangements with George; Willie to plan for some of the family's leisure needs and fun.

At the sixth session Nancy, attending with Willie, said that the arguments were much more settled but that Willie had been apprehended by the police for shoplifting. Nancy had decided to enrol Willie in the 'Big Brother' system, in which one man made a commitment to be responsible for the welfare of a younger one who had encountered some difficulties. Willie told me that eventually he wanted to become a member of the police force, but he had been advised that another episode of shoplifting would result in a criminal record, putting an end to his hopes for a police career.

I decided to see Willie individually for ten weeks to help him with his sense of identity and self-esteem, and to foster a nourishing male–male bond. Willie settled well into therapy and talked about the loss of his father, who used to take him trail-bike riding, but now showed little interest in shared activities. Willie felt cheated. 'Perhaps you felt that life has stolen from you?', I suggested. 'I wonder if that is why you stole from the shop . . . you felt you needed some compensation?' Willie continued to tell me of his losses: how he felt cut out of Sylvie's and Carla's activities. Whenever he had planned fun-time for the family, his sisters had seemed to band together against him and concentrate on their own play. However, Willie did have a companion, Jason, who lived nearby and even came to a therapy session with him to help his friend. A good mate indeed!

Nonetheless, although individual therapy appeared to be progressing well, Willie stole again about six weeks later. This time, he had taken a bicycle speedometer from a school colleague, which he had returned promptly on being caught. The police were not involved. I said to Willie, with Nancy present, that he seemed to be struggling with a little devil inside him, which tempted him into shoplifting, stealing, tantrums and general bad behaviour, and was always getting him caught. Would Willie bring me a drawing of this little devil to the next session?

Willie and Nancy both came to the next session. Nancy said that Willie had now bought himself a speedometer out of his own pocket money. When Willie showed me his drawing (Fig. 5.2), I commented that Willie's little devil did not really appear to be all that evil, in fact in appeared to be rather cute. It was a shame that such a cheeky little devil seemed likely to eventually sabotage Willie's future vocation. It was at this stage that Nancy remarked that she also felt the need for some individual therapeutic support, and I agreed to see Nancy and Willie on alternating weeks.

Nancy's individual therapy centred mainly on examining her self-talk, the messages inside her head that helped to lower her self-esteem and destroy her confidence. I asked Nancy if she would write down some of these messages, and compare them with some of the ways

Fig. 5.2 Willie's drawing.

that George had used to discount her. Nancy's list is reproduced in Table 5.1.

We discussed how George's messages had increased the intensity of her own internal sense of guilt; indeed, Nancy said that, in all previous relationships, she had chosen men who had discounted her, reproducing the original patterns of her own sexually abusing, emotionally depriving family of origin. When 11 years old, Nancy had been fondled once on her breasts and buttocks by an uncle. She had not felt free to tell her parents about this event, and had lived in fear of her uncle as she grew to adulthood. Nancy had learnt recently from Sylvie that her grandfather, Fred, 75, had done the same thing to Sylvie at a similar age.

Table 5.1 Nancy's list of George's discounts

Nancy's internal messages that invoked her guilt

I am 'just' Nancy: I am not important enough to ask for anything, I am not entitled to anything, I have no right to anything, I am not good enough

When the kids ask for something and I cannot or will not supply, I feel I am not a good enough mother

When I do not like my kids or others, this makes me feel either bad or superior, which makes me feel guilty. When I have felt good, I feel egotistical; when bad, self-pitying; when angry, avoiding and aggressive; when wanting, demanding

Needing sex is the same as being a slut

Needing help is the same as being weak or helpless

When we were building our house, I felt I did not deserve it and when we moved in, I felt out of place and less than those around me

I have entered a fancy boutique only once when I was 16; I have always felt inferior

I feel a failure – marriage, kids, weight, pregnancies, happiness, contentment, achievement, academically, philosophically, financially, now relationships with friends are breaking down

My opinions can be critical and judgmental

George's messages that invoked guilt within Nancy

You wanted everything; I worked my guts out to supply

You did not work. You never got a proper job

I am entitled to my share. You have everything, I have nothing

I am an alcoholic. You show no understanding or care. My drinking is your fault

You spent all the money. You are aggressive, demanding, critical, distant, cruel, hard, greedy, punishing. Your desire is to take me to the cleaners

Nancy had ensured that her children were never left alone with Fred again. I admired Nancy that she had believed her daughter's account of Fred's sexual abuse, and had acted effectively to protect her children. We talked about some areas of worth, her humour, perseverance and dedication to family, which she might use to develop some internal self-affirming messages, and ways that she could treat herself: to go to a fancy boutique and window-shop, rather than tell herself that she did not deserve luxuries.

Willie continued to express to me his frustration and anger at the marital split, but we shared a small moment of triumph: Nancy, who usually brought him by car to therapy, had been unable to transport him that day. I had suggested that Willie come by public utility. 'He

will never make it', Nancy had snorted. 'He is just so disorganized'.
Yet here he was, having travelled alone by train and tram! I offered my
congratulations, and gave Willie a copy of one of my recently written
stories. 'I am trying to find out which age group would be the best one
to present this', I said. 'Would you read it during a quiet moment with
Mum and let me know your opinion?'. Willie agreed.

Cheepatta, The Echidna

Cheepatta was angry and fearful. He was a young echidna whose
spines were just beginning to grow. Cheepatta's father, Gnarla,
was a fine looking echidna with strong, sharp spines. He knew all
the best places to find juicy ants to eat. Cheepatta's mother, Orlick,
also looked wonderful with her strong sharp spines. She knew
precisely where to shelter from the heat of the Australian summer
sun. Both Gnarla and Orlick knew exactly how to roll themselves
up into spiny balls to protect themselves from the wild dingos that
roamed nearby. Cheepatta loved and admired his parents. He
hoped one day that he would be just like them, with their full-
grown spines and their wisdom in the ways of the forest.

Now, Cheepatta was angry and fearful because Gnarla had left
home to live in a gully far away. Cheepatta saw his father only
occasionally – once or twice a year – because Gnarla's new house
was such a long distance from home. Gnarla seemed happy to see
Cheepatta when his son visited him, but the father was also sad
and grumpy for much of Cheepatta's stay. There seemed to be
little time for fun and play.

Orlick told Cheepatta that she and Gnarla had become too prickly
for each other. Orlick liked the forest walks whereas Gnarla would
rather spend his days looking for juicy ants to eat. They could not
agree as to how to spend their time together and had decided not
to live with each other any more. Cheepatta blamed Orlick for
Gnarla's departure. How could he grow strong, sharp spines without his father around? Would he and his mother find that they
were too prickly for each other? Would they too separate? How
would he be able to look after himself if that happened?

Orlick was upset by Cheepatta's anger and fear. She felt that she
had enough wisdom and skill to help Cheepatta grow strong,
sharp spines. But Cheepatta was scared that this would not happen
if Orlick and Gnarla did not live with him in the same house.
Cheepatta and Orlick quarrelled frequently and Cheepatta used
every trick and argument to try and convince Orlick to bring
Gnarla back home.

As time passed, Cheepatta began to trust the way that Orlick
cared for him. She took him on many forest walks and they did

not get lost. She found tasty and nourishing food and dug out a comfortable shelter for them both. Orlick also found some new friends. Some of them were men echidnas and they and Orlick were not so prickly as Gnarla and Orlick had been. They treated Cheepatta with kindness and respect. Gnarla also made new friendships and Cheepatta learnt that his father could be less prickly with other women echidnas. Gnarla was less sad and grumpy and there was more time for fun and play whenever Cheepatta visited him. Both Orlick and Gnarla were becoming happier and more confident. They were indeed changing. Perhaps Cheepatta could also change and be less angry and fearful?

Cheepatta came to understand that sometimes mothers and fathers do not live together. They may choose to live apart and build a new and different type of family. As long as they treated each other with kindness and respect and talked with each other about what they wanted for the future of their family, they could all get on with their lives. Cheepatta always regretted that Gnarla and Orlick never decided to live together again, but he learnt to get along well within his new family, and discovered some new and different ways of growing strong, sharp spines from his mother, his father, and their many friends.

At our next family meeting, just prior to Christmas, Sylvie and Carla related how their attempts at arranging access with George had proved unfruitful. George would contact them only irregularly, take them to the movies, then drop them straight back home. There was no time made for conversation. Moreover, they were angry that George was paying them no maintenance, even though he had obtained new employment. Nancy commented that, in fact, George had paid the family $400 during the five months since separation. Sylvie and Carla had decided that they would not visit George for Christmas. They wished to explore how Christmas could be different with just the family of four. Willie, however, had wanted to visit his father on Christmas day. Sylvie said how she had felt guilty when George had told her how hurt he was at their decision. We discussed for a while the words 'hurt' and 'disappointment', and decided that while family life involved many disappointments, most of which could be coped with, the word 'hurt' had been used by George more to invoke guilt in his children than to express his disappointment. Nancy said that she and Willie had perused my story of 'Cheepatta, the Echidna' and thought that it fitted quite well for adolescents as well as younger readers.

At the subsequent therapy session, the teenagers said that none of them had visited George on Christmas day, although they had seen him the previous Sunday. They had all enjoyed a leisurely day together. The fighting between Willie and his sisters had decreased to a minimum, with no fear of bodily damage. I complimented the family on their improvements, and Nancy requested further weekly individual therapy to work on her problems of loss of confidence, guilt, low self-esteem, and letting go her anger at George. Willie was happy to use my room as a drop-in centre whenever he felt the need.

Willie did attend a further session a month or two later. He sat quietly in my room with moist eyes. 'Shall I tell Dr John what it is all about?', queried Nancy. Willie nodded. 'Willie is sad', Nancy said, 'because he likes you better than his father. . . . And here is one to add to your story', Nancy continued. 'Yesterday, I was really upset and crying about it all, and this young bloke sitting here beside me gave me the biggest, most comforting hug!' Two months later, Nancy told me that George had visited his solicitor, now paid the family $80 maintenance regularly each week, and took the teenagers every fortnight for weekend access.

Six months later, the family situation remains improved and there have been no further episodes of stealing.

——————————— . . . ———————————

DISCUSSION

Although there are 'hours-long' silences in the family, and guilt plays a significant part in the way they are experiencing their world, family members agree that their main struggle is with their anger towards George.

Initially, the family is encouraged to talk about their angry feelings and examine their self-blame following George's departure. They decide that George's decision to leave is his own responsibility, and that nobody has the right to act in a way that increases their advantage to the detriment of others. A grieving task is arranged: to consider some happy times over some photos. It is often easier to let go a family member when those who remain recall that there are some good memories left to nourish them in the future. People may be left with unresolved grief if they experience the past relationship as a total loss, with no good experiences within it. At this stage, the family is also encouraged to explore some routines that might help them to function more effectively in the new situation.

The conflict settles and another problem arises: Willie's stealing. During some individual sessions, I endeavour to form a more nurturing relationship than the one he has experienced with his father. This is enhanced by the 'Big Brother' programme.

Willie's drawing of his 'little devil', and a story about separation, are used to encourage him to consider his future options. Will his personal demon sabotage his police career? Can a separated family provide the environment that Willie needs to grow to adulthood? Nancy attends her own individual sessions with me, in parallel with Willie, to work on her issues of guilt and self-blame.

During the final family sessions there are signs that members have accepted the *status quo*, having negotiated equitable access and financial maintenance arrangements with George, having spent Christmas in a new and different manner, and having reached a cooperative home routine with one another. Willie, in particular, has stopped fighting and stealing, is content to have less contact with his father, and is showing much more affection towards Nancy. Nancy says that she now feels more free to pursue her own issues in therapy.

CASE STUDY

Case 5B   Revenge

Kath, 51, a private secretary and currently unemployed, commenced individual therapy with a description of her sense of lost vitality and depression. During the past 12 months, a grandson had died of cot-death and her three-year relationship with Greg, 44, manager of a golf club, had ended six months previously. Around this time also, Kath had been made redundant following two years of employment. As we talked about her losses, Kath's voice rose in volume, her face reddened and her limbs and body began to shake visibly. 'I had not realized that I was so angry about it all', she commented.

We continued to discuss other disappointments from the past. Kath appeared to have developed a habit of forming relationships with exploitative men, herself taking the role of carer to her partners. Des, 65, a banker, had been preoccupied with his work, had abused Kath both emotionally and physically, and the marriage had ended with Kath leaving and raising her adolescents on her own for several years. Kath had determined that her children should not be exposed to the further influence of abusive men, and had waited until they were all young adults with a measure of their own independence before pairing up with Greg. She was initially attracted to Greg's sociable and outgoing nature. They shared a mutual interest in golf, but she was disappointed to learn just how sociable Greg had proved to be. He involved himself in affairs with several women ('A womanizer, just like Dad!', Kath said) during the course of their marriage. Greg was also heavily engrossed in the golf club, yet emotionally demanding of Kath for even

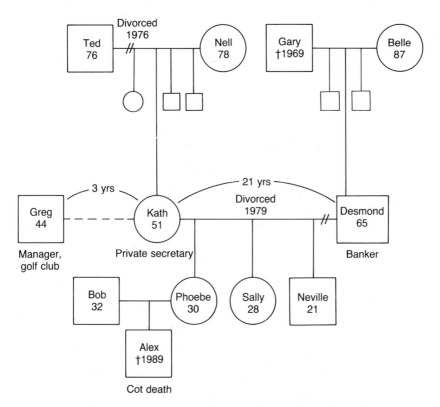

Fig. 5.3 Kath commenced therapy in November 1989.

the smallest domestic comfort. I asked Kath what her dreams, hopes and fancies were for a future life on her own. 'I will probably end up owning a country pub, but I always wanted to be a madam on a paddle steamer. I was a good kid when young. . . . I was such a pain in the bum! I always thought that tarts had all the fun!'

I asked Kath if she would draw a picture of herself as a tart (Fig. 5.4) for our next meeting, and we arranged a series of ten weekly sessions.

During our second and third sessions I encouraged Kath to express her feelings of anger. It appeared that, within her family of origin, Kath had been raised as 'carer' to other family members. Her mother seemed to have required Kath's support during a difficult marriage, which ended in divorce. Kath appeared to have carried this carer role into her subsequent intimate relationships with patriarchal men, who had expected it of her. I asked Kath to contemplate those moments in her life when she had felt cared for (Kath nominated her wedding day to Des, and the time she had spent at boarding school with her peers).

Fig. 5.4 Kath's drawing of herself 'as a tart'.

Who was there within her current social network who could tend to her needs? (Kath named some fond friends with whom she often played golf.) I asked Kath to watch the film *Never ending story* which details the stages of grief (Gunzburg, 1991).

At our fourth session, Kath was still in a fury and I asked her to write a farewell letter to Greg. She shared it with me at our fifth session:

> Dear Greg,
> This is goodbye.
> What can I say – it has been weird. Life with you was weird and life without you is weird. I need to say goodbye to preserve my sanity.
>   I would like to say I wish you well, but I don't. I would like to say I wish you good health, but I don't. As a matter of fact, I cannot bring myself to wish you anything but rotten things. I hope you live long enough to regret the opportunity you lost and mourn it till your dying day.
>   You don't deserve me and I certainly don't deserve someone like you.
>   I hope one day you eventually grow a spine and learn to stand up for yourself and not run away.
>   Still God protects drunks and idiots, and He must be looking after you well.
>   I hope our paths never cross. I hate to think what my reaction would be,
> Kath

All these efforts were to no avail. Kath's rage remained as hot as ever, and she said that she felt as if it was burning her up.

At our sixth session, we discussed what more Kath would have to do to say goodbye to Greg. Kath replied that, since she had commenced therapy, she had come to realize just how effectively Greg had discounted her. She seemed intent on avenging herself for the years of abuse, but did not quite know how to go about it. She could think of nothing else. I asked Kath if she would draw an impression of Greg (Fig. 5.5) and compile a specific list of ten curses to fall upon him. Kath brought both these items to our seventh session.

Ten curses on Greg
 1. May you suffer heart-wrenching grief without the shoulder of a loved one to lean on.
 2. May your beloved golf club burn to a cinder around your feet.
 3. May your health deteriorate rapidly and dramatically.
 4. May your precious car be stolen, stripped, wrecked and pushed over the edge of the Westgate bridge.

Fig. 5.5 Kath's drawing of Greg.

5. May you face the harsh realities of life and realize too late just what you have lost.
6. May you live in poverty for the rest of your life.
7. May your friends forsake you.
8. May your hair fall out and you grow fat.
9. May you suffocate from having your head so firmly buried up your arse.
10. May you become an alcoholic with emphysema.

This session brought about a remarkable change in mood. Kath almost giggled as I read out the curses. She said she felt that a bane had been lifted from her shoulders in doing the task. Our conversation turned to the malediction of patriarchy, with its dominating, often violent, male attitudes towards 'caring, passive' women. We discussed the importance of overcoming feelings of helplessness in the face of injustice, and the gaining of autonomy and direction. I asked Kath what were the blessings in her life that countered the effects of curses. She replied, with tears, 'Alex had an angel face. It is the memory of his angel face that keeps me going through the tough times'. Kath also told me that Phoebe and Bob were expecting another child.

The final three sessions were spent in affirming Kath's relief that her rage at Greg was lessening and that she was indeed letting go. 'These curses are a powerful voodoo', Kath commented rather anxiously. 'Number seven seems to be having effect. Greg rang me to tell me that a friend of his is dying of leukaemia'. We both marvelled that sometimes the real world does match the imaginary one that we co-create within the therapeutic encounter.

Kath also said that she was back in the swing of the golf season and enjoying it immensely.

I have not seen Kath since then. A Christmas card received a year later read: 'Dear Doctor John, Greetings and love . . . life looks a whole lot brighter since our time together . . . Kath.'

· · ·

DISCUSSION

Kath comes to realize early in therapy that her 'loss of vitality' and 'depression' are related to an underlying rage. Her losses are explored and the major fuel to her fury is found to be the abusive, discounting attitudes of her previous partners. Some grieving tasks: writing a farewell letter, and the watching of a film, are not enough to enable Kath to express her anger, and it is an activity which involves playful creativity and some good-humoured naughtiness (note how Kath wishes

Table 5.2 Therapeutic process in the case of Kath

1. Description of problem	'loss of vitality, depression'
2. Definition of underlying emotion	Rage 'I had not realized that I was so angry about it all'
3. Context of emotion	Separation from Greg; patriarchal attitudes
4. Creative expression	Farewell letter to Greg, film, drawing of Greg, list of 10 curses
5. Exploring future options	Supportive social network, playing golf again, Christmas card signals that 'all is well'

that she had been a little more wicked when young) that provides the necessary change in mood.

Table 5.2 illustrates the therapeutic process in this case study, using the schema presented at the beginning of the chapter.

. . .

CASE STUDY

Case 5C   Making his own mark

Mark, 40, an advertising consultant, told me of his feelings of desperation and the 'watch-spring'-like tension that had been building up in him over the past few months. Normally a social drinker of fine red wine, he found himself using alcohol excessively to quell the anger that kept welling up within him. He was also having trouble with Terry, 14, who was proving to have a short fuse and to be self-centred. The fights between them were increasing, although no physical violence was involved. Mark claimed that he had coped well with his divorce from Elizabeth, 33, a computer supervisor, and that there were no 'leftovers'. He described her as an emotionally empty partner, unable to give much conviviality to their relationship, and the marriage had ended several years earlier after Elizabeth had commenced an affair. Vincent, the younger son who was one year old at the time of the separation, had stayed with his mother, while Terry, at seven years of age, had moved to new lodgings with Mark. Mark said that his work was proceeding without event, and he listed as his resources walking, eating in restaurants and reading, which mainly focused on modern histories and photography. 'I have to do the walking', Mark commented, patting his paunch with a grin. 'I do so like the food and wine!'.

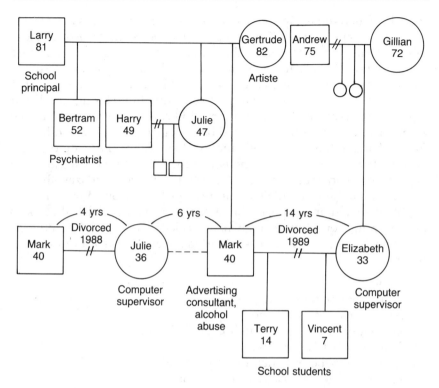

Fig. 5.6 Mark commenced therapy in May 1991.

As Mark continued to tell his story, the image of his family of origin emerged as rather bleak in emotional nourishment. Mark's father, a former school principal, had been an authoritarian, controlling, firmly principled man, very keen on rules, regulations and 'the correct way of doing things'. He was not averse to giving young Mark a 'whipping' for perceived misdemeanours. Mark's mother, an artist, seemed to have painted her social world 'black and white'. 'She was a snob', Mark said, 'no-one could do right by her'.

'So childhood must have been quite difficult for you', I responded, 'your father holding high expectations of you, your mother telling you that you could never reach them'. Mark's eyes moistened. 'Yes', he said, 'I never felt that I could approach them with any warmth, softness or tenderness'. In fact, the situation that most enraged Mark was the rigidity of bureaucratic systems. He always felt that the people within such systems, particularly those in positions above him, were trying to get at him.

I praised Mark for his sense of restraint. He appeared to have grown within a family where there were many restrictions and little fun. He must have had quite a residual store of resentment towards his parents for their unbending rules. There may be leftover sadness also for those missed fond moments within the family that he might have shared with others, had his parents been different. I was very admiring of his concern for Terry's emotional wellbeing, and that Mark had not beaten his son, as his father was wont to do with him during conflict. I wondered if Mark had initially married Elizabeth to gain some of the emotional nourishment that he had been denied earlier on, and having found that she too had lacked emotional substance (intimate partners do sometimes connect unconsciously at the level of their psychological deprivation) had sought solace in food and the bottle. Elizabeth, too, may have entered the affair in an attempt to find out how emotions might be shared and expressed in a different manner. I asked Mark to list the range of ways that he had tackled his sense of emptiness, boredom and stress in the past. Mark showed me his list at our next session.

Mark's list
 1. Drink something / go to the pub.
 2. Sex / be close to someone.
 3. Get angry / rude / sarcastic (Julie calls it 'cocky').
 4. Drive too fast / aggressively.
 5. Thump somebody (when I was younger).
 6. Go for a walk (especially beach or bush).
 7. Go for swim in surf.
 8. Watch a video / go to pictures.
 9. Take a day off.
10. Go out for breakfast.
11. Cut down trees, pull out stumps, chop wood.
12. Gardening.
13. Reading (but find it hard to concentrate lately).

I commented that Mark seemed to have compiled his own personal history. Earlier attempts at coping with stress appeared to have involved 'acting out' (drinking, violence), whereas later efforts were to do with looking after himself in a more adult fashion (exercise, gardening, reading). I complimented Mark on this progress that he had recorded about himself. In fact, Mark had not drunk at all for the past four days, and had withheld his anger at a supermarket attendant who had 'acted a bit haughty' with him. I asked Mark if, for the next session, he would write a conversation with his 'rage': what was it doing for him? What would happen if he became less forceful? How could Mark and his 'rage' strike a bargain so that Mark did not need to drink, either for comfort or to temper his anger?

At our next session, three weeks later, Mark said that he was feeling good, had not drunk since our last meeting, was enjoying a brisk five-kilometre jaunt morning and evening, and was delighted that his weight had dropped below the 80 kilogram barrier for the first time in years. He had not written down his conversation with his 'rage', but had thought about the questions that we had previously considered. Mark said that he felt his anger was largely a reaction to 'being told what to do'. The family in which he had grown up had been a rigid and authoritarian one – 'claustrophobic', and he had struggled for most of his life to gain his own autonomy. His pattern of feeling disempowered had been repeated in his arguments with Elizabeth, she demanding that he tend to her emotional emptiness, and he experiencing their relationship as a fight for freedom and flexibility. I commented that the alcohol may have served to facilitate a number of functions: being rebellious, a way to have fun, a means to cope with his anger, and that Mark was now finding more rewarding ways to take charge of his life. We discussed how Bertram might have become a psychiatrist to learn more about the rules of power and autonomy. Mark said that he had also recently felt a renewed yearning to become more creative, and had entered a course in pottery making.

'It should be fun', Mark said, 'I am looking forward to it. We always had to work so hard to have fun with Mum and Dad. Work was highly valued. Fun was very much down in the hierarchy of things to do. My parents' idea of roguishness was to go to France for two weeks' holiday and to purchase a bottle of expensive wine that would take them two years to consume!'.

'Yes', I responded, 'fun can be a very dangerous thing to a family whose raison d'être is to work dedicatedly throughout life', and I related the story of a young couple who had been recently married according to the rites of a strict, puritan religious sect. They had asked their minister if it was correct and proper to participate in sexual intercourse in the vertical position. The minister admitted that he did not know the answer to their query and said that he would take it to the head of their institution at a seminar being held that weekend. On his return, the minister informed the couple that it was expressly forbidden by their scriptures to have sex in the standing posture. 'Why?', asked the young couple, in disappointment. Came the reply . . . 'because it might lead to dancing!'

Finally, Mark told me how Terry was now constantly engaging in combat with Julie. Mark felt however that, while the endless arguments between himself and Elizabeth (which Terry must have observed) had found no resolution, his son might just have found his match in Julie.

'I was a bit obnoxious with my temper at Terry's age', Mark said. 'No-one could do anything with me. But I think that Julie is teaching Terry a thing or two. I keep my nose well and truly out of it.' Once again, I complimented Mark at this obvious sign of progress; first, that he was letting Julie and Terry develop their own relationship and negotiating style (quite dissimilar to his parents' attitude), and secondly, that he had selected a partner who might prove to be not only his friend, but Terry's also.

Mark's progress, his decreased drinking and increased exercise and recreation patterns, have been maintained over the subsequent six months.

· · ·

DISCUSSION

Defining the problem

Mark's 'watch-spring'-like tension, excessive alcohol intake and increased fighting with his son appear to be associated with the anger that keeps welling up within him.

Exploring the context

Mark says that there are no 'leftovers' from his divorce with Elizabeth, and that work is uneventful. His family of origin appears to have been emotionally depriving, full of rigid rules, high expectations and punitive attitudes. Mark's eyes become watery as he expresses sadness for those moments of tenderness and warmth that never occurred. I affirm Mark for his sense of restraint; he has never hit his son, as his father did him. I comment on how he may have searched for tenderness in his relationship with Elizabeth, a partner who also proved to be emotionally deprived, and some of the same rigidities that Mark experienced in his family of origin appear to have been repeated in this marriage. Mark had also expressed his antipathy towards rigid bureaucratic institutions. I ask him to list as many ways of coping as he can remember.

When Mark produces his range of coping skills, I take one of his personal resources (an interest in modern history) and comment that he seems to have been his own historian in recording his own progress. Mark says that he has not had a drink since our last session. I ask him some further questions on how to negotiate a future with his 'rage'.

Options for the future

Mark returns with news of significant progress: feeling fine, no further drinking, regular exercise and weight loss. He seems to have gained insight that his anger is well rooted in the attitudes of his family of origin that so lacked in fun, and he tells of his anticipated enjoyment in a pottery class for which he has enrolled. I share an anecdote about the solemnity of having fun. Finally, further improvement is reported in that Terry and Julie are negotiating in a more fiery, yet more effective, manner than he and Elizabeth ever achieved. Mark is content to take a back seat, letting them reach their own solutions at their own rate.

— · · · —

CASE STUDY

Case 5D   The three amigos

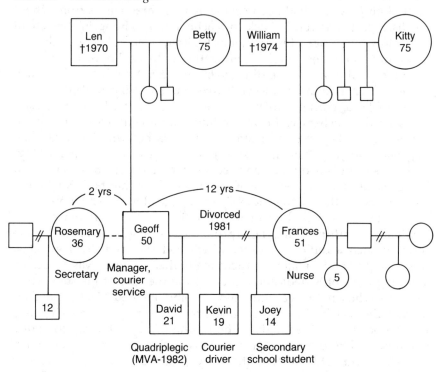

Fig. 5.7 Geoff, Kevin and Joey commenced therapy in March 1991.

Geoff, 50, manager of a courier agency, and his sons Kevin, 19, a driver in the same courier firm, and Joey, 14, a student at a private secondary college, sat in my room, the heat of their anger emanating from them like a fire with quietly glowing coals about to burst into renewed flames. Geoff told me their troubled story. His marriage had ended ten years previously, after his wife Frances, 51, a nurse had left him. Geoff claimed that he and Frances were a mismatch right from the start of their relationship. Frances had won the custody of their three children and, shortly after the split, the eldest son David had become quadriplegic following a car accident. Frances was now remarried with another daughter, and when Kevin and Joey had 'come of age' (12 years) to make their own decision, they had moved into their father's residence. Geoff, Kevin and Joey all saw David occasionally, and all seemed to have settled well into their living arrangement. During the past two years, Geoff had developed a friendship with Rosemary, 36, a secretary, who lived in separate accommodation. Both lads appeared to have accepted Rosemary's entry into the family.

Problems had come to a head over the past few weeks, and had centred on Joey. He had been suspended for three weeks from school for disrespect (answering back to teachers and fighting in the school yard). Kevin described his brother as basically a 'good kid' who did not know his limitations, often wanting things to go his own way and 'spitting the dummy in the dirt' when he did not get his wishes. Joey expressed his frustration at Kevin's freedom. He also complained about the school's unfairness. Joey had had a keyring confiscated in class ('because the teachers said I was fiddling with it') and when he went to reclaim it, the keyring had been lost. The teacher who had taken the ring had told Joey that the loss was not the teacher's responsibility. Both sons complained that Geoff seemed too preoccupied with his own life to make time for them. Geoff's response was that both Kevin and Joey neglected their domestic obligations and did not show any willingness to sit down and negotiate resolutions to their differences.

Initially, I affirmed the family on their strength in having come through such a difficult decade, which had involved divorce, catastrophic injury and a major restructuring of their group. I was especially admiring of Geoff's dedication in accepting the care of his sons when they had chosen to live with him. I complimented Geoff also that, despite the fact he thought he and Frances were a 'mismatch', they had cooperated well enough in the raising of their children to young adulthood, able to make their own choices about where to live, when to visit David, etc. Indeed, the busy routines of trying make this arrangement work may have got in the way of letting go the grief from the past. Geoff, Kevin and Joey all seemed very angry about what had happened, almost cemented into solidity by their anger, and perhaps it was now time to sieze the moment and tend to improving this aspect of their emotional life. I was very impressed with Kevin's concern regarding Joey. 'He is a great older brother!', I commented, 'Can I borrow him for the weekend?' Both young men grinned. I was also impressed with Joey's sense of equity. He knew well where the responsibility for the loss of his property lay. I wondered if he would think about how to write an appeal to the authorities to gain compensation.

During our second session, a week later, Joey said that he had thought about writing an objection to the school about the lost property. 'But I am not going to do it', he asserted. 'It will not make any difference. They will go ahead and do anything they like, without listening to anything I say.'

'That is just his usual style of getting aggro, doc', Kevin rejoined. 'When Joey gets an idea into his head he will just sit there and stick to it. He blocks out anybody else's ideas.'

'What do you do when you get angry?', I asked.

'Oh, I take myself off out of it', Kevin replied. 'I get up and take a walk around the block for a while.'

Both sons said that when Geoff 'got into a shit', he would withdraw from them, turning into himself and spending hours thinking about the problem.

'So you each have different styles for handling your emotional shit', I commented. 'Joey fires up and fights to the death; Kevin takes time and space out to settle his, and Geoff withdraws into himself to contemplate a resolution.' I mentioned how admiring I was of those times, during these first two therapy sessions, when Kevin had provided comfort to Joey – an arm around the shoulder and a kind word – when his younger brother was distressed. I wondered if Joey might be able to develop an 'internal comforter' to help him out with his anger when nobody else was around? I wondered, too, if his comforter could help temper his anger and add stability and rationale whenever he negotiated with Geoff?

At our third session, two weeks later, Geoff commented how arguments between the three of them had settled. He had been very taken with the idea of a 'comforter'. He said that he had realized during our last conversation how each of the three men had sought their own individual ways of resolving their anger, rather than facilitating each other in becoming calmer when enraged. The family had seemed much less disjointed and more cohesive over the last fortnight, and Geoff could recall at least one occasion where each of them – Geoff, Kevin and Joey – had acted as 'comforter' to the quarrels of the others, rather than siding with one against the other.

We continued to discuss family routines. One problem was that Joey still did not cooperate well with the others in doing the domestic chores. It was Joey's job to take the vegetable waste out from the kitchen to the compost bin in the back yard each Tuesday evening. He neglected to do this task regularly. Joey complained that the others were careless and that paper, aluminium cans and glass bottles would be thrown in among the vegetable waste bags (which were next to the recycling bags). He disliked intensely putting his hands in the organic slime to extricate the other materials and place them in their appropriate bags. The others acknowledged their laxity and agreed to take more care in disposing waste if Joey would promise to do his job without reminder. We talked for a while about the most effective way of processing compost, and I mentioned my surprise that we had turned from last session's topic of 'emotional manure' to dealing with the conversion of organic waste into rich compost. I said that one of my clients had once given me a silver scarab (dung-beetle) pendant, and I had thought at the time that it was a suitable emblem for a therapist – helping to turn emotional manure into fertilizer!

At our fourth session, Joey had returned to school and his marks during second-term assessment had shown improvement. Geoff said that he was proud at how his youngest son was knuckling down to the responsibility of studies this term. Joey said that he still felt that Geoff was preoccupied, with little time to spare for him. Both made a commitment to set aside one hour's 'caring' time each week for discussion. Kevin stated that he had some personal issues on which to work: self-confidence; how he saw himself as a man; and developing intimacy with women. I replied that I thought it might be best to commence a conversation about these matters with another colleague, and that I was pleased that he was using the momentum gained from the family's progress to start exploring his own internal emotional world. In the meantime, I would be happy to continue to see Joey and Geoff together to help improve the quality of their relationship. I complimented all of them on just how friendly they appeared to have become – the three amigos – and that they were now expressing concern and interest in each other that they should find their own direction towards their goals.

_____ . . . _____

DISCUSSION

Defining the problem

Geoff, Kevin and Joey describe the way they are trying to express their anger. Most affected is Joey, whose unruly behaviour at school has led to suspension.

Exploring the context

The anger is framed as a 'leftover' from previous family events: the divorce and David's quadriplegia. The family is affirmed for their coping strengths. The different styles of expressing anger are explored, Kevin's skill as comforter to Joey is admired, and a query as to whether Joey can develop an 'internal comforter' is made.

Options for the future

This family of men takes to the idea that members may occasionally comfort, rather than combat, each other, and domestic routines are discussed. A comparison of converting vegetable and emotional leftovers into fertilizer for the future is made. Kevin decides to seek independent individual help for his own struggles, whereas Geoff and Joey decide to focus on improving their time together.

SUMMARY

In this chapter we considered:
Case 5A, 'The little devil', in which the family's blaming and anger regarding the rather insensitive way in which the husband–father has left them (without maintenance or access arrangements) is normalized. Creative ways of expressing the anger are found – the rebellious son's drawing of his little devil, the mother's listing of her feelings, and the sharing of a story about a family of separated echidnas – and future options are explored relating to family routines: the establishment of access and maintenance, cooperativeness within the new family structure, and encouragement of the son's growth to young adulthood.
Case 5B, 'Revenge', in which the divorcee's blaming and anger towards her patriarchal ex-husband is channelled creatively into revenge fantasies. She writes a farewell letter, and lists ten curses on her ex-spouse. Options for the future are explored through both creativity (a drawing of herself as a paddle-steamer madam) and discussion (how she can retire from the 'carer' role to discounting, unappreciative partners, and find future independence, perhaps as the owner of a country pub.
Case 5C, 'Making his own mark', in which a man expresses his anger at his emotionally depriving and authoritarian family of origin, and empowers himself by listing the healthy ways he has learnt to cope with stress of 'being told what to do by others'. This power is translated into cessation of alcohol abuse, weight loss, exercise and interest in a pottery-making course.
Case 5D, 'The three amigos', in which three men, enormously enraged after some devastating events (divorce, quadriplegia in a family member) are encouraged to be comforters of one another, rather than combatants. The anger is expressed in this instance through creative conversation and metaphor (emotional manure being converted into useful compost),

rather than writing or drawing. Options for the future include one son entering therapy elsewhere to look at his own issues, while the other son and the father concentrate on bettering the quality of their relationship.

POINTS FOR REFLECTION

1. Think about a number of words and phrases that your clients use to express their anger. What non-verbal communications commonly accompany either the expression of anger or its suppression?
2. What creative means do you have at hand to enable your clients to express their anger?
3. Take a risk! Contemplate a conversation with your own anger. What questions do you need to ask your anger to find out more about it? How long has it been there? What are the messages that your anger is conveying to you? Does it give you strength, energy, vitality . . . or does it burden you and hold you back? What do you need to do to channel it more effectively, creatively?

What?? . . . no anger?? . . . good work!! . . . or . . . progress to Chapter 6 'Denial'.

REFERENCES

Kubler-Ross, E. (1973) *On Death and Dying*, Tavistock, London.
Gunzburg, J. (1991) *Family Counselling Casebook*, McGraw-Hill, Sydney.

Denial

6

Denial can be considered to be an initial reaction within the grieving process, and also a defence against hurt to the self. This chapter regards denial as an emotional resource, a way of coping with distressing events over time, until our clients are more able to acknowledge the events being denied and express their grief adequately and effectively.

Therapy consists of:

1. focusing on those areas which are being denied by clients as a source of loss;
2. utilizing clients' creative resources to redirect the energy underlying the denial into a productive expression of the grief;
3. considering future options.

———————— · · · ————————

CASE STUDY

Case 6A   Villains and rogues
Moira, 42, an unemployed nurse, had recommenced abusing alcohol over the past few weeks after several years' abstinence. During our first two sessions of therapy, she told me of her distress within her current relationship of nine months' standing, with Chuck, 45, a plumber, and also an alcohol abuser. They lived in separate residences.

'It is the way Chuck treats his women friends when we are out together at parties that upsets me', Moira said. 'He cuddles up to them, giving them passionate kisses and fondling their breasts. I don't like it!'

Moira described much of her past life as having been filled with fear

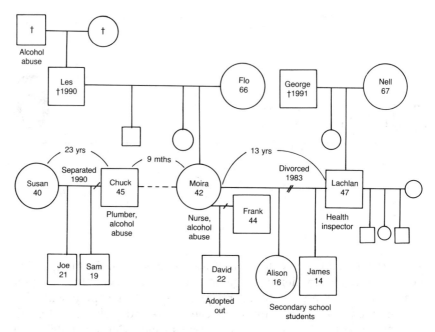

Fig. 6.1 Moira commenced therapy in May 1991.

and anxieties. Her family of origin had been a puritan, authoritarian one, with little shared leisure activities or fun. Consequently, Moira had used creative youthful fantasies to escape the rigours of her family life, travelling to far-off places and enacting exciting adventurous roles. As a young adult, Moira had entered several relationships with men who seemed to have taken advantage of her. Frank had impregnated her after a 'one-night stand' and had rapidly disappeared, leaving Moira with the decision to adopt out their son, David, now 22. Moira had entered into marriage with Lachlan, a chauvinistic man who had expected her to support him in his career of Health Inspector to the exclusion of her own, and their children's, needs, and the union had ended in divorce 13 years later. Moira had become agoraphobic two years into that marriage, which had also been stressed by financial struggles. Moira had raised the two children on her own, although recently Alison had decided to live with her father. Moira lived quite comfortably with James, whom she described as an enjoyable and stable lad. 'I just have the normal nonsense with him. When both he and his sister were with me, they fought abominably. I disagreed against Alison leaving at first, then felt it best that she should go. Although they still appear to dislike each other intensely, they both have settled into the new arrangement.' James saw his father and

Alison hardly at all. Following the divorce, two years of therapy with a female practitioner had helped Moira to gain confidence and become more assertive. So she was particularly unhappy to now find herself in such a demeaning relationship with Chuck.

I affirmed Moira's determination in seeking rewarding intimacies, and on the way that she appeared to have negotiated so that Alison and James could choose where they might live most comfortably. I commented that Moira seemed to have associated with an assortment of villains and a gallery of rogues who had never seemed to have been quite there for her appropriately when she had needed them. Frank had deserted her . . . definitely a villain! Lachlan had wanted to direct her and be her puppeteer . . . he probably tended towards villainy. That these men had behaved like this, I suggested, was not necessarily a reflection of Moira's ability to choose suitable partners, but rather that they were following an expert training as to 'how men should behave in a patriarchal western society'. Chuck appeared to be testing the limits of Moira's tolerance. I guessed that part of my task was to help Moira gather information in order to decide whether Chuck was a villain or a rogue. I wondered if he would attend a future therapy session? Moira said that she would try to convince Chuck to come along.

At our third session, Chuck, who presented himself as a 'boyish charmer', told of some of his own fears. He had always experienced difficulty, he said, developing a sense of partnership with his first wife Susan. He felt that he had never really 'belonged' to that marriage and wondered if he could develop a special relationship at all with Moira. Chuck admitted to his caressing of the ladies at various social functions ('A bit of fun', Chuck called it) and thought it all rather harmless. 'Yet Moira has said quite clearly that she does not like it', I responded. 'You appear genuinely fond of Moira and I am a little puzzled that you would persist in an activity that caused her discomfort.' I noted aloud that Chuck was born in the same year as I, and continued: 'I wonder if part of it is the way we were raised to be men in the 1950s. We saw our film heroes . . . Cary Grant, Clark Gable, Humphrey Bogart . . . ever so nicely 'roughing up' their women: 'What you need, my dear, is a good spankin' ', asserted Cary Grant with smooth assurance as he put his girlfriend over his knee and slapped her backside. Gable snorted tersely, 'Frankly, my dear, I don't give a damn'. Bogart patronized Bergman with the memorable 'Here's lookin' at you, kid'. Our idols were portrayed on the screen as delightful cads and lovable rogues but, in actual fact, much of the way that they treated their women was quite villainous . . . and, oh, those heroines were always so sweet, demure, deliciously helpless, and in such need of discipline from their men! Indeed, we males seemed to be well trained to communicate emotionally with our female intimates primarily with our fists or our genitals.' I wondered if Chuck would be willing to experiment and explore other ways of enjoying the 'softer' emotions with his women friends, rather than always going for the physical? Would Moira also consider how she could make the relationship with Chuck 'safer', so that he could feel more emotionally connected with her? We agreed to meet again after a month.

The following week, Moira requested a session on her own. She was concerned about the forthcoming weekend.

'Chuck's father is visiting and the whole family will be at Chuck's house', Moira said. 'From past experience, I will be expected to attend and tend to everyone else, but I will be totally ignored and unappreciated. I shall be treated as part of the furniture. I have spoken with Chuck about this but he keeps telling me not to be so silly, it is all in my imagination.'

We talked for a while how Moira had been 'carer' to all her men . . . incubator to Frank's unwanted fetus, supporter to Lachlan's vocation, and now helper to Chuck's family, and I suggested that she discuss with Chuck the idea of taking some time out over the weekend, the two of them spending some time away from the family, perhaps going to a restaurant, a theatre, or for a walk in the park, just to remind themselves that they were a couple.

At our fifth session, Moira attended on her own and said, with tears, that she had decided to end the relationship with Chuck. The family had gathered at the weekend, and when Moira had approached Chuck for time out he had fobbed her off: 'We'll see, we'll do it later'. And, yes, he was still displaying very much a 'hands-on' approach towards family friends who were also guests that weekend. Moira believed Chuck would never become so fond of her that he would cease fondling other women. Though Moira felt that Chuck was not really a true villain, she had decided not to accept him as a lovable rogue either. She felt that she could do better, and esteem herself better, on her own. Moira felt anxious that Chuck would successfully cajole her back into the friendship now that she had concluded it. He had proven his expertise in the use of 'guilt-hooks' in the past.

Our conversation turned to exploring some phrases that Moira might use to facilitate the process of 'letting go' Chuck:

Chuck: I miss you, really I do. I am lonely without you. I do not think that I can go on without you.
Moira: Yes, there were some good times that we shared that I miss too. It is over now and I am moving on in my life.

--- . . . ---

DISCUSSION

Defining the problem

Moira enters therapy after a series of relationships in which her male partners have used her largely for their own needs. Moira defines her lost opportunities for intimacy as being related to her own personal social inadequacies, and denies the influence of her partners' patriarchal attitudes.

Exploring the context

A joint discussion with Moira and Chuck outlines how both might have absorbed the patriarchal training of the 1950s, by examining the stereotypic images reflected in the cinema of those times: men being tough, hardy, masterly and benevolent tyrants, and women needing those masterly men to discipline them. Both Moira and Chuck are encouraged to experiment with change, Chuck to find a different way of connecting with women, Moira to explore how Chuck could 'belong' more comfortably within their relationship.

Options for the future

Chuck's reluctance to regard Moira as special within his family group, and his continued fondling of other women, confirms for Moira just how entrenched are Chuck's patriarchal attitudes. She decides on a sole life, one in which she can feel better about herself. A few statements are examined, to create distance from Chuck and to enable Moira to assert her rights within social intimacies in the future.

· · ·

CASE STUDY

Case 6B   Star search
Karl, 35, a country medical practitioner who was about to sit for his fellowship examinations for the Royal Australian College of General Practitioners, came to therapy on his own, complaining about his dissatisfaction with his work and generally feeling that he was not an integral part of the society in which he lived. Karl had commenced an associateship three years previously, with another practitioner and his wife, and the practice had blossomed since they all had joined forces. Karl said that the feedback from the practice's patients was most encouraging . . . he had proved to be a popular, respected and much-

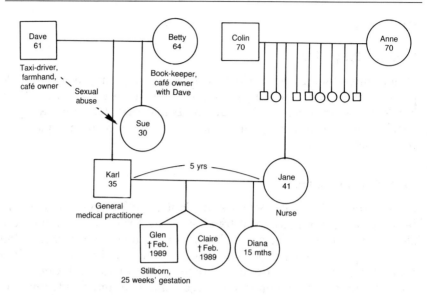

Fig. 6.2 Karl commenced therapy in May 1991.

loved doctor. Nonetheless, Karl took little pleasure in the appreciation of his clients and wondered more and more just where he fitted in.

Karl had been married for the past five years to Jane, 41, a nurse, and although he enjoyed playing with their 15-month-old daughter Diana, Karl said that Jane often commented on the lack of conversation within their relationship. Indeed, Karl had few social contacts and described himself as a bit of a loner. He said that he had always experienced difficulty opening up his innermost feelings to his intimates. Karl described his family of origin as one in which he had felt 'undervalued'. He had never been able to do well by his father, and could remember no warm moments from his childhood with either parent, although he had had no doubts about their love and concern for his welfare. Karl told of a period of time during medical school when he had felt very much a part of the student body. He had lived in residence on campus with other students and recalled many enjoyable activities – the games and banter of his peers – with some pleasure. All this had disappeared, however, with the responsibility of a career and marriage. Even an overseas sojourn and nomadic lifestyle during the two years following graduation had been more of a soul-searching, an intense exploration of self and identity, rather than a memorable adventure.

Towards the end of our second session (we were meeting weekly), I was forming the conclusion that here was an individual experiencing the rigours of 'midlife burnout', and that some sensitive Jungian counselling, hoping to facilitate the emergence of Karl's intuitive feminine side and integrate it with his well-developed analytical male side (Jacobi, 1973) was in order. Then Karl paused and said: 'You know I have told you a great deal and I have now just remembered something else. A little over two years ago, Jane and I lost twins, Claire and Glen, after 25 weeks' gestation. We have just passed the second anniversary. Do you think that it is this that could be bugging me?' We talked for a while about those good moments that Karl cherished during the twins' brief hours of life, and also of his struggles in trying to share his grief with Jane since their death.

At our third session, Karl arrived calmer, more relaxed and visibly relieved. Part of this was surely due to the fact that he had completed his fellowship examinations, but he also recounted a recent memory which he had completely forgotten until our last meeting, and also a new understanding which had offered him comfort. The week following Claire's and Glen's deaths, Karl and Jane had ventured into their back garden and had chosen two stars in the night sky, near the Southern Cross, to commemorate their lost twins. Karl had remembered that they had found great difficulty in sighting the stars at all due to the full moon's glow.

Crying gently, Karl related how he had just realized that they had called their new daughter Diana, and that this was the ancient Roman name for the goddess of the moon. 'So', I commented, also moved to tears, 'you found a way to pass on your love for the lost twins in the name you gave the new little person in your lives.' We discussed some of the risks relating to the possibility of Diana being a 'replacement' child. The danger was that she might unfairly be expected to carry some of the qualities bestowed on Claire and Glen, rather than being allowed to develop as a unique individual in her own right. Karl commented that, during the past week, he had been more able to share his sense of sadness with Jane over past events, and also had been able to enter into a conversation with his sister, Sue, for the first time, when she had wanted to talk with him about her past experience of sexual abuse by their father. Sue was currently troubled by this, and Karl had been able not only to lend her a supportive ear, but encourage her to seek professional help.

―――――――――― ⋯ ――――――――――

DISCUSSION

Defining the problem

Initially, it appears as if Karl's problems are those of midlife: he blames himself for his inadequacy in expressing emotions, he appears to suffer 'burnout' and loss of interest in his vocation, and complains of a sense of isolation within his intimate relationships. There seem to be pressures also from his studies for examinations. The temptation is to focus on these issues. Then Karl mentions the deaths of his and Jane's twins.

Exploring the context

Karl remembers the 'denied' second anniversary of the deaths of Claire and Glen, and this triggers off a forgotten memory relating to a creative response to their grief: Jane and Karl have chosen two stars in the night sky to honour their lost twins. Karl notes the connection between the choosing of the stars, the moonlight, and the name, Diana, that they have selected for their subsequent offspring, and I mention the symbolic association of passing love from those gone to future generations. Karl and I are able to share our tears together as we talk.

Options for the future

The pitfalls of unrealistic expectations on 'replacement' children are noted, and Karl says that he and Jane have been more able to discuss past sad events in their lives. He says also that he has been able to support his sister during their conversation regarding her previous experience of incest. Karl appears to be opening up to the emotional world in a way that he has not known in the past.

——————————— · · · ———————————

CASE STUDY

Case 6C   The letter
Nell, 54, commenced individual weekly therapy describing her feelings of 'emptiness, loss of energy and restlessness'. She had worked for the past 17 years as a customs officer, and had supplemented her income with a night job as computer operator. She also leased a room of her house to a university student, a young Chinese woman, of whom Nell was very fond.

There certainly appeared to have been many stresses and losses in Nell's life. Her parents had both died within the past five years, and her son Steven, 30, an accountant who had discarded Nell's informal Christian teaching to adopt a stricter puritan interpretation of the faith, had married Sarah and had moved to South Australia. They seemed to show little warmth towards Nell, and Steven in particular was constantly reminding Nell of her 'deficiencies as a mother' during his

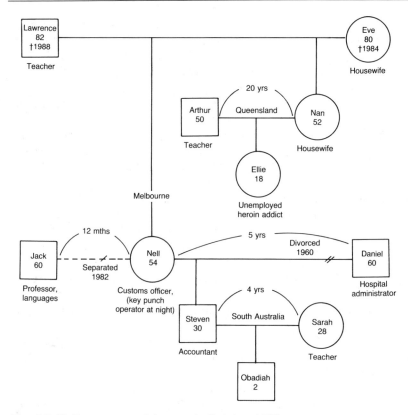

Fig. 6.3 Nell commenced therapy in October 1990.

formative years. Nell described her marriage to Daniel, 60, a hospital administrator, as an emotionally barren one. He was always dictating to her how to run family affairs, and Nell had left with her ten-year-old son. Steven seemed to have followed in his father's path: 'You should have stayed with Dad' he would still write dogmatically, 'and you should be showing more interest in Sarah and me!' Both Sarah and Steven made it quite clear to Nell that any contact with her two-year-old grandson, Obadiah, through family visits and holidays, was entirely dependent on Nell's financial support of their branch of the family.

Several years previously, Nell had enjoyed a stimulating friendship with Jack, 60, an American professor of languages, and said she had never quite recovered from his unilateral decision to return to Boston, even though their parting had been an amicable one. Nell's sister Nan, 52, a housewife, had also proved to be a person of many demands. Nan had wanted Nell eventually to settle into her and her husband Arthur's 'extended residence', but Nell felt that her sister wanted to use Nell's money to renovate her home and improve her creature comforts. Nell was also bothered by Nan's tendency to dominate her. Nan had told Nell about an extramarital affair (to be kept secret from Arthur), and Nell felt that her sister was involving her in a web of deceit. Nan's daughter, Ellie, 18, was a heroin addict and Nan was constantly asking Nell to fly up to Brisbane for a weekend to give Ellie guidance. Ellie, who was unemployed, often wrote to Nell requesting money to help defray her living costs. Nell continually worried about Ellie's welfare and felt guilty that she was not able to do more to help her niece. Little wonder that Nell was feeling thoroughly used and abused!

We discussed for a few sessions how Nell coped with the manipulations of her demanding family. She often suffered migraines and had felt that she was a poisoner of her relationships, both familial and social. She had thrown herself into her work with determination and vigour in an effort to distract herself from family expectations, and often dreamt of her eventual retirement to a small coastal villa in Spain (away from the rain which falls mainly on the plain!). I commented that there was no doubt in my mind that Nell was successful in relationships – the length of her career, the friendship with Jack, her ability to provide for a lodger all indicated that fact. I suggested that perhaps she was downgrading just how unreasonable was her family's behaviour towards her.

I asked Nell: 'Which unreasonable attitude of your family is the most troublesome to you?', and she replied, 'The constant blaming of my son. I really feel I have done my best by him; he has his career and family, yet shows no appreciation of my efforts to help him get there. I have tried to smooth the way to an easier relationship between us without success'.

'Would you compose a letter to Steven', I continued, 'and tell him just what you have related to me?'

At our next session, Nell shared the following letter, which she had posted to Steven, with me:

Dear Sarah and Steven,
This is a difficult letter for me to compose, however, here goes . . .

As you both know, way back in June I contacted you, earnestly desiring that we might resolve our conflict and hopefully learn about each other as well as learn to respect one another. (Hoping for a miracle I guess).

However, I do not believe that we have made any headway at all in this regard and I am forced to conclude that the situation between us is irrevocable.

In fact I strongly suspect that my attention and correspondence may be distressing to you Steven. This was not my purpose at all. We both know there is so much left unspoken and I suspect that is how you wish the situation to remain. So be it.

As you probably know, I reached the mature age of fifty-four last birthday and this, amongst other things, made me realize I do not need, nor can I afford, to subject myself to any further pain or anguish. I have experienced enough of life's sorrow and the time has come to call it quits. I have decided that whatever time I have left (hopefully twenty-five years!!) I intend to avoid any future unnecessary heartache.

Consequently I shall make this my final communication. I send you all my best wishes for the years to come.
> Sincerely,
> Nell

Therapy has continued for a further six months since Nell sent Steven that letter, to which no reply has been received. Nell has also created a distance between herself and Nan and Ellie, telling her sister that she did not wish to be coerced as an ally into any future secret plans. Nell suggested to Ellie that she might do better to seek professional help for her problems, rather than to keep asking her aunt for money. I commented that the emotional distance seemed now to approximate more the geographical distance from her demanding relatives. Nell described her sense of relief. Her lodger had left recently and this had proved an easier 'letting go', leaving Nell with warm memories of good times past. She said that memories of Jack were now flooding back, giving her nourishment and comfort. Moreover, Nell had experienced no migraines for the past six months.

'I never thought that I would get rid of them', Nell said, 'or of the guilt. I always thought that you could choose your friends but not your family.'

'And whose unreasonable expectation is that?', I bantered back!

— — — · · · — — —

DISCUSSION

Defining the problem

Nell describes her emptiness, her low energy levels and restless searching for solace. She blames her condition on her own inadequacies, her 'poisoning' of her relationships, and denies totally the input of her family, their unrealistic expectations and exploitative demands.

Exploring the context

I comment that Nell appears to have enjoyed several relationships in the past, and that the fault does not seem to be related to her lack of social skills. I then focus on the demand that her family makes of her: bend over backwards until your back breaks. Nell identifies Steven's behaviour as the most painful, and writes him a farewell letter to commence the process of letting go.

Options for the future

Nell continues the process of letting go, resolving her dilemmas with her son, sister and niece. She experiences accomplishment in letting go a successful relationship with her lodger (letting go need not be filled with anguish), and remembers some happy moments with her former lover. Nell appears to have broken the pattern of holding on to toxic, unrewarding relationships, even if they are flesh of her flesh. Spain definitely appears to have become a sunnier prospect!

――――――――――― · · · ―――――――――――

CASE STUDY

Case 6D   Flinders St station

Bella, 55, a bouncy, bosomy woman, who described herself as the eternal Earth Mother, told me between tears of frustration that her public service job of 20 years' standing was finally getting to her. Normally a dependable, efficient employee, with lots of energy and organizational skills, Bella was finding, over the past month, more and more difficulty in keeping up with the pace of her work. The final crisis had come when she had been passed over for a promotion that Bella said was due to her.

As we conversed, it became apparent that for the past two years Bella had been the focus of a great deal of envy from her work colleagues. Because of her competence, Bella had maintained a pleasant and stable relationship with her bosses, and her colleagues complained that she always got 'the good jobs'. For the past six months Bella had been her own boss, doing courier work 'on the road' for the department, but four weeks ago she had been transferred to another branch, where the boss had proved to be patronizing, chauvinistic and demeaning towards her. Bella believed that it was largely due to his influence that she had missed out on her promotion. She felt that she was undergoing a nervous breakdown, and had requested leave of absence.

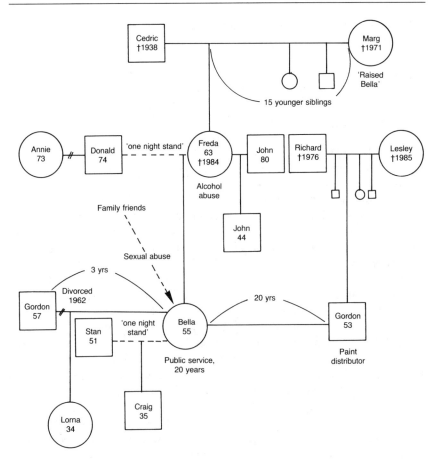

Fig. 6.4 Bella commenced therapy in May 1991.

We commenced discussing Bella's family of origin. Her mother, Freda, had conceived Bella during adolescence and out of wedlock. Partly because of the shame of illegitimacy, and because Freda had commenced abusing alcohol (this was to become a lifelong pattern), Bella was fostered out to Freda's mother, Marg, where Bella could be lost amongst Freda's 15 other siblings.

Bella had raised two children, Craig and Lorna, to adulthood, each born from brief relationships with two different partners, before settling into a marriage of 20 years to Gordon, 53, a paint distributor. Bella described this last union as respectful, rewarding and stable. I was impressed by the large size of Bella's childhood family, and wondered if it had been hard for her finding her own position and sense of identity. Had she indeed become lost?

'It all sounds rather like the bustle of Flinders St railway station', I commented, 'people always coming and going, with not much sense of contact or permanence'.

'Yes', replied Bella, 'there were always family friends popping in and out of the house, sleeping over and staying the weekend. In fact some of them had a go at me and fiddled with my genitals when I was a kid. But it is not the family that I have come to you about', Bella added promptly. 'I am here about the hassle in my job situation.'

I gave Bella four weeks' leave of absence from work, and as she left, she turned to me and yelled in a fury: 'Why won't anybody give me six months' break!!'

We continued to meet on a weekly basis. Bella felt that she was to blame – she had always been a good worker and could find no conceivable reason not to be able to do her duties now. She wanted to continue in her job for another five years, and the thought of early retirement due to invalidism appalled her. I directed our conversation gently towards the rigours of her early family life: who, of all those persons, was there to tend to Bella's youthful needs adequately and appropriately? How had she been able to cope with the demands and competition within that family? There seemed to have been little opportunity for privacy and adolescent reflection. And the sexual abuse must have been confusing and quite frightening: those troubled family friends had put their 'adult stuff' on to her and had not allowed her to enjoy her 'kid stuff'. It all sounded as though it had been hard work, and Bella appeared to have taken this family tradition of hard work into her own adult life, to serve well and diligently in her own vocation and family life. There did not seem to have been much leisure activity, no time out for Bella to refresh herself. Her autocratic boss may well have triggered off bad memories of the incest: that women are there to do service, to be abused and humiliated.

By the fourth session, Bella's fury had turned to tears. 'I cannot stop crying', she said. We talked about Bella's internal messages that accompanied the weeping. They mainly were to do with the 'hurting young child' within Bella that yearned for comfort and attention, with everyone else around her being too busy with their own needs to notice. Emotional deprivation had also been a strong family tradition; it may even have influenced Freda in her alcohol abuse. We considered what 'arguments for change' Bella might need to present to her boss: Bella said that she required an adequately furnished office, an acknowledged status, and the opportunity for appropriate promotion. There might also be the chance for a move to a different department.

At our fifth session, Bella was calmer and smiled warmly, with no tears. She had telephoned her boss to demand a recognized position within the hierarchy for her competence and this had been granted.

We agreed to continue weekly therapy for a while to discuss roles, how to avoid unrealistic expectations (especially of being Earth Mother!), and assertive skills; how to depart from Flinders St station and journey to a quieter and more agreeable part of the terrain.

———————— · · · ————————

DISCUSSION

Defining the problem

Bella presents herself as an all-giving carer who has reached an impasse in her life, and wishes to find a way to care even better for others. She vigorously denies any influence of her family of origin on her current crisis at work. A leave of absence is arranged.

Exploring the context

The family of origin is gently explored as the original source of her stress, with its emotional deprivation, competitiveness, unreasonable demands and sexual abuse. I take particular care to offer Bella an opportunity for private pauses within our dialogue, clear boundaries using words rather than physical touch, and letting Bella tell her story at her own pace without demanding too perfect a performance. Bella's anger turns to tears as she tunes in to the intrapsychic experience of her internal 'hurting child' calling out for solace.

Options for the future

Ways in which Bella can satisfy her vocational needs are discussed, and she puts these into action with significant success. Other methods by which Bella can assert herself within social situations, and gain more fun and relaxation, are also regarded.

———————— · · · ————————

CASE STUDY

Case 6E   Simon says
Simon, 41, an assistant curator of a tennis club, was telling me of his anger and frustration at the situation that had developed between himself and his wife Sandra, 38, a theatre sister, now unemployed. He described himself a failure both as a man and a husband. During the early stages of their marriage they had enjoyed all levels of intimacy:

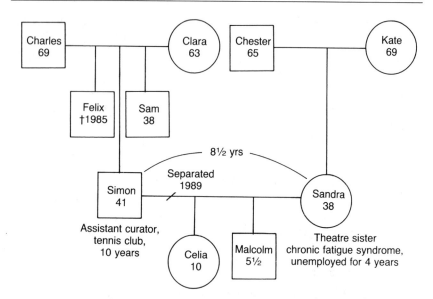

Fig. 6.5 Simon commenced therapy in March 1991.

socializing, dining out, travelling, with good conversation, great sex and plenty of fun. Though the arrival of the children had slowed their entertainment somewhat ('Nothing ruins a good marriage like kids!', Simon had quipped wryly), they had managed to cooperate and be flexible in their adaptation to parenting. Real problems had commenced with the onset of Sandra's 'chronic fatigue syndrome' four years previously, a condition which sapped her energy, depressed her mood and reduced her libido. Simon said that he had taken on extra domestic chores to give Sandra respite, but the lethargy that had commenced during the initial phases of Sandra's ailment had increased, and there was now a very tangible emotional distance, punctuated by moments of brusque fighting, between the two of them. Simon claimed that he should have been able to create an impact and lessen Sandra's debility, yet she showed no signs of recovery and he felt stagnated, flat and impotent. In fact, physical impotence was currently an aspect of Simon's struggles. The situation had come to a head two years ago when Simon had left to live in separate accommodation after a series of bitter spats. He visited the family home every weekend to be with the children and partake in the housework.

At our second session, one week later, both Sandra and Simon attended. Sandra told how disheartened she was with her body. She had wanted to return to her nursing career, to regain the zest in her marriage, to enjoy the growth of her children more, but simply could not fire up to get started. She was tired of the constant battery of examinations, investigations and general aimless guidance of the medical profession over the years. Sandra felt that Simon was always expecting more performance from her than she was able to give. He seemed constantly to be demanding of her: Let's get back to what we had. She resented any closeness with him, and wanted to be let alone for three months, with no contact, to be able to sort her feelings out. Sandra declined to come to a further session, and I thanked her for her participation and the information that she had given me.

During our next three sessions, I focused our conversation on to the process that appeared to have occurred in Simon and Sandra's marriage. It seemed that they did indeed know how to enjoy their partnership mutually as a couple: the early years had testified to that. Since the birth of Celia, however, they appeared to have slipped into a 'crisis lifestyle', with the demands of parenting and Sandra's decline. This latter occurrence had truly been problematic. 'It seems as if you are struggling to accept Sandra's condition as valid', I said. 'If it were paraplegia, multiple sclerosis or a debilitating cancer, it would be much more concrete. You might be more able to accept the changes that you would have to make to accommodate to the new situation. But because of the esoteric nature of chronic fatigue syndrome, and the doctors' vagueness about its prognosis, you seem to be discounting its effect. You appear to be assuming that it will pass, that events should all return to normal, and that your hard efforts should ensure Sandra's perfect recovery ... if only she can get enough rest! But perhaps you will have to let go your expectations that the past can be restored, and renegotiate your marriage contract according to a new agenda.'

The last two sessions were spent rather more quietly, with a tearful Simon discussing and letting go his original dreams for the relationship, and grieving over lost moments and opportunities. Three months later, I learnt from the general practitioner who had referred Simon that he and Sandra were living together under the same roof again.

···

DISCUSSION

Defining the problem

Simon tells of his anger, despair, failure as a husband, stagnation, flatness of mood and impotence.

Exploring the context

Simon blames himself that his personal efforts within the family have not led to Sandra's restoration of good health. He regards the increased emotional distance, quarrelling and resultant separation as evidence of failure. What more can he do, he says, to improve the quality of the marriage? I change the focus of our conversation from a context of 'achievement through personal endeavour' to one of 'creating change through interaction' with Sandra. Her condition has an air of mystery about it, and Simon's efforts to overcome it by manly willpower appear to be invalidating its significance. His message seems to be: If only I keep working at it, I must be able to help you to overcome it. Sandra has requested a three-month period of space for herself. If Simon gives this to her and backs off from trying to make things better, she may feel more respected and believed. If he ceases trying to restore the status quo and accepts the possible permanence of her disability (this may involve grieving and renegotiation towards a new direction), they may resolve their impasse.

Options for the future

Simon turns his attention to his own feelings of grief, expresses them quietly, dreams some new dreams, and eventually renegotiates his return to the family home with Sandra, hopefully to experiment with reconciliation under different terms.

SUMMARY

In Chapter 6 we considered areas relating to possible grief that may be denied by clients:

In *Case 6A, 'Villains and rogues'*, Moira blames herself for her inadequacies in intimate relationships, and denies the influence of patriarchal training on her exploitative male partners that has intruded into the comfort of her relationships. Acceptance of this factor allows for a more independent and self-esteeming lifestyle.

In *Case 6B, 'Star search'*, Karl has denied the anniversary of his twins' death. Discussion allows him to reflect on the love that he has passed from them on to his new daughter.

In *Case 6C, 'The letter'*, Nell is full of self blame, denying the manipulations of her family that have stolen warm moments of family life from her experience. Our conversation enables her to let go of toxic relationships and open up to more nourishing ones.

In *Case 6D, 'Flinders St station'*, Bella denies the influence of the emotional deprivation within her family of origin on her current interactional life. We focus on ways she can tend to her needs in the here and now.

In *Case 6E, 'Simon says'*, Simon denies that his wife's disability has altered the course of their marriage irrevocably. Acceptance allows planning for a different future.

Notice that, in many of these case studies, denial is not the only element related to the way the problem is being defined. In Case 6C, Nell's denial is accompanied by emptiness; in Case 6D, Bella expresses fury alongside her denial; and in Case 6E, Simon's denial is partnered with despair. There is no such thing as a 'pure' emotion that signals the presence of unresolved grief, i.e. anger, denial, depression, emptiness. Unresolved grief can be regarded as an emotional complex.

POINTS FOR REFLECTION

1. Select some of your recent case histories and construct genograms of events discussed. Are there any areas relating to unresolved grief that are being denied?
2. As you regard these genograms, do you recall the words used by clients to describe the feelings that accompany any denial?
3. Over the next month, make a habit of recording key emotional words, e.g. furious, sad, empty, stuck, that clients use to define their problems, in cases where causes for grief are being denied. What sort of vocabulary do you end up with?

REFERENCE

Jacobi, J. (1973) *The Psychology of C.G. Jung*, Yale University Press, Newhaven.

Depression

7

———————— . . . ————————

CASE STUDY

Case 7A   Educating Rita

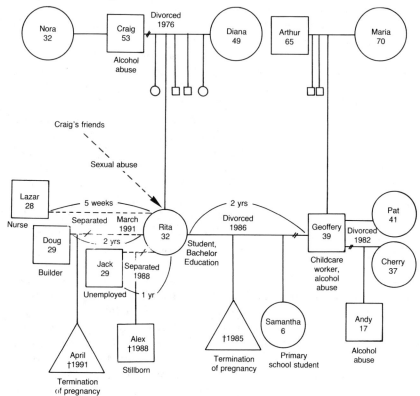

Fig. 7.1 Rita commenced therapy in April 1991.

Rita, 32, a second-year student in a course for Bachelor of Education, was telling me how her depression was interfering with her routines. She had two assignments to be completed within a fortnight, and simply could not find the energy to finish them. Rita said that she felt stressed, overworked and was bursting into tears every few hours. She could not understand how she could fall to pieces so easily.

As we talked, the many losses, missed opportunities and violations in Rita's past became evident. Her father had been a regular abuser of alcohol and violent with his fists and words to Rita, her mother and her siblings. The father's friends had sexually abused Rita on more than one occasion during her youth, and the parents had divorced when she was 17.

Rita had continued to contact partners who violated her life. When she was 25, she had married Geoffery, 39, a childcare worker who also abused alcohol. Though not physically or verbally violent, Geoffery spent most of his nights out with his drinking mates. After a miscarriage, Rita gave birth to Samantha, now 6. The marriage eventually 'died' emotionally, and the pair had separated amicably two years later. Geoffery saw Samantha regularly on fortnightly weekend access, and paid maintenance for her upkeep responsibly. Another bonus was that Andy, Geoffery's son from a previous marriage, was very fond of Samantha and happy to play 'big brother' to her. Rita had immediately entered a brief relationship with Jack, 29, unemployed, whom she described as 'unreliable and a liar'. A pregnancy had resulted in a stillborn son, Alex, and Rita agreed that she still had not come to terms with his loss. A third friendship with Doug, 29, a builder, followed. Over two years, Doug had proven himself to be a 'con man', always saying that he would do such and such, and reneging on the agreement. They had separated two months previous to Rita seeking therapy, and two weeks after separation Rita had discovered that she was pregnant. She was now deeply depressed that she had proceeded with the ensuing termination of pregnancy. She felt that, rather than supporting her, Doug had used every manipulation to make certain that Rita ended the pregnancy . . . and therein lay the source of Rita's self-blame. Since Samantha had entered kindergarten, Rita had been channelling her energies into her own development; into her education, writing and feminist literature. She had become well aware of the patterns of disempowerment and gender bias within the community, yet kept involving herself in relationships which ultimately disadvantaged her. I expressed my amazement at the variety of troubles that Rita had faced, admired her fortitude in withstanding stresses which might have driven others to drink, drugs, madness or suicide, and asked her to consider for next session the area which most troubled her.

Our second session (we were meeting weekly), was mainly centred on Alex's death: the unfulfilled hopes, the lost dreams and the regrets that remained. I commented how admiring I was that Rita had named her stillborn child, rather than letting it pass unacknowledged into insignificance, and wondered how she might remember her son's uniqueness on the next anniversary of his death.

At our third session, Rita said that she had been able to complete her two assignments and hand them in for assessment by the due date. We talked about the incestuous secrets and patterns of deceit within Rita's family of origin. We discussed how boundaries had been blurred, roles had been confused, power had been mismanaged and protection had been denied. I asked Rita if she would construct a conversation between the 'grieving Rita', who had missed out on many nourishing moments within her original family, and the 'developing Rita', who wished to explore more rewarding directions for the future.

At our fourth session, Rita showed me her conversation: 'Grieving Rita' needed time and space to let go the emotions related to past losses: anger, emptiness, despair. 'Developing Rita' required flexibility to experiment with new situations. I commented that it appeared these two parts of Rita eventually needed to negotiate and reach a compromise; Rita's developing self might enable her to move forward out of the stagnation of grief, while her greving self might give her pause not to forge ahead too rapidly without well-considered planning. Changing the focus on to Rita's expressed interest in feminism, I shared with her a paper that I had recently prepared on Michael White's work with abusive men and the women who partner them (White, 1986; White and Epston, 1990).

The restraining of the training of the shrew

In William Shakespeare's play *The Taming of the Shrew*, Baptista, a wealthy resident of Padua engages Petruchio, a gentleman from Verona, to subdue and marry his high-spirited and 'evil tempered' daughter, Katharina. Petruchio succeeds in wooing his bride, but several weeks later . . .

Act 1. Scene 1. A room. Katharina and Petruchio are seated before a wise counsellor.

Counsellor: What seems to be the matter?

Petruchio: Zounds and damnation! – I cannot make this shrew do as I wish. I gained Katharina as my wife with witticism, swagger and bravado, winning her with my winning ways, and showing her who was truly lord and master over our marriage. I commanded her: 'Kiss me, Kate!', and so modestly she did. Now the witch no longer follows the script. She lashes out with her spicy, peppered tongue, and the only way I know to tame this shameless shrew is to give her a goodly clap on the chin. I know of no other way. She goads me, my rage mounts, and I am at her throat.

Katharina: Petruchio, my lord and master? . . . Indeed! This remorseless, lecherous, treacherous villain wishes me to come at his beck and call, to serve and simper as he pleases as if I had no will of my own, to be subdued and to subordinate me to his desire. When I try to tell this brute my story, to say how it is for me, he goes for the whip and the boot. I do not wish to be whipped nor under his foot; nor shall I be silent, nor ever a servile slave . . . the Devil take Petruchio for the tyrant that he is!

Counsellor: And yet, is there no morsel of good that you two enjoy together?

Petruchio: Why yes, when Katharina is in good temper we do while away the time in exceedingly sweet pleasantries.

Katharina: And when his choler is controlled, I do confess that I warm to his company and conversation.

Counsellor: So if your passion could be better spent, would you seek to preserve your union?

Petruchio: 'Tis true, I would do so.

Katharina: And I, also.

Counsellor: Then I believe I can be of some help to you. I know another version of these happenings between you that is quite different from the one you present; truly, you may both swoon to hear of it. I find your account for these tidings and mine so dissimilar as to astound even myself. My story differs in such marked detail from yours that you may find it profoundly upsetting. This is particularly so for you Petruchio. With blanched cheek and fevered brow, you may struggle with my version. Verily, you may even attempt to flee the battlefield of confrontation, or desperately girding your loins, attack me in the attempt to defend your stance.

Katharina: Your words intrigue me, counsellor . . . I am ready to hear more.

Petruchio: Your words do strike terror into my very soul, counsellor . . . yet tend to them I must, for in truth, I do not feel well about myself when I hit Kate. I would find another way.

Counsellor: But soft you now. . . . I would warn you both not to accept what I am about to say without question, for you have been scripted well by William, a literary genius! Let us explore together the argument and see whether you can come to a resolution.

Katharina and Petruchio: We are ready for it.

Counsellor: William had a brilliant narrative skill, but was of a mind that men ruled the world. Look how Ophelia and Gertrude were done to death by the manipulations of their menfolk, Hamlet and Claudius. Note how Lady Macbeth achieved her goals with underhanded and deceitful cunning, rather than by being able to combat her male peers as equals. Observe the plotting of Richard Crookback, who murdered wife and young innocents to gain England's crown. Even the intelligence of Portia could only be of help to the merchant of Venice when she disguised herself as a male solicitor. The blame of scripting men as all-powerful lies not with William . . . this was the way of the world in his time. But do you think that if your author had held women in a different light, his stories would have read differently? Had William experienced women as exploited, oppressed, taken-over, suffocated, enslaved . . . would his characters have behaved otherwise?

You, Petruchio, were scripted to be brave and witty and charming, an all-knowing master in your house. Your story, Katharina, was written by a man, for other men. They termed your energy, liveliness and independence as 'shrewishness'. They said you should be tamed and turned to domestic humility.

Do you think, Petruchio, that you should follow this limiting and stultifying script of your author relating to power over others, or does the idea of enabling you and Katharina to become 'real people', growing in appreciation of your personal resourcefulness and empowerment seem more attractive? If you opposed these ideas about the supremacy of men, Petruchio, you would set yourself apart from other men . . . surpassing Hamlet, Macbeth, Julius Caesar, even William himself. Could you manage that much success? Could you cope with the attitudes of other men of Padua and Verona to such a change? No more duels, carousing or cockfighting! Could you face up to hearing Katharina's story without regarding her as a shrew? Or would you crumble? Might you both be so bold as to seek out some of the differences that would take place in your lives and relationship should you decide to experiment with change?

Katharina: Will you turn from falconry, Petruchio, to preparing sweetmeats in the kitchen? Will you avert your gaze from country wenches to the care of our babes whilst I attend my tuition at the college of studies?

Petruchio: My heart faints to think on it, yet . . . I will think on it.

They both leave . . . the counsellor, on seeing them reach the court-yard and give each other a hug, sings:

> Tell me where is courage bred,
> In the heart or in the head.

The fifth to tenth sessions were spent discussing a new acquaintance, Lazar, 28, a nurse, whom Rita had met at a party the previous weekend. He seemed to be different from the other men that she had selected as social intimates, more sensitive to her conversation, more able to hear accurately what she wanted to communicate. As these five weeks passed, Rita met Lazar regularly and was able to tell him clearly what she wanted from him at this particular moment; that she was coming out of a painful relationship and was seeking neither a heavy emotional nor a physical involvement; that she was not interested in long-term one-to-one commitment, and that she needed space, rather than intense contact, within their relating. As it happened, Lazar had also recently ended a friendship, and was about to go overseas for an extended vacation within the next few weeks. He appreciated the need not to create a 'deep and meaningful' bond with Rita. Rita said that it felt good to be in charge of her participation within a relationship for a change, and to be telling another person what her particular needs were.

When Rita eventually received her assignments back from her lecturer, she learnt that she had passed with distinction. A year later, Rita has commenced an eight-month tour of India with Samantha.

–––––––––––––– . . . ––––––––––––––

DISCUSSION

Defining the problem

Rita tells of her depression, says that she is falling to pieces, and that it is interfering with her study routine. She blames herself that, although she has become well educated in feminist issues, she still chooses partners who exploit her.

Exploring the context

A number of contexts relating to Rita's struggles are examined. First, the grief relating to Alex's death is expressed through dialogue. Following this, Rita is able to finish her assignments. Next, the abuse within Rita's family of origin is examined. Rita's interest in feminism is intrigued by discussing patriarchal patterns relating to the discounting of women within our wider community, as illustrated by Shakespeare. These are linked to her past personal experience within her family of origin. Rita's written conversation between her grieving self and her developing self indicates the need for these two parts of Rita to integrate and help each other move towards a more flexible, yet thoughtfully planned, future.

Options for the future

Rita meets a new acquaintance, one who seems to respect her needs. They both appear able to discuss and arrange the most appropriate relationship within the circumstances available to them, rather than fall into the same old tired 'me Tarzan, you Jane' script. Rita describes with pleasure her new experience of mutuality.

As a point for reflection here, compare the issues illustrated within Case 7.1, 'Educating Rita' that resemble those in Case 6.1, 'Villains and Rogues'.

------------------------   . . .   ------------------------

CASE STUDY

Case 7B   The procrastinator
Arnold, 55, an administrator of a health benefits fund, said that he had been depressed for many months and was bursting into tears almost every day. He lacked energy to do his job properly and was concerned about his institution making a loss that financial year.

Arnold described his youth as nomadic. Born in Germany just before the outbreak of World War Two, he moved with his Jewish family to Belgium. Arnold's father was interned in Buchenwald concentration camp. Arnold and his sister were hidden in a convent and tutored in the Catholic religion during the rest of the war, while his mother and elder brother found shelter elsewhere. The family all survived, regathered and migrated to Australia when Arnold was 13 years old. Arnold's father literally dropped dead on the wharf when they arrived.

'I always hated him for doing that to us', Arnold said. 'It caused us all such hardship during those early years.'

Arnold had performed poorly at school, had held several short-term unskilled jobs, and eventually had married Helen, a manufacturer. They had two children and Arnold described family life as lonely, disconnected and lifeless. Helen resented Arnold's repetitive periods of

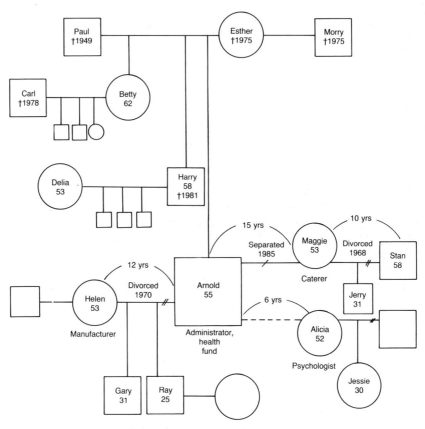

Fig. 7.2 Arnold commenced therapy in April 1991.

unemployment between jobs, and eventually she left Arnold to live with a lover. Arnold had immediately courted and married Maggie, who had recently left her own marriage with her son Jerry, 8. Maggie was a complete contrast to Helen in personality. The manager of a catering firm, diagnosed as manic-depressive, Maggie was 'loud, boisterous, vulgar, sociable, exuberant, gregarious'. She was happy to support Arnold financially, and Jerry and Arnold got on famously. However, beneath Maggie's energetic exterior lay an emotional dependency, jealousy and possessiveness that Arnold found claustrophobic. He eventually left Maggie to pair up with Alicia, 52, a psychologist. Alicia was different yet again; cultured, quiet, educated. Though Arnold and Alicia lived apart, they enjoyed many social and educational activities together, and during their relationship Arnold trained for, and obtained, a diploma of administration and had remained employed in his current position for some years. Their main problem, and the source of many arguments, was that though Arnold and Maggie had been separated for six years, Arnold had not proceeded with divorce. He had had all the relevant papers lying in a drawer for a couple of years.

'Oh, Alicia has made it clear to me', Arnold said. 'She is not necessarily pushing for marriage. She is just not comfortable with my residual legal connection to Maggie.'

I told Arnold that I admired his ability to survive such a disjointed youth: being uprooted from his home; transferral to another country as a refugee; being raised within two cultures (Jewish and Catholic); and his father's sudden death with its ensuring difficulties.

'Your father might have been room-mates with my grandfather at Buchenwald', I commented. 'They were both interned there during the same period. Coincidentally, they both died in the same year, possibly from their experiences there.'

I could well understand Arnold struggling to find out where he 'belonged' after such a disruptive passage into adulthood. He appeared to have explored where he belonged within three different relationships. One of his partners had valued her independence and privacy, another had been an organizer, full of energy and vivacity, and a third was an explorer of the world through learning and social interaction. Perhaps an issue now for Arnold was not which partner to live with, but whether he might live within a couple or alone. We agreed to meet weekly, and I asked Arnold to list for next session the pros and cons of a relationship with Alicia.

At our second session, Arnold gave the following letter to me:

To John Gunzburg,
Before involving Alicia, or for that matter anybody else, I think there are a number of points I want to clear up. Why do things stress me? Coping mechanisms? Why am I so bloody ambivalent? Why do I find it so hard to make decisions? Why am I so insecure? Do I really want to be left alone? to live alone? Why am I always a blink away from tears? What is the core of my sadness? If I have nothing to be unhappy about, why am I? Do I really care if I live or die? Why do I hide, what from, who from? If I am seen to be coping, am I coping? Depression, lack of sleep, nightmares – tablets? When I found out about having blocked arteries, I was not really worried about dying (I think) but more about the limitation on my physical activities. Why is only my work life important? Everything else is peripheral. Then I get defensive if my partner complains. Why am I so self conscious about my lack of formal education? Entailing an admiration of everyone educated, although I know there are educated idiots. Why am I still feeling guilty

about Maggie? Why do I not comply with Alicia's wishes? I know we could have had a good life. Did I 'stuff it'? Did I want to 'stuff it'? Do I want to live alone? Do I want Maggie back? Why have I never respected Maggie? Was I trying to prove something? How great and clever I was? Do I regret Maggie because she thought I was so clever? Big fish – small pond. Alicia sees through me. Did Maggie?
Why am I so angry!!
Arnold

Arnold said that he had thought about the benefits of a partnership with Alicia: companionship, creation of a family situation (his sons liked Alicia and Arnold got on well with her daughter from a previous marriage), division of labour, potential for an equitable distribution of finances, improved quality of lifestyle, availability of an 'intelligent sounding-board', and that Alicia was not 'your typical Yiddishe hausfrau' – and the disadvantages: reduced privacy, infringement of freedom and flexibility, that none of his friends liked Alicia, the competitiveness between Alicia and himself, their difficulty negotiating differences, her resentment because of his inaction in divorcing Maggie, and that Alicia was not 'your typical Yiddishe hausfrau!' However, Arnold said, he wanted to concentrate on the issues inside his skin, as illustrated in his letter.

I commented that some of the emotions Arnold talked about: stress, ambivalence, hesitancy, insecurity, depression, anger, did not seem to have risen within his skin per se, but were more related to his environment. His whole youth appeared to have been a stressful buffeting from one country to another. His ambivalence may have resulted from a clash of religious cultures, and his hesitancy and insecurity may have been due to the crises that kept blowing up in his face: war, death, poverty, illness. It was a bit like residing in a minefield, never knowing which step would be the next one that would damage or destroy him. Moreover, much of his adult relating seemed to have occurred within triangular structures. Helen had been involved with her lover for many years before she finally chose him as a partner over Arnold, and Alicia and Arnold had been lovers long before he had left Maggie. Arnold's pattern of human relating seemed to have always been within a 'crisis context'. Here he was at 55 years of age, having missed out on the benefits of an affable 'couples' intimacy and seemingly unable to set boundaries around a personal relationship with Alicia. Perhaps the emotions Arnold was now feeling – anger, depression, tears – were more to do with grieving for his lost opportunities, and rather than losing more time searching for a 'Why?', his energies might be better channelled into the 'How?' of a more nourishing future.

At our third and fourth sessions we continued the theme of a bachelor lifestyle as opposed to intimacy. Did the triangular relationships within which Arnold lived (his continued marriage to Maggie while maintaining an intimacy with Alicia could be regarded as an example of this) prevent him from gaining the information he needed to know before making a couples commitment?

At our fifth session, with both Arnold and Alicia attending, we discussed what needed to be done to change the status quo. Arnold expressed his anxieties that Alicia would not get over her resentment at his procrastination, and that he would end up with a partner who blamed him for their missed opportunities. I commented that, although Alicia and Arnold appeared to have reached an impasse of some years' duration in their relationship, I admired the respect that they were displaying towards one another, even though they were angry at each other, Alicia at Arnold's delays, Arnold at Alicia's prodding.

'I see a lot of couples sitting in those chairs tearing one another to pieces', I said. 'You two do not seem to have any of that antagonism here.'

Alicia told me a little of her own past. They both appeared to have had many past struggles. Perhaps Arnold's heart attack had reminded them that time was not infinite. I wondered how many more months would have to pass before they both realized that they deserved a better time of it, quietly rounding off their lives before the big sleep.

'After all', I added, 'why should Hitler win? Why should the damage he has wrought continue to plague your story? Would you be prepared to experiment together as to just how you might achieve closeness and permanency within your relationship?

I did not see Arnold again for a month. He told me that during that time he had signed the papers relating to his and Maggie's divorce and had forwarded them to his lawyer. His tears had ceased, and he and Alicia were starting to banter, rather than bicker, as to where to live – his place or hers? They had even spent weekends looking at properties to decide if they wanted to live together in completely different accommodation. I asked what had created the change. Arnold said that it had been a number of factors. He and Alicia had believed that their arguments were due to an irreversible cycle of events. During our joint session, it was the first time in a long while that anyone had said anything nice about them: that they treated each other with some respect, that they had displayed strength in overcoming personal hardship. And I had posed for them a question: How much more bloody time were they going to let slip by before they enjoyed themselves within a committed partnership? Our conversation seemed to have given them permission to stop blaming each other and to start to work together as a team.

···

DISCUSSION

Defining the problem

Arnold tells of his depression and the emotions related to it, and is full of recriminations for his own failings in personality.

Exploring the context

Our conversation changes the focus of Arnold's search from the intra-psychic to the interactional, and from the 'Why?' of the past to the 'How?' of the present and future.

Options for the future

Arnold and Alicia indicate that they are respectful of each other, and are asked to experiment in negotiating closeness and commitment. Arnold proceeds with his divorce and the two of them contemplate future joint residence.

      ——————— · · · ———————

CASE STUDY

Case 7C   Bagels and sponge-cake
'I have been depressed for years', said Esther, 20, a student of pro-fessional writing, during our first meeting. 'I just cannot seem to do anything about it . . . and I have got to do something about it. I am just lying in bed all day, not bothering to get up and do anything. I have got to do something about it! I have an assignment that has to be finished within six weeks.'

As we talked, Esther told me something of her youth. Her father, Jonathon, now 65, was Jewish, a pianist, witty, dependent on his wives for emotional support, and an abuser of alcohol. Her mother, Liz, now 50, a secretary, was Anglican, fair-minded, loving and funny. They had divorced when Esther was seven. Esther had always enter-tained feelings since childhood that she was unlovable. She related how a teenage 'friend' had raped her when she was 12. Esther told how, as she entered young adulthood she was constantly controlling of her relationships – being 'dominating, choosy and finicky', and she was concerned that her current two-year friendship with Calvin would

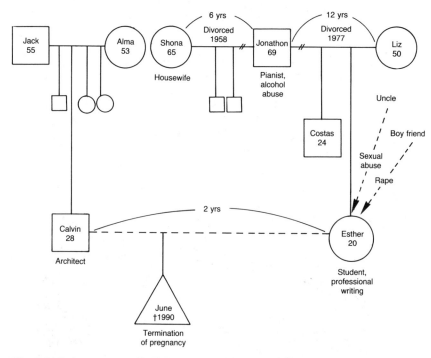

Fig. 7.3 Esther commenced therapy in February 1991.

end soon when Calvin accepted an overseas job opportunity that had recently become available.

'There has always been a bit of a battle between Cal and me', said Esther. 'Especially around the time of the baby.' Esther had undergone termination of pregnancy nine months previously, felt that Calvin had offered little support, and that he had, in fact, leant heavily on her to seek an abortion.

We agreed to meet weekly.

Esther had nominated music, poetry and drawing as her resources, and I wondered if she would take some time to draw her experiences of the rape. Her description of this event seemed to have been the most evocative, producing tears during the session.

Esther showed me her sketches at our next session (Figs 7.4 and 7.5). She described the feelings that had been let loose as she had drawn the pictures: emptiness, fear, rage.

'Today, I just have this huge, great hole inside me', she said. 'There is nothing else there inside me, just this big, empty space.'

We discussed for a while how the men in her life had not been available for her emotional nourishment. Her father had left her in her

Fig. 7.4 Esther's drawing: 'How I felt about the boyfriend who raped me'.

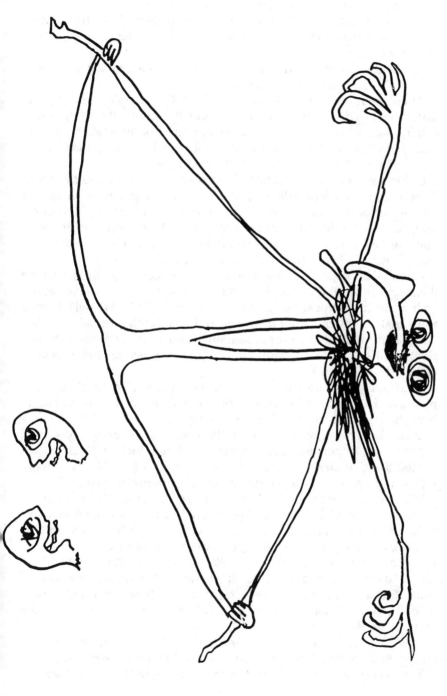

Fig. 7.5 Esther's drawing: 'How I felt about myself after being raped'.

youth, as he had the children of his first family. Her teenage acquaintance had responded to her affection with violation.

'That was not the only incident of sexual abuse', Esther added. 'When I was five, I went to live with my grandmother for a while and an uncle touched me up.'

Calvin also had forced his views on to Esther at a time when she was vulnerable and required his support.

'These men all seemed to have drained you', I said, 'sucking the matter out of you, drying you up, emotionally, spiritually, so that what is left inside of you is not the sweet substance of an English sponge-cake, but rather the emptiness of the hole in the centre of a bagel.'

Esther smiled – just a little – for the first time.

Esther was still staying in bed until noon every day. I spent the next three or four sessions talking about how she might nourish herself during her time in bed: making sure there was a tray of provisions – fruit, juices, that did not require preparation – by her bed and ensuring that the bed was warm and comfortable. How, in fact, could Esther make resting in bed a treat rather than a retreat?

At our sixth session, Esther fumed into my room. Calvin had ended their relationship unilaterally without consultation or conversation. Esther was murderously angry and mentioned suicide. We talked about ways that she might care for herself: residence with a friend for a few days? the possibility of hospitalization? Esther stood up abruptly and shouted at me, 'I do not want your bloody suggestions! I just want to be heard!'

I did not sleep much that night. Esther was not accessible by telephone and I wondered what sort of correspondence I should send to her. She arranged to see me the next afternoon.

'I am just so angry that Cal has broken it off without any sort of negotiation', Esther said, with energy and determination. 'I will not be treated like that any more. He told me when he left that he was doing it this way because it was kinder to me . . . patronizing bastard!'

We discussed the sort of information that Esther needed to know to enable her to let Calvin go, and she decided that it would be reasonable of her to demand another meeting with him to clarify exactly how he had come to his decision to separate. A genuine intimacy of more than two years seemed to preclude a unilateral split by either party. Were Cal to decline such a meeting, it would further affirm his lack of suitability as a respectful partner for her. Esther requested, and I helped her to obtain, a two-month deferment of her project on the grounds of 'depression'.

A week later, Esther said that she had lunched with Calvin and the arrangement to separate had been discussed much more clearly.

Two weeks later, I met Esther bouncing along in the street. I was on my way to the bank, she was going towards the milliner's shop, the time was 10.30 a.m.!

——————————— · · · ———————————

DISCUSSION

Defining the problem

Esther recognizes that she has been depressed for years, and her problem of lethargy is currently confining her to bed and interfering with her studies.

Exploring the context

There are many losses: the parents' divorce, childhood and adolescent sexual abuse, termination of pregnancy, the threat of relationship breakdown. The rape is explored pictorially and the feelings under-lying Esther's depression are expressed.

Options for the future

Esther's boyfriend ends the relationship without discussion. Esther demands a further meeting with him and successfully negotiates a separation. Her project is deferred and she no longer languishes in bed.

——————————— · · · ———————————

CASE STUDY

Case 7D   The art director
Les, 40, an art director, said that he was disheartened and depressed following the end of a recent relationship with Amy, 34, a writer who worked in the same office as he. They had commenced their affair six months previously – it had been filled with passion, fun and excite-ment, and had risen out of the premise that Amy was leaving her seven-year partnership with Todd, 36, an accountant. Amy, however, had informed Les one month ago that she was reconciling with Todd, and Les was left feeling distraught that he had invested so much emotionally into this friendship only to have it blow up in his face.

Les told me about his nine-year marriage with Susan. They had been good mates, but their union had lacked flair and vitality. The marriage had ended after Susan had become involved with Sanchez, 25, a fiery

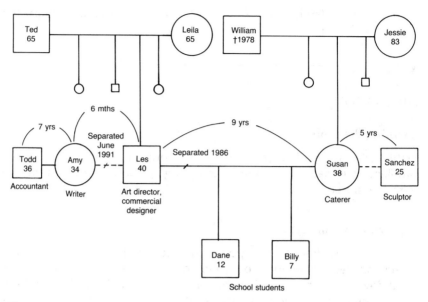

Fig. 7.6 Les commenced therapy in July 1991.

Spanish sculptor. Despite their initial distress, Susan and Les had remained friends and Les saw their sons Dane, 12, and Billy, 7, regularly on fortnightly access.

As we talked, it became clear that Les was grieving. He had not, as yet, cemented a permanent relationship with a partner and he did not seem to have found the emotional balance that he required within intimacy. His long-term experience with Susan had lacked vivacity, and several shorter encounters had all been 'disastrous'. Each partner had started out as loving, energetic, committed, yet after a few months had always proved to have had someone waiting in the wings – a former spouse or another person within their social network – for whom they had rejected Les. 'So when you achieve stability over a length of time, your passion decreases', I suggested, 'and when you find fire, you all too readily lose your cool. I wonder if you would take time out to script a conversation between your "passion" and your "cool", and discover whether they could negotiate a suitable compromise within a future intimacy?'

At our second session, Les shared his dialogue with me:

A conversation

Les and Gian-Carlo were identical twins, separated at birth by a cruel twist of fate far too lengthy to deal with now. Suffice to say they had totally different upbringings, one in Australia, the other in Italy and they met for their first time just after their fortieth birthdays. Les has agreed to show his brother around during his first visit to this country.

'I like this place, Les. What did you call it?'

'The Dog's Bar. There's a little feeding bowl with water in it out the front.'

The bar was quite empty, maybe ten people, which Les found a little disappointing. He wanted to show his long lost brother a good time.

'It reminds me of some of the bars home in Milano.'

'Good. Sorry it's so empty, it'll be buzzing in an hour or so.'

'Tell me about your life so far, Les.'

'Nothing to tell. I'm married, got two kids.'

'What do you do for excitement?'

'Excitement? Me? Give us a break. I left that behind years ago. The job and the mortgage keep me busy enough. I don't need to complicate my life any more than it is. What about you?'

Gian-Carlo just smiled and looked down into his drink.

'I've been seeing this girl. She's so cute.'

'So why didn't you bring her out with you?'

'I don't think the guy that she lives with would be too happy about that.'

'She lives with a guy? Are you crazy?'

'No way! She loves me. It's cool.'

'How can you stand it? I mean she goes home at night and gets into bed with another guy.'

'No, I don't think she does. I think he sleeps out the back.'

'So she says. I thought you Italian guys were supposed to be jealous types. I couldn't handle that.'

For the first time the smile dropped just a bit.

'How many girlfriends have you had?'

'Heaps. The ones I really like usually dump me and then you get these ugly ones that hang around ringing you up all the time making your life a misery. But I just can't stand being stuck with the one woman. Imagine waking up to the same face every morning.'

'But the ones you really like, wouldn't you like to settle down with one of them?'

'Funny you should say that but that's what I think about quite a lot. But don't tell anyone! No. What I really like is that hit you get when you start getting on to someone new.'

'Hit? You mean like a drug?'

'Better than any drug I've tried. No I can't explain it, it's just this gut-wrenching, heart-thumping feeling. Like living on the edge of a blade. It's such a high.'

'And you're an addict!'

Gian-Carlo laughed loudly then sat pensively for a moment.

'Well if you don't chase women, what do you do?'

'Well, the house keeps me busy, I'm fixing up the garden. Then there's the kids. You can't get started on anything without being interrupted by one or other of them looking for some help. I dunno. There's always my mate Stan, too. He's in the same boat as me. He's into computers too so we've got a lot in common.'

'Sounds like a real exciting guy.' The voice was tinged with irony.

'We get involved in all these weird projects, like starting a fan club for the Legendary Stardust Cowboy.'

'Who?'

'He's this crazy guy in the States who had a record in about 1969 called 'Paralysed'. It was a bit of a hit over there, and has been included in every collection of 'The World's Worst Records' ever since. We decided he needed a fan club. It's sort of a club for people who would never consider joining a club.'

'Sounds like Groucho Marx.'

'So do you, only you say "Any girl that would have me I wouldn't want to know".'

Another big Italian laugh followed by the pensive silence.

'Maybe.'

'Well look at it. You're always going for girls who are attached. Do you figure that that is some kind of seal of approval?'

'What do you mean?'

'Well, like if they've already got a guy they must be OK. If they can't get a guy there must be something wrong with them. You know.'

'Hmmmm . . .'

By now the bar was starting to fill up and Les could see that he would have trouble holding Gian-Carlo's attention.

'Don't you ever get tired of chasing women? I mean it's a pretty shallow existence . . .'

'No way. Just look at that one over there, I think she was checking you out. You should do something about that. Life is not a rehearsal, you only get one shot at it, so go for it!'

'You never give up, do you. I'm not interested. She is kind of nice, though. What am I saying . . . You're a bad influence, Gian.'

'You must have thought about it. You can't make me believe that you don't come to places like this and don't check out the girls.'

'Check out, maybe, but I'd never do anything about it.'

'Yeah, just dream about it. It's all the same. If you think about doing something you might as well have done it.'

'Sounds like something from the Bible. What was that? Something about committing adultery just by imagining it. I didn't know you were so religious.'

'Hey. I'm Italian.'

'Right. You guys think it's OK to do what you like on Saturday night as long as you say a few Hail Marys the next day in mass.'

'It's a wonderful system, so don't knock it.'

'Sure.'

The exchange had been light-hearted but discussions about religion are always dangerous so Les took a different tack.

'Don't you ever get lonely? You know, when you're between girlfriends?'

'It comes with the territory. You gotta have the good with the bad. That's not something I'd admit to just anyone though.'

'So can you see yourself with just one woman?'

'Never! Actually I really like the girl I'm seeing now but you know the situation. I'll tell you something I've never admitted to anyone. If she'd leave him, I'd marry her just like that.'

'But she won't?'

'Who knows. I think if she was going to she would've by now. I mean the perfect opportunity would have been to run away here with me. I was thinking about it this morning in the shower. I was thinking this is really great, so warm and comfortable, but I gotta get out. But it's so cold out there, so I'll stay in a bit longer. Yeah it's fantastic, but if I don't get out soon the hot water's gonna run out and having a heap of cold water dumped on you is much worse than just leaving the shower. Shit it was hard to get out, though.'

'Sounds like you crave a bit of security in your life.'

'You know, seeing you with your gorgeous wife and kids did make me a bit jealous. But don't quote me on that.'

'Funny you should say that, but I was thinking before how I wouldn't mind your lifestyle for a while. I wish there was some answer, some way to balance things.'

'Perhaps we could swap lives for a few weeks each year!'

'Good idea. Another drink?'

Les told me that, on writing this conversation, he had thought about the many short-term partners, and Amy in particular, who seemed to have 'dumped cold water' on to their relationship, denying him the security for which he craved. He had ended up feeling used. Even though he had enjoyed the warmth of their passion, he had hated being doused. We continued to talk about the various family contexts within which people endeavoured to satisfy their needs. The popular media frequently promoted the excitement and novelty of extramarital affairs, whereas a reality was that, on entering triangular relationships, people often found themselves intimately connected to their lover and married to their enemy. On the other hand, monogamy was often presented as sterotypically stale, without life or leisure, or a 'battle of the sexes' with constant sparring and malicious trickery. I commented that Les, in his conversation, had outlined quite clearly the dilemmas that he faced. Perhaps, arising out of this exercise, Les might continue to explore some new opportunities for the future.

At our third session, one month later, some surprises had occured. Sanchez had decided to return to his home town of Barcelona, and Susan had requested, and obtained, respectful support from Les. We discussed if a future prospect for reconciliation existed. Les thought not. He had written and posted a 'letting go' letter to Amy, expressing his feelings of being used and dumped. And he had met Debbie, 29, who worked in media.

'You could have knocked me down when after our second date, she told me she was leaving a marriage', said Les. 'I seem to have a real knack for picking them attached!'

Nonetheless, Les had discussed with Debbie the ground rules for a further friendship, including maintaining distance and not becoming too involved. They had decided to enjoy the occasional restaurant and film outing together, without too much emotional intensity and sex at this stage. This was a different situation for Les. He was usually an eager starter for 'red-hot loving', and was finding the cooler contact of social dialogue quite rewarding.

Our conversation concluded with a few ideas on how to assess a person's ability to make commitment to an intimacy: What is their past track record? What is their current lifestyle? Is the language they use respectful and sensitive to the emotional context of relationships, or focused largely on self-needs?

——————————— . . . ———————————

DISCUSSION

Defining the problem

Les speaks early in therapy about his disheartenment and depression, and relates this to the recent ending of an intimacy with Amy.

Exploring the context

The marriage with Susan has ended amicably and appears to present no problems. Les sees his sons on regular access, and his vocation is proceeding without mishap. Les describes his inadequacy at maintaining passion in his long-term 'safe' marriage with Susan, and in achieving stability and security within briefer, though passionate, friendships. A written conversation helps Les to clarify his dilemma: does he wish for safety and security, excitement and variety, or a bit of both?

Options for the future

Les lets go of his previous, painful relationship with Amy in the form of a letter. He supports his ex-spouse respectfully during a stressful moment, and experiments by negotiating some different ways of commencing a new social intimacy with Debbie.

—————— · · · ——————

CASE STUDY

Case 7E   Black Peter

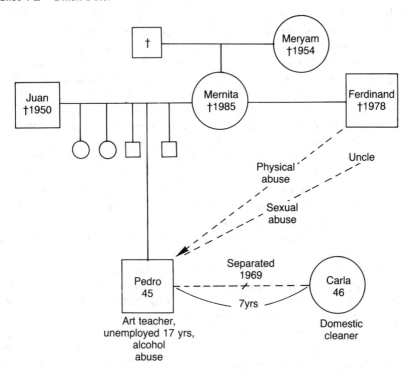

Fig. 7.7 Pedro commenced therapy in February 1989.

Pedro, 45, an unemployed art teacher, came to therapy during one of his recurrent episodes of depression. He had migrated to Australia from the Philippines as a young man, and had gained a teacher's certificate, entering the state education system in the late 1960s. Pedro had lost his job after a 'nervous breakdown' during which he had 'heard voices', and he had not worked since the early 1970s. He had experienced bouts of depression many times since then. During these times he would eat poorly, consuming junk food, or abstain altogether. Sometimes he became agitated and wandered aimlessly around the neighbourhood. More often, he would lose energy and lie listless in his room. Between 1986 and 1989 Pedro had abused alcohol in his attempts to console himself. He had been sober since 1989. An intimacy of several years with Carla, 46, a domestic cleaner, had ended in separation in 1969, and Pedro said that he had been celibate since then.

Pedro's main problem was his conviction that he was 'full of poison', able to entice young men sexually and corrupt them. He believed that he was the cause of much provocation among his room-mates at the hostel where he lived, and he was often engaged in yelling matches with members of the public, having been cautioned by the police on more than one occasion for loitering and making a nuisance of himself. Pedro felt that he was putting out 'bad vibrations', persuading others to think evil and erotic thoughts about him. Often he could not deduce whether the thoughts were arising within himself or those others around him. Pedro said that he was constantly bothered as to whether these vibrations were part of the physical or part of the spiritual world, and felt at times as if he were 'possessed by demons'. On occasions, Pedro felt quite disorientated and disintegrated. He said that doctors had placed him on stelazine (for a schizophrenic illness) during the 1970s, but that he had been medication-free for the past decade.

It was many months before Pedro trusted me enough to tell his story of life as a youth. The early stages of weekly therapy were spent in affirming Pedro's qualities: his beliefs in social justice, his relationship with a merciful and friendly God, his determination to find contentment even though troubled by depression and bizarre experiences. We talked how one could recognize elements of the material world, discussing the St. Kilda seascape and Blessington Botanical Gardens, musing about the fragrances and tastes of the Acland St restaurants, examining various physical signs and symptoms and relating them to bodily systems. Nonetheless, Pedro was not able to accept the idea of a psychological world, with its projections and perceptions, communication patterns and behaviours, and clung to the concept that his feelings resulted from demonic possession, thought control and telekinesis. I did not challenge these beliefs; rather, I expressed my curiosity as to how these phenomena might occur.

After about one year, Pedro told me of his childhood. It seemed that he had been raised in a family in which emotions had been extremely primitive and extreme, boundaries had been fuzzy and roles were almost non-existent. Juan, the father, had died when Pedro was six, and Mernita, the mother, had remarried soon afterwards. Pedro remembered both parents as fierce, argumentative, threatening characters. When Pedro was eight, an uncle regularly performed fellatio on him while the lad lay reading his comic books. Pedro said he found this confusing but not frightening. More sinister were the beatings that his enraged stepfather used to give him during adolescence, whenever Pedro took out a girlfriend on a date.

'I think that my stepfather fancied me', said Pedro, 'and wanted me for his own pleasure.'

'It certainly sounds as if he treated you like a lover who had betrayed him', I commented.

As therapy progressed, Pedro began to remember more past events and to reclaim forgotten history.

'Do you know what the word "Avshalom" means?', Pedro asked one day. 'I heard a voice saying it during a dream last night.'

I expressed my surprise that a good Catholic boy should know this word; it is the Hebrew name of King David's son.

'Ahhhh!', continued Pedro, 'my grandmother Meryam used to read me stories about King David when I was a boy. She was a Syrian Jewess, a real tough cookie! But she was also a sweetie. I always knew that she loved me and was kind to me. I miss her. . . . I was ten when she died.'

On another occasion, Pedro had dreamt of fires, explosions, volcanoes and burnt children's bodies. I was remarking to Pedro that such dreams are common among victims of sexual abuse, when he recalled that the Japanese had bombed his village when he was a toddler during World War Two.

'Yes', I thought to myself, 'we do remember reality as well as metaphorical images of violation!'

All this narrative unfolded over some two years, and during this time, Pedro made some significant changes. He had initially entered therapy dressed in a black tracksuit, with long hair gathered in a pigtail. After six months, I asked Pedro that if he wanted to change his name, which one would he choose? Pedro had replied: 'I think I would like to be known as Black Peter.'

'That is the name of the pirate flag as I recall it', I suggested, 'and in truth, you do sometimes look a bit like a rascally sea-dog, or a bandido or toreador. I wonder if the way you present yourself to others frightens them a little?'

Within several weeks of this conversation, Pedro came to sessions wearing a grey tracksuit with a pink jumper, and carrying a small brown furry toy dog in a pouch hung from one shoulder. He said that people in public places were treating him much more kindly now, and I complimented him on the manner in which he was signalling his friendliness. Twelve months into therapy, Pedro began to complain of stiffness, pain and spasm in his neck. Being trained as a masseur, I offered him regular neck manipulation. This seemed to relax not only his neck but his whole body. Pedro had also begun to go for walks on the beach and to enjoy Tai Chi in the park, but all throughout those two years, he believed that people could get into his mind and control him, and that his 'evil vibrations' remained a dangerous influence to others.

I drew for Pedro the diagram illustrated in Fig. 7.8. I talked with him about how I admired his gifted and intuitive awareness of both the material and the spiritual spheres. He knew about tastes, colours,

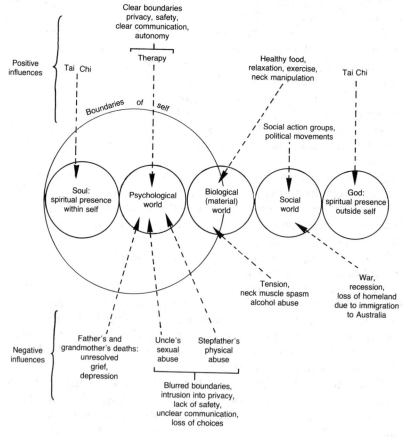

Fig. 7.8 John's drawing for Pedro.

shapes, fragrances, and also about the soul within and the Divine Presence without. Yet events within Pedro's psychological and social worlds, I suggested, may have separated the material from the spiritual. First, the death of Pedro's father and grandmother may have left for him a pervasive sense of grief, heavy and depressing. Then, the uncle and stepfather's sexual and physical abuses may have blurred boundaries, decreased his sense of safety and privacy, made communication unclear, and deprived him of his freedom of choice. War and economic recession also appear to have added to his insecurity. Perhaps these psychosocial violations had intruded into Pedro's youthful emotional world, and he now 'remembered' them as 'evil vibrations and demonic possession'. Indeed, the internalized voices he had experienced during his schizophrenic illness may have been the remembered 'screams of his violated youth'. Pedro appeared to have suffered many losses due to his demons; his peace of mind, vocation, intimacy with Carla, sexual enjoyment. He had already found ways to overcome some of these: eating healthy foods, exercise, meditation, relaxation, pursuing therapy with its provision of safe territory, confidentiality, clear boundaries, sensitive conversation, creativity, flexibility and encouragement of autonomy. Perhaps Pedro could seek further integration of the material with the spiritual, and pursue social justice through action groups, such as feminist meetings and MASA (Men Against Sexual Assault) and TAGS (Towards A Gentler Society)?

When I gave Pedro's neck a twist at the conclusion of this session, his muscles and vertebrae released some enormous clicks.

'Wow!', he exclaimed. 'That is good . . . that is very gooood. . . .'

Pedro appears to have become unknotted.

Six months later, Pedro has not complained of any depression, no longer speaks of possession, and has had no altercations with the community or police.

--- . . . ---

DISCUSSION

Defining the problem

Pedro describes well his long history of depression, and ties it to possession of his spiritual world with demonic presences.

Exploring the context

It takes over a year to build up enough trust for Pedro to explore a different context for his depression. He has had many losses: his father's and grandmother's deaths; loss of his childhood innocence due to the abuses of the uncle and stepfather; loss of his homeland; loss of his employment; and the end of an intimacy. The influence of the abuse and wartime experiences are highlighted in a diagram, and a point is made as to how psychological violation may be experienced as possession by evil spirits.

Options for the future

Pedro appears to be taking better care of himself, presenting himself as friendly, and adopting a healthier lifestyle. Perhaps the search for social justice can be realized through human contact within an action group.

SUMMARY

In Chapter 7 we considered five cases in which clients defined their problem primarily as depression.

In *Case 7A, 'Educating Rita'*, Rita's depression is linked with the violent, exploitative, patriarchal attitudes of her male intimates. A paper on abusive men highlights the entrenched influence of gender bias within our society.

In *Case 7B, 'The procrastinator'*, Arnold's emotions are ties to his war experiences: his uprootedness, undeveloped sense of self and lack of belonging, especially within deeper intimacies. A letter demonstrates the 'Why?' questions that Arnold keeps asking of himself, whereas the therapeutic conversation focuses more on the 'How to?' obtain his goals.

In *Case 7C, 'Bagels and sponge-cake'*, Esther appears to be burdened with 'leftovers' from her parents' divorce, and describes her sense of unlovability. She seems to have sought intimates who might fill up her 'emptiness within', and one of her acquaintances rapes her. The anger underlying Esther's violation is expressed pictorially, and she is more able to ask for her needs to be met appropriately during the ending of a recent friendship.

In *Case 7D, 'The art director'*, Les appears to be troubled by modern male mythology: lengthy stale relationships or passionate unstable ones? And affairs are fun! A written dialogue between his 'passion' and his 'calm' helps to outline his dilemma, and he negotiates some more satisfactory ground rules within a newly forming couples relationship.

In *Case 7E, 'Black Peter'*, Pedro relates his depression to demonic possession and his story reveals details of grief through parental death, sexual abuse and physical abuse within his family of origin. Therapy pays heed to creating a safe environment, with stable boundaries, privacy, clear communication and autonomy. An illustration offers Pedro a possible description of the negative influences within his biological, psychological and spiritual worlds that might be perceived to be possession by devils. Ways of counteracting them are also explored.

POINTS FOR REFLECTION

1. Select five recent case histories at random. What words do your clients use to express the emotions associated with their depression?
2. Consider a moment in your life when you experienced depression (make sure that it was not a time of extreme depression!). Draw a picture of the depression. What feelings are evoked by your picture? Are you able to script a dialogue between yourself and your depression? What questions do you ask of it? What replies do you receive?
3. What novels, plays, essays, films, paintings do you know which express the elements of depression, including its resolution? Are there any that you might utilize in the therapy of your clients?

REFERENCES

White, M. (1986) The conjoint therapy of men who are violent and the women with whom they live, *Dulwich Centre Newsletter*, Spring.
White, M. and Epston, D. (1990) *Narrative Means to Therapeutic Ends*. W.W. Norton, London.

Emptiness

8

—————————— · · · ——————————

CASE STUDY

Case 8A   Birds on the wing
Andrew, 37, an arts council coordinator, described the emotional vacuum in his life that had been present since childhood. His youth had been a lonely experience.

'Dad was a placid man', said Andrew, 'but I always found him to be

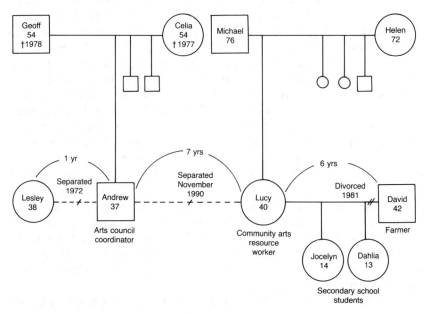

Fig. 8.1 Andrew commenced therapy in February 1991.

withdrawn and out of reach. I could never extract any substance out of him. Mum was pretty much the boss, always ordering us what to do. I could not get too close to her, she was too prickly!'

Andrew said he had never really felt a part of that original family, always seeming to be the odd one out and this appeared to have been carried over into his relationships.

'I have never really belonged to another person', said Andrew. 'My first real relationship was with Joanne when I was 18. She dumped me after a year, telling me that I bored her silly. I never really tried another friendship for years after that because of the hurt.'

He had started a friendship with Lucy, 40, a community arts resource worker, seven years previously, and this had proved to be an on–off affair. Andrew would stay at Lucy's house for some months, apparently enjoying the company of Lucy and her daughters Jocelyn, 14, and Dahlia, 13. Then he would develop a yearning to be free and leave. Andrew's last sojourn with Lucy had ended six months before, and since then they seemed to have been bringing out the worst in each other, pushing all the wrong buttons and squabbling at every opportunity. Now, they could not decide whether to separate or not.

We talked for a while about Geoff and Celia, Andrew's parents, who had both died of cancer within several months of each other. Both had taken years to die, and Andrew remembered it (with tears in his eyes) as a daunting period in his life. I commented that Andrew had been relatively young (24–25 years old) to have lost his parents, and suggested that sometimes we resolve our feelings of grief over death of our parents later on during midlife. I wondered how Geoff had handled his own midlife, and asked Andrew if he would write a conversation with his father on the theme of midlife change. And I asked if he would approach Lucy about coming to a future joint therapy session to help me gather the information that I needed to know to be of use to him.

At our second weekly session, Andrew said that although he had not written his conversation, he had thought a lot about his experience of his 'midlife' father – a gentle, sensitive man who seemed to have 'observed' the world, who had offered little emotional nourishment to those around him, appeared not to have acknowledged that which was given to him, and who took few risks in experiencing the world. I commented that, although Geoff may have taught Andrew the skills of 'doing' (both men having demonstrated themselves to be industrious and determined workers), and had given Andrew a quiet appreciation of the world, the father seemed not to have modelled for his son the emotional flow of closeness–distance within intimacy. Andrew said, as we concluded our session, that Lucy wanted to consider a while whether or not to enter therapy.

Our third meeting continued with the theme of 'observing/experiencing'. Andrew said that, like Geoff, he felt he was an avid observer of the world, but what deterred him from experiencing the world, especially within relationships, was a fear of failure. I suggested that perhaps his fear of failure was itself producing an unsatisfactory outcome with Lucy: keeping him aloof from her presence within the friendship and denying himself the closeness that he sought. Andrew mentioned that another lesson he might have learnt from his father's reticence was that to ask for one's self needs to be met equated with creating a problem for others. Certainly, Andrew had taken great pains to accommodate to the requests of Lucy and her daughters without asking much for himself. Then, after some time had lapsed, he would feel drained and unacknowledged and would feel the need for space, wanting to be free.

Our fourth and fifth sessions took up the theme of 'self/other' needs. Andrew said that he had difficulty asking reasonable demands of colleagues, and was often left feeling resentful after business meetings. We discussed ways of asking for what he wanted without feeling guilty: 1) How could he assess exactly what he wanted? 2) How could he frame his requests clearly? 3) Could he tell when other colleagues were using 'guilt-hooks' to get him to accede to their wishes?

Lucy decided to attend the sixth session with Andrew. She said that she very much wanted their relationship to develop warmth and togetherness. We discussed ways in which they could affirm their sense of belonging and uniqueness within their union.

Lucy described her frustrations with Andrew. He was, she said, 'a little boy who was continually searching for self and wanting to go off on his own to find his answers'. Lucy related how her own family of origin was one which 'looked within', valuing their own resources and talking among themselves as to how to achieve their needs. They seemed to have achieved flexibility and traded positions in their efforts to help one another. I contrasted this situation with Andrew's original family: the parents who maintained rigid 'dominant/passive' roles, and who conversed little between themselves. Andrew appeared to have always sought his social supports outside the family. So Lucy's and Andrew's relationship could also be regarded as having adopted rigid 'pursuer/escaper' roles, with Lucy constantly trying to contact Andrew, whether it be by affectionate touch, argument, or involvement in conversations with Jocelyn and Dahlia. Andrew's response would be to withdraw, to leave the scene and contemplate his solutions on the periphery of the action.

'When you fight', I commented, 'you seem to be a little bit like Spitfires and Messerschmidts engrossed in an air battle. But did you know that in the Battle of Britain about a fifth of the Spitfires lost in action were shot down by 'friendly fire'? It would be a pity if one of you mortally wounded the other in your sparring, especially if it turned out that you were both on the same side. I wonder if, in your conversations, rather than resembling fighter planes you could be more like birds on the wing? You might fly together in a pair, curving and swerving through the skies. Occasionally one of you, then the other, might wing away for a while to explore your own territory. Then, when satisfied you could join the other in your travels together again.'

At our seventh session, ten days later, both Lucy and Andrew said that their arguments had ceased, and that they were hopeful that they could create a different future together. Both had been helpful to each other with family interpersonal conflict. Andrew had supported Lucy in a necessary confrontation with her father. Lucy had offered Andrew suggestions as to how to increase contact with his brothers, whom he rarely saw. I congratulated them on their progress and we decided to end therapy for the present.

Four months hence, Lucy and Andrew returned to therapy. Lucy said that she was totally confused and disappointed. Andrew told me that he had made a unilateral decision to separate. Lucy's confusion centred on Andrew's 'mixed messages'. Although he still lived separately and made his enjoyment of his freedom quite clear, he participated warmly within the family as though he intended to remain a permanent member of it. Lucy did not know whether his amiability was within a context of 'coming together' or 'separating'. For her, it felt as if they were a piece of elastic stretching until it must break. She reiterated that Andrew still clung to his 'little boy' attitudes.

'He wants me to mother him', she said, 'and then he wants to go away and have his fun by himself.'

Andrew believed that they were indeed separating, but for him the experience was quite different. It was as if the decision to end the relationship had been surely made, and he was moving back and forth between his and Lucy's residences, 'letting go'. We discussed their different ways of experiencing the separation. Lucy's process could be regarded as: head, action, feelings. She was working out what she wanted, setting up a structure to reach her goals, and letting her feelings (of grief) follow thought and behaviour. Andrew's process could be considered to be: feelings, head, action. He was letting his emotions flow freely, waiting for some ideas to arise from his feelings, and then acting upon them. We talked about how they could add more formality to their differing experiences of separation so that the event might proceed more smoothly and less painfully. Lucy commented: 'The quicker the better for me'. Andrew agreed to a series of social meetings with Lucy to decide a time and agenda for separation, division of property, and the possibility of a workable professional and social contact. We all shared hugs and sadness as we parted. Lucy felt no further need of therapeutic contact, but Andrew requested a few more sessions to help him express his sorrow effectively. During these meetings, Andrew told me that no matter how fond he had become of Lucy, he felt that a life on his own, with some lighter social intimacies, was the most rewarding direction for his future. Andrew commented that he felt he and Lucy had been flying as a pair during their four months of experimenting before returning to the therapy room. However, whenever he had winged away from her he had become more and more comfortable within his own airspace, and had eventually opted for solo flight.

· · ·

DISCUSSION

Defining the problem

Andrew describes his internal vacuum and relates it to his isolation and lack of emotional contact within his family of origin.

Exploring the context

The father's poor modelling of emotional expression and the parental deaths are linked to Andrew's emptiness and lack of intimacy skills. Lucy and Andrew discuss the differing interactional patterns within their families of origin, and the 'pursuer/escaper' roles that they appear to have adopted. The metaphor of flight is used to illustrate a cooperative mode of relating, rather than a combative one. They are asked to explore more flexible ways of achieving mutuality, closeness–distance, and getting their needs met.

Options for the future

Andrew and Lucy describe how they have supported each other with issues arising within their families of origin, demonstrating that they have made some changes. Nonetheless, four months later Andrew decides to end the relationship and some separation counselling is arranged.

· · ·

CASE STUDY

Case 8B   Crossing her bridges
Joan, 44, a psychology student and trainee family therapist, was telling me of her loss of energy, aimlessness and general lack of purpose to her life. Joan could recall many episodes since 1980 when her life

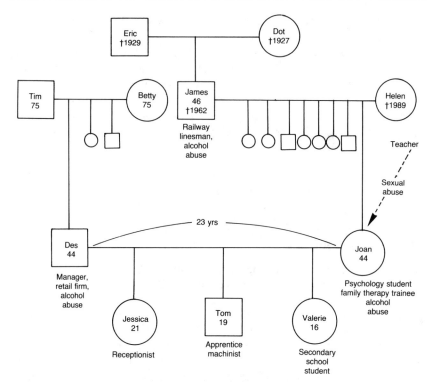

Fig. 8.2 Joan commenced therapy in February 1990.

seemed to 'fall away'. She could find no motivation to complete her day's work and would feel bored and emotionally flat.

'It is as though everything of value within me has vanished', Joan said. 'There is nothing there. I feel completely worthless.'

Joan also described her fear of crossing bridges. She would have fantasies of driving over the edge, or of stopping her car and jumping off the bridge. She also was afraid of jumping out of windows from the upper levels of tall buildings. Consequently, Joan would travel along routes that involved no bridges, and this often meant avoiding whole suburbs. She would also remain at ground level within buildings. Her opportunities to obtain employment were thus considerably limited.

Joan's family of origin appeared to have groaned at the seams with its overwhelming mass of humanity. There were ten of them in all. James, Joan's father, a railway linesman, had regularly abused alcohol for much of his life and, although a gentle man, had appeared to be emotionally inadequate during conversation with other members of the family. James had died in a motor vehicle accident when Joan was 16, and her mother, Helen, had raised the eight children to adulthood on her own. Joan described her as 'strict but fair'. Joan told of a high-school teacher, a man, who seemed to pick on her in sadistic fashion in front of her classmates when she was 12. He would mock her, frequently find fault with her, and during more than one detention after lessons had fondled her genitals. Joan said that she had been too frightened and ashamed to tell other adults about these events. Joan said that her current family was supportive and caring. Her husband Des, 44, manager of a retail firm, tended to behave like a benevolent autocrat, though he was not verbally or physically violent. Joan's main dissatisfaction with Des was that, like her father, he would offer the family practical support (money, home help) but was not open to dialogue emotionally. Des also drank alcohol to excess, and would spend many mellow hours relaxing in his beloved lounge chair, watching television or drowsing. Their daughters and son appeared to be entering young adulthood without too many problems. Joan's main concern was that she, too, was exceeding her usual limit of three glasses of red wine a day, and that she would come to rely on alcohol as a source of solace. Joan recalled her hospitalization during a 'mini breakdown' in 1981, when she experienced depression, anxiety, fears, panic, and had been prescribed antidepressive medication. Joan feared that the same course of events would now take place again.

I commented that Joan's main emotional expression during the narration of her story seemed to have occurred when she had told of James' lack of emotional presence in her original family. I wondered if she was grieving the absence of a father–daughter relationship in her youth. Would Joan write a letter to James and ask for his help now? What would his reply be? We arranged to meet weekly.

At our second session, Joan showed me her letter to her father, and his answer.

> Dad,
> It is much more difficult to write this note than I originally thought. My childhood relationship with you did not include confiding in you. Because of being the eighth child and sixth daughter, I have often had some anxiety of not being wanted by you (another mouth to feed). However, Fay explained some important 'facts' that related to the time I was born.
> My difficulty at the moment is to explore my life experiences in order to discover if there is an underlying cause for my anxiety when driving in unfamiliar places, driving off a bridge or jumping out a window. This fear prevents me from driving wherever I want to go. I haven't always experienced this fear so what triggered it off?? I would be grateful for your help.
> Joan

Dear Joan,
We didn't have a close relationship because I had difficulty controlling my emotions and I didn't have the knowledge or words. Your mother was the strong one and she dealt with those things that troubled you.

In order for you to reach a greater potential, I will continue to support you in your search for inner knowledge. I cannot give you the answers now because it is in the search you will find them.

You have your mother's strong will and I have no doubt you will become a more fulfilled person through this searching to overcome these fears and anxieties.

I hope some day soon you will see me as a more loving father.
From Dad

As she had written, Joan had exposed an underlying fear that she had been an unwanted child. She had explored this during a conversation with her sister Fay, ten years her senior, and had decided that this was not the case. Fay said there had been much joy in the family after Joan's birth.

'I realized', said Joan, 'just how frightened I had been of Dad. He was a big, lumbering man and I was always scared as a child that he would fall on to me in one of his drunken stupors and crush me to death.'

We discussed the difficulties and strengths of being raised in such a large family, and I encouraged Joan to see the Daniel Day Lewis–Brenda Fricker film *My Left Foot*, dealing with the dynamics of a large family in which the husband–father abused alcohol yet was obviously concerned for the welfare of his children.

'I wonder if your fear of Dad falling on to you has something to do with you falling off bridges or out of windows', I ventured. 'It must have been difficult for you to walk anywhere in the house without the fear of Dad falling upon you. Your home, which should have been a haven, was filled with danger. I can understand you mistrusting seemingly stable structures such as bridges and skyscrapers. I wonder what bridges there are for you to cross in the future for you to succeed in your search for a fulfilling life?'

At our third session, Joan showed me a list of her bridges that she had yet to cross.

Hopes in my life . . .
1. Control over alcohol intake.
2. Control over cigarettes.
3. To remain healthy.
4. I don't want to die yet.
5. A part-time job (How can I accept being paid? Maybe I'm not good

enough at anything? Why am I so convinced that I am no good??? who said so and why do I continue to let this control me?).
6. Continue with Family Therapy training? (Maybe I won't be accepted? Can I bear failure again? Would it be better not to apply and so not take the risk of rejection?)

We talked about Joan's indecision regarding family therapy training. She shunned confrontation with other trainees, keeping a low profile in the training group, and was bothered about future conflict with colleagues in the workforce. I commented how sometimes hidden anger within families can influence family members not to challenge one another. Any sort of debate might cause a volcanic eruption of rage! Certainly, Joan's family, apart from some sibling squabbling, seemed to have avoided negotiation, argument and problem resolution at all costs. Joan had rarely seen her parents differ. James would be asleep most of the time in his armchair, and Helen appeared to have suffered in silence. Perhaps, I suggested, the whole family had been frustrated by 'father's indelicate condition' but had agreed to a secret agenda not to comment about it?

Joan turned to some happier memories of James. He had loved painting scenery in oils. Joan felt that her father had shown real potential which had never been realized. I commented how creativity seems to necessitate its own discipline. A spontaneous flow of talented ideas does not appear to be enough. There also seems to be required the creation of a structure within which ideas can be expressed in a medium of the artist's choosing.

'Is this your dilemma?', I queried. 'You have admitted to lapses of discipline, in your drinking and smoking, and a lack of confidence in your own abilities. Yet you want to become skilled in family therapy, which is certainly a creative field. Will you be able to make it? Do you have what it takes?'

Joan had appeared to enjoy discussing her father's artistry.

'Do you have any other good memories of your Dad?', I asked. 'Sometimes happy moments spent with intimates can hold solutions for the future.'

Our third session arrived and Joan shared with me some other memories of James which she cherished:

1. I have a photo of Dad pushing me in the pram.
2. He sat beside my bed one night when I was sick and told me about his brother who had injured his arm.
3. I remember singing a song to him and he sat and listened and enjoyed it.
4. Walking to church with Mum and Dad.

5. His weather-beaten face that was often serious but gentle. There was a faraway look in his eyes.
6. He was overwhelmed by events with my sisters, who were nuns . . . Poor Dad!
7. He had an ability to sit and think and reflect, particularly when in the veggie garden.
8. He did his best . . . just that I didn't understand him.
9. He provided for us . . . never had days off. He was a responsible man in many ways.

[He was drunk at my sister's 21st and I was disgusted. I was frightened of him. He died and there was no time left.] He cooked my breakfast just the way I liked it.

At our fourth session, Joan expressed her ambivalence towards her father. Composing her list of good memories had given rise to feelings of tenderness for the way he spent time with her, pushing her in the pram, walking with her to church, singing to her and reflecting with her. She had developed an admiration for him as a responsible man who had done his best. Yet there had also developed feelings of disgust, fear and abandonment. Joan had written, of her own volition, a short essay about her mixed emotions:

> I am sick of the feelings of being torn between loving him and hating the way he was. I admire him for his sensitivity and hate him for not being there for me in the way I wanted. He couldn't be relied on to be alright if I brought friends home. He had a very hard life and there wasn't any energy left for me. I feel like the victim but when I look at it from his point of view, I get caught between his needs and my needs. I didn't provide him with what he needed to be alright. I think I failed him as a daughter . . . maybe we all did. I blame his drinking for this, also my fear of him. We really hardly ever connected . . . maybe I didn't try hard enough . . . I just don't know any more. I see males as being fairly selfish bastards and life is supposed to operate around them and their demands. They have an incredible power.

I admired Joan for the clarity in which she had expressed her increased awareness of her struggles with her feelings.

Joan had also noted similarities between Des and James: the sensitivity and practical help, their emotional 'absence' in the family, their unreliability, her inability to bring her friends home because of Des' inebriation. She did feel that James had been selfish, self-centred and ruled the roost. We discussed the possibility of Joan having been raised in the role of carer to her father. She did feel guilty that she had failed him. Did she feel the same way about Des? If so, did Joan want change? If so, how could she get it?

Our fifth to eighth sessions were spent exploring how Joan could face her fears. Joan had appeared to have grown up in a family in which there was 1) emotional deprivation; 2) a role planned for her that seemed more suited to other people's vicarious needs than her own; 3) a lack of intimate relating skills. I shared with Joan an essay on 'Aggression' (Gunzburg, 1991). I could understand how Joan, coming out of such an environment, might fear crossing her bridges, proceeding forwards to new territory that might involve confrontation with others, and be unable to ask others to have her needs reasonably met. I could realize also how she might well want to drive off the bridge rather than progress to a possibly dangerous area over the other side. Yet I greatly admired how Joan had entered family life, had raised three young adults and had studied successfully up till now. She did seem to have the resources to cope in the adult world. Perhaps she needed to remind herself more constantly of her gains, finding a way of valuing and prizing herself, and getting her intimates to tend more to her emotional needs because she was indeed worthy of receiving such attention?

At a review session seven months later, Joan said that she had decided to apply for second-year family therapy training and had been accepted. She had deferred her psychology studies for a semester. She said she no longer abused alcohol, limiting herself to her usual glass with each meal. Joan reported that Des seemed to be responding more kindly to her. When I expressed my pleasure at this news and asked her how this had come about, Joan told me that she had begun to focus more onto the practical side of their relationship. Rather than continuing to wish that Des be more romantic, Joan was initiating outings to films, restaurants and concerts. Des appeared happy to follow her lead . . . as long as he did not have to plan too much about what they were going to do.

One year later, Joan works as a counsellor in a local government agency. She still experiences some anxieties when approaching bridges, but crosses them nonetheless . . . that's courage!

--- . . . ---

DISCUSSION

Defining the problem

Joan describes her episodes of energy loss, lack of motivation and emptiness that have been recurring since a major depression ten years earlier. She also tells of anxieties associated with specific situations: crossing bridges and climbing to upper floors of buildings. Joan says that she has lost her confidence, does not feel like continuing her studies, and that she has started to abuse alcohol.

Exploring the context

Joan appears to have come from an emotionally depriving family. She may be grieving over the father–daughter relationship that she missed during childhood, due to her father's alcohol abuse and restricted emotional range. Joan is encouraged to 'recreate' a relationship with her father through writing a conversation with him and recalling some good moments with him. She also composes a list of hopes for the future. Joan ascertains that she was a 'wanted' child. Her fear of her father falling on to her and crushing her child's body during a drunken bout is brought to the fore. I introduce the metaphor of 'falling off bridges, out of windows, during life's passage' into the therapeutic dialogue to link this remembered context of danger with Joan's current anxieties. Joan's emptiness seems to be replaced by warmth at the remembered soft moments with her father, and also by energizing anger as she becomes more aware of a common pattern concerning James' and Des' emotional unavailability. We discuss ways that Joan might value herself and get her needs met, whether at home or in the workplace.

Options for the future

Joan defers her psychology course, enters a second year of family therapy training, and finds ways to invite Des to 'cross some bridges' with her towards a more satisfying marriage. She ceases abusing alcohol and her anxiety attacks are much lessened.

─────────   . . .   ─────────

CASE STUDY

Case 8C   The lost boy
'I do not know what is wrong with me', said Terry, 35, an unemployed art and crafts teacher, during our first meeting. 'I should be the happiest man alive. Marie is expecting our first child next May, but I haven't any enthusiasm towards the delivery. I have just about lost interest in everything.'

Though unemployed in his profession of training, Terry worked part-time as a teacher of English to migrants and, although his superiors praised Terry's competence at his job, he found his work boring and unsatisfying. Terry described how he wanted eventually to enter a

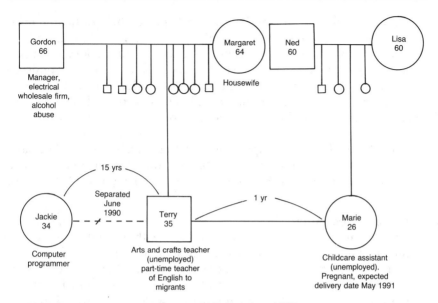

Fig. 8.3 Terry commenced therapy in December 1990.

career which created more impact. He was fairly useful with his hands at woodwork, and fancied himself as a maker of fine furniture, but he lacked the energy to commence such a venture. He thought of himself as a writer also, but could not get the motivation to set down his ideas on paper. His mind was always 'on-line', constantly flowing with ideas, yet he could not get a hold on them long enough to make them concrete.

'My head is filled with buzzing', said Terry, 'but there is silence in my heart.'

Terry's family of origin also appeared to have been continually 'on-line', buzzing with activity. Terry's father, Gordon, a manager of an electrical wholesale firm, who regularly abused alcohol, was constantly engaged in verbal crossfire with Terry's mother, Margaret, who seemed 'overwhelmed' with the raising of ten children and Gordon's demeaning manner. In fact, Terry remembered his siblings as having 'dragged themselves through their youth' without too much adult help. It seemed to have been very much a family without adults! Terry did recall some happy moments, largely due to the episodes of wagging school with his brothers and playing in the bush, climbing trees and making their own fun. Most of the time, however, was spent coping with their abject poverty, competing with his siblings for food, clothing and attention. Terry could remember no real or meaningful connection with his parents. He had gained no sense of his own uniqueness or belonging within that family, and now rarely contacted any member of it.

I thanked Terry for his candour and commented how difficult it must have been to develop a sense of himself, his own potential and his direction within such an environment. Gordon had modelled one role of fathering to his children which had seemed less than ideal. I wondered if Terry was concerned, and not a little despondent, about the fathering role that he was going to model to his first-born child? Did he have what it takes? Would he write a description of what it meant to be an adequate father?

Terry showed me his composition on fathering at our second session, one week later. He told me that Marie's obstetrician had informed them that the ultrasound had indicted that their baby was likely to be a son.

Being a good father

I hope that I can develop a connectedness with my child, investing time and energy, in hopefully a pretty spontaneous way to create a loving, respectful two-way relationship. I hope that I don't have too many expectations of my child, but let him seek out his own path within a supportive environment. I want to be a friend to my son. I don't want to pretend that I'm always strong and have all the answers. I think that it's important to be emotionally honest with kids if I'm angry or sad or what have you. I think it's best my son is able to see that clearly and that I'm not too afraid to express my emotions without too much cover-up.

So an honest expression of emotions was very much a major theme within Terry's essay. Terry added that, to achieve a 'loving, respectful two-way relationship' with his child, there needed to be the same sort of relationship within his marriage, and our conversation turned to another area in which he was troubled: his 15-year friendship with Jackie, 34, a computer programmer. It had appeared to be a stable, cyclic affair. Jackie would offer Terry support, comfort, 'mothering' even, for several months, then they would separate for a while but would not let go of each other, returning to their 'carer/cared for' roles. Even now, though married to Marie and having ended the physical side of the friendship with Jackie years beforehand, Terry still felt dependent on Jackie's support and he said that Marie had often expressed her resentment at Jackie's presence within their lives.

'It sounds to me as if you were a "lost boy" within your original family', I suggested, 'present, but unacknowledged. Even though you describe your family as active, chaotic even, it can happen within such a situation that a child is left out and feels isolated, alone, uninvolved, unloved . . .'

Terry was quick to assure me that he believed that his parents had loved him.

'There was always bread and jam on the table for us after school', Terry said, 'and plenty of clothes from the opportunity shop to wear. It is just hard for me to remember the occasions when they did show their affection to any of us. They never hugged or kissed. It was screaming and yelling all the time, mainly Dad at Mum or us kids.'

'I can understand how you might have been attracted to Jackie in the first place', I continued. 'You must have missed the support from your Mum, who seemed to be occupied in just surviving herself. It must have been a bit of a heartbreak to you not to have too many soft moments or warmth with her. Perhaps, as in J.M. Barrie's great classic *Peter Pan*, Jackie played Wendy to your "lost boy" and it was good for you to receive some of the mothering and emotional nourishment that you missed as a kid. It helped you to set aside your grief for the mother you never had. It must have been good too for Jackie to have been able to help you grow and feel special. Yet when you and Jackie wanted to have a more adult relationship, with intimacy, togetherness, sex, it must have been a bother to you both. Mothers and sons don't do that sort of thing. So perhaps you came together to be 'nurturer/nurtured' and separated when the guilt of lusting for each other became too strong. You both may have genuinely wanted to get past the original mother/son contract, but were not able to make it.'

With Marie, Terry's relationship seemed to have had a completely different agenda. Marie was energetic, spontaneous, generous and able to make her husband feel special, whereas Terry was quiet, accommodating, sensitive and wanting to have lots of passion and fun. Marie's and Terry's union appeared to have developed a complementary pattern that might lead towards mutuality much more than his alliance with Jackie. Marie might stop Terry from sinking towards the depths of despair, while Terry might prevent Marie from sailing away above the clouds. Perhaps it was time for Terry to say goodbye to Jackie, to grieve at her passing and the loss of 'mothering' that both Jackie and Margaret represented, and affirm his commitment to Marie.

Our third to fifth sessions were spent in exploring issues that arose out of our first two meetings. Terry's family of origin had been described as chaotic and energetic. How could he learn to set limits within his current family? Because of the anger and bickering within his original family, Terry's tendency was to avoid conflict with Marie. How could he negotiate openly and tolerate constructive criticism without withdrawing and holding on to resentment? Terry had played truant with his brothers to find fun. Could he now enjoy happy times within his family, without needing to run away to find them? Terry felt that he had not been able to compete successfully with his siblings. How could he now learn to compete successfully with his peers? I also asked Terry to plot a chart of the days on which he felt emotionally empty or fulfilled. I suggested that this might give Terry some information as to the pattern of his moods.

We broke for a month's holiday, and at our sixth session Marie attended with Terry. She affirmed her belief in Terry and their marriage. Marie said she was delighted that Terry seemed to be drawing Jackie less and less into their conversation. She mentioned how she, too, was still grieving the uprootedness left from her family's migration from Belgium to Australia during her adolescence. We talked about how Marie and Terry could 'enjoy the moment', planning good days, relaxing, treating themselves without too much concern for the future. How could Terry fill his 'empty space' with nourishing moments experienced within their relationship? How could they both find their own roots within their marriage?

At a review session, just after the birth of their son, Terry said that he had decided to continue his part-time job and add to his career the

Table 8.1 Terry's daily record of his emotional changes

Sun	Mon	Tues	Wed	Thurs	Fri	Sat
Mar. 10	Mar. 11	Mar. 12	Mar. 13	Mar. 14	Mar. 15	Mar. 16
7	5	6	7	7	6	6
Mar. 17	Mar. 18	Mar. 19	Mar. 20	Mar. 21	Mar. 22	Mar. 23
7	5	5	7	7	10	7
Mar. 24	Mar. 25	Mar. 26	Mar. 27	Mar. 28	Mar. 29	Mar. 30
6	6	6	5	6	6	7
Mar. 31	Apr. 1	Apr. 2	Apr. 3	Apr. 4	Apr. 5	Apr. 6
7	7	7	6		8	5
Apr. 7	Apr. 8	Apr. 9	Apr. 10	Apr. 11	Apr. 12	Apr. 13
6	7	7	8	7	8	5
Apr. 14	Apr. 15	Apr. 16	Apr. 17	Apr. 18	Apr. 19	Apr. 20
7	6	7	7	7	7	7
Apr. 21	Apr. 22	Apr. 23	Apr. 24	Apr. 25	Apr. 26	Apr. 27
7	7	6	7	8	6	7
Apr. 28	Apr. 29	Apr. 30	May 1	May 2	May 3	May 4
6	6	8	6	7	7	7
May 5	May 6	May 7	May 8	May 9	May 10	May 11
6		6	7	7	8	8
May 12	May 13	May 14	May 15	May 16	May 17	May 18
7	8	7	9	9	8	8
May 19	May 20	May 21	May 22	May 23	May 24	May 25
8	7	7	7	8	8	7

Scale:
  5 = struggling
  6 = not coping very well
  7 = coping
  8 = coping well
  9 = coping very well
  10 = enjoying

post of house-husband. His chart showed a definite increase in the number of days on which he felt emotionally fulfilled (Table 8.1). Both Terry and Marie had decided that, when their baby was old enough, they wanted to travel to join in a community aid programme overseas, in India, or perhaps Asia. They believed that they would both discover during this venture a way to belong, not only to each other, but to a group that was creating its own impact within society.

Eight months after the birth I met the whole family in their general practitioner's waiting room. They had just completed the medical examinations preceding their journey overseas. Terry and Marie introduced me to young Joshua, who flashed me a great smile of welcome. He seemed to be just like his Dad at that moment . . . with mind content and heart full.

* * *

DISCUSSION

Defining the problem

Terry describes his lack of enthusiasm, loss of interest, buzzing mind and empty heart. Even though his wife is expecting, and he has creative talents, he feels like giving up and not doing anything.

Exploring the context

Terry's family of origin, though chaotic and energetic, appears to be one in which Terry felt isolated and disconnected. The only fun was obtained by missing school and spending lighter moments with his brothers in the bush. Terry's parents seem never to have been there for him. I ask Terry to explore in an essay the qualities of 'good fathering'. We discuss his long-term friendship with Jackie. Perhaps Terry hoped to receive from her some of the mothering on which he missed out earlier. I use the 'Peter Pan' metaphor to outline Terry's search for a mother in Jackie, and highlight the better chance he may have of mutuality with Marie. I suggest to Terry that perhaps it is now time to grieve for the nurturing he has not adequately received from Jackie or his parents, and to make a commitment to a more balanced life with Marie?

Options for the future

We discuss ways that Terry might achieve a balanced relationship with Marie: setting limits, negotiating conflict, arranging leisure activities, competing equally. During a joint session, Marie affirms her belief in the strength of their marriage, and mentions her residual sorrow at leaving her Belgian homeland. Terry charts his moods and indicates steady improvement. He determines to retain his part-time job, devote some of his time to parenting, and both plan for a vocational direction overseas. Their son is born without mishap, and the plans to participate in a community aid scheme abroad are under way.

―――――   . . .   ―――――

CASE STUDY

Case 8D   Dear G'd!

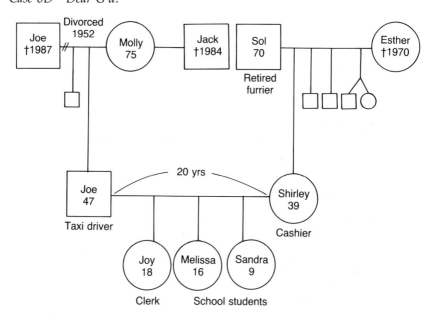

Fig. 8.4 Shirley commenced therapy in July 1991.

'It is no good, doctor', exclaimed Shirley, 39, a cashier. 'What is my life all for? I am tired of waiting. Joe and I have worked and worked for 20 years and nothing ever changes. We have had no mazal (luck). Joe is a man who can make a small fortune . . . out of a large one! He has had 14 jobs over the past 20 years. I am tired of it all. There is nothing in it for me. I want a rest. I want my cousin's life in England. She has got my life, doctor; a house, lots of money, holidays every year . . . what is the use of it all?'

Shirley continued to tell me of the stresses that had beset her ever since her family had broken family tradition and migrated from Liverpool to Melbourne when Shirley was eight.

'I thought that my cousins, uncles and aunts would follow us', said Shirley, 'but they must have hated us for leaving. They have had very little to do with us since we moved.'

There were many other losses besides those of Shirley's homeland and extended family. Shirley had given up her schooling to care for her mother, Esther, during the many years of a protracted illness. Esther had died when Shirley was 18. She had married Joe when she was 19, and they had never earned more than just enough to provide the basic needs. Two years after the marriage they had sold their family home to repay debts. They had rented accommodation, and some years later they had purchased another house. They expected to be mortgaged and remortgaged until retirement (whenever that would be!).

More and more, Joe and Shirley were arguing. 'If only you would get a proper job so that I did not have to work', Shirley would say to which Joe would respond, 'Why can't you appreciate how hard I work for you and the girls?'

Joe worked six days each week driving his taxi, and there was virtually no shared time or closeness between them . . . except for their fighting. In spite of the tension, Shirley said that their daughters were doing well at school and employment, had many friends, had avoided the pitfalls of youth (drugs, vandalism, promiscuity) and were 'nice kids'. Shirley's father, Sol, 70, a retired furrier, had kept an Orthodox Jewish perspective until the death of his wife, when 'he had thrown it all away'. Shirley described herself and Joe as informal in their religious observances.

'But I believe in God', Shirley hastened to add. 'I have asked and asked Him for help. Why won't He listen to me?'

Our conversation concluded by highlighting the extent of loss that Shirley had experienced. Her life seemed to have been filled with so much grief that she may have needed to create some emotional barriers to shield her from the assaults of a harsh and uncaring world. Behind these barriers, I suggested, Shirley might be experiencing an emptiness, a hollow space that was not able to be filled by any warmth or tenderness shown towards her. The barriers seemed impenetrable. I wondered how she could transform these fixed barriers into emotional filters, capable of letting in nourishment from the positive aspects within her family life, i.e. Joe's devotion, her daughters' successes. We agreed to meet weekly.

At our second session, Shirley mentioned her impending 40th birthday. She was facing it with dread. It represented so many missed opportunities. I commented how our ancestors, the Israelites, had wandered in the desert for 40 years before reaching their much-sought-for territory. I wondered who were the characters within her family who were important to her during her wandering. Shirley remembered Esther's father to be a leader of men, hot-tempered, forthright and dominant. He was quite different from Sol, who was quiet, patient, stable and even-tempered – a follower of leaders. I commented that, with all the crises that had occurred, Shirley might have found difficulty finding her place within that wandering family.

'Yes', she replied, 'I always seemed more like a sister to my mother than a daughter, because I had to do so much for her during her final illness. After she died, I felt more like a mother than a sister to my sister and brothers, because of all I had to do for them. It is not fair. I have had no childhood. How can I be expected to be a proper wife to Joe with all that I have missed out?' I wondered when Shirley's wandering would come to an end, and when she would 'be at home'?

At our third session we discussed how Joe's mother Molly, 75, would deny them emotional and financial support, and would often pull the rug out from under Shirley whenever her daughter-in-law expressed any hope. When Shirley had recently mentioned how she wished she and Joe could spend a holiday in sunny Queensland, Molly had retorted: 'You cannot afford a trip up north. Stop dreaming. I had it hard when I was your age too. Put up with what you have got.' I suggested that Molly seemed to be saying that, because she had suffered, Joe and Shirley were not allowed to suffer more than she, nor express their discontent. Shirley sighed: 'There is no light in my life', she said. Our conversation turned to the topic of lights, and Shabbos (Sabbath) candles. It is a Jewish tradition for families to light two candles every Friday evening, one flame representing light in this world, one flame representing light in the world to come. Shirley remembered Shabbos candles from her father's house.

'But Joe is always too busy driving taxis on Friday nights. It is one of his most hectic periods.'

'So who says that Shabbos has always to be on Friday night?', I bantered back. 'Is there any other evening on which you and Joe could enjoy a Shabbos experience, with candles, Kiddush (wine), good food, songs?'

Our fourth and fifth sessions continued earlier themes. Shirley's extended family was in the United Kingdom, and her father, embittered by Esther's death, offered little emotional contact. Joe was often away at work. With whom could Shirley talk and affirm herself? Shirley mentioned Joe's aunt and some girlfriends who were reliable conversationalists. Yet here was also a problem. Although Joe was usually unavailable for leisure, he was jealous of Shirley's social group. 'Why don't you make arrangements to go out with me?', he would say. 'Why aren't you around to go out with?', Shirley would reply. Shirley was resentful that Joe rarely challenged Molly's discounts. Shirley felt unsupported and unprotected, though she was always ready to admit Joe's dedication to the welfare of herself and their daughters.

Both Joe and Shirley attended the fifth session. Joe pinpointed four areas in their lives which he felt were of particular irritation to them both: 1) confronting Molly; 2) confronting Shirley's father and her siblings; 3) Shirley's attention towards Shirley's friends, to his exclusion; and 4) Shirley's envy of Sonya and Alex, a married couple within their social group.

'They have everything that we don't, and boy do they let us know it!', said Shirley 'Do they flaunt it!'

We discussed budgetry. Shirley and Joe claimed that they could not afford cinema, restaurants, weekends away, yet there were always funds available to repair refrigerators, fix cars, purchase new clothes to replace frayed ones.

'So you value tzoros (trouble)', I said. 'You can always find money when something goes wrong, but you can never find enough to give yourselves a treat or buy something special for yourselves. It is a bit sad what is happening to you, really. Sometimes, God says 'No'. I struggle with that one: Why does God say 'No' so often and to so many people? I cannot explain to myself why God says 'No' so frequently. But I do know that when God does say 'No', it is important to get your resources together and weather the storm until it passes, rather than bickering and blaming one another about it. I wonder if you would write a letter to God, just to find out why He has said 'No' to you for so long?'

At our seventh session, Shirley shared her letter with me:

Dear G'd,
How are you? Well I hope. I just thought I'd drop you a line. I've tried to phone you but nobody picks up the phone. I dropped by but no-one was home. I just cannot get in touch with you. It's impossible. I have prayed and prayed to you, but still you take no notice. I'm starting to take this whole thing personally. After all you know and I know, let's be honest, I've been a good girl (maybe a few mistakes, but I'm only human). And I really believe it's time I deserved a break. So how about it. Can't we be friends? I keep telling my therapist that you're punishing me. He says it's not punishment, that I don't come across as a bad person. Well if it's not punishment, why do I feel punished? (Maybe I was a murderer in my last life and I'm copping it in this life?) Whatever it is, I'm tired. Why can't I find the shalom (peace) and security that I'm longing for. Please listen to me, help me. When I lost my Mum (G'd rest her soul) my father stopped believing. He felt you had

taken away his beloved wife in the prime of their lives. But I always believed in you. Why won't you believe in me? I want to win this fight. I want to ENJOY the rest of my life. You've watched Joe and I work hard. Now I want you to watch us play. Please G'd, just one small thing I ask. 'SMILE ON MY 3 DAUGHTERS'. I want them to have a good life. And maybe while you're in a good mood, just another smile for me and Joe. And while I'm asking for favours a little LIGHT with the smile would be wonderful. Now I don't want to overdo it, but just one more favour. I don't want to hurry you. But could you do it while I'm young enough to enjoy it.

My love always.   Shirley   x x x x x x
x x x x
x x x
x

Shirley said that Joe had read her letter and had written one of his own:

Dear G'd,
It's 3.30 A.M. and you just got me out of bed because I could not sleep after reading my wife Shirley's letter to you. She's right, you know, we don't ask for much. You blessed me with her and my 3 daughters but that's all.

Tell me something, why is it that you seem to bless the ones that go to shool (synagogue) and read the prayer book and because I don't you seem to punish me. Is it not good enough that I worship you with my heart and soul and not with words? I would read to you and go to shool if you would give me the time to do so. I work six days a week. When do I get the time? Give me the time to do so and I will.

I don't ask for miracles. All I ask for are a few comforts for Shirley and the children. Myself I don't care about. I just want them to be happy, with a roof over their heads and food on the table.

Please G'd, I'm 47 years. Nearly half of my life is gone and I have not enjoyed one bit of it. I figure that if you had guided me I would not have made all the mistakes that I have made, but where were you when I needed you? I could go on and on, but if you read this letter I think you can understand my plight. Just remember I still love you too.
Kind regards,
Joe

A week had passed without any fighting, and they had spent Sunday night enjoying a candlelit dinner.

At our eighth session, Shirley could not understand some of the lovely events that were beginning to happen to her. Sonya had entered hospital for a week's recuperation, and Alex had asked Shirley out one evening to keep him company. They had planned to see the Billy Crystal film *City Slickers*, a comedy about midlife change. Joe had expressed his disappointment . . . he had wanted to see this film with Shirley himself. Alex and Shirley had arrived at the wrong cinema and had seen a different film instead. Joe had been delighted with this outcome. Shirley said that two male friends had commented on how wonderful she had been looking recently, and indeed she said that she had begun to glow inside.

The next week, Shirley said that Joe had woke her at midnight and taken her to the dining-room for supper by candlelight. 'You don't know just how deeply I love you', he had said, and had started making passionate love to her. Shirley could not remember when he had behaved with such intensity before.

'What's happening to me, Dr Gunzburg?', asked Shirley. 'I really like this therapy. I thought that when I first came all you were offering me was a load of nonsense, what did I need it for? Now I am really beginning to believe that I have needed this therapy!'

'When you missed *City Slickers* with Alex, you were afforded the opportunity of seeing it at a later date with Joe, which is exactly as he wanted. I wonder if this, together with Joe's midnight dalliance, in a small and simple way, is an example of God saying "Yes".'

——————— . . . ———————

DISCUSSION

Defining the problem

Shirley tells of the lack of meaning and direction in her life, her unfulfilled marriage and arguments with Joe, and her resentment towards others who seem to be having a better time of it than she is.

Exploring the context

There are a number of losses: migration from the United Kingdom, lost opportunities for advancement, and Esther's death. More recently, financial stresses have been the focus of family distress. Shirley speaks of her belief in God, and I choose a spiritual context within which she can write a letter to God seeking some answers. We discuss how Joe and Shirley seem to value troublesome moments more than treating themselves, and how they might arrange leisure time and search for social support.

Options for the future

Joe and Shirley join together in their petitions to God, and their arguments cease. They start planning some pleasant surprises for each other. Shirley makes a Shabbos meal for Joe one Sunday night. Joe invites Shirley to a candlelit supper, with a little lust for dessert!

SUMMARY

In Chapter 8 we considered people whose unresolved grief was experienced as some form of emptiness.

In *Case 8A, 'Birds on the wing'*, Andrew describes the emotional vacuum in his life. During the therapeutic conversation, he grieves the lack of intimacy with his father, and the death of both parents. Rigid roles and patterns of relating within Andrew's family of origin are examined, and cooperative ways of relating with his current partner Lucy, rather than combative ones, are explored. Andrew finally settles for life on his own, and separation counselling is arranged.

In *Case 8B, 'Crossing her bridges'*, Joan tells of her energy loss, lack of motivation to continue her studies, and her abuse of alcohol. Grieving for her missed father–daughter relationship, owing to the father's alcohol abuse and lack of intimacy skills, is encouraged. Her anxieties regarding the drunken father falling and crushing her youthful body are linked to her current fears of crossing bridges and falling out of windows. Creative resources are used to enable Joan to recall good moments with her father. Joan becomes angry and energized at 'men who are emotionally absent from their families', and makes some reasonable demands of her own alcohol-abusing husband Des, with some success. Joan rearranges her studies, ceases abusing alcohol, and commences to cross some new bridges.

In *Case 8C, 'The lost boy'*, Terry says that he lacks enthusiasm towards his wife Marie's pregnancy and his work. His chaotic family of origin, in which he appears to have been a 'lost boy', and the manner in which he continued a prolonged and unrewarding relationship with Jackie to receive some of his missed mothering, are explored. Using creative resources, Terry is encouraged to let go the emotional deprivations that he has experienced within his original family, and with Jackie. He is asked to consider what makes an adequate father, and to explore ways of achieving mutuality with Marie. A baby is born and Marie and Terry plan a joint vocation overseas.

In *Case 8D*, *'Dear G'd'*, Shirley describes her general lack of meaning and direction in life. Various losses: emigration, parental death, marital hardship and the grief relating to them, are discussed. Shirley, and her husband Joe, who are constantly fighting, both correspond with God. The arguments stop and the two commence to affirm, rather than discount, each other.

POINTS FOR REFLECTION

——————————— . . . ———————————

CASE STUDY

Case 8E   The lonely guy

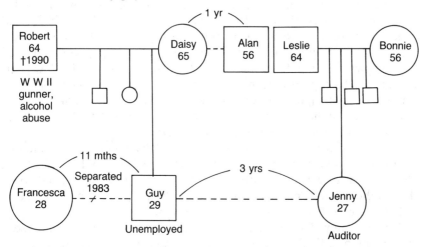

Fig. 8.5 Guy commenced therapy in August 1991.

1. Consider Fig. 8.5. Guy complains of his lack of vitality and inability to plot any future course for his life. What do you think is the most likely context for his emotions? How would you intervene? Compare your answers with Guy's story at the end of this chapter.
2. I am in no way suggesting that the emotions related to unresolved grief are confined to the four that I have selected in this section, i.e. anger, denial, depression and emptiness. Choose three case studies of your own which have an emotion related to unresolved grief running through them; it might be stagnation or panic or sadness or irritability. Write a series of descriptions for these case studies similar to the format used in Chapters 5 to 8. Then you will have a chapter of your own to add to this book.

Guy, 29, unemployed for 12 months, complained of his lack of vitality and inability to plot any future course for his life. He had experienced a gamut of emotions: depression, lethargy, despair, anxiety, and had not felt confident or adequate for many months. Guy said he was lonely, disconnected, emotionally drained, and wondered at times if he was going mad.

Guy described living within his family of origin as having been an 'empty' experience. Robert, his father, had regularly abused alcohol. Though Robert was a decent, practical man who participated in home duties and earned a steady income, Guy was always bothered by his father's 'short fuse'. Guy seemed to have inherited this character trait from his father. However, although both men could be extremely cutting in their remarks, they had never lashed out with their fists. Guy's mother, Daisy, was a down-to-earth woman who accepted her husband's occasional outbursts of temper as leftovers from his experiences as a World War Two gunner. Since Robert's death she had been enjoying a much more peaceful relationship with Alan. After a brief friendship with Francesca several years previously, Guy had lived on his own, feeling fairly lonely and isolated. He had held various unskilled jobs for only several months at a time. His relationship of three years with Jenny was going well, and was quite unlike his first one. Francesca had been a 'wild thing' and they had been always arguing. With Jenny, life was secure and stable.

I wondered if there was any grief left for Guy relating to his father's death. Was anything left unsaid between Guy and his father? Would Guy write a conversation with Robert telling him how he had felt about their father–son bond? Did Guy need to write a letter of goodbye to Robert? Guy left the session, visibly saddened.

A week later, Guy said that he had not been able to compose a conversation with Robert. When he had tried to do so, it had proved too painful. Yet Guy said that he had thought much about their relationship. He said that Robert seemed to have lacked confidence to take risks and make his own way in the world. Guy felt that his father had settled for 'second best', and had missed out on several opportunities to develop himself. We discussed ways in which Guy might reimagine his future so that he would not die with his potential intact.

At our third and fourth weekly sessions, Guy was more energized and said that his mood had lifted. The possibility of obtaining a shipwright's apprenticeship and also a job at the Commonwealth Scientific Institute and Research Organization had risen during the week, and Guy had completed application forms for both positions. He was also interested in participating in a programme for helping AIDS victims. I complimented Guy on his efforts. He appeared to have overcome his stagnation and was commencing a journey along a new path.

We discussed some future goals to which he might be moving. Guy mentioned the importance of home ownership and the desire to travel overseas with Jenny.

At our fifth session, Jenny attended with Guy and aired her thoughts that Guy's main struggles seemed to be focused on Robert's death. In fact there had been a number of losses in the past year. Greg, 29, a dear friend of Guy, had died of melanoma.

We discussed an area of conflict. Jenny regularly visited her parents on Wednesday evenings for a family dinner. Guy, though fond of Jenny's folks, declined to join her in this routine. Jenny was upset by this, feeling that Guy was hesitant to belong to her family.

'I wonder if visiting Jenny's family regularly is a bit risky for you', I suggested to Guy. 'To see them regularly might mean that you would increase your emotional investment with them. And that may be a bit dangerous. People whom you have loved have died on you.'

'I had not thought about it like that before', Guy responded.

'Yet you are risking such a situation in helping AIDS victims', I continued. 'You will develop a deep emotional bond with them even though you know they will die on you sooner rather than later.'

We talked about how Jenny's family closeness had been unusual to Guy. Guy's family, though practically supportive to each other, were not emotionally expressive.

'I don't even think I saw my mother smile, or even remember Dad giving her a hug', Guy said.

Guy's relationship with Francesca may have been an attempt to experience some passion, and it had not lasted. With Jenny, he had stability, security and commitment, but was Guy concerned that he would end up 'trapped' in an empty existence with his partner, similar to the relationships in his original family? We finished our conversation considering some ways to fire up their match.

——————————— . . . ———————————

DISCUSSION

Defining the problem

Guy describes his lowered energy levels, loss of direction and decreased confidence in his abilities.

Exploring the context

Guy's grief over the loss of his father seems to be the most obvious ground for his feelings of stagnation. I ask Guy to script a conversation with Robert expressing his feelings. The task proves too painful to complete, but Guy does contemplate how Robert appeared not to take risks and perhaps missed opportunities in his life to grow and be different. Guy becomes more energized after the conversation around Robert's death.

Options for the future

Guy applies for two possible job opportunities. The relationships with Francesca and Jenny are contrasted as attempts to explore different modes of intimacy. Jenny mentions the recent death of Guy's friend Greg, and we discuss ways in which Guy is confronting his reactions to death, by entering an AIDS rehabilitation programme. Perhaps Guy can risk increasing his emotional investment within Jenny's family, and discover that not everyone to whom he becomes close 'dies on him'?

REFERENCES

Gunzburg, J.C. (1991) *Family Counselling Casebook*, McGraw-Hill, Sydney, Chapter 27.

PART THREE
Exploring the Context

Truth-finding should be compared with situations where someone can see something that other people cannot see; not because they have a special kind of eyes but because they have a position in space which others do not have.
Johansson, I. (1987) Beyond objectivism and relativism. *Radical Philosophy*, Autumn, **47**, 13–17.

Physical abuse 9

In Part Two, the therapy of unresolved grief was considered with an emphasis on defining the problem as an emotional state with which clients were struggling. A sequence was then followed. Having defined the problem, the most likely context within which those emotions arose was explored. Creative resources – conversation, writing, artistry – were then utilized to express and redefine the emotions, so that clients could expand their options for future growth and choose new directions along which to proceed.

Part Three places the emphasis on exploring the context. Cases have been grouped within each chapter according to the most likely context, i.e. physical abuse, divorce/separation, chemical abuse, that gave rise to problems. The choice to do this has been quite an arbitrary one, so that readers can reflect on descriptions of casework relating to a common context, rather than to a description of a client's emotions. However, another dimension of the therapeutic process is also highlighted.

When therapists encourage clients to define their problems, the therapists can be regarded as gaining an understanding as to how clients are constructing their view of the context in which their problem arose (Table 9.1). Often the questions that clients are asking of themselves are linear and accusatory: Why am I feeling this way? What is behind this problem? Who caused it? Who is to blame? How can I discipline myself? How can I overcome or punish those people who are causing my distress?

When exploring the context within which clients' problems arose, therapists can be regarded as being able to see a 'different reality' relating to the problems. As the statement by Johanssen which opens Part Three suggests, this is not because therapists have any special kind of eyes, but rather because so much of their experience has been in conversing with such a variety of people about unresolved grief that they are able to occupy a position in space which the clients do not have.

Table 9.1 The process of affirmation, deconstruction and reconstruction during therapy

Stage of therapy	Therapeutic process	
Defining the problem	Therapists encourage clients to describe their emotions related to unresolved grief; therapists gain an understanding as to how clients construct their view of the context within which those emotions arose.	
	(1)	(2)
Exploring the context	Clients relate their problem to loss. Therapists affirm the clients' view, highlight their strengths, and utilize creative resources to express unresolved grief.	Clients relate their problem to a cause other than loss, often involving blaming and linear thinking. Therapists deconstruct their clients' view, offering another context in which to view the problem. Therapists then affirm clients' changes and utilize creative resources to express unresolved grief.
Options for the future	Therapists and clients mutually reconstruct a context which offers autonomy, increased options, freer emotional expression, creative and holistic thinking, and new direction towards a more rewarding life and agreeable relationships.	

There are two tracks that can be taken. Where clients directly relate their problems to an underlying loss, their view can be affirmed and creative ways to enable them to express their emotions can be found. In Case 5C, 'Revenge', Kath stated that she was experiencing difficulty getting over her divorce. Artistry and prose were used to help her express her revenge fantasies towards her ex spouse. In Case 4D, 'Images', Richard complained that Rosa did not appreciate the depths of his feelings of loss for his ex wife and two children of that marriage. A metaphor was chosen during conversation with this couple that encouraged them to cooperate with each other in 'letting go' the hurts of the past. Where clients are denying loss, and are blaming themselves or others in their family for their woes, ways are sought to deconstruct the 'blaming' context so that they can view the problem from a different angle. In Case 7A, 'Educating Rita', Rita blamed her disastrous relationships on what she saw as her poorly developed intimacy skills. Using an essay 'Restraining of the Taming of the Shrew', a different sociological context was offered: that her boyfriends' exploitative behaviours were more to do with communal patriarchal attitudes, rather than any innate tendency on Rita's part to choose abusive partners. In Case 7E, 'Black Peter', Pedro believed himself to be infested with devils. A diagram introduced him to the impact of psychological mechanisms, rather than demonic influences, within his life. When deconstruction is successful, clients can then be affirmed in the changes they have achieved in overcoming their emotional stagnation. After affirmation, or deconstruction followed by affirmation, clients can participate mutually in the reconstruction of a new context, one which fosters autonomy, independent choices, creative rather than linear, blaming thinking, freer emotional expression and the move towards more rewarding relationships.

Returning to Case 8E, 'The lonely guy', the discussion might be organized as follows.

DISCUSSION

Defining the problem

Guy's description: Guy speaks of his depression, lethargy, despair, anxiety, lack of confidence, inadequacy, loneliness, disconnectedness, feeling drained, feeling empty.

Guy's construction: Guy wonders if he is going mad.

Exploring the context

Therapist's deconstruction: The therapist relates Guy's feelings to the 'emptiness' that he first experienced within his family of origin. There was a lack of contact and nurturing with Robert, the father, followed by Robert's death. Guy is asked to script a conversation with Robert, expressing his feelings. The task proves too painful to undertake, but Guy does contemplate how Robert appeared not to take risks and perhaps missed out on many opportunities in his life to grow and be different. Guy becomes more energized after the conversation concerning Robert's deficits and death. He applies for two jobs and enters a programme to support AIDS sufferers. The therapist admires Guy for his efforts. Jenny's construction of the problem is that Guy's struggles are founded on Robert's death. The relationships with Francesca and Jenny are compared and contrasted as attempts to explore some of the different modes of intimacy that he may have missed in his original family.

Options for the future

Mutual reconstruction: Jenny mentions that Guy has been affected by the recent death of his friend Greg. Our conversation frames Guy as a courageous explorer, confronting and redefining his reactions to death by investing emotionally in a relationship with an AIDS sufferer, a young person who is fairly certain to 'die on him' in the short term. Too many people seem to have 'died on' Guy in the past. Perhaps through this new activity, Guy will learn to invest emotionally in the other relationships that he has been avoiding: with Jenny, with members of her family. Hopefully he will discover that the rewards of belonging within a mutually intimate relationship and within a cooperative family far outweigh the pain of loss that inevitably occurs with death and/or separation.

Note the therapeutic process illustrated here:

1. Guy offers his description and construction of the problem: that his feelings are a measure of his developing insanity.
2. Guy's view is deconstructed, connecting his current emotions with deprivations initially experienced in his family of origin, and he is encouraged to think on his father's death.
3. Guy introduces new information; he remembers his father's reluctance to take risks and perhaps missing out on opportunities to develop his potential. Guy becomes more energized and starts to plan new ventures for the future.
4. Guy's changes are now affirmed. Jenny shares her view that Guy's struggles are related to Robert's and Greg's deaths. Guy's relationship with Francesca, rather than being regarded as a failure, is described as an exploration of intimacy that he missed within his family of origin. His friendship with Jenny seems to be a more successful exploration.
5. Guy tells of his entrance into a support programme for AIDS sufferers. During conversation between Guy, Jenny and the therapist, this information is used in the mutual reconstruction of a new social context within which Guy can examine his feelings towards death. Through overcoming his sensitivity towards intimates 'dying on him', Guy hopefully will learn to trust and deepen his current relationships.

Note that it is Guy (with Jenny's participation) who introduces the details that are to be affirmed, deconstructed and reconstructed. This helps to ensure their autonomy and keeps the focus on Guy and Jenny, not the therapist, as the persons most advantaged by the therapy. One of our major tasks as therapists, then, can be regarded as maintaining a space in relation to our clients from which we can respond to their descriptions with other descriptions.

1. Clients describe their problems and their construction of those problems.
2. Therapists respond with a description that either affirms or deconstructs their construction.

3. Clients describe their expression of feeling or shift in perception regarding their problem.
4. Therapists offer a description that affirms their expression of feeling or change in perspective, and explores options for the future.
5. Clients describe new efforts that they are making towards continued change.
6. Therapists forward a description that aims to encourage their progress, and maintain/increase their gains.

As readers will have already noted, the creative resources of clients and therapists are often utilized in framing descriptions.

If therapists put their learned theories, expert analyses and dogmatic interpretations aside, and concentrate on offering an appropriate and richly descriptive response to their clients' descriptions, new solutions arise that were not apparent before. This approach can be regarded as the ability to introduce good 'banter' into the therapeutic conversation.

——————————   · · ·   ——————————

CASE STUDY

Case 9A   The mouth
Leila, 33, an unemployed receptionist, and Jonno, 30, a forklift driver who had been made redundant two weeks previously, had been fighting for most of their year-long marriage.

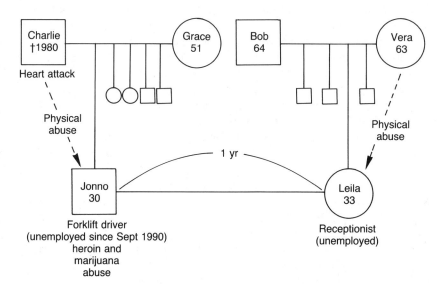

Fig. 9.1 Leila and Jonno commenced therapy in September 1990.

'Leila has got a mouth, doctor!', Jonno asserted. 'She doesn't know when to button her lip. Off she goes, and I do my block and clobber her one!'

'But Jonno is always walking out on me', Leila retorted. 'Whenever I want his attention, he ducks and weaves the other way. No wonder I have to nag at him! Besides, every now and then I hit him back as good as he gives to me!'

Both Leila's and Jonno's stories were replete with descriptions of physical abuse. Jonno, a towering giant of a man, covered with tattoos and sporting a gold earring, had been beaten 'to a pulp' on several occasions by Charlie, his alcohol-abusing father. Jonno had run away from home when 12 to live as a street kid. In his late teens Jonno had been gaoled, on a charge of assault, for 18 months. He had used heroin recreationally until three years ago, and nowadays regularly smoked marijuana. Jonno admitted to having hit Leila on several occasions, 'but always with an open hand, Doc, never with my closed fist'.

Leila acknowledged that she had a short fuse and an acerbic tongue, and that when she got going she could be aggressive and provocative. Her mother, Vera, a discounting and critical person, had frequently taken to Leila with a strap or broom handle. Jonno and Leila told how they had lost their house four months previously due to the current economic recession.

We discussed their losses. There had been no sense of 'family' for either of them in their youth. Jonno's violent nature had led to penal servitude and Leila's temper had cost her many friendships. Recently they had lost both employment and accommodation. Despite their fierce altercations, Leila and Jonno said that they both loved each other and wanted to see if there was a way to continue their liaison.

I remarked that I was horrified at the amount of physical abuse in their lives. It was tragic that they were tearing each other apart during this difficult period, rather than supporting each other, and I wondered how much of the heat of their arguments was due to grieving: anger at having missed out on so much in their lives. I noted the tradition of physical abuse in their families of origin. I could well understand that, when stressed, Jonno and Leila would resort to combat to settle their disputes. I said that I would not do therapy with them unless they made an arrangement to abstain from all physical abuse, and that the goal of therapy would be to help them maintain a non-abusive relationship. If they made such an agreement, I would bend over backwards in my efforts to help them achieve a more rewarding union. I asked Leila if she knew the telephone number of a women's refuge. I especially emphasized my expectation of Jonno that he accept responsibility for his physical abuse of Leila. I asserted that many of us men feel entitled to certain patriarchal privileges from our female partners and that, when we do not receive them, we become physically abusive. I saw it as part of our masculinity to learn restraint, expressing our emotions in a responsible manner. Jonno made a commitment to cease physically abusing Leila, we arranged to meet weekly, and I asked them if together they would try to identify some of the trigger points at which they started quarrelling. I also asked Jonno what life would be like if he maintained his commitment not to hit Leila?

At our second session, Leila and Jonno produced their list of trigger points:

1. We keep on harping about same things for hours on end.
2. We keep on bringing up things from the past.
3. We call each other names such as: slime ball, scum cutter, why did I ever marry you?, pig, poo-breath, shit head, fat slob that sits on arsa and does nothing, hit me . . . go on do it!

Jonno shared his essay on life without violence:

> I know it would be completely different to see people walking away and talking their problems out instead of using their fists, feet, etc. I would really like to find total inner peace and not find violence seething through my pores and not on my wife or things around me. But until I can overcome my violent fits of rage I will find it hard to find inner peace and tranquillity. It would be good to see less youngsters (youth) on the street drinking and then violence occurs on passers by or themselves. If there were more youth clubs and places for the youth to go when there is no home life the world might get along a lot better because the youth of today could see that people actually care and not turning a blind eye.

I complimented Jonno and Leila on their mutual efforts to discover the humiliating remarks with which they incensed each other, and praised Jonno for the sensitive manner with which he wanted to be responsible for controlling his violence, and the way he had connected abuse in the home with violence in the streets. Leila said that she had never heard Jonno speak like that before. We considered some other ways of expressing their differences in a mutual fashion:

1. Giving each other a 'haircut': for five minutes each day, one of them was to express their dissatisfaction with everything else except their partner, and for five further minutes their partner would reciprocate.
2. They were to sit for 30 minutes each week to share their problems.
3. They were to use 'I' messages to express their feelings, e.g. 'I feel disrespected when you walk away from me', or 'I feel provoked when you call me a fat slob who does nothing all day'.

By the third session, the fighting had settled (though Jonno had not hit Leila since our first meeting) and Leila had obtained work doing child-minding. We took a month's break for holidays.

At our fourth session, the situation had deteriorated. The old patterns of combative arguing had re-emerged, with two episodes of Jonno pushing Leila against the wall. Both blamed each other for being provocative, Leila with her nagging, Jonno with his withdrawal. If only the other would change, they maintained, their relationship would improve. I asked Jonno to renew his commitment of non-abuse. This he did. I asked Leila if she felt safe enough living with Jonno to continue with the status quo, and persist with therapy. She said yes. I asked them if they would draw, for the next session, the demons that they saw within each other and experienced within themselves when they were angry.

'Jonno', I continued, 'you keep saying that Leila always treats you badly. But I wonder if she does in fact do some nice things for you and you miss it? Would you, Leila, do something very special, very subtle, for Jonno and see if he picks it?'

Our fifth session, a week later, indicated that the couple had improved once more and were good-humoured. Leila had bought Jonno a Stephen King novel, which he had appreciated. In return, he had brought Leila a cup of tea in bed. We talked about their drawings of each other (Figs 9.2 and 9.3).

Leila had shown Jonno's demon to be half good guy, half bad guy, and unpredictable as to which half Jonno was going to be at any moment. Jonno drew his own demon as going red with rage. Both portrayed Leila's demon as having a large mouth! Over the next several weeks, I focused our conversation on increasing their ability to overcome their demons and affirm their relationship. We discussed how Jonno was accommodating to the 'prison' of his unemployment, coping with his boredom by reading and doing jigsaws, and how they could budget for his marijuana habit. Nonetheless, a cycle of abuse, although no longer physical, still seemed to persist. There would be outbursts of arguing at home (though Jonno now abstained from any physical abuse), they would come to therapy to discuss their differences more reasonably and have their successes affirmed, and leave therapy beaming, then go home and argue once more. I wondered if I was going to become a permanent member of their family!

'It's her bloody mouth, Doc!', Jonno snarled at our 15th session. 'Why does she always have to bad-mouth me? Why can't she keep saying nice things about me? I like it when she does that.'

'It's a bit true', added Leila with a mischievious grin. 'I do keep having a go at him. I can't seem to stop myself.'

I seized the moment and said: 'Perhaps Jonno is right! We have been

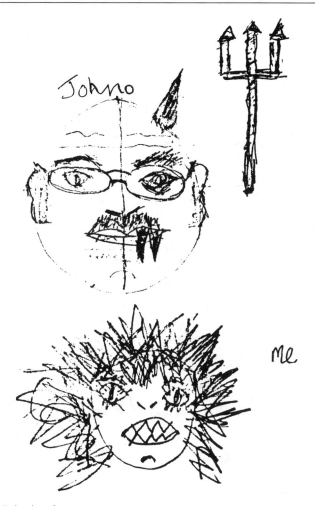

Fig. 9.2 Leila's drawings.

concentrating for weeks on how to control his temper, yet you both admit that he is improving. Perhaps we are missing something here. Perhaps we should be admiring Jonno for his show of restraint, rather than focusing on his past misdemeanours. You, Leila, agree that you are clever with use of your words. Would you turn your words into praise for Jonno's victories whenever he holds back from violence, rather than reminding him of those times he has lashed out?' I wondered if they would write a record of the nice things that they were starting to do for each other.

At review, three months later, Jonno had obtained employment as a storeman. Leila said that, although they still shared some heated

Fig. 9.3 Jonno's drawings.

moments, all the fearsome quarrelling had ceased and that Jonno's hands had taken to caressing, rather than cuffing, her. They were sitting down together at least once each week to talk about their differences.

'It's real good!', Jonno told me, 'Leila's saying some lovely stuff about me.'

They shared with me the lists they had composed of the treats that they were now giving to each other:

Jonno's list:
1. Leila has been good, just a little bit of yelling.
2. I travelled to get hot dogs at 1.00 p.m. for the pair of us, not just for me.
3. Told Leila not to turn the knob on the washing machine while out. Got told 'f––– off!'. She didn't continue to abuse me after that.
4. Leila was very sweet and went to the shops to buy my smokes without me asking, no argument.
5. Leila has been rather nice. Makes me feel needed, wanted and important. Love her heaps!

Leila's list:
1. Jonno got friend to ring and tell me he was on his way home.
2. Jonno arrives on time.
3. Jonno thanks me for going out at 1.00 p.m. and getting us a snack.
4. Jonno tidies house and goes shopping.
5. Jonno lets me sleep in.
6. Jonno more compassionate towards friends and me.
7. Jonno makes me breakfast.
8. Jonno makes me cup of tea in bed.

After they left, my receptionist commented: 'You have done rather well with those two. He usually paces up and down in the waiting room while she sits in the corner, looking glum. Today, they were sitting holding hands and giggling.'

Six months later, there have been no episodes of physical abuse.

––––––––––––––––––   . . .   ––––––––––––––––––

DISCUSSION

Defining the problem

Leila's and Jonno's description: They tell of their episodes of recurrent fighting; Leila contacts Jonno, who withdraws. Leila then pursues Jonno with her clever use of words and Jonno lashes out at her with his hands.
Jonno's and Leila's construction: They claim that each is making the other angry and is responsible for the outbursts. If only the other would change, their marriage would improve.

Exploring the context

Therapist's deconstruction: After ensuring Leila's safety and Jonno's commitment to non-abuse, their view that 'the other is to blame' for their distress is deconstructed and a suggestion is made that their anger is related to 1) grief for their many losses, and 2) a family tradition concerning use of violence when negotiating differences. They are encouraged to experiment within a different interactional context; both examine the trigger points to their violence; Jonno describes what life without violence might be like. Leila and Jonno are affirmed in the manner in which they have cooperated on these tasks, and we look at further ways to express anger and negotiate effectively. After a relapse of violence, they are asked to draw their demons and to see if Jonno can detect when Leila is being nice to him. He can (when she buys him a book), and further means to overcome their demons and affirm their relationship are considered.

Options for the future

Mutual reconstruction: A reconstruction has already begun with the introduction of new ways to express anger and negotiate cooperatively, within a different interactional context. Jonno comments that Leila always reminds him of the times he has been violent, to which Leila agrees. I suggest that perhaps it is time to remind Jonno of his achievements in this area, rather than his failures. Both return to a review session to tell that all ugly arguments have ceased, there has been no violence, there is increased affection, and that negotiating meetings are taking place regularly. Both of them list the ways that they are treating each other as special.

——————————— . . . ———————————

CASE STUDY

Case 9B   The secret garden
Sara, 39, unemployed, and currently a student of Japanese, English and mathematics at a tertiary institution, had no problems identifying where her feelings of sadness, depression, lethargy and emptiness came from. Her story was filled with a series of quite horrifying abuses and deprivations.

Sara had been raised in Lebanon, and had migrated to Melbourne with her parents when she was 20. Her mother, Amira, was a Catholic and her father, Ibrahim, belonged to the Druse faith. Consequently, Sara had never been able to attend a Druse temple nor a church, because of the teasing of others that she came from a mixed marriage. Sara was also very dark in complexion, and she had been teased cruelly by her cousin and step-siblings for being 'Sudanese', and an

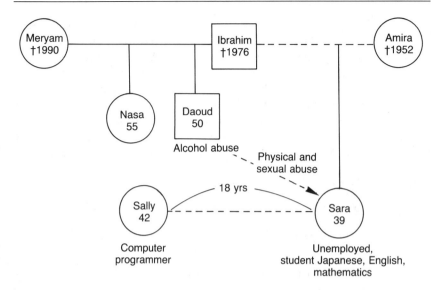

Fig. 9.4 Sara commenced therapy in May 1991.

outcast. Her elder step-brother, Daoud, from Ibrahim's first marriage, had abused alcohol for much of his life. Daoud had beaten Sara during most of her adolescence and had raped her when she was 16.

Sara said that she had been depressed for most of the 20 years since she had come to Australia. She felt that she had a huge black hole of 'nothingness' inside her, and that she was worth very little. Her main despair now was that she had no energy to study. Sara was facing examinations soon, and she was frightened that she would fail them. Sara listed as her resources operetta, Beethoven, Mozart, and her friends at a local ashram, where she meditated regularly. Sara described God as her friend, who had constantly supported her during hard times.

I affirmed Sara's faith and her dedicated efforts towards improving her life. No matter how harshly her peers had treated her, Sara appeared never to have given up hope of a better future. In fact, she seemed to resemble those composers that she admired who had also beaten the odds: Beethoven, who continued composing despite his deafness; Mozart, who wrote his last three brilliant symphonies against a background of poverty and malnutrition. Sara described Ibrahim as a kind man who had always believed in her future, and I wondered, if she wrote a conversation with him, what sort of advice might he give her?

Our next eight weekly sessions were spent in building up Sara's sense of safety within therapy, and discussing how she could structure her time so that she could study more effectively. We talked about planning a study routine that was not too demanding, and ways that Sara could refresh herself at leisure: warm baths, nourishing food, yoga relaxation, massage, good company. At our third session, I wondered if Sara would draw up a strategy to facilitate her ability to study. At the next session, Sara showed me a battle plan that she and her friend Sally had drawn up (Table 9.2).

At our fifth session, Sara said that she had called the Salvation Army to take away her television set. She was very pleased about this as she had found the TV too easy a distraction from her studies. Sara also

Table 9.2 Sara's and Sally's battle plan

Battlefield	
Lack of discipline	
Laziness	
Bad health	
Lack of confidence	THE ENEMY
Lack of finances	
Difficult goals	
(high standards)	

GOAL!!!! (Pass at school)

	Free time
	Outside moral support
	Good health
	Concentration and
MY ARMY	relaxation
	Environment
	Intelligence
	Will
	Good teachers
	Study allowance

Battle plan

ENEMY	against	SOLDIERS OF MY ARMY
Lack of finance	against	Austudy* Part-time work
Laziness	against	Intelligence
Lack of discipline	against	Will Outside support Good teachers Environment
Bad health	against	Treatment

* Australian Students' Financial Support Scheme.

expressed her fears that Sally might be trying to take over her life and direct her, just as so many others had done before. Sara gave me a letter that Sally had asked her to give to me and I read it out to Sara.

Dear Dr Gunzburg,
Why is Sara my friend?
The question never occurred to me because when somebody becomes my friend, there are no explanations as to why . . . it just happens.
I like Sara because she:
fights against the odds
is hurt by others, which shows to me a sensitivity found only in people whose heart can still respond
tries, again and again, even after defeat
accepts me, even if she cannot always understand me
understands the depth of me most of the time
wishes the best for me and the rest of the world
helps me try to find 'my' solutions
was never either helped nor lucky
had a bad start in life and never blamed anybody for it
is true and is free of all that I despise in a person
likes dancing and singing
responds to the same humour as me
I personally believe that Sara has the brain, the spirit and the courage to finally find a meaning to her life, although it seems to me that a 'bad force' (I cannot think of another word) keeps spoiling every progress, every step forward that Sara makes, as much in her studies as in her behaviour and attitude towards life in general. Her health has been partly destroyed and it is very difficult for Sara to keep being very strict on herself ALL THE TIME. She is capable (and does it so often!) of going to extremes of any diet or therapy recommended to her by her naturopath, reversing in fact the effects that these cures would do for her.
   I sincerely do hope that I have been of some help to you to help Sara. She needs help. She deserves it. I would do a lot for her because she is my friend.
   Sally

On hearing this letter, Sara said that no-one had ever spoken about her as warmly as that, and believed that Sally had written more as a concerned, loving companion than a person who wished to dominate her.
   At our ninth session, Sara told me that she had been thinking about writing a conversation with her father during the week, and had remembered a dream from the previous night. She was walking with

me through the most beautiful garden filled with sturdy trees, sparkling brooks and flower beds that were a glory of colours and fragrances. Sara saw her father in the garden, floating in the air towards us. Her father gave me a bunch of crimson carnations. I expressed my amazement and admiration that Sara could have had such a wonderful vision.

'Your description is almost like the Garden of Eden', I wondered. 'You must have a marvellous spiritual strength within you. Many people who have experienced violations and abuses in their lives dream of fires, volcanoes, explosions, wars. You have this very special, peaceful, nourishing garden inside you where you can refresh yourself. God must truly be your companion. Most of us are like Noah who walk, as children, with God (Genesis VI: 9), our Parent. You are like Abraham, walking before God (Genesis XXIV: 40), your Friend. What a lovely gift to have me share your secret garden with you! Your father seems to be happy with me also as your therapeutic friend.'

Sara passed her examinations and our discussion turned to how she wished eventually to join the Jewish faith. Apparently, the Druse religion shared many events in common with Judaism: the Sabbath is on Saturday; milk and meat foods are not eaten at the same meal; men and women pray separately; and many biblical characters, such as Abraham and Solomon, are revered. Sara had been mingling with many Jewish people in Melbourne – employers, acquaintances at the ashram – and regularly practised Jewish rituals such as lighting Sabbath candles, eating apples and honey at the New Year, fasting and meditating on Atonement Day, and fixing mezuzot (symbols of Jewish identity) to the doorposts of her home. A visitor had criticized Sara for this last practice, saying that the mezuzot were the cause of her troubles. Nonetheless she had persisted. I praised her courage at withstanding the intolerance of yet another violator. Sara had been struggling to read a very complex cabbalistic work, and I offered her some different reading instead: *This is my God* (Wouk, 1959). Sara said that she wanted to attend a Passover service and I gave her the address of the Beth Din, the organization that deals with conversions.

'They will discourage you several times from converting', I said. 'It is not a personal thing, they do it with all potential converts. They wish to test your sincerity. It may take a year before they accept your application. However, when they do accept your application, then they are obliged to support you one hundred percent.'

'Thank you for warning me', Sara replied. 'I would have taken their initial refusal as rejection. I would have thought that they were being nasty and not wanting me, like so many others have done.'

· · ·

DISCUSSION

Defining the problem

Sara's description: Sara describes her sadness, depression, lethargy, emptiness, black hole, and feelings of little worth.
Sara's construction: Sara says her current feelings stem from the teasing and abuse in her youth. She is concerned that these dark moods will prevent her from completing her studies.

Exploring the context

Therapist's affirmation: Sara is dedicated to improving her life, like the musical predecessors she so admires, who overcame their disabilities. Her spiritual strengths are admired. Sara has developed a Garden of Eden inside her, despite the social violations which she has experienced.

Options for the future

Mutual reconstruction: Sara coopts Sally to help her plan an effective study routine. Sally shares a letter of concern and affirmation about Sara. Sara gives her television away to concentrate on her studies, and passes her examinations successfully.

Sara expresses her wish to belong to Judaism. She is quite involved already in Jewish practice. A contact point through which Sara might formalize her entry into Judaism is given, and she is warned that she might experience the early stages as rejection. Sara expresses her readiness to take that risk.

------ . . . ------

CASE STUDY

Case 9C   Déjà vu

As I introduced myself to Lawrence, 26, an honours student in philosophy, he looked up from the magazine that he was reading in my waiting room and said:

'What a coincidence! I just noted that the name of the model in this photograph was Marilyn, and when I turned the page, I discovered that her surname was Black. That is the name of one of my friends in my university course.'

'Marilyn Black?', I responded. 'That is a common enough name.'
Lawrence's face paled and he walked solemnly into my room.

As Lawrence told me his story it became obvious that Marilyn Black

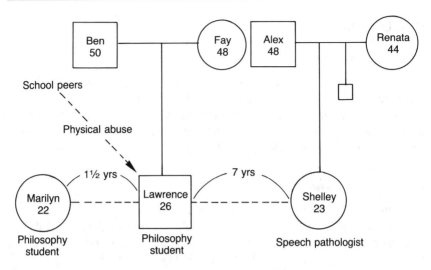

Fig. 9.5 Lawrence commenced therapy in May 1991.

was a central character. Lawrence described himself as very much an observer in his tutorial groups, always maintaining the image of the 'wise old man' whom others could approach with their queries. Lawrence had adopted an analytical, intellectual stance towards them, and often thought of himself as their 'counsellor'. He had been able to maintain this sense of detachment throughout the first three years of his course, but this had been disturbed by events over the last two months in his relationship with Marilyn. Lawrence felt that Marilyn was warming towards him, wanting to develop a romantic interest. When he had asked her about this on several occasions, she had denied it. He had been receiving repeated phonecalls from someone whose voice sounded identical to Marilyn's. She had denied making the phonecalls also. Lawrence was starting to doubt his perceptions and was becoming obsessed by the whole matter. He was certain that he had seen Marilyn, wearing a red cardigan, going up the stairs in front of him. When they reached the top of the stairs, she was wearing a white blouse. He wondered if he could be starting to hallucinate? Lawrence denied any recreational drug usage.

Lawrence feared that he was going mad and, in fact, had become so despondent with the situation that he had attempted suicide two weeks previously by placing live wires in a bathtub full of water. When he had thrown the switch, nothing had happened except a mild tingling in his legs.

I expressed my appreciation at Lawrence's candour in what was a first therapy session. It must have been really frightening for him to have found himself doubting the validity of his perceptions. We made a contract to meet for ten weekly sessions. Lawrence made a commitment not to act in any destructive way during that time.

At our second and third sessions we explored Lawrence's early experiences. He had migrated to Melbourne from Lebanon as a young lad with his family, and was always perceived as different by his school peers. This was partly because he was 'a bloody wog' (a common Australian epithet for an alien), and partly because he wore corrective footwear. He was bullied and teased between six and 12 years of age, often being bashed by gangs of youths after school. Lawrence had come to accept that his role in life was to be 'whipping boy'. At 12 years, Lawrence gained a hint that the way he was being tormented was not the normal way of the world when he saw the disgust on the school bus-driver's face at the way the others were treating him. The bus-driver had put an end to the torture for that moment. Between 12 and 14 years, Lawrence developed anorexia/bulimia. At 15 years, for the first time in his life, he had hit back, knocking down the chief bully. At 16, Lawrence's eating problems disappeared, and by 17, he was leader of the gang and spent a year bashing other boys. At 18, Lawrence decided to put aside his aggression and channel his energies into other areas. He became an A-grade student, and had developed a seven-year friendship with Shelley, now 23, a speech pathologist. All had been going well until the upset with Marilyn. Indeed, Shelley had been supportive of Lawrence as he struggled with his obsession, though she was becoming troubled at how often Marilyn's name had crept into their conversations, and she was concerned about Lawrence's suicide effort.

The next five sessions were spent contemplating the losses in Lawrence's life: his country of birth and adjustment to a new culture, his self-image due to wearing corrective shoes, and his sense of safety as a youth due to the bullying. Lawrence's basic perception was that the world was a cruel, unrelenting place, and this had only been challenged at 12, when he had noted the bus-driver's reaction to his mistreatment by other students. I wondered if the period of anorexia/bulimia might have been grieving for the nauseating events in his life. Then Lawrence appeared to have taken charge, first by becoming the aggressor, then by channelling the aggression into study and developing an intimacy.

'Yes', Lawrence commented, with sadness, 'I never felt good about myself being the bully. It was good not to be bashed, and it was something that I had to do, but I never felt that I was really doing the right thing.'

'And when persons are treated cruelly, it is often difficult to for them to get an accurate perception of the world', I said. 'Some people remain aggressors all their life. I am very admiring that you have overcome the primitive, vengeful emotions and have learnt to enter the adult world in a constructive way.'

'You know, Dr Gunzburg', Lawrence responded, 'you will never convince me that life is worth living or that happiness is to be found.'

'Bugger happiness!', I continued, 'Let's settle for contentment, and a few genuine regrets. I wonder if Marilyn is treating you a bit cruelly also? You seem to be approaching her courteously to clarify your and her relationship, and she prevaricates, leaving you feeling diminished. I wonder if it is not Marilyn's problem rather than yours? You seem to be behaving rather like her unpaid therapist, without any of the protection that the usual formal therapeutic structure offers. In such a situation, your 'client' can really push your buttons, and cause a lot of psychological pain.'

At our ninth session, Lawrence said that he had felt much more comfortable in Marilyn's presence that week. They had sat next to each other in lectures and he had not been bothered by her company. Shelley was happier at this outcome also. She had noticed how Lawrence's preoccupation was less during their conversation.

'Do you remember at the beginning of our first session that I was rather startled by you?', Lawrence asked during our tenth and final session. 'When you said to me: "Marilyn Black? That is a common enough name"', I had a recollection. Ten years ago, I had a dream in which a person who looked just like you said exactly those same words to me in a doctor's waiting room.'

We talked for a while about *déjà vu* experiences and the phenomenon of prophecy, so well documented in a wide range of world literature.

'Perhaps you have a unique prophetic skill', I ventured. 'You are able to connect with future events. Perhaps the Marilyn you saw going up the stairs in a red cardigan was a brief vision of the future, and when you reached the top of the stairs, you returned to the present.'

Lawrence seemed intrigued and well pleased by this idea, and said he would consider it further. He has continued to pass his examinations with distinction, and there have been no more suicide attempts.

——————————— · · · ———————————

DISCUSSION

Defining the problem

Lawrence's description: Lawrence discloses his depression and suicidal feelings.

Lawrence's construction: He fears that he is going mad.

Exploring the context

Therapist's deconstruction: Lawrence has experienced many losses: emigration to Australia; not belonging to the group due to his being of different ethnic origin; decreased self-image due to corrective shoes; diminished self-esteem due to severe humiliations. These events may have blunted his ability to check out accurately his perceptions of the world. His anorexia/bulimia may have been part of a grieving process.

Therapist's affirmation: Lawrence appears to have stepped outside the pattern of being abused, first by becoming gang leader, then by adopting a more adult approach. Lawrence is admired for entering study and an enjoyable intimacy.

Options for the future

Mutual reconstruction: Lawrence is encouraged to consider who owns the problem, he or Marilyn? He is asked whether he is taking on the role of informal therapist, with all the dangers of psychological and emotional bruising that entails. He is queried as to whether he might have a prophetic skill.

. . .

CASE STUDY

Case 9D   Sex, lies and therapy

Felicia, 27, a vocal lead in a rock band, sat in my room with her head bent towards the floor, her limbs shaking, and speaking in a soft, halting voice. She had been experiencing episodes of dark despair for many years, and at present was thoroughly confused. Her story, as she told it to me, could well have risen from a horror script by Edgar Allan Poe.

Jack, Felicia's father, an alcohol abuser, had beaten her several times weekly since she was a toddler. Jack would regularly confront the family, sitting with a shotgun on his knees, playing with the cartridges and threatening to shoot them all before he finally settled into a drunken snooze. When Felicia was 14, Jack had raped her, and he had terrorized Felicia by holding his shotgun to her head and vowing to kill her if she ever told anyone about the rape. All throughout her youth, Felicia had felt disempowered, unprotected, and had believed that she would not live to reach adulthood.

Felicia's current relationship with Neville, 34, a computer programmer and political scientist, had been an on–off situation for five years. Neville, her first love, appeared to be a withdrawn, non-expressive

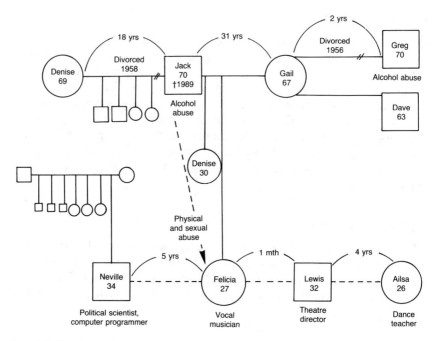

Fig. 9.6 Felicia commenced therapy in June 1991.

man, quite the reverse of Jack. Felicia was certain that he would not physically violate her, but Jack did tend to discount Felicia and she often felt stupid and inadequate in his company.

'I thought that Neville was quiet and calm, so unlike my father that I was sure to find happiness with him', Felicia said. 'But I feel unloved and unlovable.'

They had lived together and separated many times. Recently, Felicia had commenced an affair with Lewis, 32, a theatre director.

'Is that Lewis Lonelyheart that you are dating?', I asked, with sinking heart.

'Yes', replied Felicia, 'but I am not sure about him. When I went to his flat for the first night, Lewis immediately pointed to a photograph on the wall and said: "That is Ailsa, my ex girlfriend." Why would he say that to me so suddenly unasked? I am not sure that I trust him.'

I felt cold, anxious and frightened. Felicia must have seen the pallor of my face. She looked around at the chairs in my room that I use for family therapy, and remarked: 'He has been here, hasn't he? Lewis was the person who advised me to seek help from you. He has been here! He has been seeking therapy in this room with his girlfriend!'

I had been seeing Lewis, 32, and Ailsa, 26, a teacher at a dance school, together for several months. One of the issues they had discussed recently was whether or not they would continue to be involved in sexual relationships besides their own. Lewis had previously enjoyed multiple relationships, while Ailsa wanted a change to monogamy. They had decided on a trial of fidelity a month ago. Now, Lewis had referred his new and apparently secret lover to me. I felt a sense of outrage, violation, betrayal and vulnerability. I believed that Lewis had placed me in a position where I might breach confidentiality and be liable to court action.

'You are exceptionally perceptive and intuitive, Felicia', I said gently. 'You have worked out something of the nature of Lewis' relationship with me, and you probably know that, because of confidentiality, I am not in a position to confirm your suspicions. But let us do an 'as if' . . . as if you have worked out correctly what the current situation is. In such a circumstance, I, as Lewis and Ailsa's therapist, would not be serving either your or their best interests if I accepted you as my client. In referring you to me, Lewis is continuing the pattern of violation and betrayal which has been so much a part of your life: discounting your needs, and thinking largely of his own. Had he genuine concern about you, he would have enabled you to find a completely impartial therapist. I believe that if I continued to see you therapeutically, I would be continuing this pattern of violation; perhaps exploring if I was clever enough a therapist to deal with the complexities of this situation, rather than doing what is best for you. In becoming your therapist, I would, I believe, deny you the security and efficacy that you deserve. It would just lead to the continued grief that plagues you because of the way that men have disregarded you. I want to refer you to another therapist who is completely free to tend to your needs.'

Felicia burst into tears. She said that she had warmed towards me during the session. Now she would have to go through the whole thing again with another person. I told her that under different conditions, I felt that we could have achieved an excellent therapeutic relationship.

'Lewis is a bastard!', said Felicia. 'Last night, he invited me to a party, and spent the whole time talking to Donna. I am sure he was chatting her up.'

I expressed my outrage that perhaps Lewis had set Felicia up . . . and perhaps me and Ailsa also. He had placed Felicia in a position where it was inevitable that I would have to reject her. Perhaps he deliberately wanted me to breach confidence, so that he could sue me and make his fortune. Then he could dump both Felicia and Ailsa, and sail off into the sunset with Donna, his new conquest. We talked a while about the film *Sex, Lies and Videotape*, with its deceptions, hidden alliances and painful resolutions, and I made arrangements for Felicia to attend another therapist within the fortnight.

At the next session with Lewis and Ailsa, I was 'closed', defensive, monosyllabic, angry. . . .

'What is the matter?', asked Lewis, puzzled. 'You keep cutting me off in mid-sentence. You are not usually like this. I cannot talk with you today.'

'You know exactly what the matter is, Lewis', I replied icily, 'and you know very well that I am not able to tell you what bothers me in this session.'

I stood up with my hands held behind my back. 'This is how I am doing therapy with you today . . . hands tied!' Sitting once more, I continued: 'Lewis, you need to have a private conversation with Ailsa concerning the secret agendas in this session.'

Lewis stormed out of my room. Ailsa seemed to catch my eye knowingly and left with a sign. I never did see them again.

I received a phonecall from Felicia a week later. 'I have broken off with Lewis', she said. 'It was hard to accept what you told me, but it has just hit me how manipulative his actions have been, and how disabled you were by them. I just wanted to thank you for what you did and to say that I take no personal offence with you for not continuing to see me.'

During another phonecall, one month later, the therapist to whom I had referred Felicia said that she was coming regularly to sessions and appeared to be settling well into the process.

This case affirmed for me how important it is to ascertain clients' referral sources at the commencement of the first therapy session.

———————— · · · ————————

DISCUSSION

Defining the problem

Felicia's description: With eyes diverted downwards, trembling body, and in a halting voice, Felicia describes her dark depths of despair and total confusion.

Felicia's construction: Felicia terms herself 'unloved and unlovable.'

Exploring the context

Therapist's reconstruction: Felicia's moods are connected to Jack's brutality towards her in the past, and Neville's current verbal discounting of her. These are men who have not learnt to treat women with respect. Lewis' behaviour towards Felicia is highlighted as another example of a man who does not value ethical action within his relationships, rather than any inherent unlovability on Felicia's part.

Options for the future

Mutual reconstruction: Felicia appears to be seeking therapy to explore areas of intimacy and love. Her perceptive and intuitive skills have already been affirmed. The basic need for safety, security and flexibility within the therapeutic relationship before these other issues can be tackled is emphasized, and an 'uninvolved' therapist is found. In a joint session, Lewis is encouraged to 'come clean' with Ailsa.

SUMMARY

In Chapter 9, we considered:

1. the processes of affirmation and deconstruction in therapy;
2. Case 9A, 'The mouth', in which Leila and Jonno learn to change their violent patterns of negotiation;
3. Case 9B, 'The secret garden', in which Sara, abused by her family in youth, learns to find integration using both personal and traditional religious resources;
4. Case 9C, Déjà vu', in which Lawrence, abused by his school peers until late adolescence, learns to understand his perceptions within a metaphysical framework;
5. Case 9D, 'Sex, lies and therapy', in which Felicia, abused by men until the current date, is offered the chance to explore intimacy within a more secure therapeutic environment.

POINTS FOR REFLECTION

1. How do you secure safety and a commitment of non-abuse in families where physical abuse is occurring?
2. Select two cases from Part Two which involve physical violence, one which demonstrates the process of affirmation and one which demonstrates the process of deconstruction.
3. Consider one of your own case studies which involves violence. Describe it according to the following schema:

   A. Affirmation
   Defining the problem
   Client's description
   Client's construction

   Exploring the context
   Therapist's affirmation

   Options for the future
   Mutual reconstruction
   (From now onwards, this formulation will be referred to as the 'Affirmation Schema'.)

B. Deconstruction
Defining the problem
Client's description
Client's construction

Exploring the context
Therapist's deconstruction

Options for the future
Reconstruction
(From now onwards, this formulation will be referred to as the 'Deconstruction Schema'.)

REFERENCE

Wouk, H. (1959) *This is My God*, Abe Wouk Foundation Inc., London.

Divorce/separation   **10**

─────────── · · · ───────────

CASE STUDY

Case 10A   The haunting

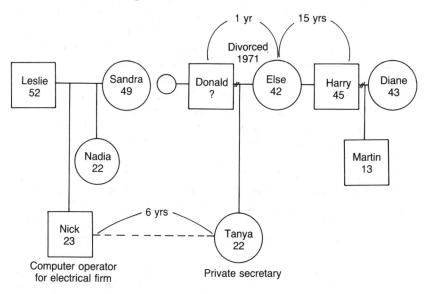

Fig. 10.1 Tanya commenced therapy in April 1991.

Tanya, 22, dressed in smart personal secretary's attire, told me of the panic attacks, neck spasms and headaches that had been making her life a misery for several weeks. Tanya believed that her distress was related to work pressures, even though she had received compliments from her superiors about her competence and there appeared to be no conflict with her colleagues. Tanya had entered her employment about 18 months previously, around the same time that she had moved into a flat with Nick, 23, a computer operator. Tanya and Nick had known each other for six years and Tanya described their relationship as rewarding and fun. Tanya told me that she thought of herself as a perfectionist. She had what she termed a pathological fear of vomiting, and avoided invalidism at any cost, often working far more diligently than was required of her. Tanya said that she had a tendency to 'go out of control' since early childhood. She would become 'ratty' and lash out, using her very extensive vocabulary, at any unfortunate bystander who happened to be nearby.

Tanya described her biological father, Donald, who had left her mother, Else, for a lover when Tanya was two years old, as a 'complete bastard'. He had never maintained the family financially and on the one or two occasions that Tanya had seen him, had appeared to be burly and intimidating. Else had married Harry when Tanya was seven. Tanya said Harry was a decent man of whom she was very fond. Tanya listed her resources as sewing, reading (particularly ghost stories), soft music and hockey.

'I wonder if your panic attacks and headaches and neck pains are more to do with cementing your relationship with Nick, than with your work?', I queried. 'Your bosses seem pretty happy with your performance and you are liked by others. When Dad left your family, and ignored his obligations to you, I wonder if he sensitized you, at too early an age, to the risks and possible losses inherent within intimate relationships? You are now developing your own bond with Nick, which entails the same possible risks and losses. Your father seems to have left you a legacy of fear and anxiety. Would you write a letter to him expressing your feelings about that?'

At our second session, Tanya told me of the anger, bitterness and depression that she had felt towards Donald since our last meeting a week ago. She said that she had always been sickened by the cavalier manner with which he had disregarded her and Else's needs.

'Perhaps that is why you are so scared about vomiting?', I ventured. 'There is so much sick feeling inside you, that once started, you may never stop.'

As we continued to talk, Tanya's sense of equity and fair play became more and more obvious. She particularly liked Harry because of these qualities. I praised Tanya that, despite the traumas of her youth, she had been able to develop her own sense of ethics and had applied them to achieve competence within her vocation and social life. I remembered Tanya's interest in tales of the macabre. Using a basic hypnotherapeutic technique, I exclaimed suddenly (to capture her attention): 'I have just thought of an idea!'. Then lowering my voice (to induce a trance state and offer a hypnotic suggestion), I continued: 'Although Donald deserted you and Mum he appears to have left a thoroughly unpleasant ghost that has haunted you to this day. Your father seems to have been unaware of the consequences of his actions. He did not seem to realize just how disabling his absence and disinterest in you would be. His departure left a gap in your family which perhaps, as a young girl, you tried to fill. Perhaps you were haunted by this ghostly 'absence', and tried to overcome it with determination, dedication and tenacity. You would not even allow yourself to be sick, so well did you have to fill the space until Harry came along. Yet the haunting did not paralyse you completely. You managed to achieve independence, work success, intimacy. I wonder if, now, it is the effects of the haunting that plagues you with panicky feelings, headaches and muscle tensions? I wonder how you have managed to avoid many of its more crippling effects as you grew to adulthood?'

At our third session, Tanya presented me with a list of ways that she had overcome the haunting (Table 10.1). Since Tanya had completed this list her symptoms had disappeared entirely! We discussed some other aspects relating to the panic attacks: the insecurity of a family member not being there, being unilaterally 'dumped' by an intimate partner, and I congratulated Tanya that she had found a method

Table 10.1 Tanya's list of ways that she had overcome Donald's haunting

Dad's Haunting	Ways I beat it
He was overweight	I lost three stone
His broad shoulders were intimidating	My broad shoulders are good for hockey power; give my shape a nice line
He paid no alimony	We survived by living with what we could afford, e.g. I am not choosy, picky about food; I look after my money, try not to spend on stupid things
He had no love for Mum or me	I now have a kind, sensitive, step-dad who actually has adopted me and cares for me
He is a very impulsive man; jumping from project to project no matter the cost	I stick things out; carry through with them; I am a quiet achiever
He has no respect for family	I am a very family orientated person; love my Mum/Dad, grandparents very much
He has no respect for marriage	I have strong principles about marriage and children

of reminding herself of her strengths and restoring her confidence whenever she felt anxious or down-hearted.

One month later, Tanya remains unpanicked!

———————————   . . .   ———————————

DISCUSSION

Defining the problem

Tanya's description: Tanya tells of her panic attacks, neck spasm, headaches. She also describes her perfectionism and her tendency 'to go out of control'.

Tanya's construction: Tanya relates her troubles to work pressures, even though she appears to be working well and reports no hassles with her employers and colleagues.

Exploring the context

Therapist's deconstruction: Tanya's problems are connected to her relatively recent commencement of a live-in friendship with Nick, and the residual emotional struggles left from her father's desertion when Tanya was two. Perhaps Tanya is sensitized to the potential risks of loss in her new relationship?

Options for the future

Mutual reconstruction: Tanya's competence in achieving independence, intimacy and ethical values is affirmed, and she is asked to contemplate whether Donald's absence has haunted her, urging her to work harder than she might need to, and causing some of her anxiety and somatic pains. Tanya is asked to explore ways of overcoming this haunting. She composes a checklist of her capabilities, removes her distress, and finds a way to remind herself of her resources whenever she is struggling emotionally in the future.

———————————   . . .   ———————————

CASE STUDY

Case 10B   The structure of time

Glen, 24, a building supplier by day and guitarist by night, said that he had been a loner for as long as he could remember. He had always felt vulnerable within intimate relationships, and had great difficulty

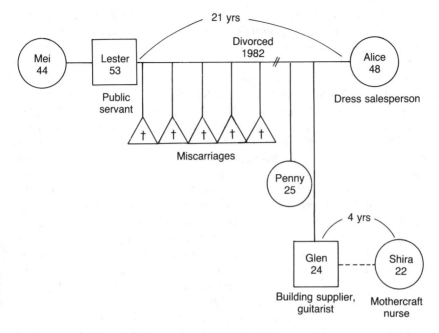

Fig. 10.2 Glen commenced therapy in April 1991.

commencing and maintaining conversation in a social situation. Glen
said that he experienced a lack of power in relationships and an inability
to take charge and ask for what he wanted. Glen was bored by his
daytime job and although he enjoyed his music, he had been basically
depressed and disenchanted with life for the past three years.

Glen described his family of origin as having been empty and
emotionally flat. His mother Alice and father Lester had rarely talked
to each other. They seemed to have been more lodgers residing together
than intimates, and they had drifted apart when Glen was 15 years
old. Alice had endured five miscarriages before she had given birth
to Penny and Glen. After Glen's birth, Alice had suffered postnatal
depression severe enough to require hospitalization and electrocon-
vulsive therapy.

Despite his reluctance to enter relationships, Glen had enjoyed a
friendship of four years with Shira, 22, a mothercraft nurse. They
lived separately and were together several times each week. Shira
was at present touring Europe and America, and Glen expected her
to return in about two months. Glen believed that many of his emotional
problems stemmed from his youthful experiences, and that this was an
appropriate time to sort out some of his own issues.

Over the next eight weekly sessions, we discussed the leftovers from the past. Glen told me of his sense of dislocation that had resulted from Lester's and Alice's divorce. Regarding himself as the only man in the house, Glen had experienced a great expectation to perform well and not make waves. Even before the divorce, he felt he had worked hard to keep the peace at home, and that he had let the family down when the split had occurred. Glen described his mixture of attitudes resulting from the divorce: no-one really gives a damn what happens in this world, life is unfair, one has to keep up appearances and never show one's true feelings. I admired Glen for having survived what must have been an emotionally 'heavy' environment in his family, following Alice's miscarriages, her absence during postnatal depression which may have deprived him during his first 12 months of life, and the divorce. We discussed ways of coping during those times when he was feeling downhearted: 1) giving himself messages of confidence; 2) distracting himself from his despondency, e.g. going for a walk in the bush, writing; 3) making contact with supportive friends. I described how, at times of stress and confrontation, Glen might regress to mid-adolescence and re-experience some of the pain and insecurity that had occurred during that period in his life.

At our ninth session, Glen said that he had been enraged at the memory of how he had had to 'parent' Alice when he was 15. She appeared to have been helpless and childlike, always wanting Glen to be around her during the evenings and weekends. Glen felt that he had missed out on many joyous times during adolescence, and that Alice had deprived him of guidance and the opportunity to explore his teenage world.

'I wonder if Alice was overcome with grief when she and Lester parted?', I queried. 'Perhaps she felt immobilized and needed your young strength to help her proceed?'

Glen settled during the session as we discussed how affectionate and supportive Shira had been during their friendship. Shira seemed to have supplied some of the 'mothering' which had been denied to Glen earlier. He had also talked with Bob, a friend whose parents had divorced when Bob was four years old, and had found comfort in their conversation.

At our tenth session, Glen said he was feeling well in himself and eager to reunite with Shira once more. I praised Glen for being able to regain his equanimity through therapeutic contemplation and nourishing contact within his peer group.

Our eleventh session was filled with despair. Shira had returned from overseas and had told Glen of her brief affair with a New Yorker. Out of this, she had decided that her relationship with Glen was too heavy and restrictive, and she wished to negotiate a trial separation.

'It is all my fault', Glen berated himself. 'Shira has wanted us to marry for months, but I always thought that I was not ready. I needed to sort myself out first. Now I want marriage very much and Shira does not.'

I expressed my admiration that Shira had requested a mutual agreement for trial separation. It indicated her genuine respect for them both and might prove to be a positive quality in the long term. Perhaps all was not doom and gloom. I suggested that we discuss how Glen might accommodate to the new situation.

The next three sessions focused on Glen's grief at the possible lost relationship: would he become stuck and helpless like Alice? Was this yet another missed opportunity, as in adolescence? Was Shira's decision more to do with her own personal needs and stage of development than a personal rejection of Glen? How could he stop blaming himself, live with uncertainty and learn to belong to the relationship in a different, more mutual way?

'I wish that we could go back to the way it was', said Glen. 'It is hard to know that I am ready for a couples relationship and Shira is not.'

Glen had told me during the first sessions of therapy of his love for science fiction, particularly space travel sagas: *2001*, *Star Trek* and *Star Wars*. I recalled a concept in Stephen Hawking's book *The Structure of Time* (Hawking, 1988) as to how time can be regarded as an arrangement of molecules as well as a progress forward from moment to moment, and decided to use this idea as a metaphor.

'It is easy to believe during a trial separation', I said, 'that people remain the same in character and all that has to change is their attitudes towards the situation. But it is an illusion that the Shira who separated from you some weeks ago is the same Shira who exists now, or is the same Shira as the person whom you want back. You would both have changed quite essentially in character over this passage in time. To recreate the happy illusion you wish, you would have to rearrange the molecules of the universe to exactly the same positions that they occupied before Shira's trip overseas, when things were going well for you. And even then, this circumstance would not be entirely satisfactory. The old friendship between Shira and Glen was not strong enough to prevent a dalliance outside the relationship. Any future friendship between Shira and Glen would have to have ways of preventing such heartache. It may be better to regard yourself as a time-traveller progressing forwards in time, rather than backwards; proceeding through the cosmos as an uncertain explorer rather than trying to rearrange the stars with your intergalactic technology.'

Returning to planet Earth, I suggested that perhaps at some stage Glen and Shira needed to court each other anew. We continued to meet weekly. Talk of Shira ceased, and we conversed on ways that Glen could increase his self-esteem and comfort as a single man.

Several weeks later, Glen told me that Shira had telephoned him and had asked him out on a date. They were seeing each other quite regularly again, and he was enjoying the journey more this time, discovering some new aspects about each other without trying to regulate the momentum or control the outcome.

————————— · · · —————————

DISCUSSION

Defining the problem

Glen's description: Glen describes himself as a loner, vulnerable, lacking in power, bored, depressed and disenchanted.
Glen's construction: Glen states that his problems commenced when his parents divorced.

Exploring the context

Therapist's affirmation: Glen is admired for having survived the family's heavy burden of grief, stemming from the miscarriages, postnatal depression and divorce.

Options for the future

Mutual reconstruction: Glen's attitudes are considered: no-one gives a damn, life is unfair, one has to be emotionally defensive to survive. Plans are constructed for coping with his episodes of despondency: how Glen can affirm himself, distract himself from his lowered mood, and gain support from friends. He practises some of these activities and restores his self-confidence.

When Shira asks for a trial separation

Glen's construction: Glen blames his procrastination as the source of the split; if only things could be as they were before. . . .
Therapist's deconstruction: A suggestion is made that the situation is more to do with Glen's and Shira's differing needs and stage of development, rather than Glen's personality defects. To restore the situation as it was might bring the risk of a new infidelity in the future. Shira's respectful approach is affirmed and is seen as a positive sign. Perhaps time itself will produce the changes in character necessary for reconciliation. A conversation with Glen considers how he might proceed comfortably on his own. Perhaps another way of developing their

relationship, discovering each other more spontaneously with less control, would be appropriate in the future? Shira contacts Glen, who says that they are courting anew, and that this time around he is anticipating the future rather than trying to engineer it.

─────────── · · · ───────────

CASE STUDY

Case 10C   Old bones, new bones

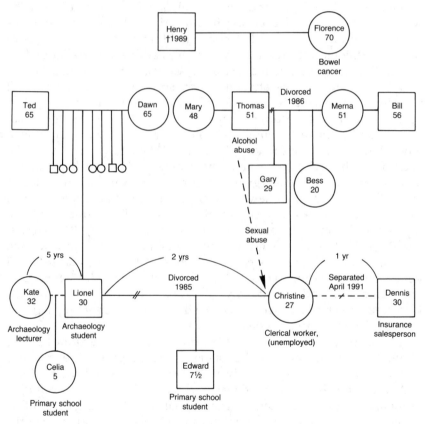

Fig. 10.3 Christine commenced therapy in April 1991.

Though Christine, 27, an unemployed clerical worker, was quietly spoken, there were flashes of anger in her voice as she told me of the depression and lack of direction since she and her friend Dennis, 30, an insurance salesman, had separated two weeks previously. They had known each other for one year and had split because of 'philosophical differences'. They both had divers needs and aspired to alternative lifestyles. Christine described herself as perfectionist, guilt-ridden, low in confidence and insecure, with little rootedness or belonging. She depicted Dennis as self-assured, sociable, easygoing and basically unruffled.

Christine said her family of origin was a nomadic one, due to her father Thomas's entrepreneurial nature and a sequence of varied careers. She recalled attending 11 schools during her youth. Consequently, there had been little time to make firm friendships with her peers. Thomas was often drunk and had sexually abused Christine when she was ten. Christine had been too frightened to tell anyone about this event at the time. She had left home at 18, and had held a series of clerical positions until recently, when she had been made redundant due to the current economic recession. Christine had married Lionel, now 30, an archaeology student, when she was 19. Lionel had left Christine two years later to live with his lover Kate. Kate, now 32, had been his archaeology lecturer. They had a five-year-old daughter, Celia. Lionel's and Christine's son Edward, now seven and a half, had been a toddler at the time of Lionel's departure. When Edward was six, he had gone to live with Lionel and Kate because of Christine's prolonged depression and lack of energy to care for him. Edward had returned to live with Christine when he was seven. Lionel and Kate spent many of their working weeks at archaeological digs, and said that they felt capable of devoting themselves to only one child during those times. Lionel made it clear that he was not dumping Edward, and wanted him for regular fortnightly access. Christine had felt she had regained her abilities in tending to Edward and was delighted to have him back. She could not understand why she was now so down in spirits. Christine listed her resources as playing the flute, concert-going, writing, eating out and painting in oils.

We talked about the losses in Christine's life: the insecurities due to Thomas' drinking, the sexual spoiling of her childhood, her parent's divorce, Lionel's infidelity, Edward's two-year sojourn with Lionel and Kate, and the job redundancy. I could understand the feeling of uprootedness due to her family's transitional lifestyle during her youth. I suggested that perhaps the recent parting with Dennis had stirred grief associated with the earlier events.

A week later, Christine said that she and Dennis had reconciled. After our conversation, Christine had decided that she had expected too much in the way of comfort for past hurts from Dennis. She believed that she would be better to continue the relationship making fewer emotional demands on him, and exploring ways to increase her own self-reliance. Dennis, too, was keen to pursue the friendship.

He had missed Christine's dedication, determination and vitality. I congratulated Christine on having achieved a resolution, and we discussed other areas in which she had created impact and had influenced positive outcomes. Christine asked if she could bring Edward to the next session. He had been moping for a while, and Christine was concerned that he had caught her depression. Perhaps he was grieving also?

At our third weekly session, Edward, a pleasant, quiet 'good' lad, told me of his frustrations during access weekends with Lionel. Edward wanted to play with him ... Scrabble, checkers, dominoes ... but Lionel would always be in his study with Kate, examining fossils and recording observations.

'Perhaps Dad has forgotten that young bones are just as interesting as old bones?', I commented. 'Would you write him a letter before your next access telling Dad just how the weekend could be made more fun if you spent some real time together? Perhaps you could buy a game to play just for yourself and Dad?'

'I think that Kate might be a bit jealous of Edward', added Christine. 'I think that she might not want Lionel to give more time to Edward than he does to Celia.'

At our fourth session, a major event had occurred. Christine had contacted her father, whom she had not seen for years, and had arranged to lunch with him. She had done this for the express purpose of clarifying the sexual abuse and obtaining an apology from him. Thomas had insinuated, during the meal, that his ten-year-old daughter had been seductive and partly responsible for the events that had occurred. Christine had resisted his interpretation and had said goodbye ... perhaps for good. Later that day, Christine was able to share her experience with, and receive support from, her sister Bess, who had left school in a fury at 16 years of age, when Thomas and Merna had split, and had charted a course of her own. Edward had written his letter, and a portion of the subsequent access was spent in playing Monopoly, a game that Edward had purchased.

By the time of our fifth session, Florence, Christine's grandmother, had died of bowel cancer. Christine told me of her sadness in having lost a friend. Florence had been a wise helper on many occasions during Edward's early years. The sixth and seventh sessions continued the quiet expression of grief, and we considered ways that Christine could lift her self-esteem and confidence during future low moments.

At our eighth session, Christine said that Edward was beginning to throw tantrums at school. I wondered if his anger could be a reflection of his grief at Florence's death also? (see '...a time to be sad...', Chapter 2). A further joint session revealed that Edward was being teased at school, as a wimp, for his placid attitude. We discussed arrangements to enable Edward to channel some of his energy into more assertive activities: joining Cubs, boxing lessons, or self-defence courses. This episode reminded me that, within a situation of loss, not all youthful anger is grief!

———————— . . . ————————

DISCUSSION

Defining the problem

Christine's description: Christine tells of her depression and lack of direction. She describes herself as a perfectionist, guilt-ridden, lacking in self-confidence, insecure, with little belonging. Her voice indicates her underlying frustration and anger.
Christine's construction: Christine relates her feelings to the recent separation from her friend Dennis.

Exploring the context

Therapist's affirmation: The split with Dennis is linked to the many losses in Christine's past, and a suggestion made that those previous grieving emotions have been stirred up by the more recent events.

Options for the future

Mutual reconstruction: Christine reconciles with Dennis and states her intention to become more self-reliant. We consider Edward's struggles with access arrangements, and he is encouraged to make his dilemma known to his father. He does this successfully. Christine confronts her father about the past sexual abuse, and when he denies responsibility, she lets him go. Christine is readily able to experience her sadness at her grandmother's death. Edward's tantrums are found to be more related to teasing at school than to the loss of Florence, and some assertiveness activities are arranged.

———————— . . . ————————

CASE STUDY

Case 10D   Sent by parcel-post
Marty, 35, a part-time mechanic and taxi driver, and his son Darren, 14, both attended the first therapy session. Marty told me of his concern for Darren's future welfare. Darren had proven verbally abusive

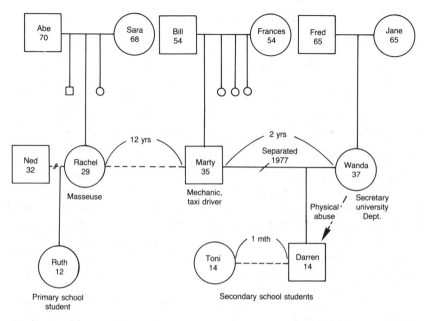

Fig. 10.4 Marty and Darren commenced therapy in July 1991.

for the past three years, and had been suspended from four different schools over that time for threatening his teachers with violence, swearing at them and shaking his fist in their faces. Darren sat quietly and sombrely as his father continued their story.

Marty had married Darren's mother Wanda, now 37, at the time she had conceived their son. They had been very much involved in an alternative culture, freely using recreational drugs, living within a commune, eschewing conservative values for a bohemian existence, and indeed Marty presented himself still very much a non-conformist, with flowing beard, shoulder-length hair and ancient, casual clothes. Wanda had left Marty when Darren was two months old, to travel interstate. She had obtained employment as a secretary in a university department, a position which she currently held. Marty said that he had been initially attracted to Wanda's passion and energy, but this had translated into continuous arguing within the marriage. He had been devastated by Wanda's sudden and unilateral departure, but he had learnt rapidly how to care for Darren, a task which he had taken to heart. Wanda had returned to Melbourne to visit Darren when he was 18 months old. Marty said that he was even more devastated to discover that Wanda, having taken Darren for an outing one afternoon, had 'kidnapped' and taken him interstate with her. Marty felt that he did not have the financial resources to recover Darren, and had decided that leaving him in his mother's custody was the best recourse.

Marty had no contact with Darren over the subsequent 12 years. Letters were returned unopened and phonecalls remained unanswered. Finally, Wanda had moved to an unknown address. The first that Marty knew of Darren's situation was a knock at the door nine months ago. Darren was standing there with a suitcase. He said that Wanda had become fed-up with his misbehaviour at, and expulsions from, school and had put him on a flight for Melbourne, having ascertained Marty's current abode from the telephone directory.

Marty may have appeared non-conformist in appearance, but he quickly assumed responsibility for Darren. He was now worried that the same disruptive actions on Darren's part were disrupting his school life in Melbourne. Darren had been suspended from one school already, and two months after having shifted into his new college, he was throwing tantrums and giving cheek to the staff. Moreover, Darren and Marty were constantly embroiled in noisy, though not physical, fights, and Marty just did not know where to seek help next.

'I know he is my son', said Marty, 'and I want to do my best by him. I want to be fond of him, but he is a stranger to me. I don't know all the subtleties of his character, how to respond to him, what he wants. I don't know how to handle his outbursts.'

Though there were many heated exchanges between Darren and Marty, Darren appeared to like Rachel, 29, Marty's live-in companion of 12 years, and Ruth, 12, Rachel's daughter from her previous marriage. In fact, Rachel had been in a similar situation to Marty. Her first partner, Ned, had left her when their daughter was an infant, and Marty had found much comfort in fathering Ruth to early adolescence.

Darren described his life with Wanda as a series of emotional and physical abuses. She had told him constantly that he would never amount to any good, and had strapped him two or three times weekly to teach him some discipline. Though Wanda had several lovers, some of whom had also beaten Darren, she had not settled into a steady relationship. Clearly Darren had no model of a stable, adult intimacy.

First, I affirmed Marty's concern and responsibility that he was here now with Darren requesting help. I asked Darren if he believed that his father was genuinely interested in his wellbeing, and could provide a safe home for him.

'Yes', replied Darren. 'I don't know why I am such an arsehole to Dad. He is not a bad bloke, but he says something that I don't like and I get going at him. I can't seem to stop.'

I told Darren that I could well understand the depths of his rage.

'It is a bit like you have been sent here and there by parcel-post', I commented. 'Mum kidnapped you and took you interstate when you were a toddler. Perhaps she had the best intentions at that time to give you a good home? Who knows what her own past was like? I understand that she was adopted herself. Perhaps your Mum was struggling with her own feelings of loss relating to the loss of her natural parents? People can act irrationally when they are grieving. Perhaps she was abused herself as a kid by her adoptive family and found out later that she did not have what it takes to raise a child herself? People who abuse others have often been abused themselves.'

Darren said that he remembered his mother's mother, Jane, as a rather harsh and bossy old lady.

'It doesn't make it right what your mother did to you', I continued, 'the beatings and the criticisms, but if she was abused herself, it does give us an indication of the world where you are both coming from . . . the Planet of Physical Abuse! Perhaps Mum has passed on all the abusive laws and traditions that she learnt on that planet to you? Now here you are, 14 years old, an angry survivor of abuse. You have been denied many opportunities to enjoy your childhood and the danger that I see is that you may deny yourself many opportunities to become a responsible, rewarded adult. Do you want to learn another way to be an adult, rather than an abusive one?' Darren answered yes.

As we conversed, it became obvious that there were many occasions during which Darren did not respond abusively to Marty and his teachers during disagreement. I complimented Darren for showing restraint at these times, and expressed my curiosity: 'How many times do you *not* lose your temper when you are provoked? What would the score be on a scale of ten?' Darren thought that he could keep his cool 6 times out of 10. I was impressed!

'So you only get into trouble a minority of times. It seems a shame that your education is going down the gurgler for a minority offence. You must be able to tell yourself inside your head to keep cool at most times. Would you write down some of the messages that you tell yourself to keep cool?'

Darren seemed to warm to this idea. I also asked him to draw a picture of his anger. I suggested that Darren and Marty were both working hard to achieve a more gentle family atmosphere. They deserved a treat. Would they go out for a meal sometime? And would they discuss the values that they shared, and were developing, as men?

I saw Darren on his own a month later. Marty sent his apologies, saying that he was tying up a business deal. Darren told me that he had had no tantrums, either at school or at home, since our last session. He showed me his drawing of his anger. I was confronted by the image of a boy holding the barrel of a revolver to my eyes! (Fig. 10.5). I complimented Darren on the quality of his artistry and queried whether he had thought about a career as a cartoonist/animator? Darren

Fig. 10.5 Darren's drawing, which represents the frontal view of a 14 year old boy holding a pistol in his hand with the barrel of the gun in front of his face, pointing at the viewer's head.

acknowledged his interest in this area. I suggested that Darren store the picture in a safe place, so that the anger would not escape and overcome him. Darren also showed me his list of self-talk (Fig. 10.6). I commented how some of the messages seemed to affirm the needs of

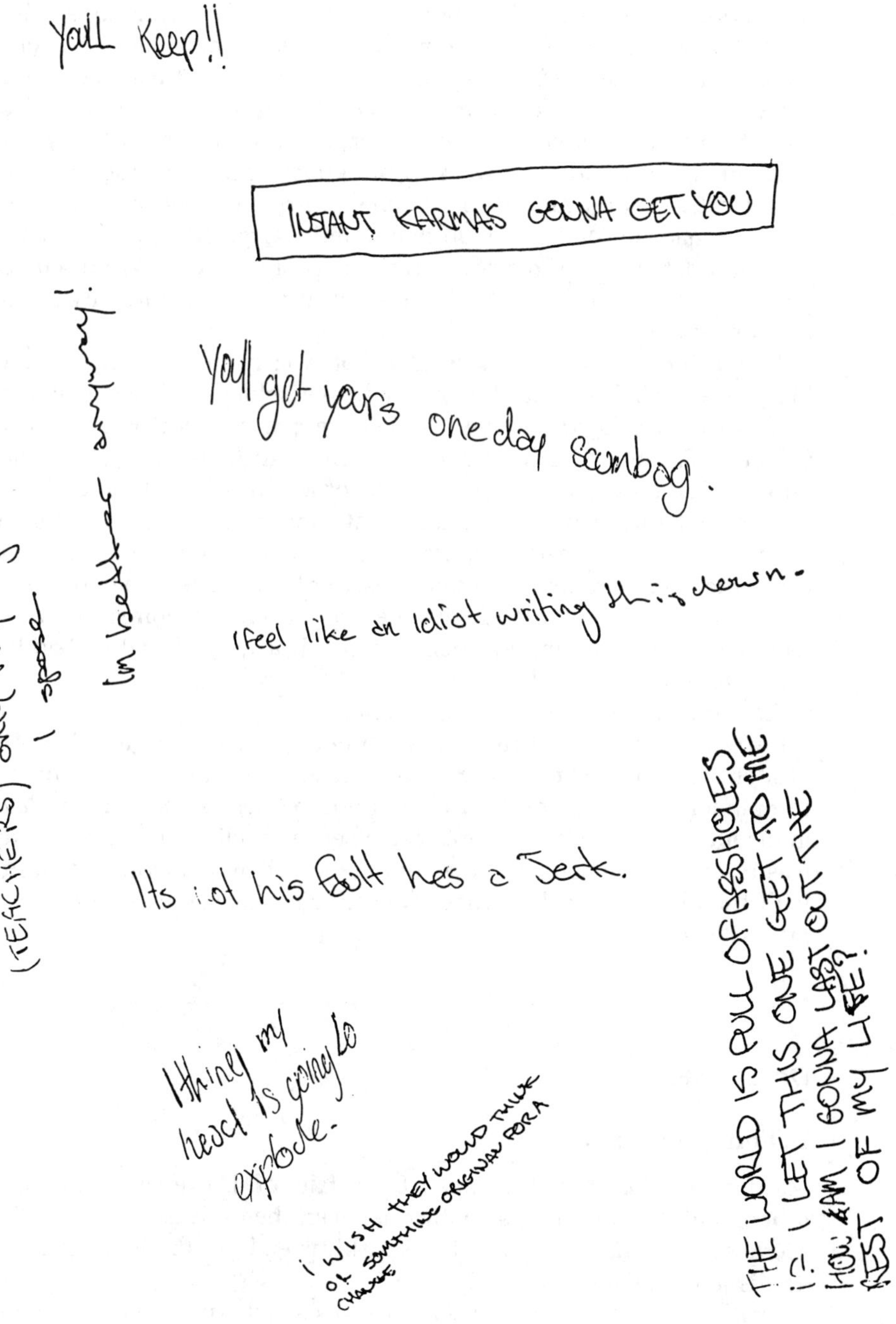

Yall Keep!!

INSTANT KARMA'S GONNA GET YOU

Yall get yours one day scumbag.

I feel like an Idiot writing this down.

Its not his fault hes a Jerk.

I think my head is going to explode.

i WISH THEY WOUD THINK of something ORIGINAL FOR A CHANGE

(TEACHERS) only want to furthur me & thier own goals

I'm better than my.

I spose I furthur

THE WORLD IS FULL OF ASSHOLES i(.) LET THIS ONE GET TO ME HOW AM I GONNA LAST OUT THE REST OF MY LIFE?

Fig. 10.6 Darren's list.

the people who made him angry (Teachers, only trying to do their good, I spose), some showed compassion (It's not his fault he's a jerk), whilst others indicated a playful sense of revenge (Instant Karma's going to get you). I told Darren of my admiration . . . not only did he have a wide and varied range of messages inside his head to regulate his temper, they had been working superbly for the past month!

Our conversation turned to Darren's girlfriend problems with Toni, 14. They had decided to be 'an item', and Darren had just learnt that Toni had dated two of his peers over the past weekend. We discussed how important to Darren the qualities of honesty and integrity within relationships were.

At our third session, ten days later, both Marty and Darren attended. Marty was delighted that Darren had now settled and was spending much of his weekend playing his newly purchased electric guitar with a friend. The noise of his tantrums seemed to have been channelled into musical creativity, a different sort of loudness! Marty and Darren had treated themselves to a restaurant dinner and had shared some common values: honesty, respecting each other's needs, learning about each other's limitations and boundaries. Marty had entered a partnership with another mechanic and, despite the current economic recession, requests were increasing for their services. Darren said that he had lost the picture of his anger!

'Lost picture, and lost anger', I commented.

Darren told me about his new girlfriend, Francine. 'I gave Toni the flick', he said. 'I told her that I did not want any lying in my friendships.' I complimented Darren on his decision not to tolerate abuse at any level in his life, and inwardly experienced a sense of relief. Now that Darren was restraining his anger, we were in an excellent position to continue with the difficult, weekly work of developing his self-esteem and intimacy skills.

–––––––––– . . . ––––––––––

DISCUSSION

Defining the problem

Marty's and Darren's description: Both talk of Darren's tantrums at school and the continuous conflict between themselves.

Marty's construction: Marty believes that Darren has a discipline problem and is jeopardizing his future.

Darren's construction: Darren says he does not know why he treats his father so badly; he just goes off. Both Darren and Marty blame Wanda's abusive actions for the current situation.

Exploring the context

Therapist's deconstruction: Wanda's actions are placed within the context of possible unresolved grief relating to her own adoption and abuse within her own family of origin. Perhaps she had passed on the traditions of abuse to Darren? My suggestion does not imply that Wanda's actions were ever correct, but it may enable us to understand what Darren is struggling with . . . his own sense of loss and anger. Did he want to change?

Options for the future

Mutual reconstruction: Both Marty's concern for his son and Darren's confidence that his father can provide a safe home for him are affirmed. A suggestion is made that they are both struggling towards a gentler future. Darren is asked to draw a picture of his anger and to list the messages he tells himself during times of restraint. He and Marty are also asked to treat themselves to a meal, and discuss the values that they share. Having completed their tasks, Marty secures a new business venture and Darren's tantrums cease. The lad turns his noise into music, and he finds a more rewarding girlfriend.

SUMMARY

In Chapter 10, we considered:
Case 10A, 'The haunting', in which Tanya's panic attacks and muscle tensions are resolved by connecting her fears relating to the future of her current relationship with her father's desertion of her mother when she was a youth.
Case 10B, 'The structure of time', in which Glen's loneliness is related to surviving his family's heavy burden of grief: miscarriages, his mother's postnatal depression, parental divorce, and his recent split from his girlfriend Shira.
Case 10C, 'Old bones, new bones', in which Christine's depression is connected to many past losses, including her previous divorce and current separation from her boyfriend Dennis. Her son Edward is encouraged to enjoy more rewarding access with his father.
Case 10D, 'Sent by parcel-post', in which Darren's tantrums are linked to possible unresolved grief relating to adoption and possible abuse within his mother's family of origin, Wanda's own abusive actions and discounts towards Darren, and Darren's sense of dislocation and lost youth.

POINTS FOR REFLECTION

Review some of your own casework involving separation/divorce. Was affirmation or deconstruction the main process used during therapy? Consider writing up the cases utilizing the Affirmation and Deconstruction Schemas to describe your outcomes.

REFERENCE

Hawking, S. (1988) *The Structure of Time*, Bantam, London.

Chemical abuse $\qquad$ **11**

CASE STUDY

Case 11A   Schnudri

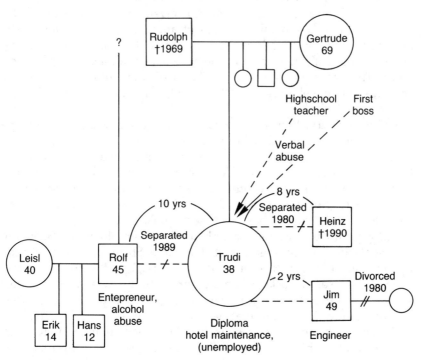

Fig. 11.1 Trudi commenced therapy in October 1991.

Trudi, 38, trained in hotel management in her homeland of Switzerland and currently unemployed, was telling me of the despair and lost meaning in life that had troubled her for years. Trudi was tired of her experience of always battling to survive.

Trudi said that she remembered her childhood as a happy one. Her father, Rudolph, and mother, Gertrude, had appeared contented and treated each other respectfully and affectionately within their marriage. They had appeared devoted to all their children, but Trudi's battle had commenced early, at four years of age, when she had asserted to her parents: 'I am not going to be a mummy when I grow up . . . it is too hard!' Her father had laughed and replied: 'That is not the way it is done around here, kiddo!' Nonetheless, all throughout Trudi's educative years, she had expressed her intention to follow a career, much to her parents' disapproval.

In fact, Trudi had performed well at school despite a reading disability. To cope with this, she would get her younger sister to read to her the stories that the teacher set for homework. The teacher was duly impressed by Trudi's comprehension even though he could not understand why she was so hesitant to present the stories in class. Trudi passed her school examinations adequately, the only problem being a verbally abusive teacher, who seemed to have taken a particular dislike to Trudi when she was 13, and made her the butt of his jokes. Trudi's response was to remain silent and not make waves. Trudi excelled in sporting activities and made waves of another sort, eventually being included in the Swiss National Yachting Team. Her parents were always embarrassed to see her name in the newspapers for a sporting achievement. They continually reminded Trudi of their disappointment that she was not developing into the sweet, feminine, 'Heidi' of classic fictional fame.

Rudolph died when Trudi was 18. When she was 19, Trudi met Heinz, a quiet man with whom she maintained a friendship of eight years, leading to engagement. Trudi eventually broke the arrangement because she was disturbed by Heinz's continually sombre nature. Trudi was also bothered by two other events at this time. Her brother had just been responsible for the death of his own fiancée in a motor vehicle accident, and a boss was very abusive towards her with his seemingly unfair criticisms. Trudi had left that employment. Soon after leaving Heinz, Trudi was attracted to Rolf. She found him exciting, passionate, debonair. Rolf pressed for marriage but Trudi was not so certain. He was a socialite, to be sure, but he was also extremely secretive. To this date, Trudi knew nothing about the details of Rolf's original family. She know that he had recently divorced his first wife, and that access to his two sons had been denied to him. Rolf had blamed it all on his ex wife's difficult nature. Still, Trudi pursued the relationship and when she was 33 they migrated to New South Wales and purchased a farm. Trudi had immediately taken to the Australian bush. She said that its beauty complemented her love of classical music.

Rolf's character changed soon after the move. Always fond of wine, he began to abuse alcohol and became even more secretive and possessive. He had demanded that Trudi stay at home and not travel overseas when her mother was seriously ill two years previously. Rolf had fired a shotgun at her to emphasize his point, and it was this incident that had convinced Trudi to leave and 'disappear' to Melbourne. Rolf had described his business activities outside of farming as entrepreneurial, but Trudi had discovered, after their separation, that this had included dealing in marijuana and heroin. Trudi said a great grief had been that she had left her dog Schnudri back at the farm.

More losses followed. Trudi loaned a considerable sum of money to newly made 'friends', who vanished without repaying her. A year later, Trudi had attended her brother's wedding in Switzerland, and had been saddened to learn of Heinz's recent suicide, at 34 years of age. On returning to Melbourne, Trudi was involved in a car accident, resulting in fractured vertebrae and chronic pain in her lower back. Trudi had saved some money to travel to Canada and join the family at the birth of her sister's first child. Now, the money had gone towards car repairs (the family eventually pooled their financial resources so that Trudi could go). Trudi had found when she came to Melbourne that her Swiss diploma in hotel management held no weight, and she had worked in a series of administrative jobs. Trudi had not worked since her accident. Trudi said that she was constantly stressed, had lost her confidence, and felt a fool to have persisted with Rolf for so long. Jim, 49, an engineer, had been her current live-away companion for about a year. Trudi was in no hurry to cement the friendship.

I expressed my appreciation to Trudi for her candour in what was an initial therapy session, and commented on just how many losses she had experienced over the past five years: her family and friends due to migration; her hotel management qualifications being disallowed in Australia; her peace of mind due to the relationship with Rolf; her beloved Schnudri and bushland around the farm; the effect of Heinz's suicide; the money, due to her acquaintances' duplicity; her health; and further financial stress since the accident. I wondered which loss had created the most impact? Trudi mentioned how much she missed her dog.

'Does the name Schnudri have an English translation?', I asked, and Trudi replied, with a twinkle among the tears: 'Yes, it means "the bugger!"'

I continued: 'I wonder if something that bothers you is that you have left Schnudri rather like a deserted child? Would you write a letter to Schnudri explaining exactly why you took the action that you did?'

At our second weekly session, Trudi said that the letter to Schnudri (written in German) had helped her to achieve a different view of the situation. When she had bought Schnudri he had become very ill, and on his recovery Trudi had admired his will to live. Trudi had promised that she would always look after Schnudri, and felt that she had betrayed him when she did leave. Now, on reconsideration, Trudi believed that she would never have been able to give Schnudri the quality of life that he enjoyed on the farm, especially with so many of the traumas that had occurred. Writing the letter had also stirred a memory. During a clandestine visit to the farm ten months previously (she had made sure that Rolf would be away), Trudi had seen Schnudri. He had leapt all over her with joy and she had been able to assure herself that he was being cared for well. Our conversation turned to the way people had exploited Trudi throughout her life: the parental expectations on her to conform and give them pleasure; the teacher and boss using her as their emotional garbage bin; Rolf's treatment of her as property. I was not surprised that Trudi had lost her confidence, yet there were many areas in which she had excelled: sailing, education, a sensitivity towards nature and music. Would Trudi list ten ways in which she boosted her confidence when low?

At our third session, Trudi appeared enlivened. Compiling her list, she said, had given her a wonderful feeling of power. She felt sure of herself when skiing, playing with animals, talking herself out of her miseries, mountain-climbing, bush-walking, relaxing with Mendelssohn and Mozart, sailing, swimming, reading philosophy and absorbing herself in the study of numerology. We discussed what some of these activities represented for her. Trudi said that self-talk enabled her to step back from a problem and examine it better. Mountain-climbing was all about progress, achieving goals, seeing the world as a whole from the peak. Sailing gave her the opportunity to see a morning sunrise, an experience that remained 'always new' for her.

'When I am distressed emotionally, I always go to the water, sailing or bathing', Trudi remarked. 'When I am thinking out a problem, then it is the bush for me . . . walking or just sitting there meditating.'

I expressed my admiration at the rich variety of ways that Trudi used to nourish herself. Trudi told me of a 'first': she and Jim had agreed to a weekend activity and Jim had suddenly changed his mind. Trudi had spoken with Jim of her disenchantment at his unilateral change and he appeared to have taken her seriously, sitting down with her to sort out the matter. Previously, Trudi had avoided mentioning her concerns to Jim because he had often dismissed her without comment.

At our fourth session, Trudi continued to tell of some further small triumphs. She had been contented for the whole week until yesterday evening, when her mood had plummeted. Usually Trudi would have spent a restless night obsessing about the Why? and Wherefore? of her depression, but she had managed to talk herself out of it.

'I told myself to behave', said Trudi, 'that I can do better than being just a bloody victim...I can live!' She had rested well, and had awoken refreshed.

'I have also stopped whingeing to myself about lack of money', Trudi continued. 'I now have an account with $15 in it and am saving $5 a week, just for myself.'

We looked at some directions that Trudi could take to develop herself: commencing a Council of Adult Education course in revising study techniques, and eventual completion of an Australian tertiary degree.

Six months later, Trudi has commenced her tertiary studies, has moved into much more affordable accomodation, and has committed herself to developing a long-term intimacy with Jim.

--- · · · ---

DISCUSSION

Defining the problem

Trudi's description: Trudi speaks of her despair, lost meaning in life, stress, lack of confidence and feelings of foolishness.
Trudi's construction: Trudi says that she has always had to battle for what she wanted... she is tired of having to fight so hard for so little apparent gain.

Exploring the context

Therapist's affirmation: Trudi's many losses are emphasized and her academic and sporting achievements are admired. The loss which most grieves Trudi is ascertained, and she is asked to write a letter to Schnudri expressing her sentiments on having left him.

Options for the future

Mutual reconstruction: Writing the letter seems to have given Trudi much comfort. She remembers a visit to the farm, after her departure, where she had found him well. Trudi is asked to list ten ways which she uses to boost her confidence. This exercise appears to help Trudi recollect many resources. She asserts herself to Jim over a unilateral change of plan, and gives herself a lift when she feels low in mood one evening. Trudi discusses how she is now disciplining herself to save money, and we look at ways in which she can renew her studies and develop a future career.

———————— . . . ————————

CASE STUDY

Case 11B   The waiter

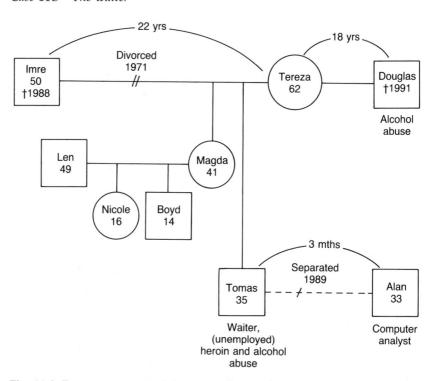

Fig. 11.2 Tomas commenced therapy in February 1991.

Tomas, 34, trained as a waiter, had been depressed and lacking in energy and direction since he lost his job, three years previously, in a well known restaurant which had changed management. Until then, his references had been impeccable, but Tomas suspected that he had been 'let go' because the owners had found out that he was gay. The current economic recession had dried up employment and Tomas was despondent about ever working again.

Tomas recalled his life in his original family with fear and distaste. His parents, Imre and Tereza, had migrated to Melbourne as refugees after the 1956 Hungarian uprising, when Tomas was a baby. From his earliest moments, Tomas remembered Imre as a violent man, who took to Tereza with his fists and to Tomas with a strap. Tereza had divorced Imre when Tomas was 15. She had then married Douglas, who, although an abuser of alcohol, was gentle and kind. Tomas had become very fond of Douglas. Tereza had constantly reminded Tomas that he would never be able to repay her loyalty to him as a mother, first for withstanding Imre's brutality, then in finding him a suitable stepfather. Tomas, in fact, was extremely angry that his mother had not left Imre earlier, sparing them pain and taking them both to a better life. Tereza had hoped that her efforts would be rewarded by Tomas entering a profession, and she was disappointed that he had chosen waiting as a career. However, she seemed to accept Tomas' choice of male intimate friends. Tomas said that he grew up always feeling obligated to his mother, and three years ago, after Imre had died, he had moved to Sydney to escape her influence. Sydney had proved to be a rough town. He had fallen in with the wrong crowd and begun to abuse alcohol, marijuana and heroin. After 18 months Tomas had entered a methadone programme and had been free of all chemicals for the past year. Tomas said that his last real intimacy was a brief one two years ago with Alan, 33, a computer analyst. Alan had continually berated Tomas for being 'a drain, and a shoddy housekeeper'. This last remark had particularly incensed Tomas, as he prided himself on his domestic skills. Indeed, during his sojourn in Sydney, most partners had been interested only in transient physical liaisons, whereas Tomas had wanted longer-term partnerships that centred around conversational intimacy. He had been both robbed and bashed for being a 'pansy boy', and since Alan, Tomas had been content to remain single and celibate. On his return to Melbourne about a year ago, Tomas had been invited back into Tereza's house. Initially, life had been better. Tereza and Douglas were contented, but Douglas had died suddenly some weeks previously. Another source of comfort for Tomas had been his teenage niece and nephew, Nicole and Boyd, but since their mother Magda had learnt of her brother's homosexuality, she had forbidden any contact.

I commented on the amount of loss in Tomas' life: his European homeland and culture; his lack of happiness during childhood; his career in waiting; the death of his hated father and beloved stepfather; his disconnection with other loved members of his family. . . . I wondered if he would compose a letter to his father expressing his feelings?

Tomas arrived at our second weekly session furious! He had not written the letter to Imre, but thinking about what he might say regarding the injustice of it all had made him livid. He was angry, too, that Tereza had stayed for so long in the unhappy relationship, leaning on Tomas for support and now expecting him to support her emotionally for the rest of her life in return.

We talked about how difficult it must have been for Tereza to actually leave Imre and live as a single mother in the 1960s. She was new to the country, did not speak the language well, and had little means of financial and emotional support. There were no women's refuges at that time, and the community had paid little heed to the plight of violated women. Might things have been worse if she had left during his infancy? Poverty? Desolation? Total despair? Tereza's early death, or suicide, leaving Tomas entirely at the mercy of Imre? Could Tereza be regarded as a person who had stayed to fight for her rights? And Tomas was proving to be a fighter too, striving to pursue his own career against Tereza's expectations, and showing the courage to subdue his addictive tendencies. I encouraged Tomas to watch *Her Story: Sanctuary*, a television programme concerning women who endured constant beatings at home, and the opening of the world's first refuge in 1971, the year that Tereza actually did leave Imre. Some of the women found safe haven within the refuge and some did not. I wondered, if Tereza had been offered such a facility earlier, would she have sought shelter with her son and overcome their plight?

At our third session Tomas was more settled. I decided to weave into our dialogue the themes of 'serving' and 'waiting'. We talked of how Tereza might have regarded Tomas as being born to serve. He might well have slipped into the role of waiting on his mother in her distress with Imre, and translated this into a career of waiting on others. Certainly Tomas had been waiting for a long time to achieve contentment and stability in his life! We also spoke about Tomas' lack of belonging. He remembered the family moving from one rented flat to another many times before the divorce, as his father attempted this job and that one, always seeming to become belligerent with his employers, moving on and dragging his family with him. Though Tereza accepted Tomas' homosexuality, his extended family had cut him out of their activities. Participation in both Sydney and Melbourne gay communities had brought him little companionship and solace.

I complimented Tomas on his persistence in pursuing relationships. He had sought friendship even though he had been troubled by many of his contacts. Obviously, he valued human interaction. I was admiring, too, of his dedication in completing the methadone programme within six months, and the strength he had shown in abstaining from mood-altering substances since then. I asked Tomas if he would compose a self-advertisement for the next session, including some of his other qualities besides his sensitivity, dedication and strength.

At our fourth and final session, Tomas said that he was calmer and more confident about coping in the future. Our conversation about his tenacity in overcoming his chemical abuses seemed to have had an impact. He had thought about advertising himself, and he would include such qualities as commitment, loyalty, humour, affection, not being intrusive, being independent, willingness to cooperate and patience. He was quite comfortable with the idea of serving and waiting on a future partner as long as this was returned in some measure with kindness and respect. Tomas was in the process of arranging with a friend to share rented accommodation well away from Tereza's house, and he had applied for two job interviews. Previous to this, he had not sought employment for six months. I was impressed with the progress that Tomas had made over a relatively brief period, and asked him what had been the most effective aspect of therapy for him. Tomas replied: 'Being able to come and talk to you about whatever I want, and not being treated like shit!'

· · ·

DISCUSSION

Defining the problem

Tomas' description: Tomas tells of his depression and lack of energy and direction.

Tomas' construction: Tomas ascribes his mood to loss of his job as a waiter, and the possible discrimination involved at that time due to his homosexuality. He is well aware of the effects of his father's beatings and is also very much into mother-blaming.

Exploring the context

Therapist's affirmation: Tomas's depression is highlighted as a reaction to the many events in his life that have involved loss: Imre's beatings, Tereza's demands, death, violations, being 'cut off', uprootedness. He is praised for having overcome his chemical abuse. Tomas is asked to write a letter to his father expressing his feelings. His mood lifts. Tomas is furious at his father's actions. He blames his mother for her tardiness in leaving. We discuss Tereza's difficulties in leaving her violent husband, and the lack of community awareness and support during the 1960s. Could she have managed the situation better, or might it have been worse for Tomas if she had left earlier? Some of the qualities that Tomas has brought into play during his struggles are admired: his sensitivity, dedication and strength. Tomas is asked to consider some of his other characteristics and to write a self-advertisement.

Options for the future

Mutual reconstruction: Tomas tells of his calmer attitude and return of confidence. He talks of his commitment to intimate relationships, and preparedness to care for another as long as this is appreciated in mutual fashion. Tomas makes arrangements to live with a friend and procure future employment.

— · · · —

CASE STUDY

Case 11C   The lotus eaters
Lana, 31, a cashier controller, sought help because of the increased violence between herself, her partner Leslie, 33, a part-time storeman and artist, and their daughter Mandy, 11, a secondary school student.

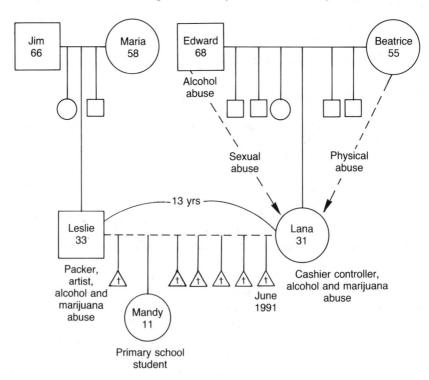

Fig. 11.3 Lana commenced therapy in July 1991.

Lana had yelled at Leslie last week, he had slapped her in the face and she had threatened him with a kitchen knife. Lana had then spent the rest of the day screaming at Mandy. Lana blamed her 'short fuse' for the problems in the family, saying that she should know how to handle their quarrels better, and that she was 'doing it all wrong'.

The tradition of violence in Lana's original family had been a lengthy and dedicated one. She remembered her mother, Beatrice, and father, Edward, continually screaming at one another, smashing household objects and throwing missiles at one another, and often taking to each other with their fists, feet and teeth. Lana's five siblings were also frequently involved in scrapping with each other, and life had been a bit like trench warfare: Lana had not known when to raise her head above the edge of her foxhole for fear of having it blown off by a passing shell. To compound her confusion, Edward, an alcohol abuser, had taken Lana as his lover when she was four, until 14 years, of age. Much later, she was to learn that Edward had also sexually abused her sister. Lana had received no protection from Beatrice, who lashed out at the kids during her conflicts with Edward, and Lana had been unable to tell anyone outside the family about any of the abuse.

Lana felt that now she was experiencing a similar circumstance with Leslie. They had endured an on–off relationship, living together then apart, for many years. Leslie would always be the one to move out, and Lana would eventually plead for his return. When Lana lived with Leslie, she felt manipulated by him. He was very good with his words and this was not the first time that he had hit her. When living away from him, she felt vulnerable without his companionship and presence.

I asked Lana to describe the good aspects about the relationship. Lana described Leslie as a caring father to Mandy. He had never beaten her, she had no doubt that he would not sexually abuse her, and whenever she and Leslie were separated he had always kept in contact with their daughter. He was quite a talented artist, who at times showed softness and sensitivity. The best times were spent when they shared a bong and drank wine. They had done this a few evenings every week for many years. These were tender moments, filled with pleasant conversation, great sex, sweet contentment. It sounded to me as though they enjoyed the carefree existence of two lotus eaters.

'We really enjoy each other', commented Lana, 'then we are so unpredictable, and blow up at each other. I thought I had avoided all this. Leslie's family is so unlike mine, so quiet and calm, not a bad word between any of them. I had hoped for so much when I met Leslie. I wanted some peace. But then I get angry over some little thing and do my block, Leslie remains Mr Cool, I get even angrier and have a go at him, and then we both explode.'

I asked Lana if she felt that Leslie might eventually do her some injury, and if she wanted to stay in the relationship? Lana replied: 'Leslie is fearsome when aroused but he won't do me any real harm. I would like to see if we can improve our situation.' I then suggested that Lana and Leslie might be struggling with some violent and angry monsters within their relationship. These monsters might have invaded their household from Lana's original family. Would Leslie come to a future session to discuss their situation? Would they both draw some pictures of the monsters that were disturbing their peace? Lana's child-hood had been a horrible one, and she had been denied many happy events. Some of her anger might be grieving for her lost youth. Would she list some of those happy times that had been stolen from her?

Leslie and Lana both attended the next weekly session. Sure enough, there had been a number of verbally violent arguments since our last meeting. Mandy's class had been found to be infested with lice. Leslie had wanted to cut her hair before treatment. Lana wanted Mandy to keep her hair long. Leslie was furious that Lana had let his mother's dog, Pintar, out of the house. They had been minding the dog while his mother was on holiday, and now Pintar was lost. They shared their pictures of Lana's anger (Figs 11.4 and 11.5).

Leslie experienced Lana's rage like something originating from the Planet of the Apes. Lana said that her fury was like a wild tornado. As they continued to argue in my room, their dance of anger became clearer. Lana would raise her voice, endeavouring to get Leslie to change his attitude. Leslie would first try to mollify Lana with eloquence, then yell her down, and when that failed, he would turn the back of his chair to her. Lana would then get angrier. We discussed how they appeared to be avoiding settling their conflict . . . the more Lana chased Leslie and argued for change, the more he would try to settle things down and eventually withdraw.

First, I expressed my admiration that, despite their difficulties, they were both obviously committed to their daughter's welfare. Then I suggested that they seemed to be adopting the styles of communication that they had witnessed in their original families. For Leslie there were never any arguments . . . perhaps differences were never discussed? For Lana, her family ground round and round in their fighting, never achieving resolution.

As we talked about their families' negotiating patterns Lana and Leslie seemed to settle. Then they burst into renewed fighting, in my room, accusing each other of responsibility for their troubles. I com-mented on the ugliness of the moment, that I was frightened by their intensity, and that perhaps it might be best for them to separate rather than continue exposing themselves and Mandy to their rage. After they had left my room, I did not expect to see them again.

A week later Lana came on her own, saying that Leslie felt that joint

Fig. 11.4 Leslie's drawing of Lana's anger.

counselling was pointless and that he would not be returning. As it
happened, their relationship had settled. Lana had agreed to let Leslie
take charge of Mandy's delousing and he had arranged to have her
hair cut short . . . which is what Mandy had wanted anyway! Pintar
had returned home safely. I commented that, during our last session,
the battles concerning the lost dog had resembled the darker qualities
of a Harold Pinter script. Lana said that she had seen the Dirk Bogarde

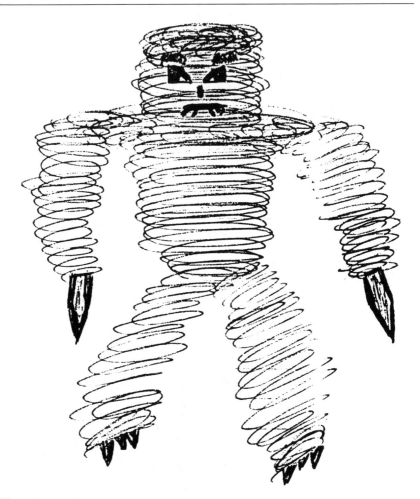

Fig. 11.5 Lana's drawing of her anger.

film of Pinter's *The Servant*, and I asked her if some of the power plays shown in that tale did not resemble her and Leslie's struggles?

Lana read out her list on what she had missed as a child.

What I missed as a child
My childhood was one where no love could be felt, no hugging or kissing allowed and no affection between my parents or other siblings.
There was never any security, I was never safe, nor was I happy.
I never had praise for my efforts at school or home.
I could never invite a friend over to my house, my home was not safe.

I never felt confident or beautiful, my birthdays were not days to look forward to, I was never made to feel special, even though I was referred to as 'Dad's little girl' this had no substance. I never had anyone to talk to.

This could go on, however I feel as though this is a 'poor me' story, and I am whinging.

Over our next three sessions our conversation included themes from this list: Lana's feelings of being cheated, too many kids in the family and not enough care, an inappropriate introduction of sexual knowledge into her childhood. Lana said that Leslie had resigned from his packer's job and was dabbling with his artistry. Over this time, however, he was sleeping in bed until noon and making no effort to exhibit or market his work.

Lana and I considered ways that she could step back from the situation about which she was angry. I asked her to examine the messages that accompanied her anger, and she wrote them out for our sixth session.

How I feel when I am angry
1. frustrated
2. I am 'right' this time surely
3. rejected
4. cheated
5. uncompromising
6. tunnel vision; I can only see what is making me angry
7. alone
8. powerful

We looked at ways to counteract the messages, e.g.
I am frustrated: What am I doing about it constructively?
I am 'right' this time surely: What is the evidence that I am 'right'?

We discussed issues of family responsibility. Leslie claimed that he wanted a more rewarding family life. Was his current behaviour consistent with such aims? What did it mean also that Leslie had refused to attend further joint sessions of therapy with Lana when she was so obviously distressed? Our dialogue turned to the many terminations of pregnancy that Lana had undergone during their relationship. Lana said that she had felt bludgeoned by Leslie into having the operations. We talked about how the series of terminations may have reflected Lana's dilemma: she desired to have more children, siblings for Mandy, yet was reluctant to raise them in an unstable family environment.

At our seventh session, Lana was furious. Mandy had told her that Edward had touched her 'in the wrong way' during an episode of child-minding. Lana had told Leslie, and he was one hundred percent supportive of Lana taking preventative action. I asked Lana if she would bring Mandy in next time?

Mandy, a bright and sociable child, came along and described how she had told her grandfather to back off when he had started to lay hands on her. I expressed my admiration at Mandy's assertiveness, and asked if she was confident that Lana could protect her from further abuse.

'Yup', Mandy replied, 'No problems.'

This answer seemed to give Lana a huge boost in mood. I commented that Lana might not have been able to prevent her own sexual abuse, but was now able to care very well for her daughter. We discussed how Lana might arrange 'safety meetings' with other members of her family to ensure that her young nieces, nephews and cousins would be protected from Edward.

Our eighth to eleventh sessions focused on resolving Lana's and Leslie's relationship. He was now regularly grabbing her and pushing her around. Once he had thrown Lana to the floor. Lana said that Leslie accused her of provoking him. Once more I expressed my uncertainty about Lana's safety. I said that I would not accept that Lana merited a physically abusive response from anybody.

'You are a person of many ideals', I suggested, 'But I am concerned about the cost to you of following those ideals. You decided not to bring babies into an unsafe world, and risked damage to your body through repeated termination of pregnancy. Are you now trying to preserve the ideal of an intact family at the risk of bodily injury also?'

At our 12th session, Lana said that Leslie had moved into rented accommodation elsewhere. She was confident that this was a permanent shift, as previously he had stayed either with his parents or friends.

· · ·

DISCUSSION

Defining the problem

Lana's description: Lana describes her short fuse, her lashing out at both her partner and daughter, and her threats to Leslie with a knife.
Lana's construction: Lana ascribes her actions to her own lack of discipline. She sees herself as being definitely at fault.

Exploring the context

Therapist's deconstruction: The traditions of abuse in Lana's original family are emphasized, rather than any personal defect on her part. She is asked to invite Leslie to a future therapy session and for them both to draw the monsters that seem to have accompanied Lana from her original family into their relationship.

At our joint session

Leslie's construction: Leslie asserts it is all Lana's fault. Things would be much better if she did not provoke him. Leslie's and Lana's dedication to parenting is affirmed. They share their drawings of Lana's anger. We talk about their patterns of communication during the session; Lana engages Leslie, who initially tries to calm her with eloquence, then speaks forcefully to her, then withdraws. Lana pursues him and Leslie retreats further. These patterns may have been learnt in their original families. Our conversation seems to escalate their arguing. I express my genuine fear of their reactions, and suggest permanent separation as an outcome.

Options for the future

Mutual reconstruction: Leslie declines further therapy. Lana and I discuss her many losses. She lists what she has missed in childhood and the messages that go with her anger. We look at ways that she can step back from angry situations. We talk about the terminations of pregnancy. Lana tells of Leslie's cessation from earning income, and his seemingly non-productive artistry. I suggest to Lana that, although Leslie presents himself as a victim of her irrationality, it appears as if he tries to coerce her into submissive behaviour. Is he committed to a mutually responsible relationship?

Lana is furious at Edward's attempted seduction of Mandy. Mandy attends a joint session, her assertiveness is affirmed, and safety meetings for other vulnerable family members are arranged. Lana says that Leslie has become much more physically abusive towards her, and blames herself for the increased distress. I state my belief that blows are never an appropriate response to words, and the couple proceed to lasting separation.

· · ·

CASE STUDY

Case 11D   The accountant
Archie, 55, an invalid pensioner, described his life as 'a mess'. He had been depressed for weeks, and felt like giving it all up. At times he

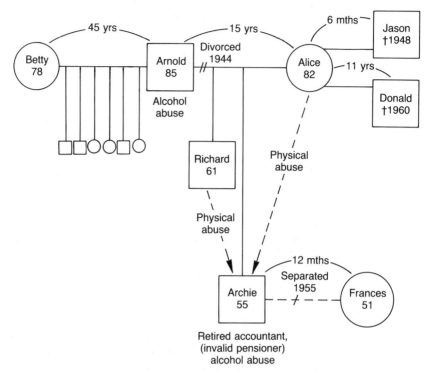

Fig. 11.6 Archie commenced therapy in January 1991.

would put his head inside the gas oven, then decide that this was not what God wanted for him, and he would proceed onwards.

In fact, the 'mess' in Archie's life had begun at an early age. His original family resided in a New South Wales regional city. Archie's father Arnold, now 85, had been an alcohol abuser for many years, and although not verbally or physically abusive, he would spend most of his time sleeping on the sofa, and offer little conversation or emotional support. Archie's mother Alice, now 82, had divorced Arnold because of his inebriation, when Archie was eight. Arnold had eventually remarried and Archie remembered regular weekly visits to the new family, and some happy times with his six step-siblings. Life with Alice and Archie's elder brother Richard, now 62, took a turn for the worse. Alice had remained single for five years, and Archie could remember her beating him frequently. Richard had constantly bullied him without Archie being able to obtain much protection from his mother. Archie recalled a time, when he was about ten, when Richard had sat on him, holding his mouth open, while Alice had force-fed him. Alice eventually married Jason, who Archie said was very kind to him. All the torment had ceased. Much to Archie's regret, Jason had died six months later. Alice soon married Donald, a dignified Englishman. Archie warmed to Donald, also who taught him the custom of sharing a glass of port by the fire on a cold winter's eve. Donald had died when Archie was 24. When he was 19, Archie had pursued boxing as a career. He said that he was quite adept and had trained for the 1956 Melbourne Olympics. He had taken to drink in a big way, saying that he would down 30 beers and a good deal of Scotch and gin in one sitting. In his early 20s, Archie had trained as an accountant, and moved to Sydney to pursue this vocation. He became proficient and had made progress until he was 27, when he was hospitalized with hallucinations. Archie had been diagnosed as schizophrenic, and given medical treatment. He had obtained an invalid pension and had not worked since then. Archie had settled in Melbourne when he was 40.

Archie's relationships with Alice and Richard had softened somewhat. His mother visited him every Christmas, and Richard, now a retired successful executive in Queensland, regularly sent Archie sums of money to help him sustain himself. But Archie was extremely lonely, living in a hostel with only three other residents, and he would visit several doctor's clinics each week, as well as his cousin Roger, the vicar, Grow, AA, and the local hotel, where he would restrict himself to lemonade. Although Archie had ceased taking alcohol many years ago, he had replaced it with tranquillizer abuse, and one of the problems, as our neighbouring pharmacist told it to me, was that Archie would present numerous prescriptions for sedatives supplied by the various practitioners he visited, unbeknown to each other. Archie was costing the community a considerable amount of money in medical payments. Another problem was that Archie, although never drunk, would frequently become involved in fights at the hotel, and he had spent several nights in police custody for disorderly behaviour. There was no doubt that Archie was mentally disabled from the effects of his alcohol abuse, and his psychiatrist had given him a diagnosis of 'burnt out' schizophrenia. His difficulties were compounded by increasing deafness and poor eyesight. I saw my task as 1) providing a safe place where he could converse; 2) decreasing his visits to the medical practitioners; and 3) stimulating his resources. Archie identified himself as a Christian and sought much solace from services and reading the psalms, and he was already involved in a number of community activities. He liked to draw in his spare time, and also to listened to music.

We agreed to meet weekly. We negotiated a time structure. Archie would see me once weekly, one general practitioner every fortnight to receive his Modecate injection, and he would visit his psychiatrist every quarter. Archie often would drop into the surgery wanting to see me every day. Occasionally, when he was obviously distressed, I would see him twice weekly, but we discussed the problems of me being charged by the authorities for over-servicing. In such a circumstance, Archie would not be able to see me at all, and within eight months he had settled into a weekly routine without undue demands on me or other practitioners.

Archie could well remember his skill as an accountant, and we spent some time grieving his losses: his lack of happy childhood, the deaths of parents, his disjointed family and few friends, the past engagement that did not work out, career opportunities.

'Yet you are no down and out tramp', I commented. 'You always come to sessions beautifully groomed, seem to have a kind nature and basically wish others well. You have managed to maintain your dignity.'

I asked Archie if he would bring an example of his drawing to our next session. He showed me his picture (Fig. 11.7) and we talked about how he might place some flowers in the empty vase.

A few sessions later, Archie read to me a section of Omar Khayyam's *Ruba'iyat* (Avery and Heath-Stubbs, 1981).

6
If the heart could grasp the meaning in life,
In death it would know the mystery of God;

Fig. 11.7 Archie's drawing.

Today when you are in possession of yourself, you know nothing.
Tomorrow when you leave yourself behind what will you know.

I decided to weave the theme of 'searching' into our conversation; how many of us spend a significant part of our lives seeking our own meaning, and quoted a subsequent verse . . .

10
The cycle which includes our coming and going
Has no discernible beginning nor end;
Nobody has got this matter straight –
Where we come from and where we go to.

At our next session, Archie shared another verse with me . . .

120
The New Year breeze is delicious on the rose's cheek,
In the wide meadow fair is the face of the enflamer of hearts:
Anything you can say about the day that is passed is bad –
Be happy and do not talk of yesterday, today is good.

I smiled. I suggested that Archie had brought a flower in literary form to rest in his vase. We chatted about how some people find meaning in their lives by enjoying 'the immediate moment', including enjoying liquor, and I read out . . .

122
Take the cup in your hand as the tulip at New Year does;
If you have the chance, gleefully gulp wine
With the tulip cheeked, for this blue wheel
Brings you down to dust suddenly enough.

The next week Archie was in more sombre mood, and offered verse 229 . . .

Were I to find fruit on the branch of hope
I'd find the end of my life's thread there;
How much longer must I be in existence's narrow straits?
If only I could find the door to oblivion.

I did not believe that Archie was seriously suicidal at this particular moment. Nonetheless, he seemed to be suggesting that constantly exploring life's meaning can lead to stagnation and despondency. I decided to introduce the theme of 'acceptance': knowing that it is time to end the search, and recited. . .

231
How long . . . will you chatter about the five senses and the four elements?

What matter if the puzzles be one or a hundred thousand?
We are dust, strum the harp . . .
We are air . . . bring out the wine.

We both agreed that Omar Khayyam's pessimism may have resulted from too much gulping of wine 'with the tulip cheeked'. I added some lines from Ecclesiastes (Soncino, 1980):

Chapter 12; 12–13
And furthermore . . . of making many books there is no end; and much study is a weariness of the flesh.
The end of the matter, all having been heard: fear God, and keep His commandments: for this is the whole . . .

Archie offered some consolation from the psalms (Singer, 1962)

Psalm 23 (p. 414)
. . . though I walk through the valley of the shadow of death, I will fear no evil; for you are with me: your rod and your staff, they comfort me.
Psalm 27 (pp. 90–91)
The Lord is my light and my salvation; whom shall I fear? The Lord is the stronghold of my life; of whom shall I be afraid?
Psalm 91 (p. 24)
. . . you shall not be afraid of the terror by night, nor of the arrow that flies by day; of the pestilence that walks in the darkness, nor of the plague that ravages at noon day . . . for You, O Lord, are my refuge.

Archie still visits me weekly and I expect him to continue indefinitely. He maintains his medication, sobriety and dignity, having had no further fights or contacts with the police. At last encounter, Archie was engrossed in *Captains Courageous*, Rudyard Kipling's classic tale of troubled souls on storm-tossed seas, who eventually find safe haven after overcoming their trials.

DISCUSSION

Defining the problem

Archie's description: Archie tells of his 'mess' of a life, his long-standing depression, his suicidal fantasies, his tendencies to violence and his loneliness.
Archie's construction: Archie attributes his problems to the beatings he received at the hands of his mother and brother. He acknowledges his alcohol abuse, and also his treatment for schizophrenia.

Exploring the context

Therapist's affirmation: Archie and I discuss his many losses, and expression of the grief through conversation is encouraged. Archie is admired for his sense of dignity in presentation and manner.

Options for the future

Mutual reconstruction: Archie seems to be creating a social context out of the medical profession! We arrange a structure in which he visits doctors less and peer groups (Grow, Alcoholics Anonymous, Church) more. Archie communicates his emptiness in his sketch of a vase without flowers. We gradually fill the emotional hiatus through sharing verses dealing with the search for life's meaning, enjoying 'the now', acceptance and spiritual contentment. Archie settles for less medical contact and no physicality.

SUMMARY

In Chapter 11, we considered:
Case 11A, 'Schnudri', in which Trudi has had to battle to develop her own identity against the expectations of others, including her alcohol-abusing partner.
Case 11B, 'The waiter', in which Tomas, physically abused by his father, has sought calm through using drugs.
Case 11C, 'The lotus eaters', in which Lana and Leslie, both very much participants in the drug culture, need to find a resolution to their violent conflicts.
Case 11D, 'The accountant', in which Archie, debilitated by his chronic alcohol abuse, struggles to fill the emptiness in his life.

POINTS FOR REFLECTION

1. Compare Case 9A, 'The mouth', with Case 11C, 'The lotus eaters'. Why do you think that the outcomes were different?
2. Describe some of your own case studies involving chemical abuse, using the Affirmation and Deconstruction Schemas.

REFERENCES

Avery, P. and Heath-Stubbs, J. (1981) *The Ruba'iyat of Omar Khayyam*, Penguin, London.
Cohen, A. (ed.) (1980) *The Soncino Books of the Bible: Ecclesiastes*, Spottiswoode Ballantyne, London.
Singer, S. (1962) *Daily Prayer Book*, Eyre and Spottiswoode Ltd, London.

Physical illness

12

———————— · · · ————————

CASE STUDY

Case 12A   Bad luck

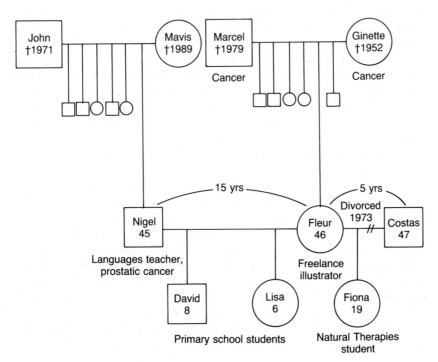

Fig. 12.1 Fleur commenced therapy in March 1991.

Fleur, 46, a freelance illustrator, sat hunched in her chair during our initial session. She told me of the long-term depression that she had experienced for many years, her lethargy and lack of motivation. She was, she said, crushed by the burdens of her life. Raised in poverty in postwar France, her mother Ginette had died of cancer when Fleur was seven. Her father Marcel had continued to care for Fleur and her five siblings on his own. As a young woman, Fleur had trained as a graphic artist, had married her first husband Costas when she was 23, and had given birth to Fiona four years later. During the pregnancy, Costas had begun to behave erratically and had been diagnosed as paranoid schizophrenic. He had proved to be an unreliable husband emotionally, economically and practically, and Fleur had separated from him when Fiona was two. A year later, after the divorce, Fleur and Fiona had migrated to Australia to seek a brighter future. Another year passed, and Fleur met and married Nigel. Soon after their marriage, Fleur learnt that Marcel had died, in France, of cancer. She had not seen him since her emigration. Two children were born, David, now eight, and Lisa, now six. The family took to farming for a while, then settled into city life. Nigel began working as a teacher of Greek, Latin and English whilst Fleur obtained part-time work as a freelance illustrator. Fleur's current crisis had been precipitated by the diagnosis of widely spread prostatic cancer in Nigel one and a half months previously. Their relationship had been strained for the past two years but, since the diagnosis, they had been fighting constantly.

I acknowledged the many stresses in Fleur's life: the curse of cancer that had robbed her of two parents and now threatened to take her husband; the poverty in childhood; the first difficult marriage. I shared my thoughts that much of Fleur's depression may have been sustained grieving for her losses, and asked whether she and her husband might come to a future session. Fleur said that she was certain he would come.

At our second weekly session, Nigel, filled with intellectual justification and fury, blamed a number of causes for the demise of their marriage. Fleur, he said, had proven inadequate in every sphere of their relationship, her depression clouding everything that they did. Their sexual life had decreased since David's birth, with complete abstinence for the past two years. Fiona, too, had been a problem.

'She is a complete bludger and wastrel!', Nigel asserted. 'Fiona dabbles in these natural therapies without trying for a real job. She spends our money like water. She is a moral danger to David and Lisa, posing half-naked as a photographer's model and showing the children the pictures. She entertains her young men friends in her room with the door closed. And Fleur damn well supports Fiona against me. I remember not long ago when Fiona snarled at me: "I am going to take your wife away from you". It is all their fault . . . Fleur's bloody depressions, always siding with her daughter . . . all this stress has caused my cancer. Well I am not going to stand for it any longer. I want Fiona out of the house now!'

I thought to myself: 'Even though Nigel appears distressed by his illness, his right wing seems to be flapping rather forcefully'. I leant forward, looked at him directly, lowered my voice, and said: 'What if you are wrong? What if it is not the problems with Fleur and Fiona that have caused your cancer? What if it is bad luck that you have got this disease, and you are now going to throw away whatever chance of reconciliation and happiness that you may have with your family . . . and all because of bad luck!' They left quietly.

Both Nigel and Fleur came to our third session, warming towards each other! They said that they had moved back into the one bedroom and bed, even enjoying an occasion of sex together. We talked about how they could maintain the cordial relations that had commenced: what did they hope for in the time left to them? What shared experiences might continue to nourish them? I asked if Fiona would come to a joint session?

At our fourth meeting, with Fleur, Nigel and Fiona all present, Fiona expressed her sadness at the loss of Nigel's and her relationship when David was born. She said that they had enjoyed a pleasant contact, talking and doing many activities together, and this had all stopped about eight years ago. Nigel seemed to have focused on David, then Lisa. Fiona had felt rejected and hurt. She had turned to her mother as her 'only source of conversation and comfort' at the time. Fiona had believed since that time that Nigel had wanted to expel her from the home. I commented that a new baby at the time of an elder sibling's beginning adolescence can be a tricky business. Just when the adolescent needs all the adults she can get to help her grow to maturity, an intruder comes along! Fiona said that there was still a spark of love within her for Nigel, and I asked how she might tend to that flame, gently blowing on it and adding more fuel, so that it might increase to warm them both?

At our fifth session to tenth sessions, I continued to see Fleur individually. We talked about how she could emphasize her bond with Nigel so that he remained aware of her support for him, and how to increase Fiona's sense of safety within the home. We considered the messages that Fleur might give to herself when her self-esteem was low, and how she could step back and let Nigel and Fiona redevelop their relationship.

At our eleventh session, Fleur told me that she and Nigel had decided to separate. Fiona and Lisa were to live with her, while David had asked to remain with Nigel. I asked how they had come to their decision. Fleur replied that while there had been marked improvement initially, Nigel frequently reverted to his blaming attitudes about her 'incompetence' and Fiona's perceived competitiveness. Over the past two weeks, Nigel had shown more interest in a 19-year-old male acquaintance and computer games than in family negotiations. Nigel had told Fleur that he felt more supported by his friends than by Fleur or Fiona, and that if these were going to be the last years of his life he wanted them to be completely stress-free, spending them with people who cared for him. Since their decision, Fleur had felt more optimistic about achieving her own peace, and less depressed now that a stable resolution had been reached. She requested an end to therapy.

Fiona came to a session on her own a fortnight later, confirming that Nigel was more interested in intellectual discussions with his friends deep into the night than involvement in family life, and that he was absorbed for hours on end with the computer. She expressed her pleasure at the new arrangements, and the hope that the family situation would improve.

I saw Nigel a month later. He said that Fleur, Fiona and Lisa were in new accommodation and that a group of his friends had moved into the family home. They and David all seemed to be getting along famously. He was calmer than he had been for years. David saw his other family regularly, as Nigel did Lisa. In fact, Fiona had become much softer to Nigel since the split, even offering Nigel 'an ear' should he ever need one.

— — —   · · ·   — — —

DISCUSSION

Defining the problem

Fleur's description: Fleur tells of her lengthy experience of depression, lethargy and lost motivation.
Fleur's construction: Fleur attributes her depression to the hardships and heavy burdens of her past. She relates her current mood as being due to Nigel's recently diagnosed cancer.

Exploring the context

Therapist's affirmation: Fleur's many losses are acknowledged and a session with Nigel is arranged.

Joint session

Nigel's construction: Nigel blames Fleur for her inadequacy, calls Fiona competitive, and states that their stress on him has caused his cancer.

Therapist's deconstruction: I suggest that it may be 'bad luck' rather than any human intervention that has brought about Nigel's illness, and that he may waste whatever life he has left to him seeking a pointless and unjust revenge. At a family session, Fiona expresses her sadness at the loss of relationship with Nigel that seemed to have occurred around the time of David's birth.

Options for the future

Mutual reconstruction: There are signs of immediate improvement, Nigel and Fleur resuming cohabitation. Fleur and I continue individual therapy, discussing ways of boosting her self-esteem, supporting Fiona's safety, affirming her and Nigel's bond, stepping back and letting Nigel and Fiona redevelop their contact. Eventually, Nigel reverts to his blaming behaviour and the couple make a mutual decision to separate. Fleur says that she hopes to find contentment living with Fiona and Lisa, free from Nigel's discounts, and pursuing her career as an illustrator. Nigel says that he feels more supported in his illness by the male friends who have moved in with him. He appears committed and effective in his parenting of David, who continues to reside with him. In the new situation, Fiona offers emotional comfort to Nigel should he wish it.

---   · · ·   ---

CASE STUDY

Case 12B   Lady in red

Charmaine, 28, an employee in a book administration company, presented at our first session very much as the 'lady in red', with scarlet dress, moon face ruddy from the effects of long-term cortisone usage, and emotions red-hot with fury. Charmaine said that she had battled against asthma since childhood, and had been admitted to hospital overnight on a monthly basis during the past three years with episodes of wheezing. Her three children, Jimmy, 3, Fay, 2, and Richard, 1, had all been unplanned, though not unwanted, due to 'failed' contraception. After the last pregnancy Charmaine had experienced a massive vaginal prolapse, which had resulted in hysterectomy. She had been alternately raging and depressed since then. Charmaine said that she was happy in her employment, though she often lacked the energy to get her work done. She described Damien, 30, an officer in the Australian Trade Commission, as a lovely partner, caring and supportive, whom she felt she was tormenting with her erratic outbursts of screaming and tears, and her inadequacies as mother and wife. Charmaine remembered life in her family of origin as a happy one. She had been

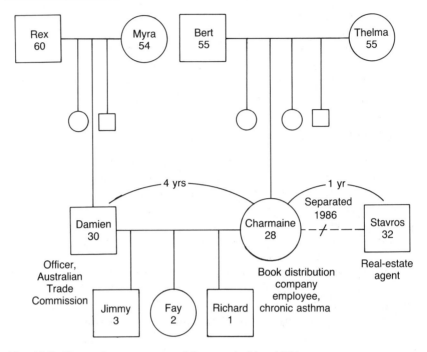

Fig. 12.2 Charmaine commenced therapy in May 1991.

engaged to Stavros, a real-estate agent, but they had separated due to their continual arguing: he had wanted to travel the world for a while, she had wanted a more sedate lifestyle, with children. Charmaine had enjoyed many sporting activities – netball, hockey, orienteering – until the asthma had become too burdensome. Another disappointment was that she had embarked on a medical career, completing her first year with high academic achievement, but had found that her illness, and the children, had interrupted her plans. Charmaine listed her resources as her Catholicism, writing and sketching.

We spent the rest of the session discussing her losses. I said that I could well understand her low spirits, but felt that she was unkind to blame herself for not coping. The strongest spirit would, I believe, have been daunted by the challenges that Charmaine had faced. In fact, I saw her as exceptionally tenacious and optimistic, forging ahead to seek satisfaction in several areas of life: family, job, spirituality, creativity. It seemed to me that Charmaine was grieving the loss of 'the Charmaine that was '– slim and graceful, energetic, sports-loving, vital, a successful medical student. Would she write a letter to 'the Charmaine that was', saying goodbye?

Charmaine shared her letter with me at our second weekly session.

Well, you asked me to write down a conversation with myself. The first thing you will notice is that I am a prolific writer. The second thing you will notice is that I have already gone beyond the task that you have set me. This is Sunday, on Wednesday I might have written about the task that was set, but I am afraid that today I will just write about what I have thought and where I am currently in that process of 'thought'. (I also do not edit my work, and my mind goes faster than my pen, so you will just have to try and decipher it).

You were right about 'letting go of who I was'. I did idolise the person that I was, after all I loved her dearly, and I felt that I was 'dead', and I resented the fact that I had to start 'anew' and form a new person. After all, I was quite happy with the old one. Anyway it hit me that I could never be that person again, no more than I could be 21 again. I cried. Then I suddenly realised that I always felt older than my years anyway, and when I was that person, all I wanted to be was a woman. I can definitely say that I am a woman now. I was hard on myself, judging myself as a failure by the standards that I set myself when I was young. Instead, I should have been proud of myself for being able to get through the last four years and be as good as I am now. After all, it is no use being upset that I did not reach my previous goals, because life threw me a curly ball, and despite my best efforts I found myself pregnant three times in four years. I did not even have the opportunity to reach those goals.

I am proud of myself, and I realise that there was nothing wrong with me that a good look in the mirror and some serious assessment would fix. I looked in the mirror and assessed. You helped me to look in that mirror, a mirror I was frightened to look in, because there was a different person looking back. All I wanted was a knight in shining armour to come and tell me that everything was all right, and to let me hide in safety for a while. The problem with that is once you hide, it is very hard to get out again, so you finish up hiding from life for the term of your life. If there is one thing about myself I know, it is that I would not be happy hiding forever, so sooner or later I would have to face the world again, so why not sooner. I was afraid that all life had to offer me was more of the same pain that I had been through, which had happened despite my efforts to be positive. It was just one of those times in your life when nothing goes right. What got me through all those hard times was my faith in God, that suffering was something that we all did, but each to their own degree. However I still saw that things can be beautiful despite the ugliness. What I have been doing recently is concentrating on the ugliness and unfairness in the world, and that led to despair which led to a belief that life held nothing but blackness, and more of the same pain of the past. Yet as my children laugh and play at my feet, and my husband looks longingly into my eyes, I thank God for each breath I take.

All of my despair was that I felt everyone including myself makes demands on me. I felt such a failure that I did not want to look God in the face, for I felt shame at deserting Him and unable to feel His presence. Then I remembered something that He told me to write down for future reference. It goes something like the following and relates to the secret of life.

We are all born, and we must all play the game of life, except that each is handicapped with their own set of blinkers and set upon a road which is full of obstacles. The trick is that the rules often change as we go along, but like all games, we improve as we play. Yet what we do not realise when we come to an obstacle is that it is an optical illusion. It seems insurmountable, but nothing is insurmountable, at least no obstacle that is set. Often we choose to avoid the obstacle, and only in retrospect do we realise that we could have in fact won over that obstacle. Death is certain, the game will always end, even if we choose not to play, eventually everything will stop. We are given companions to help us and keep us company in our journey. The answer: – it is only a game, nothing stays the same forever, things will always change, some things will be in our control, some will not, the trick is just to live and survive, grab at the happiness that is around you, and do not take yourself or life so seriously. There are few true answers. Enjoy . . . death will come soon enough.

I take life too seriously. I know that I have been given an infinite amount of strength, each time I hit rock bottom, the strength seems to swell again like the tide. I know for certain that I will be confident (because I believe that whoever I am now, and it involves a lot of soul searching, will be a person to be proud of, so I have no intention of losing my confidence). I was a wonderful person who has been through hell, and survived, so now I am also a wonderful person, just battle weary.

We spent the next two sessions talking about further mobilizing Charmaine's spiritual and creative resources. She had always wanted to resume her medical studies, but now thought that it might be more realistic to enter a second-year science course. I asked her to compose a structure for the future. At our fourth and final session Charmaine showed me her list.

Needs and wants for a newer, happier life:

1. Happier, more sharing marriage, involving mutual admiration and caring, being able to do things together that we like and allowing ourselves that pleasure.
2. Being separate beings, having Damien more able to go and do things he likes like sport, so I can do things I want without feeling guilty or that I have to justify it.
3. Being more involved with the children, rather than just being ill or working and resenting them when I need time to myself, or when I am busy with the housework. Playing with them, spending more time as a family, having some good times.
4. Study – being free to study.
5. Health – maintain weight level, be active, exercise.
6. Accept illness – it may be with you a long time. God made you strong, so you can endure harder things than most!
7. Avoid unnecessary worry or strain, in bed early, take all medication.
8. Avoid financial stress.
9. Enjoy your sex life for what it is, not always wishing for more.
10. Cannot have any more children, stop feeling so guilty about it.
11. Stop comparing your life with someone else's.
12. Write yourself a list of three or four feelings: positive ones when you are feeling happy to remind yourself of what it is like to feel good; negative ones when you are feeling low so that you know how to look after your self when you are feeling down.
13. Do not concentrate on past struggles; look to the future! Live, Charmaine! At the moment you are too ready to die, too busy thinking about past and present illnesses and hardships, condemning yourself before the vote is cast. Build a future, it only takes courage and strength and that you have plenty of!'

We discussed the possibility of Charmaine taking a holiday while Damien cared for the children.

'Much more preferable to having a holiday in hospital', I commented. Perhaps she could include into her routine regular weekends of rest and refreshment away from the family?

I received the following letter two months later.

Dear John,

As you have probably gathered by now, I have stopped coming to see you. Part of the problem has been working full time which has not left me much time. The other reason is that I feel totally in control. The depression has lifted, my health has improved with being away from the children, and I feel like my old self again.

I want to thank you for helping me to break away from the chains of the past. You certainly got my brain thinking again, and I guess, considering the rate my thoughts move, that was all I needed.

Anyway, if I find myself regressing, I will certainly be in touch again. I won't let myself fall down to the level I was when I saw you, because it is just that much harder to get up again.

Thanks for your help, I certainly have appreciated it.
Regards,
Charmaine

Six months later, Charmaine remains content and has had no further admissions to hospital.

--- . . . ---

DISCUSSION

Defining the problem

Charmaine's description: Charmaine tells of her recurrent battles with asthma, and her alternating moods of depression and anger.
Charmaine's construction: Charmaine largely blames herself for being an ineffective wife, mother and person.

Exploring the context

Therapist's construction: After affirming Charmaine's strengths in her struggles against almost overwhelming odds, I suggest that her moods may be due to grieving rather than personal weakness. She is asked to compose a letter of farewell to 'the Charmaine that was'.

Options for the future

Mutual reconstruction: During the writing of her letter, Charmaine discovers some of her forgotten resources and starts to give herself some self-affirming messages. We build on this progress and Charmaine constructs a routine to become strong and healthy again. The theme of 'rest and recreation' is woven into our conversation, Charmaine takes a vacation away from the family while Damien minds the children, and she stabilizes her emotions, breaks the disabling cycle of her asthma and renews her enjoyment of life. These improvements are maintained for the subsequent six months.

CASE STUDY

Case 12C   The gerrymander

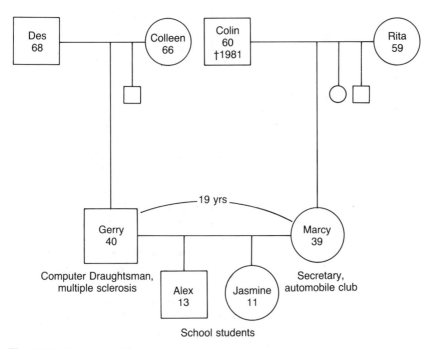

Fig. 12.3 Gerry and Marcy commenced therapy in March 1990.

Gerry, 40, a computer draughtsman, and Marcy, 39, head of the travel department of an automobile club, were telling me of their disjointed and crisis-laden experience during much of their 19 years together. They said they had 'come to the end of their tether, and did not know what to do next'. Marcy was the principal speaker, her lively and colourful narrative often being replaced by lengthy pauses of quiet fury. Gerry was largely silent, adding occasional monosyllabic detail.

They had spent their initial period of marriage establishing careers (Gerry had worked in his vocation for the past 22 years, while Marcy had entered business administration and worked her way up to her current post, which she had held for six years), setting up domestic routines and purchasing a home.

Problems seemed to have begun after Alex's birth, 13 years previously. Forty-eight hours after delivery, Marcy had received an anonymous telephone call, in her postnatal ward, expressing condolences on his 'stillbirth'.

Five years later, Alex had been mailed an unsigned 'sympathy card', on his birthday, conveying the sender's grief on hearing of the joint deaths of his parents in a motor vehicle accident. Marcy thought that both these cruel hoaxes were perpetrated by an aunt well known for her caustic sense of humour, but Marcy had never felt enough confidence to approach her relative on this matter.

Around that time, Marcy's father, Colin, had died in an industrial accident.

Three years later, Gerry suffered loss of vision in his left eye and tingling in the fingers of one hand. He had been diagnosed as having multiple sclerosis, and had been free of all symptoms since this initial episode.

During the subsequent year, Marcy's boss had asked her to help him 'kidnap' his 30-year-old son from the living quarters of a religious cult. The cult had been exposed by the media as seemingly exploitative of its members, and an official inquiry into their activities was under way. The retrieval of the son proved successful. Marcy had warmed to her boss and his family during this venture, and shortly afterwards, Marcy had found his body slumped on the floor of her office. Postmortem indicated heart attack as the cause of death. The sadistic aunt had died during that year also.

Gerry had spent most of his life working diligently for a firm that kept him in a subordinate position, with little status and low pay. He had consistently refused to confront his bosses regarding promotion, and it had been up to Marcy to seek better jobs to improve the economic quality of their lives. Though Marcy earned a good income, Gerry insisted on managing the budget without her influence. This had led to numerous arguments. It was only eight months ago that Gerry had changed placement for better conditions.

'We have stopped quarrelling all right', snorted Marcy. 'Now we say nothing to each other!'

'Oh, it is not all that bad, really', countered Gerry. 'We do talk sometimes.'

Marcy described their social life as dull, their sexual enjoyment as negligible, and their children as good kids with adequate grades at school and many friends.

I expressed my amazement at the number of traumas that Gerry and Marcy had suffered over the past several years, and the disruption that this had caused to their pleasure in life. They did not seem to have had any reasonable time to grieve over one loss when another pressure would rise and distract them. I admired the strength and tenacity with which they had persisted in raising their children and struggling with their problems, and asked them what the most oppressive issue was for them at the moment.

'Oh, that is an easy one', Marcy replied. 'Definitely Gerry's multiple sclerosis! He thinks that he is dying. He has given up on everything. Gerry talks of throwing it all away and leaving us.'

Gerry sat silent at this moment, with shoulders slouched, hands held limply in his lap, and eyes gazing out the window.

'Yet you have recently changed jobs, Gerry', I commented, gently trying to draw him more into our dialogue. 'You must be hopeful for something better.'

'Could be', Gerry replied dispiritedly. Marcy sighed.

We agreed to meet a week later to see if we could explore ways in which Gerry might renew his interest in life.

At our second session I wove the theme of 'living with danger and insecurity' into our conversation. With so much turmoil, and the rearing of young children, it would have been difficult to find opportunities to nourish and support each other. This broached another issue: how Marcy and Gerry handled 'emotionality' within their relationship. I explained that I saw Gerry as cool and collected, quietly seeking his wisdom, wanting to sort out his own problems in an independent fashion, whereas Marcy appeared to be the 'go-getter', initiating and making contact, ever eager for emotional interaction. I regarded Marcy as offering colourful descriptions of family life, while Gerry occasionally affirmed, clarified, and sometimes redirected, her story.

We discussed how, until recent decades, men in our society were encouraged to be 'Leaders of the Nation', rugged, thoughtful and practical, whereas women were trained to be 'Earth Mothers', in charge of emotional expression, particularly their softer feelings of warmth, nurturing and sadness. I commented that Gerry and Marcy appeared to be reflecting these patterns and wondered out loud if they had learnt them within the families in which they had been raised.

As it happened, both families of origin appeared to have been gerrymandered towards the preservation of 'men's rights'.

'Dad was always right', Marcy said, 'and none of us would dare to cross him.'

'We were always rather pleased with our three-man football team', remarked Gerry.

Both fathers appeared to have had the final say over finances, children's education, family holidays and entertainment. Mothers were expected to keep a tidy house, transport the children to various functions, support their husband's vocations, and allow their men time out with their mates on evenings and weekends. Any income the wives earned was seen to be subsidizing that of their husbands. A major difference was that Marcy had often talked with her sister during their youth about the apparent unfairness of 'men having it all their own way' in the family. Another important difference was that Marcy and her sister were fearful that their father might fly into a punitive rage if they ever did contradict him. Within Gerry's family, everybody considered men's privileges over women's needs to be the norm. A challenge was never considered necessary.

Nontheless, both Gerry and Marcy described their childhood memories as happy ones, and their parents as having been contented within their marriages. They had experienced no violence or sexual abuses, and were fairly certain that there had been no infidelities or other family secrets. As long as the 'masters of the house' had been obeyed, peace and order had been maintained.

At our third session, I continued the theme of 'men of granite' and 'women of silk'. Gerry's favourite childhood heroes had been Clint Eastwood, John Wayne and Clark Gable. We discussed how, in his films of the Wild West, Eastwood, 'the good guy', overcame 'the bad and the ugly villains' without injury to himself; how John Wayne appeared to have won World War II single-handed several times over; and how Vivienne Leigh seemed to have melted into Clark Gable's arms as he boldly swept her up the stairway to the boudoir, in *Gone With The Wind*.

I suggested that perhaps Gerry had been unable to grieve his illness. After all, who had seen Eastwood, Wayne and Gable weep on the screen? Gerry might have lost his sense of 'mastery', and not permitted himself to experience his sorrow, resulting in a prolonged period of depression, with loss of energy and lack of motivation and drive. Perhaps it had been easier for Gerry to argue with Marcy than be sad?

'There may be something else important here also', I said. 'Marcy and her sister always wanted to change the way men related to women in their original family, but Gerry and his menfolk were happy with the status quo. Perhaps some of your arguments have been about changing and staying the same. Marcy has been arguing for change and Gerry has been supporting stability. I wonder what would happen if you reversed those roles? What would happen if Gerry was able to vent his feelings, even going over the top a little? What would happen if Marcy took charge of the family's practical needs? Would you, Gerry, before our next session, write a list of the emotional supports that you might need from your family? Would you, Marcy, prepare the family budget for the next month entirely free from Gerry's input?'

Marcy mentioned an anxiety similar to the one she had experienced with her father: if Gerry did let her know his 'real' feelings, he might prove aggressive towards her and she would get hurt.

I did not see either of them again for a year, when Marcy came on her own. She said that their situation had initially improved somewhat. Gerry seemed to have been more talkative and a participant in family life, but the onus of supporting them all emotionally had remained largely on Marcy's shoulders. Finally they had separated, eight months after their last session.

We discussed some of the factors related to the split. First, coming to therapy had emphasized for Marcy that men can relate towards women differently from the model that she and Gerry shared. Both the general practitioner who had referred them, and I, had presented as men genuinely concerned with her and her family's welfare, rather than Gerry's aloof, withdrawn manner. Secondly, Marcy had realized much more how frustrated she had been with Gerry's self-focused attitudes. For years he had centred his energies on to his job, relying on Marcy for support, but never really asserting himself until recently to better himself financially. All the events that had happened to them, culminating in Gerry's malady, had drawn Marcy more and more into the 'carer' role. Gerry had not been there for her during the times of the hoaxes, Colin's death or her boss's crises. What had finally affirmed for Marcy that Gerry was unlikely to change was her mother's recent debilitating illness. Gerry had offered no time to listen to Marcy's concerns and anxieties about Rita's demise.

Since the separation, Gerry had moved back with his parents. He had told them, and Marcy, that he was not going to stay with a wife who was not committed to giving him her full attention in his 'final illness'. Gerry's parents had appeared quite eager to accommodate him. Alex and Jasmine enjoyed regular fortnightly access with Gerry, and reported that they shared much of the visits with their grandparents, while their father, who had ceased his employment and was on an invalid pension, sat around at home watching reruns of old westerns on the television. Over six weekly sessions, Marcy expressed her feelings of guilt that she had left a 'dying man'. In retrospect, she had been considering leaving Gerry several years previously, but the onset of his multiple sclerosis had influenced her to stay. We talked for a while about fantasy and reality. The reality was that Gerry had a potentially serious and disabling condition, but that the likelihood was that he might well be able to support his family if he chose until their children were young adults and independent. I wondered how much of Gerry's decision to give up the fight was linked to his not maintaining the patriarchal privileges that had seemed so dear to him. We finished by discussing Marcy's future options: assertiveness to her in-laws and their expectations; dealing with possible power plays; laying down boundaries around her own territory; and countering community attitudes towards her as a 'deserting' wife.

· · ·

DISCUSSION

Defining the problem

Gerry's and Marcy's description: They tell of their frustration and dis-jointed experience of marriage. Gerry feels that it is not as severe as Marcy states.
Marcy's and Gerry's construction: Both relate their stresses to the many crises which they have experienced.

Exploring the context

Therapist's affirmation: The strength with which Gerry and Marcy have persisted with their struggles is admired, and a suggestion made that perhaps there has been no time to grieve. We discuss the families of origin and how interaction has been gerrymandered more towards the satisfaction of men. Marcy comments that she and her sister always found this a bit unfair, whereas there had been no objection in Gerry's family. We talk about stoic male heroes and their gentle, supportive women, and they are asked to reverse roles: would Gerry take charge of expressing emotions while Marcy look after the practical aspects of family life?

Options for the future

Mutual reconstruction: After ceasing therapy, and an initial improve-ment, Marcy and Gerry decide to separate eight months later. Marcy tells how she learnt in therapy that men can respect women and not expect them to be an appendage of their experience. Gerry states to Marcy that he wants her total attention now that he has a final ill-ness. His parents offer to give him that sort of care and he moves in with them, also retiring from work. The children visit him regularly, and Marcy begins to see her life differently, asserting her own needs and wants.

——————————— · · · ———————————

CASE STUDY

Case 12D   Halloween
Jane, 42, secretary in a cytotechnology department, and her sons Patrick, 14, and Michael, 12, attended our initial therapy session principally because of Michael's increasing nightmares. These had commenced a few months previously following Patrick's hospitalization for an episode

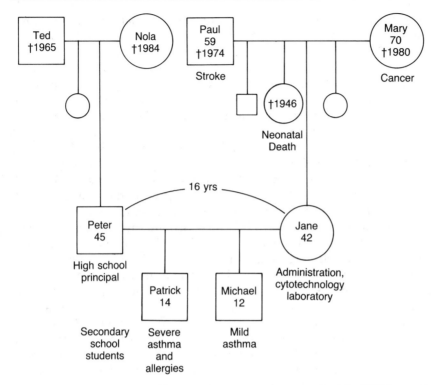

Fig. 12.4 Jane, Patrick and Michael commenced therapy in July 1990.

of asthma, during which he had almost died. Indeed, much of the family's activities over the past several years had centred around Patrick's condition. Not only had he been hospitalized two to three times annually, the whole family's diet and the house furnishings – carpet, curtains, pillows, interior of sofas and chairs – had been changed in an effort to alleviate Patrick's skin and eye allergies. Michael, usually a sufferer of mild asthma, was also experiencing increasing difficulty with his breathing, and an exacerbated cough.

Jane described her husband Peter, 45, a high-school principal, as a caring partner and father. Peter and Jane had not known whether Peter's presence would be necessary at our first session, and he was certainly prepared to come in the future if need be. The boys were achieving above average academically, and they seemed to get on well with both their teachers and peers.

Being focused on Patrick's illness for so long, and involved in busy and fulfilling careers, Jane and Peter spent little leisure time together and with friends, and there were few occasions when the four enjoyed each other as a family. Another problem was that both Peter's and Jane's parents had died, and there was little extended family support. Jane said that she and Peter felt isolated in their struggles.

I asked Michael about his nightmares. He told me that he continually dreamed of the horrific personage of Michael Myers (the character portrayed in the film *Halloween*) stalking him with a huge blood-dripping knife. Michael Myers would almost slice him, when he would wake up screaming in a sea of sweat.

I wondered in my mind whether Michael was angry at the whole situation and, in his dream, was taking the anger out on himself. I also wondered how much of Michael's anger was due to grieving over lost attention, little family fun, death of the grandmothers, and fear of Patrick's future decline. I decided to keep those musings to myself.

I commended the family on the sensitivity and care that they showed towards each other. I was very impressed that Patrick, though enduring his own serious stresses, was concerned about Michael's distress and had come along to this session. Their family had undergone a great deal of crisis and loss – illness and death – over the years, and it was a nice thing to see two brothers loving each other in such circumstances. I asked Michael if he liked drawing, and when Michael nodded that he did, asked him if he would create a picture of Michael Myers locked away in a safe place from where he could not escape. I also asked Patrick if he would plan a fun activity for the family; they were all hard workers and deserved a treat. We agreed to meet again in a month.

During our next session, which Peter also attended, Michael said that his nightmares had ceased and his asthmatic symptoms had eased. Michael showed me his picture of Michael Myers (Fig. 12.5), banished to the depths of Hell! Michael had even singed the edges of the picture with flame to increase the effect.

'Your Michael Myers is smiling', I noted. 'Perhaps he is contented being in Hell? Perhaps he will stay there and not bother you any more?'

Patrick said that the family had spent their treat during an afternoon at a ten-pin bowling alley.

I congratulated Michael for having handled his fears so effectively, and Patrick for enabling the family to reward and enjoy themselves. Our conversation turned to ways in which the family could continue to support each other more adequately. Because of work and school routines, they did not often sit down together, even at mealtimes. We planned a family meeting once a week, during which everyone could express their successes and concerns. I commented that, when struggle and crises were predominant in families, it was often difficult for people to feel good about themselves and one another. Would they put a 'gold star chart' on the wall, and every time someone did an act

Fig. 12.5 Michael's drawing.

that made another feel good about themselves, would the beneficiary award the giver a gold star?

I did not see the family again in therapy. Six months later, Michael has no further nightmares and both boys' asthma is well contained on their medication.

――――――――― . . . ―――――――――

DISCUSSION

Defining the problem

Family's description: The family describes the distress of Michael's nightmares.
Family's construction: The family considers the problem to be Michael's, and express their wishes to help him.

Exploring the context

Therapist's affirmation: I wonder if the dreams represent Michael's anger and grief over the grandmothers' deaths and lost opportunities for family fun, and fears regarding Patrick's illness and possible imminent death? These ideas are kept to myself. Family members are complimented on their dedication to each other, and particularly Patrick on the support that he gives his brother. Michael is asked to draw Michael Myers locked up safely, and Patrick is requested to plan a family fun activity.

Options for the future

Mutual reconstruction: Michael shows me his picture, Patrick tells of the family treat, the nightmares are gone, and Michael's asthma is improved. We plan some activities for future contact (weekly family meetings) and affirmation (gold star chart).

SUMMARY

In Chapter 12 we considered:
Case 12A, 'Bad luck', in which Nigel blames Fleur's depression as the cause of his cancer.
Case 12B, 'Lady in red', in which Charmaine is encouraged to review how her self-image has changed within the context of her chronic asthma.

Case 12C, 'The gerrymander', in which Gerry's diagnosis of multiple sclerosis alters the power balance in the family.
Case 12D, 'Halloween', in which Michael dreams up and draws out his anger.

POINTS FOR REFLECTION

1. Compare and contrast Cases 12A, 'Bad luck', and 12C, 'The gerrymander'. What similarities and differences do you note?
2. I am not entirely satisfied with the outcome in Case 12C. Perhaps I did not engage Gerry adequately in therapy? What else might you have done to involve him more in the therapeutic process?
3. Describe some of your own cases involving physical illness using the 'Affirmation' and 'Deconstruction' schemas.

Remarried/blended families

13

· · ·

CASE STUDY

Case 13A   The law clerk

Tracy, 25, a law clerk, said that she had been depressed for a few weeks and requested therapy to consider her past and present relationships and to make some informed choices about her future. Her experience with men had always been somewhat painful, commencing with her father Nicos, whom Tracy described as a strict, moral autocrat who seemed to represent 'justice without mercy'. Nicos had died of cancer when Tracy was 16. When she was 20, Tracy became involved with Carlo, a builder. An only son, Carlo had proven devoted to his parents, spending many evenings and weekends visiting them. Tracy and her boyfriend quarrelled frequently about how much time they were to spend with his family, and after four years, Carlo ended the relationship. Soon afterwards, Tracy fell in love with her boss Murray, 32, manager of an airline company. Tracy worked in the administration section of the company as Murray's secretary, and they began an affair. Murray had told Tracy on several occasions that he loved her deeply and eventually wanted their marriage. He said that he was in the process of leaving his wife, but had found the idea of 'deserting' his children distressing. Frustrated with Murray's hesitation, Tracy had endeavoured to end the relationship. She stopped seeing him and formed a friendship with Dave, a forklift driver. Tracy described Dave as 'pleasant but dull', and they had parted six months later. Murray had approached Tracy to 'try once more' and, five months ago, had left Nicole, 32, a medical receptionist, and his children Boyd, 6, and Lara, 3, to live with Tracy in rented accommodation. Six weeks ago, Tracy had resigned as Murray's secretary to obtain her current position as a law clerk.

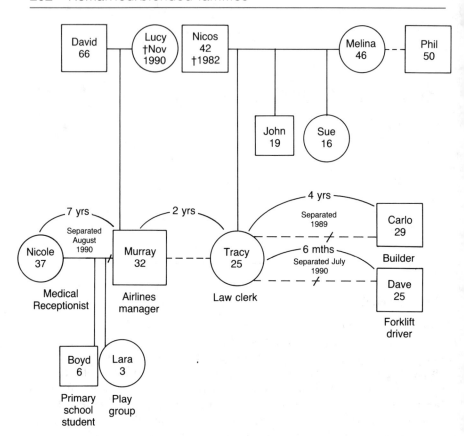

Fig. 13.1 Tracy commenced therapy in January 1991.

Tracy's current dilemma was that, although Murray said that he was committed to their eventual marriage, he had kept their relationship secret and seemed unwilling to discuss future plans in a concrete way.

'I am bothered about Murray's whole attitude', Tracy said. 'He won't make any legal moves towards divorce. He won't talk about running our household. He is always stressing how he misses the kids and how hard his work is, and the cost of living. It is hard for me too! And he is always running over to his family, fixing tap washers, repairing gutters, whenever Nicole calls for help. He is a bit like my Dad, always wanting to run the whole show how he sees it, not listening to anyone else. I want a husband, not a bloody manager!'

I praised Tracy for her persistence in her search to eventually find a rewarding intimacy; many others might have given up by now. I could also understand her anger, considering the discounting treatment she had experienced in several of her relationships with men. Perhaps some of this anger was now inwardly channelled and contributing to her low spirits? I asked Tracy if she would encourage Murray to come to a joint therapy session, and if she would compile a list of pros and cons for continuing the relationship.

At our second weekly session, still attending on her own, Tracy shared her list with me (Table 13.1). Tracy said that she had experienced herself getting angrier as she wrote of Murray's delays in contributing mutually to the costs of the household, and telling his family and friends about their relationship. There were too many secrets. He had hesitated also about coming to therapy, saying that he needed a little more time to think about it. I decided to work with Tracy on her relationships with men. I asked her if she was willing to wait to see if Murray did attend therapy, to continue to invite him along, and to write a list of things that they did have in common. Tracy agreed to wait a little longer.

At our third session, Tracy showed me her list of things that she and

Table 13.1 Tracy's list of pros and cons for continuing her relationship with Murray

Pros	Cons
Intelligent	Short temper
Handsome	Being taken for a ride by his wife
Confident	Won't talk about our future
Sensitive, most of the time	Won't contribute his financial share
Well dressed	of bills, i.e. only pays for rent. I have
Gets on well with people	to buy groceries, things for house,
Always tells me how much he loves	etc.
me and how happy he is to be with	Won't see a solicitor for his rights as
me	a separated husband, just pays wife
Looks after his health and fitness	what she asks for
Is a good provider for his wife and	Too serious about his sport i.e.
children, i.e. he financially supports	triathlons to the extent that he feels
them	guilty if he misses training etc.
Always looking for things to do,	Hasn't told his family about me
places to go rather than sit at home	Hasn't told me much about his past
Helps with housework . . . sometimes	family (I feel like there's so many
Brings me flowers out of the blue	secrets)
Rings me up during the day to tell	
me he misses me	
Helps with my family, e.g. ideas as	
to how to approach my younger	
brother and sister about their	
problems as teenagers	
Helps others, e.g. friends with their	
work problems etc.	

Murray had in common: music; both getting along with other people; being on an equal footing in a crowd; being mentally synchronized; food; same line of work; films and television shows; appreciating nice scenery, e.g. beaches, forest; both being affectionate, e.g. we can express our love for each other, kissing, cuddling; love of children.

Over the next three sessions we discussed the qualities represented in Tracy's list and the other elements necessary in successful intimate relating: knowing the resources and limitations of a partnership; knowing one's needs and how to ask for their satisfaction; dealing with rejection; learning about our intimates, and avoiding 'mind-reading' – assuming that we know what our partners want without checking it out; planning future routines and negotiating respectfully; and, more specifically, problems related to divorce and remarriage. I commented that Tracy might have had some difficulty learning about these qualities in her youth. Her father seemed to have been a man unwilling to entertain the idea of mutual interaction within relationships, or of acknowledging other people's needs. Tracy said that Murray had informed his parents of their friendship and I congratulated her on getting her point across, something that she had rarely been able to do with her Dad.

At our sixth session, Murray came with Tracy. He described Tracy as too impatient, and that she was not giving him enough time to leave Nicole, Boyd and Lara. Murray affirmed that not only had he approached his parents about the new situation, he had also approached a lawyer for advice regarding divorce. As we talked, it became clear that both Murray and Tracy had invested a great deal of energy in living up to the expectations of their previous intimates. Though highly competent in his work environment, Murray had yielded to Nicole on almost every family decision.

'That is the way that Mum and Dad used to do it', commented Murray. 'Mum was a great organizer and Dad used to help her at every turn.'

As an only child, and shy of his school peers, Murray had rarely discussed or seen other modes of family life during his formative years. On the contrary, Tracy had rarely deferred to Nicos, who had wanted a traditional lifestyle for his daughter, with marriage to a kinsman, lots of babies and much play between grandparents and grandchildren. Tracy felt that she had spent much of her life rebelling against this. So, in their families of origin, Murray appeared to have been the 'sensitive and caring helper' always supporting his family's needs over his own, and Tracy might be regarded as the 'person who kept things cooking', always trying to stir the pot and introduce a new flavour.

I decided to weave the theme of 'lost opportunities' into our conversation.

'It sounds, Murray, as if in your original family your role was to help keep your home calm and peaceful', I said. 'Mum was the prime mover and you and Dad supported her. Perhaps you slipped into the same role with Nicole, constantly following her lead? Yet you may have regretted, and be grieving, the many lost moments when you wanted to create your own impact. Tracy, you sound as if you were the revolutionary in your original family, always wanting to improve the variety of family life. In so doing, you appear to have antagonized your Dad, and may now be sorrowing to have missed out on many warmer moments with him. Murray appears to have missed out on independence, and Tracy on closeness, and you both may feel it important now to achieve these things in your new relationship. Yet your roles seem to me to have changed. Murray, you now appear to be the independent revolutionary in leaving Nicole for Tracy and setting up a new life with her, and you, Tracy, seem to be asserting your desire for closeness in wanting a stable, secure and committed match with Murray. Perhaps some of your current struggles are grounded in getting used to these new roles. Would you, Tracy, write a letter to your father describing how you are experiencing your relationship with Murray differently? Having told your parents about Tracy and sought legal advice, would you, Murray, continue to plan a direction that offers safety for you both?'

At our seventh session, Tracy read out her letter to Murray and me:

Dear Dad,
You know I always found it hard to talk to you. The fear of you and my respect for you prevented me. I always wanted to tell you that I loved you and felt your pain as you tried to raise us the way you thought was best. It was very painful and frustrating for me because I missed out on a lot of fun that the other kids were having. I understood your reasons were justifiable to you because as far as you were concerned you were doing it for my own good. You did not realise that you were taking a lot away from me. I was scared and embarrassed in front of the other kids because they laughed and thought I was unsociable. They could not understand why I did not want to participate in such harmless behaviour as walking home from school together. It was even harder to answer their questions, to make excuses. The worse thing is that I feel as if it was never resolved, even to this day.

It is still hard for me to talk to you because I still fear your responses. I know that you would not be agreeable with the way I have conducted my life. In a sense I do not agree with it either. All along I wished and prayed that I would meet a Greek person, marry him and have his children; all done the 'proper' way as you would have approved of. But the harder I tried, the further away I got. I spent years of my life trying so hard to give everything to someone who would grant my wish and yours but in the end he just walked away. I was ashamed of myself. I felt cheated and used. I felt your disappointment in me. I can still feel that disappointment. I tried to start anew, swore to myself that it would not happen to me again. But it did – it is still happening and I am so scared. I know you are not in approval. He is not Greek. He is married with children belonging to another woman. I know he is not son-in-law material. I know that his upbringing was completely different to mine. I know that he has all these faults and more, but what I know the most of all is that I love him so very much!! I want him to be there for me forever. I want him to become that man that I have always dreamt of marrying. I want him to father those children that I have for so long dreamt of having; those children who would be your grandchildren. I want you to accept him so that I too can accept him totally. I want to stop feeling that I am doing wrong by pursuing this road. I want you to help me through the rough times. I need your approval.

I want to be able to put the past away. I want the guilt to stop haunting me so that I can make this relationship work. This is what I want more than anything else in the whole world. I want to be given the chance mentally to make my life and my future a success.

I know Murray has his hang ups and he is quite stubborn at times and I wish it would be easier for him to let go of his past and his guilt associated with his past so that the effort can be put into us and our future together. But on the same token I am proud of him for providing for his family. I am glad he did not just walk away without second glance. It proves that he is a caring and sensitive person. I know too that if it were not for his responsibilities to his family, he could be the sort of person you might approve of; except his nationality, of course. I know however that in time you would probably be able to overlook that 'flaw'. I know also that you would not be able to overlook that he was married and had his own family. I know that you would believe that I would never be as good to him as his first family, that he would always put them first, think of them first, feel sad for the things he would be missing in their lives. I know this for a fact because I am a part of you, you created me and I think exactly the same things as you would. I know you would be saying that I deserve better. I know that you were proud of me and that you want me to be worthy of your pride. I want that too, more than you will ever know. Please do not feel that I have let you down. I

could not handle it! I need the chance, the courage, the trust and the love to make it work. I do not want a miserable future, it is not what I am aiming for. I am seeking happiness and fulfillment and when I get it, I can prove to you the worthiness of your pride in me.
Love,
Tracy

This letter introduced many themes for conversation: Did Tracy and Murray's relationship have to succeed so that Tracy could gain Nicos' approval, and was this inducing Tracy to pressure Murray into action? Was Tracy choosing Murray as a partner for his own worth, or to gain the love that she had missed out on from Nicos? Did Tracy desire children so that she would prove to be a kinder and more understanding parent than her father?

Murray said that he had started to express more of his feelings to Tracy: sadness at the loss of his family; guilt at leaving his first family for what he believed would be a more rewarding experience with Tracy; anxiety at the admonishment that might come from their friends when all was made public. Murray had been pleasantly surprised that Tracy had tended to his feelings. He had thought that 'all women are the same', getting on with their own lives and wanting their men to be competent and undemanding followers. Both Tracy and Murray had sat down together and organized a sharing budget!

Our last five sessions were spent building on these successes. We considered issues of respecting private time when each was occupied in activities away from the other. We talked more about how Murray could express his anger respectfully, rather than withdrawing into the position of being a resentful follower. We discussed how Boyd and Lara could fit in to family routines more comfortably whenever they visited during access. Previously, Murray had always visited the children at the family home, but by the time of our last session, Boyd and Lara had spent their first Saturday afternoon with 'Daddy and his friend Tracy', and divorce proceedings were under way. Finally, I commented that both of them had mentioned that they carried a large amount of guilt and shame from the past, and we looked at ways that they could support each other. I mentioned that my wife wrote on a recent 20th wedding anniversary card that 'our failures can be seen as stepping stones to wiser actions', and I often find that thought a comfort.

DISCUSSION

Defining the problem

Tracy's description: Tracy tells of her depression and her desire to make some informed choices about her relationships.

Tracy's construction: Tracy discloses her many unhappy relationships with men, commencing with her father, and culminating in her current struggles with Murray whom she wishes to marry.

Exploring the context

Therapist's affirmation: Tracy's determination to achieve a successful relationship given her past distressing experiences is admired, and her anger validated. Tracy is encouraged to invite Murray into therapy, and through writing, to examine the strengths and danger points of their friendship.

Joint session

Murray's description: Murray blames Tracy for being impatient and not allowing him enough time to get used to the new situation.

Murray's construction: It becomes clear later in therapy that Murray believes that 'All women are leaders of men', and he is resentful of this.

Therapist's deconstruction: We discuss Murray's and Tracy's families of origin: how in Murray's family cohesiveness was preserved at the expense of individual independence, and how in Tracy's family individuality and change were achieved at the expense of closeness. I suggest that perhaps Tracy and Murray have reversed roles in their new situation: Murray, the follower, is finding a new direction (telling his parents about Tracy, procuring legal advice), while Tracy, the explorer, is seeking firmer ground (wanting mutual negotiations, planning a household budget). This may be stressing them. Tracy is asked to write a letter to her father expressing her feelings, and Murray to explore how his new direction can lead to safety for them both.

Options for the future

Mutual reconstruction: Tracy's letter reveals how her feelings about Nicos may be influencing her attitudes towards Murray. Murray has been telling some of his sorrow to Tracy, who tends to him. Some issues for the future: dealing with guilt; budgeting; arranging access for Lara and Boyd; progressing with the divorce, are considered and put into action.

CASE STUDY

Case 13B   The hero

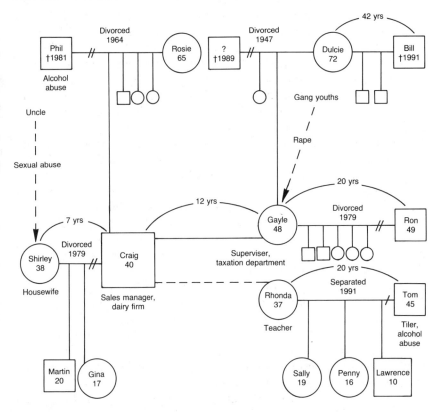

Fig. 13.2 Craig commenced therapy in October 1991.

At our first session, Craig, 40, sales manager with a dairy firm, told of his frustration and despondency in pursuing intimate relationships. He wondered if he would ever be able to make a rewarding and durable match?

There had been numerous women in his past. Craig said that he always had 'a bit of an eye for the ladies' during his youth, and this had led to a 'shotgun' wedding with Shirley when he was 21. Although he had made a commitment to monogamy, Craig continued to have a series of lovers unbeknown to his wife, and they had finally separated and divorced when Craig was 28. Shirley had moved interstate with their two children, Martin and Gina, and Craig had little contact with them. Craig had been involved in an affair with Gayle, a tax department supervisor nine years his senior, for about two years before he and Shirley parted, and they soon married. This was a different experience from Craig's first match. Gayle was perfectly happy to plan and organize much of their lives, together with those of her five children from her marriage to Ron, her first husband. Craig said that he felt more like an 'elder brother' than a parent to Gayle's children. After the children had all grown to young adulthood and left home, some ten years later, Craig had fallen in love and commenced an affair with Rhonda, a primary-school teacher, who was in the process of leaving her own violent, alcohol-abusing husband, Tom, a tiler. Rhonda and Tom had separated 18 months later and Craig visited Rhonda, Penny and Lawrence, who lived in the country about two hours' drive away from Melbourne, on weekends. The eldest daughter Sally lived with Tom, and appeared to support his case against her mother. Craig had recently informed Gayle about his relationship with Rhonda. Gayle was encouraging her husband to end the affair and work on their marriage. Craig said that he was now filled with doubts, and a sense of shame concerning his various infidelities: Could he ever maintain a monogamous relationship? How could he make a permanent and enduring commitment to a partner? Should he proceed with reconciliation with Gayle, or follow a new future with Rhonda?

I agreed to meet with Craig weekly and asked him two questions: If he were to invite Gayle or Rhonda to a joint therapy session, which person would come with him? and, would he compose a list of qualities that he, Rhonda and Gayle contributed to their relationships?

At our second session, Craig said that he had thought long and hard about who would join us in therapy. He had decided that, in the first instance, he did not want to invite Gayle at all, and secondly, he chose at this stage not to hassle Rhonda, who was struggling to counter Tom's vehement and threatening phonecalls.

'It sounds to me as if you have decided a future path with your lover', I suggested. 'You seem very protective of Rhonda, that she avoid more stresses than she can handle at present, and do not want Gayle involved in our conversation in any way. I wonder if you are being fair to Gayle? She seems to be working hard to resuscitate your marriage, while you appear to lean towards separation. Should you be residing with Gayle, offering her false hope, if you have definitely determined to leave?'

We examined Craig's list (Table 13.2)

'I wonder if there is something Freudian and Oedipal going on here?', I commented to Craig, who had read a number of psychological texts. 'The qualities you have noted for Gayle sound very appropriate in a mother, whereas the traits that you attribute to Rhonda, even

Table 13.2 Graig's list of qualities that he, Rhonda, and Gayle have contributed to their relationships

Craig	Rhonda	Gayle
Positive qualities		
Caring	Caring	Caring
Sensual	Sensual	Sexually acquiescent
Hard-working	Hard-working	Hard-working
Logical	Fun-loving	
Monogamous?	Monogamous?	Monogamous
Loyal	Loyal	Loyal
Law-abiding	Law-abiding	Law-abiding
Supportive	Supportive	Supportive
Sensitive	Sensitive	
Gardener	Gardener	Cook
Self-sufficient	Self-sufficient	Clings
	Communicative?	Frugal
	Erotic	
	Daring	
	Psychologically equal	
	Houseproud	
	Exposes underneath	
	Mothering	
Accepts family	Accepts family	
	Intelligent	
Negative qualities		
Uncommunicative		Uncommunicative
Moody	Moody	Unexpressive
Overworks	Fiery	Lacks confidence
Perverse	Illogical	Narrow interests
Dogmatic	Naive	Unaccepting of family
Frugal	Spendthrift	Ex in-law contact
Undomesticated		Poor budgeting
Flirt	Flirt	

though you have included 'mothering', describe a lover who might well develop into a mutual partner. Perhaps an original agenda with Gayle was to receive more sound 'mothering' after your prolonged and tempestuous 'adolescence' with Shirley, and having settled, you now want to try a more balanced 'adulthood'? Is that your dilemma? – to change the nature of your marriage with Gayle, who is willing to try, or proceed with Rhonda, whom you experience more as an equal?'

We discussed Craig's family of origin. His father, Phil, had been a ferocious, alcohol-abusing husband to Craig's mother Rosie, often beating her. Craig remembered climbing out of the window on more than one occasion to call the police. As we talked about Phil's violations, Craig recalled that both Shirley and Gayle had been sexually abused during their adolescence, Shirley by an uncle, Gayle by a gang of youths. I decided to continue the 'Freudian' theme.

'Perhaps you were cast early, by your original family, into the role of hero? – rescuing your mother and wives from the clutches of villainous men? Perhaps part of your struggle is that you want to change this pattern, but now find yourself rescuing Rhonda from a snarling Tom? Will you and Rhonda be able to develop a respectful love for each other out of this, or are you condemned to follow a script that was written for you by others long ago?'

Our next four sessions dealt with lost opportunities that often occur when people follow scripts written for them by others. Craig must have missed out on a great deal of protection, safety and security when he was growing up, due to Phil's violence. Phil and Rosie could hardly be said to have modelled adequate social skills for him. Perhaps some of his adolescent and young adult sexual encounters had been a desperate attempt to develop different social skills, and fill the emotional emptiness and comfort the sorrows within him? Or perhaps he had been continuing to play the hero, rescuing fair maidens at one level or another? It sounded as if he had found stability and nurturing in the early years of his marriage with Gayle, but had discovered a different way of relating with Rhonda. Now he appeared to desire a permanent bond in a future marriage that would not be troubled by the patterns of the past. Considering Craig's story, I could well understand his despondency and grief, that he felt his attempts at intimacy had led to nowhere and that he was in danger of becoming a lonely old man.

During our seventh session, Craig said that he was experiencing panic attacks. I suggested that these might be stage fright, and that he seemed to be in the position of having to make a definite decision: to continue the patterns of the past, perhaps leaving Gayle and Rhonda to find a new person to rescue, or to act with integrity to himself and others, tell Gayle of his intentions, leave, and progress so that he and Rhonda could support each other more effectively.

By our eighth session, Craig said that he had left Gayle and was now living with friends and was looking for rented accommodation. Over the next six sessions many events occurred. Gayle started to express her anger and bitterness towards Craig. Craig had previously told me that he thought that Gayle would be furious and vengeful towards him if he did leave. I suggested that Gayle's anger appeared to be reasonable, part of her own grief, and Craig came to accept this without becoming defensive towards her. They were now entering into a constructive property settlement. Tom, who was known to the police for drug dealing and other criminal activities, continued his harassment of

Rhonda. Sally visited Rhonda's house one evening when Craig was visiting and smashed up his car thoroughly with a baseball bat.

'Perhaps Tom has put out a contract on you', I queried, 'and used Sally as his hit-woman?'

Craig and Rhonda arranged police and legal protection, and Sally and Tom are now repaying the costs of damage. Penny had left for 14 months' schooling in Japan as an exchange student. Rhonda had obtained enormous emotional support from Penny, and was grieving her departure. Craig had discussed with Rhonda how he might offer support of his own.

I complimented Craig on these achievements. It is not an easy task to divorce turbulent partners. He and Rhonda may have found the experience a bit like living in the front-line trenches of Europe in 1916, not being able to move forwards or backwards, and not knowing when or where the next artillery shell was going to land. Perhaps the only thing to do in such circumstances was to live day by day, supporting and comforting each other, while waiting for the powers that be to end the war. Would he continue to explore with Rhonda ways to nourish each other and gain some rest and recreation during these tough times?

Six months later, Craig, Rhonda and Lawrence have moved into joint accommodation.

· · ·

DISCUSSION

Defining the problem

Craig's description: Craig describes his frustration, despondency and sense of shame at his repeated infidelities. He doubts whether he will ever form a stable intimacy, and does not know whether to choose his wife or his lover as a future partner.

Craig's construction: Craig believes his struggles to be due to personal inadequacies in forming relationships.

Exploring the context

Therapist's deconstruction: First, Craig is asked to consider his current position: Who would join him in therapy – Gayle or Rhonda? What similarities and differences do he, Rhonda and Gayle share? Out of these conversations, it seems that Craig has decided to leave Gayle and partner Rhonda, and I comment on the equity of his present stance in residing with Gayle, who wants reconciliation.

We examine Craig's family of origin and his loss of emotional security and safety during youth due to Phil's violence. I comment that most people coming out of abusive families struggle with what they have learnt in them. Rather than a sign of personal weakness, some of Craig's past tempestuous relationships might be regarded as a desperate attempt to learn about social skills differently from the model he witnessed in his parents, or an 'acting out' of his grief, or playing the role of 'rescuer to helpless women', as he appears to have done with his mother. I suggest that this may be part of Craig's current dilemma – to change the patterns of the past, or to continue them? Craig develops panic attacks and his need to make a decision promptly is emphasized.

Options for the future

Mutual reconstruction: Craig leaves Gayle, faces her anger respectfully, and commences negotiating a fair property settlement. Sally smashes Craig's car and he and Rhonda seek protection and compensation successfully. Penny leaves for overseas and Craig offers support to Rhonda. Craig's achievements are affirmed, and he and Rhonda are encouraged to continue finding ways of nourishing one another until their crisis is over.

——————————— · · · ———————————

CASE STUDY

Case 13C   Another design

Wanda, 43, an award-winning fashion designer, sought help for her increasing sense of depression, emptiness, loss of energy, lack of confidence and obesity. Wanda's feelings had become troublesome to her about six weeks ago, when she had remarried her ex husband Edwin, 45, a theologian. Wanda and Edwin had decided on the arrangement after he had entered what was believed by his doctors to be the final stage of AIDS. Edwin had informed Wanda that his solicitor had advised remarriage as the best means of distributing his assets to their daughters Nerissa, 16, and Dahlia, 14, after his death. As it turned out, Wanda had just discovered that Edwin had nominated his current friend Daisy, 37, a choreographer, executrix to his will, and there was precious little property to leave the daughters anyway! Wanda said she was overwhelmed at Edwin's seeming duplicity.

Three generations of Wanda's family had been touched by some of the major upheavals of our century. Her maternal grandparents were killed in Russia during the Stalinist purges of the 1930s, and the first family of her father Solomon, 81, was lost in a Nazi concentration

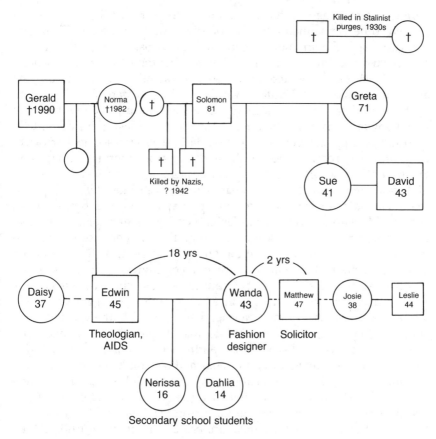

Fig. 13.3 Wanda commenced therapy in May 1991.

camp. Wanda's childhood memories of her mother Greta, 71, were of an angry person continually berating the often withdrawn and uncommunicative Solomon. When her father did respond, it was usually in a disparaging and demeaning manner. They did not seem to have had much time to spend with their daughters. Wanda and her younger sister, Sue, had found solace in each other's company in this unhappy situation, and were still close. Sue was contented in her present marriage with David, though they had not been able to conceive children. Wanda left home and pursued a career as fashion designer. At 27, she had become attracted to Edwin for his physical and intellectual attributes and his apparent sensitivity and sense of fun. Greta and Solomon had objected vociferously to the relationship, and when Edwin and Wanda married the parents refused all contact with them and, eventually, their granddaughters. Though stable during the initial period, the marriage started to founder in the early 1970s, when Edwin proved to be very much a 'seeker of Truth' outside the family sphere. He would spend many hours at encounter groups, communes, ashrams and poetry readings, and rarely devoted his time to earning income. It had been up to Wanda to support the family financially, as well as raise Nerissa and Dahlia. Wanda finally decided she wanted to continue on her own, and although she and Edwin parted without too much obvious acrimony, he rarely showed an interest in his daughters. Solo life had proven rewarding. Wanda had progressed in her career until she had reached her peak, and she was offering Nerissa and Dahlia both a secular and a Jewish education. They were achieving high academic results, and appeared to be well liked by their peers. Wanda looked forward to the time, perhaps five years hence, when she would be able to retire from fashion designing and follow her great love of portrait and landscape painting. Part of her disenchantment with her vocation was that, although she had risen to the top of her profession, the male members of several committees in which she was involved appeared to discount her input because she was female. She was tired of countering their 'conservative attitudes'. Two years previously, Wanda had entered a friendship with Matthew, now 47, a solicitor. She had been attracted to his eloquence, intelligence and charm. Wanda was to discover that Matthew lied eloquently, embezzled company funds intelligently, and charmed several lovers outside their relationship. Matthew was currently involved with Josie, 38, lead singer in a rock band, who had seen her own mother murdered several years ago in a South American revolution. Josie was married to Leslie, and both Matthew and Josie seemed undecided about the future of their affair. It was all very complex. Wanda said that she was aggravated that she had made the same mistake twice – having been attracted to men who seemingly respected her, and finding out later that they were unreliable and irresponsible. Wanda said she felt a 'fool in love'!

First, I affirmed Wanda's successes regarding her career and daughters. Then I decided to weave the theme of 'patriarchal privileges' into our conversation. We discussed how, so often, many men consider their female partners as appendages of their experience. For many men there seemed to be a basic injunction within our society: 'I am entitled to certain inalienable rights, and you, my female partner, are responsible to ensure that I receive them'. Both Edwin and Matthew seemed to follow these codes. Initially, the 'chemistry' between Wanda and her partners seemed to have been right – matching physical, emotional and intellectual qualities – but the men appeared soon to have begun demanding their 'patriarchal privileges' and ignoring Wanda's, Nerissa's and Dahlia's needs.

'I wonder if this was one of the reasons that your Mum appeared so infuriated at your Dad?', I queried. 'Did he slot her into a similar subordinate role?' I asked Wanda to write out a list of what she desired in a rewarding relationship, and would she draw a 'rogues' gallery' of all the men in her life who had mistreated her?

'It is funny that you should ask me to do that', replied Wanda. 'I am already halfway through painting it!'

At our second weekly session we discussed some of the other influences that might have contributed to Wanda's difficulties within intimate relationships. Having to cope with the effects of violation from the Stalinist and Nazi eras, her parents may have been unable to offer Wanda the emotional stability and nourishment that she needed to feel comfortable about herself during her formative years. Wanda may have then sought 'to be loved' by Edwin and Matthew, and this need to be loved may have initially blurred her vision towards some of the more detrimental aspects of her partners.

Wanda showed me her list of needs in a relationship.

What I am looking for in a relationship –
Love, respect, consideration and appreciation of my talent and my needs arising from it, freedom, intelligence, humour, humanity.

Wanda had seen Greta and Solomon continually discounting each other. It must have been a welcome change to have been valued, at first, by her intimates, and offered some of those qualities represented in her list. We considered whether Wanda had married Edwin to create impact, and be different from her parents. We discussed the possibility of Edwin's not-too-distant funeral. Would Wanda attend, and how would she cope? We talked about some of the struggles of children of Holocaust survivors. Some appeared to be superachievers, determining to influence the world positively so that such a tragedy would never occur again. Others seemed to be superfertile, endeavouring to replace the souls that had been lost. Yet others appeared to give up completely, sinking into depression and despair: 'What is the use of doing anything', they seemed to be saying, 'if it can all be swept away by such madness?'

I concluded with the following anecdote: In the late 19th century, a young man, Moshe, saw his father captured and burnt at the stake by the Cossacks during a pogrom in Russia. Immediately Moshe started consuming huge amounts of food until he weighed about 180 kilograms. His friends asked him: 'What are you doing, Moshe? Why are you behaving like this and making yourself so fat and unsightly?' Moshe replied: 'Because when the Cossacks come to burn me, I want them to know that it is not so easy a thing to kill a Jew!'

Over a further six sessions, Wanda seemed to gain in energy and hope for the future, and lose in weight! Edwin died of his AIDS, and

Wanda was able to attend the funeral without undue discomfort. She was not bothered to see that most of the gathering lent their support to Daisy. The event affirmed for Wanda how far into her past Edwin had actually receded before his death. Wanda was now in the process of sifting through her friends, retaining those who gave her mutual support, letting go those who were demanding of her. Matthew had telephoned Wanda for a date after some weeks' absence. Wanda had told him to 'go jump in the lake!' Matthew had been stunned. We talked about future intimacies: What questions did Wanda need to ask of her male companions, during the initial stages of a relationship, to assess whether they were centres of their own universe, or sensitive to others' needs? What observations did she need to make about their past track record regarding relationships? Were they many-times married? Had they left their former partners without paying maintenance or being committed to any form of access with their children? Nerissa and Dahlia were invited to a joint session. They also had let many of their emotional ties with Edwin go before his death, and they expressed their confidence in Wanda that she would see them through to their independence.

At our tenth and final session, I asked a slimmer and more contented Wanda what aspect of therapy did she experience as most helpful towards some of the changes that she had made.

'It was when you asked me to do my list', Wanda replied. 'It convinced me that I had a right to ask for those things on my list in a friendship, and that what I wanted was reasonable and realistic. I feel now that I can stop worrying about what has happened in the past and look more at what I want to do with my future.'

—————————— · · · ——————————

DISCUSSION

Defining the problem

Wanda's description: Wanda tells of her depression, emptiness, loss of energy, decreased confidence and obesity. She traces her symptoms back to when she found that her spouse Edwin had deceived her regarding his will.

Wanda's construction: Wanda says that she feels stupid for having mismanaged two important relationships in the past.

Exploring the context

Therapist's deconstruction: After having affirmed Wanda's vocational and parenting skills, her struggles with her intimates are linked more to the values of her patriarchal partners (and perhaps society in general), rather than to her personal relationship skills. Wanda is asked to list what she desires in an intimacy, and to draw a 'rogues' gallery'. We discuss other events that may have influenced her choice of relationships: her emotional deprivation in youth; her need to be loved; wanting to create an impact on her parents; and the possible effects of being the child of Holocaust survivors. We discuss the possible stresses relating to Edwin's approaching death. An anecdote is told which suggests that Wanda's obesity might be regarded as her protection against future hurts.

Options for the future

Mutual reconstruction: Wanda's mood lifts and she starts to lose weight. She attends Edwin's funeral with no mishap, and Nerissa and Dahlia come to discuss their father's death and give their mother a vote of confidence. Wanda examines her social network, retaining only those friends who are nourishing to her, and discusses how to assess early whether relationships are exploitative or not. She says that composing her list was the most powerful therapeutic event in helping her to consider more reasonable choices for her future.

· · ·

CASE STUDY

Case 13D   The good lad

Alan, 37, an accountant, was anxious, confused and paralysed, unable to make any intelligent decisions about his future. He had enjoyed a stable and pleasant marriage to Fran, 37, a pharmacist, for 12 years. They had pursued their careers, socialized, got on well with each other's families, and spent happy hours with their two sons David and Peter. All had appeared idyllic until Alan had become infatuated with Molly, a speech therapist, at a local Gilbert and Sullivan production two years previously. They had both taken part, Alan as the Judge and Molly as Angelina, the jilted maiden, in *Trial by Jury*, and had commenced an affair during the time of rehearsals. Molly was also one of Alan's current clients.

The affair had been wonderful! quite different to any relationship that Alan had previously experienced. As a gawky, shy, obese adolescent, he had shunned social contact, preferring to spend his leisure at tennis, football and amateur theatre. Alan said he had married Fran because 'it was the right thing to do' and because he feared that no-one else would accept such a 'fat, ugly slob' for a husband. In fact, Alan

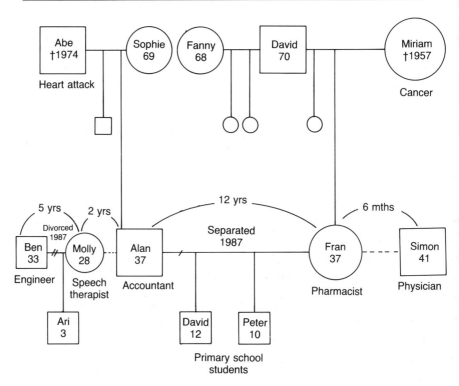

Fig. 13.4 Alan commenced therapy in May 1989.

had lost 25 kilograms in weight the year before he met Molly. She was a 'stunning beauty', and it had been a real boost to his self-image when they had agreed to become lovers. Molly had just divorced her first husband Ben, an engineer, and she had custody of their son Ari. The affair had lasted six months and then Alan had ended it. He had told Fran about it and had determined to see if he could make a go of it with Fran, who wanted to continue their relationship. After a year, Alan left Fran, with both of them deciding that the distance that had developed between them was too large to close. Fran was currently dating Simon, 41, a physician.

Alan's current struggle was how to proceed forwards along his future path? He had no doubt that he and Molly would enjoy a rewarding partnership. They were far more open conversationally than he had ever been with Fran. They enjoyed better sex, were emotionally comfortable, and their social group recognized them as a couple. Moreover, Alan and Ari liked each other and David, Peter, and Ari had become quite good playmates when Alan and Molly shared their weekends with them. However, Alan said that he was plagued with guilt for having betrayed Fran and breaking up their match, and grieving that David and Peter would never know the pleasures of a 'normal family'. Reconciliation with Fran was not an option. Molly was pressing for marriage and more children. To go ahead with these plans would be to lose the dream of a 'normal family' forever.

Alan remembered the early years in his family of origin as happy ones. His parents Abe and Sophie had run a traditional Jewish family. Abe had died of a heart attack when Alan was 20. He had been fond of Abe, a 'wise man', and Alan often wished that his father could be there for him now. Sophie always appeared to have high expectations of both her sons in almost every facet of their lives. Alan had learnt rapidly that it was best for him to be 'the good lad', keeping Sophie contented and proud of him. He rarely contradicted her wishes. Sophie was, of course, devastated by the split with Fran and, although she liked Molly, constantly reminded Alan of the adverse effects of divorce on her grandsons.

I affirmed Alan's determination to understand more about himself, to stop hurting others, and to find suitable solutions that would achieve integrity and fulfilment.

'It sounds as though your affair with Molly might be seen as a bit of naughtiness on your part, against your Mum's wishes', I suggested. 'She seems to have wanted the very best for you: to have a career, marry a nice Jewish girl, have children. Your affair revealed another side of you, one over which she had no control. I wonder what would have happened if you had taken a lover of another faith?'

'You may be right', Alan responded with a half smile. 'I may have wanted to stir Sophie up a bit with my affair, to show her that I have my own independence, but a non-Jewish lover? . . . you want me to kill her off?'

We agreed on weekly therapy, and that future goals would include a lessening of Alan's guilt and sense of disloyalty to Fran, exploring how a 'remarried' situation could succeed, and discovering what actions would be in Alan's best interests, as well as the interests of those close to him.

As therapy progressed, I wove different themes into our conversation which I hoped would shift the focus away from Alan's guilt. There was the theme of 'stagnation': Alan and Fran appeared to have become stuck in a rigid routine. I suggested that sometimes people have extra-marital affairs to learn new information and bring this into their primary intimacy. Alan had endeavoured to enliven his relationship with Fran after his affair with Molly, and this seemed not to have worked. Then there was the theme of 'roles': Fran and Alan appeared to have adopted fixed roles in their marriage that had ultimately proved to be unsatisfying. Could Alan and Molly avoid the same error? Molly came to our fourth session. She stated that she wanted Alan to commence divorce proceedings and move into joint accommodation with her. Molly wanted the focus of their activities to shift on to their future together, rather than remain on Alan's 'emotional leftovers'. It was important for Molly to be able to attend David's approaching Barmitzvah, not as 'the other woman', but as a person recognized by Alan's family with some dignity and status. Molly could only foresee this happening in a circumstance of marriage, and Alan was quick to agree with her: mistresses were not widely respected at Barmitzvahs! Molly said that she was willing to wait for Alan to make a move, but not forever.

As Alan and I continued to meet weekly, we discussed the 'pleasantness of not deciding': being constantly in transition offered Alan the illusion that he had many options open to him, and thus a fair amount of power over his future. Making a definite decision seemed to narrow his range of choices and involved risk-taking. I asked Alan to see the William Hurt–Geena Davis film *The Accidental Tourist*, a film about Macon, a man sleep-walking his way through life (unmoved even by the murder of his young son) until he meets Muriel, a quirky dog trainer who opens his eyes to the emotional aspects of relating with humour and affection. Alan and I considered other themes: commitments – could Alan keep them?; change – travelling towards the unknown; there is no loving without pain; there is a process of letting go after divorce; and Alan's seeming need to control outcomes – attempting to avoid the stresses of change. I reminded Alan of Molly's statement that she would not remain in waiting indefinitely, and asked him what would he be telling himself on his 70th birthday? Which chosen scenario would leave him the bitter, old man?

The topic of reward and punishment came to the fore. Alan had committed adultery and broken one of the major ten commandments. Had he expected to be struck down by a lightning bolt? If so, it had not happened. Was he waiting for the final Divine blow? Sometimes people test the mercy of the Almighty. It was unfortunate that Alan had become involved in an extramarital relationship, but perhaps that is all it was . . . regrettable. Alan seemed to carry a sense of tragedy about the whole event, with its agony, sorrow and struggle. Perhaps he was giving himself a lifelong sentence of guilty suffering for his misdemeanour and denying himself further happiness because of it? Yet would it not be truly evil to keep hesitating and vacillating in this situation, robbing himself, Molly, Fran, their sons and their possible future children, of a more secure and perhaps enriched family life?

Continuity became a theme for discussion. Fran appeared to have been fairly dependent and clinging on Alan, always asking him for advice and guidance. Molly was now requesting closeness. Did Alan interpret Molly's wishes as clinging, whereas perhaps what Molly wanted in fact was continuity, i.e. more contact and availability for refreshment between them? Our final theme was responsibility. Molly had been Alan's client when he had commenced his affair with her. Did Alan feel that he had abused his professional position in entering a sexual relationship with a client? Molly relied on Alan's accounting skills for her taxation preparation and investment of financial assets. This was certainly not as intense a relationship as between doctor and patient, solicitor and client, or lecturer and student, but nonetheless, did Alan feel that he had been professionally irresponsible and unethical in his dealings with Molly? What should judges do when they fall in love with jilted maidens over whom they have to make a judgement? If Alan did feel that he had acted with some lack of integrity, how could he redress that situation?

Therapy lasted for five months. Alan felt considerably less anxious and more comforted by our conversations, but had made no practical moves to resolve his dilemmas.

I saw Molly and Alan together for six weekly sessions about a year later. There had been major changes. Alan was going ahead with divorce proceedings, and he and Molly were living together. The Barmitzvah had passed without any family ostracism of Molly from Alan's family. Alan had moved into a more spacious office. As a result, his practice had grown and he had employed an associate. Alan and Molly were now seeking help because of increasing arguments, largely over the boys' discipline. David had asserted to Molly: 'You cannot tell me what to do. You are not my mother!' Alan commented: 'I told you so, John . . . make a move towards commitment and it all goes awry'. Molly could not understand the nature of the heat between them. She was happy with their progress and felt more than ever that they were a couple, yet everything seemed to be falling apart.

'It is all going wrong', Molly said.

I suggested that, rather than being a deterioration, their fighting was more to do with accommodating to the new situation and changing for the better than falling apart. This was a common circumstance at the beginning of a family's formation. We discussed the negotiating patterns between Alan and Molly, and those that they had observed in their families of origin. Both families had designated men as cool thinkers and women as passionate expressers of emotion. I commented that both these aspects of problem-solving were important: cool thinking to consider all information offered, and passionate expression to persevere, brainstorm and find solutions. The only possible problem, as I saw it, was that these roles had been fixed according to gender. Would Molly and Alan reverse places, Molly becoming the rational person and

Alan the emotional expresser? We discussed a theme concerning the discipline of children within remarried/blended families, that I had previously found useful: rather than be seen as surrogate parents to each other's children, Alan could be regarded as Molly's support in the discipline of her son Ari, and Molly could be seen as supporting Alan in his care of David and Peter.

A year later, Alan has secured his divorce and the new family – Molly, Alan and Ari – are well settled in their abode, with regular fortnightly access visits from David and Peter.

· · ·

DISCUSSION

Defining the problem

Alan's description: Alan describes himself as anxious, confused, paralysed, indecisive, disloyal and wracked with guilt.
Alan's construction: Alan sees himself as the betrayer of the principles which he and Fran laid down at the beginning of their marriage.

Exploring the context

Therapist's deconstruction: After Alan's determination to solve his dilemmas is affirmed, his affair with Molly is described as an attempt to break free from the expectations set by his family of origin. We discuss a series of themes that attempt to defuse Alan's sense of guilt, and open him up to future options: how to overcome his sense of stagnation, give up his illusions of power, make commitments, cope with the stresses of change, let go, stop punishing himself, and make some responsible decisions. At a joint session, Molly states her wish for stability and recognition by Alan's family. Alan is asked if he misinterprets Molly's desire for continuity in their relationship as clinging.

Options for the future

Mutual reconstruction: Alan commences divorce proceedings, enlarges his accounting practice, and moves in with Molly and Ari. Alan and Molly tell of the increasing fights between themselves. They fear that their relationship is falling to pieces. Their quarrelling is ascribed to the process of accommodation that often occurs in the formation of blended families, and we consider another way of regarding the discipline of children, other than replacement of the missing parent.

SUMMARY

In Chapter 13, we considered:

Case 13A, *'The law clerk'*, in which Tracy overcomes the expectations of her father and cements her relationship with Murray.

Case 13B, *'The hero'*, in which Craig continues his growth towards adult intimate relating.

Case 13C, *'Another design'*, in which Wanda fashions another model within which to form friendships.

Case 13D, *'The good lad'*, in which Alan lets go of his guilt and expectations of a 'normal' family.

POINTS FOR REFLECTION

1. Compare Cases 13B and 13D. What are their similarities and differences?
2. List some of the common themes that enter your conversations with remarried/blended families.
3. Describe some of your own casework dealing with remarried/blended families, using the Affirmation and Deconstruction schemas.

Incest

14

· · ·

CASE STUDY

Case 14A   Tomahawks and Scuds

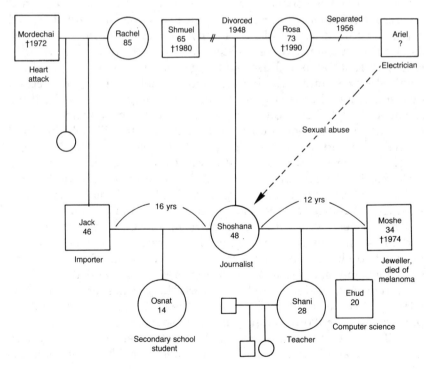

Fig. 14.1 Shoshana commenced therapy in December 1990.

During our first session of therapy, Shoshana, 48, a journalist, told me of her unhappy marriage to Jack, 46, an importer, and her anger at her daughter Osnat, 14, a secondary-school student.

'My marriage', Shoshana said, 'has been a dead duck for years. Jack has no interest in me . . . he doesn't want to go out with me, he doesn't want to mix with my friends, he doesn't want to make love with me . . . he is a real cold fish. There has been nothing between us since Osnat was born.'

Shoshana had been involved in an affair five years previously. She had enjoyed her lover, who seemed to have treated her with respect, sensitivity and warmth. Shoshana and Jack had separated, and when the affair had ended six months later, Jack had convinced Shoshana to return home 'for Osnat's sake'. Shoshana was now regretting this decision, as Osnat was proving a difficult teenager in recent years.

'Osnat keeps telling me that, if only I could be happy with Daddy, everything would be OK', Shoshana commented. 'You know, it is funny. Everyone at work thinks I am terrific. They say I am very good at my job, friendly, helpful, and never thrown off balance by any upsets . . . a real tough cookie. They have no idea of what goes on at home. They would get a real shock to know how things are. Look at me . . . I am a lousy wife and mother!'

We discussed Shoshana's family of origin. Her mother, Rosa, had divorced her father, Shmuel, when Shoshana was six, and they had emigrated from Russia to Israel shortly afterwards. Rosa had married Ariel, an electrician, two years later. Ariel proved to be a savage man who physically abused Rosa, and began sexually abusing Shoshana when she was nine. This had continued until Rosa left her second husband when Shoshana was 14. Shoshana said that she had felt too ashamed to tell her mother about the sexual abuse, and had not mentioned it to anyone until now. She had felt humiliated, dirty and tainted, and had avoided social contact until she had met Moshe, a jeweller, when she was 20. Moshe was a quiet and caring man, and their marriage became warm, safe and protective for Shoshana. Two children, Shani and Ehud, were born, and the family migrated to Australia to gather some sound financial assets and eventually return to Israel. Twelve years after their marriage, Moshe died of melanoma, and Shoshana described her grief, loneliness, and the demands of raising two children on her own, as too overwhelming to bear. She soon met and married Jack, who appeared strong and dependable. Jack, however, had declared very early his wishes of running the relationship in a traditional, patriarchal manner: Jack wanting lots of practical and emotional support from Shoshana, leaving little time for his wife's needs to be acknowledged or met. After Osnat's birth, Jack had turned almost completely to his career for fulfilment, whereas

Shoshana channelled her time into rearing the children and completing a Bachelor of Arts degree, with majors in media and psychology. Shani and Ehud had both left home, and appeared to be pursuing their lives successfully elsewhere.

I expressed my admiration at Shoshana's honesty and clarity in this first therapy session. I felt touched by her trust. I was impressed, too, with her persistence in raising a family and pursuing a career despite all her struggles. Rather than an inadequate wife and mother, I saw her as an extraordinarily strong woman who had needed to use most of her personal energies to survive the violations and upsets of her past. I asked her if she would talk with Jack about their future: What did he want? Would he come to a joint session to discuss the issues between them? We agreed to meet weekly, and I concluded our session by reading Shoshana the story of Wendy, an incest survivor who had experienced struggles within her own intimate relationship (Gunzburg, 1991). I gave Shoshana an essay that Wendy had offered me at the end of our therapy:

Please hear what I am not saying
Do not be fooled by me. Do not be fooled by the face I wear. I wear a mask. I wear a thousand masks – masks that I am afraid to take off: and none of them are me.

Pretending is an art that is second nature to me, but do not be fooled. For God's sake, do not be fooled. I give the impression that I am secure, that all is sunny and unruffled within me as well as without; that confidence is my name and coolness my game, that the water is calm and I am in command; and that I need no one. But do not believe me, please. My surface may seem smooth, but my surface is my mask, my ever varying and ever concealing mask.

Beneath lies no smugness, no complacence. Beneath dwells the real me in confusion, in fear, in loneliness. But I hide that. I do not want anybody to know why I frantically create a mask to hide behind – a nonchalant, sophisticated façade – to help me pretend, to shield me from the glance that knows. But such a glance is precisely my salvation, my only salvation, and I know it. That is, if it is followed by acceptance, if it is followed by love.

It is the only thing that can liberate me from myself, from my own self-built prison wall, from the barriers I so painstakingly erect. It is the only thing that will assure me of what I cannot assure myself – that I am really something.

But I do not tell you this. I do not dare. I am afraid to. I am afraid your glance will not be followed by acceptance and love. I am afraid you will think less of me, that you will laugh, and your laugh will kill me. I am afraid that deep down I am nothing, that I am no good and that you will see this and reject me.

So I play my game, my desperate, pretending game, with a façade of assurance without, and a trembling child within.

And so begins the parade of masks, the glittering but empty parade of masks. My life becomes a front. I idly chatter to you in suave tones of surface talk. I tell you everything that is nothing and nothing that is everything, of what is crying inside me. So when I am going through my routine, do not be fooled by what I am not saying.

Please listen carefully and try to hear what I am not saying, what I would like to be able to say, what for survival I need to say, but cannot say.

I dislike hiding, honestly. I dislike the superficial game I am playing, the superficial phony I am being. I would like to be really genuine and spontaneous and me. But you have got to help me. You have got to hold out your hand even when that is the last thing I seem to want or need. Only you can wipe away from my eyes the blank stare of the breathing dead. Only you can call me into aliveness. Each time you are kind and gentle and encouraging, each time you try to understand because you really care, my heart begins to grow wings, very small wings, very feeble wings – but wings.

With your sensitivity and compassion and power of understanding, you can breathe life into me. I want you to know that. I want you to know how important you are to me; how you can be the creator of the person that is me, if you choose to. Please choose. You can remove the mask, you alone can release me from my lonely prison. So do not pass me by. Please do not pass me by. It will not be easy for you. My long conviction of worthlessness builds strong walls. The nearer you approach, the blinder I might strike back. It is irrational, but despite what books say about a person, I am irrational, I fight against the very thing I cry out for.

But I am told that love is stronger than the strongest walls, and in this lies hope. MY ONLY HOPE. Please try to beat down my wall with firm but gentle hands – for a child is very sensitive, very fearful.

Who am I, you may wonder? I am someone you know very well FOR I AM EVERY WOMAN YOU MEET. I AM EVERY MAN YOU MEET. I AM RIGHT IN FRONT OF YOU
Anonymous

At our second session, Shoshana said that she had spoken with Jack, who had stated that he definitely wanted a divorce and did not see the need for any therapy to help him reach that goal. Osnat had told Shoshana that she was unsure about attending a joint session, but would think about it. Shoshana expressed a mixture of feelings on hearing Jack's decision: relief, anger, sadness, panic, isolation. I commended her on having achieved such a significant change for the future.

Over the next seven sessions, our conversation included many themes which endeavoured to increase Shoshana's self-esteem and improve her self-image: 'achieving safety' – Shoshana, having been violated by her stepfather Ariel, may have sought security first with the quiet and sensitive Moshe, who had died, and then the strong but self-centred Jack, who did not tend to her needs. How could Shoshana 'take charge of her life'? Perhaps she had studied psychology in an effort to understand herself better, and gather information to become more independent from the abuse and emotional deprivation that she had experienced? Could Shoshana now find safety in a life on her own, perhaps with the support of a group of friends, rather than a marriage?; 'letting go' – how would Shoshana benefit from the separation? Over what aspects of the marriage would she grieve? What memories would Shoshana take with her to nourish her in the future?; How could Shoshana 'plan a separation routine and budget'?; How could she counter Jack's 'guilt-hooks' and vengeful remarks? He was already accusing her of 'stealing his money, driving his car, buying her food with his resources', rather than sharing their financial assets during the process of separation. We talked of leaving with dignity, maintaining boundaries and protecting her territory. Jack had threatened Shoshana with assault, and she had contacted the police; they had cautioned Jack. Shoshana said she would have considered such an action unthinkable several weeks earlier.

Osnat came to our tenth session. She was an energetic and likeable teenager who described her parents' decision to separate as a move for the better. Her problem was choosing where she wanted to live. Jack was now settled into his own flat. Osnat believed that she could get on well with her father; he was a practical man definitely interested in her welfare. However, Osnat said that she did enjoy warm feelings towards her mother, and would be prepared to stay with her if only she would be less negative and protective. Shoshana listed her many complaints regarding Osnat's rebellious nature, including rejecting the food that Shoshana cooked for her (Osnat had been diagnosed as having mild iron deficiency anaemia, and Shoshana was concerned that her daughter was 'not eating right'), and wanting to go out at night and on weekends without telling her mother any details of her whereabouts. We agreed that Osnat would take responsibility for her own diet during the coming week, and that she would leave a telephone contact whenever she went out. Shoshana said that she would only use the telephone number in emergency and not to intrude into her daughter's activities.

We continued our weekly joint sessions discussing privacy in bedrooms (Osnat objected to Shoshana's entry into her bedroom, but often burst into her mother's room without knocking); how to assert their needs to each other with respect; how to address Shoshana's impression that Osnat was simply a boarder, using her mother's services without any special regard towards her; and how they aggravated each other when expressing differences. Osnat still missed meals and only occasionally left her mother a point of contact whenever she went out for any length of time. Shoshana said she felt disrespected. The 1991 Gulf War had just concluded, and I commented after one of their angry interchanges during a session: 'You know, when you two fight it is as though you are both using Tomahawk missiles to get your message across. There is no escape when you use Tomahawks; they are too accurate and devastating. They always hit and destroy their target. Perhaps you should use the occasional Scud missile so that you can have some hope of surviving each other's attacks, and not be completely blown to pieces?'

After a month's break for holidays, Shoshana, attending on her own, told me that although the fighting had settled somewhat, Osnat was now living with Jack. Osnat had told her mother that she had stayed initially because she was worried that Shoshana would feel rejected if she left, and would fall apart. Osnat said that, following our joint sessions, she believed her mother was stronger now and would be able to handle her departure. Shoshana said that she felt bitter about the outcome.

'Osnat thinks she is going to have it easy with Jack', she said. 'She will learn that it is not going to be all sunshine with Daddy. Still, she is almost 15, old enough to know for herself. What more can I do?'

I complimented Shoshana on giving Osnat a chance to take charge of her own life. Such a situation had been denied to Shoshana during her own adolescence. I said I believed her acceptance showed a confidence both in her own mothering skills that she had raised a daughter capable in caring for herself, and that Osnat would indeed prove a responsible young adult. In fact, Osnat had visited her mother since leaving on more than one occasion, and they seemed to be reaching a different understanding of one another.

We spent our two final sessions contemplating Shoshana's future on her own. She expressed her sadness at the end of an era, her fear of being alone for a lengthy period of time, and also her sense of optimism that she might at last find some of the peace and comfort that had eluded her for much of her life. Shoshana said that she had gone out socially that week with a group of friends for the first time in many months. She had feared ostracism from her peers. What would they think of her now that she had 'deserted Jack and thrown Osnat out of home'? Actually, her friends had expressed their pleasant surprise that Shoshana had managed to arrange a separation with Jack and Osnat, who they considered had treated her rather shabbily for years.

———————————   · · ·   ———————————

DISCUSSION

Defining the problem

Shoshana's description: Shoshana describes her unhappy marriage with Jack, and her anger at her daughter Osnat's rudeness.
Shoshana's construction: Shoshana blames herself as an ineffective wife and mother.

Exploring the context

Therapist's deconstruction: After details of the many losses and violations in Shoshana's life are gathered, her honesty and clarity of description, and her determination to succeed in family life and career, are affirmed. Shoshana is asked to discuss the future with her husband, invite both Jack and Osnat to a joint session, and we share an essay on 'being heard and tended to' that another sexually abused woman has offered me.

Options for the future

Mutual reconstruction: Jack announces his intention to divorce, and means whereby Shoshana can strengthen her self-esteem and take charge and achieve security in a life on her own, are discussed. Jack leaves, and during a series of joint sessions Osnat and Shoshana consider ways that they might cooperate more in the new situation. Osnat decides to reside with her father. Shoshana chooses to accept her daughter's decision, grieves, and starts seeking support from nourishing friends rather than aiming for a deeply intimate relationship.

———————————   · · ·   ———————————

CASE STUDY

Case 14B   The kiss of death
Suzy, 30, a marketing officer with a major insurance company, told me of her longstanding depression, and despair that her six year marriage

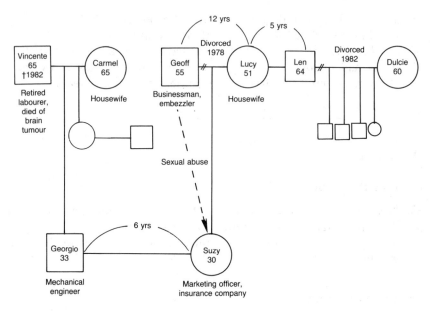

Fig. 14.2 Suzy commenced therapy in August 1989.

with Georgio, 33, a mechanical engineer, was coming to an end. Suzy described her husband as a kind, decent and rather obese man, who attended to many practical details of their relationship but did not seem to acknowledge the emotional side. Although affectionate and cuddly, Georgio would frequently withdraw into himself when Suzy wanted him to listen to her when she felt low. During leisure times they often enjoyed themselves at restaurants, cinema, day trips, usually in the company of friends. The physical side of their marriage had never been very active, and they had participated in sexual intercourse perhaps once or twice every year over the last half of their marriage. Suzy said that Georgio was considerate and never forced himself upon her. Suzy's asthmatic wheeze, present since childhood, was also worsening, and she had been prescribed increased medication.

There were several areas of distress during Suzy's early life. Her father, Geoff, a businessman, had been a negative, discounting man who had told Suzy continually that she would never amount to anything much. Geoff appeared to be well learned in the ways of disrespecting women. He had indulged in numerous covert extramarital affairs during the whole of his marriage, and would leave his wife, Lucy, suddenly for weeks on end, never revealing his whereabouts. When Suzy was 13, he had fondled her and given her a passionate kiss. Suzy remembered being totally confused by this episode: erotically aroused, disgusted and humiliated. She had wondered: 'Why is Dad doing this to me if he is married to Mum?' Suzy had felt far too ashamed about this event to have told anyone about it, including her mother and Georgio. Suzy's subsequent adolescence and young adulthood was fraught with anxiety and mistrust of her peers. She felt that she had no sense of control or influence within relationships, and this feeling had remained in relation to Georgio. When Suzy was 19, Lucy divorced Geoff. Geoff had also conducted quite a successful career as an embezzler, until he was caught and imprisoned when Suzy was 22. Around this time, Suzy had experienced rather severe repetitive stress injury in her wrists, which had limited her career options. Nonetheless, she had pursued a vocation in insurance and currently was in charge of a large sector with considerable responsibility. Suzy loved her job and enjoyed an excellent working arrangement with her colleagues. When she was 24, Suzy married Georgio and this had led to another area of apprehension with Geoff. Her father hated Italians and knew nothing of Suzy's marriage. Suzy was fearful that, on his release from jail, he would find them and attempt to do some harm to Georgio.

I said that I admired Suzy's determination to forge a rewarding life for herself. She had withstood the rigours of asthma and RSI, the insults and assault of her father, and the trauma of parental divorce. Suzy had also chosen a partner who appeared respectful of her, and had succeeded in a career. I asked her if she would invite Georgio to our session next week?

At our second session, Suzy said that Georgio had a work commitment that day and would attend next time. We talked more about Suzy's fear of being hurt within relationships. She seemed unable to answer challenges on contentious issues. Suzy was worried that a co-worker, Marcy, whom Suzy liked, knew about her past and would discount Suzy if she ever discussed it with her. I asked Suzy if she would be willing to take a risk: would Suzy tell Marcy about her concerns of being ridiculed by her, and discover if they were justified?

At our third session, Georgio and Suzy agreed that their marriage lacked shared enjoyment. Suzy had told both Marcy and Georgio about the sexual abuse. Georgio had been furious at Geoff's injustice, and Marcy had been gently supportive. Suzy had been pleasantly surprised at both reactions. She had never seen Georgio so fired up before.

Georgio said that he often experienced Suzy as 'demanding, clinging, and at times, a burden'. They were never able to complete negotiations, as Suzy would always push him for rapid, ready answers to problems. He would rather withdraw and take time out to think about the situation over a longer period. We discussed how much of Suzy's 'pressuring' of Georgio may have been due to her need for safety, stability and structure. Suzy seemed to have a need of a plan for the future, whereas Georgio appeared more contented to flow along and let solutions arise. A major issue was whether they were to have children or not. I asked them whether they would consider this topic for next session, and explore which facets needed to be addressed?

At our fourth session, Georgio said that he had always been a bit nervous of having kids. He had never been really fond of them and was a bit bothered about 'dropping them, and all that!' Georgio remembered always having to compete with other members of his original family to get attention, and felt that if he and Suzy had children he would find himself in a similar situation. Suzy wanted children very much, so that she could offer them a better life than she had had.

Suzy had been upset that week because her pet budgie, Cindy, had died. Suzy had wept inconsolably for days. We discussed how people who have themselves been hurt in childhood often find it difficult to lose their pets. One of Georgio's hobbies was artistry, and I asked him if her would draw a memorial picture of Cindy for Suzy? I also wondered what would happen if Suzy gave Georgio some leeway: Suzy was keen on planning all her arrangements with Georgio. Georgio had complained of their lack of fun, and his frustration at having to compete with Suzy for her own needs. Would Suzy trust Georgio enough to let him organize a weekend entertainment without her knowing what it was beforehand?

We discussed Suzy's fear of Geoff hurting Georgio. I suggested that Georgio's Italian background might in fact prove to be a deterrent to Geoff. If Geoff did make threats, could they quietly give Geoff the message that Georgio might consider putting out a Mafia-style contract on him?

From our fifth session, Suzy and Georgio seemed to grow in confidence and optimism. Suzy said she treasured Georgio's drawing of Cindy (Fig. 14.3). Georgio had arranged a picnic to Sylvan dam, which had proven delightful for them both. I asked Suzy if she would write a letter expressing her feelings to Geoff?

From our sixth session, Suzy's depression began to lift and her asthma had improved markedly. She had vented a great deal of anger in her letter to her father, and said that she seemed to have let a burden go in composing it.

Dear Dad,
No! Maybe I should just call you Geoff because I cannot think of a time when you were a father to me?
    My memories of having a father are filled with fear and loathing. When Georgio's dad died I really wished it was you. Certainly I can't think of anyone who would be sorry to hear you had died.

Fig. 14.3 Georgio's drawing for Suzy.

I always thought fathers should be friends to their children, someone to look after them. The only kind thing I can ever remember you doing for me was easing the cramps in my legs at night and showing me how to do it for myself. The rest of the time, as far back as I can remember, spending time with you was uncomfortable. We never had anything to talk about, you were always disapproving and nothing was ever good enough.

When I was tiny, I remember wanting and trying to spend time with you but you always made me feel like I was in the way. Anytime you played with me, I would always get hurt and cry. Once I got older you made me feel like my interest in boys was dirty. You made me feel worse when you tongue-kissed me.

I could never understand how you could do that to anyone – let alone your daughter – when you were trying to reconcile with Mum. Either you wanted to be faithful and get back together or you didn't. As it turns out you didn't. I spent the next six years terrified of being alone in the house with you in case you tried to do something worse. It was only a couple of years ago that I realised that this was incest. It was only then that I began to understand just how evil it was and how lucky I am that it wasn't worse. At the same time I remembered the stories I heard from girls at school and what their brothers had done to them. No-one treated it as a problem – one girl was thought of as a hero, the other as a liar. I know I never really believed their stories and I felt very guilty and ashamed that I had not.

You are a very manipulative and cruel man. Whenever you have contacted me or tried to, I know it is not because you are sorry. You have never ever apologised or said you would try to change or improve the situation. You build relationships because they are useful to you. You want something from me when someone else has dumped you. You played me for a sucker when you and Mum finally separated. You tried to turn her against me, and separate me from my dog.

I HATE you so much. You have really tried to ruin my life. You have not succeeded but you have caused some damage.

Because I was a girl, you never let me think about a career. In fact you and Mum blatantly discouraged me from studying. I think in Mum's case, a lot of it was ignorance. She just does not understand about studying and exams and projects. But you! You wanted me to stay in the gutter with you. I was learning to do things that you had had to bluff your way through. I was gaining knowledge that would reveal your scam, and heaven forbid, I was a woman. I could never be allowed to be equal or better than you in anything.

The way you treated me has meant that Georgio has to live with the scars. And I am very sorry for that. It isn't his problem but he has to live with it daily. He paid for my education so that finally I can have a career. I have probably turned a profit for him by now but he hated the time I spent studying. I won't have sex with him because I do not want to be too close or intimate with him. I have seen and felt how painful close relationships are. And sometimes Georgio will say something and it reminds me of you. I begin to feel like the little girl who could never be good enough, struggling because she thought that what she had done was good. You never told me you loved me. You never said I did something well. You never said you were proud of me.

I was never important to you. I was just useful – a substitute when nothing better was around like a woman for you to screw, shop and do your washing. Even in my last farewell letter to you when I told you it was over, you made me feel guilty about saying goodbye. After all the terrible things you had done to me, I still wondered if I was being too harsh.

I really think you are the loser. You have a daughter you do not know who is quite a nice person with good friends and a good job. You do not know anything about me or my life. The only thing you have ever been interested in is trying to humiliate me, frighten me and prevent me from reaching my full potential as a person.

You are a loathsome, vile person. I think you have no friends because no-one will ever be able to get close to you.

I do not want to be like you in any way. I am ashamed that you are my father. I have thought about telling people that my father is dead but have decided the honest approach is better. My father is a creep. A real bastard. I do not want ever to see him or communicate with him ever.

I hate you. You are vile. It will be good when you are dead because then you cannot frighten me.
Suzy

Having written this, Suzy had started using her mother's maiden surname at work, rather than her father's surname which she had used up till now.

I described Geoff's action in terms of a curse, a 'kiss of death' that had left Suzy filled with hatred and loathing, and had meant death to any closeness, comfort and sexual enjoyment within her relationships. I said that I wanted to see Suzy individually for a while to see if we could beat this wicked spell that Geoff had placed on her, and that perhaps every six weeks, Georgio would join us to toss ideas around about how they were progressing. I also stated that I liked challenges. I warmed to overturning wicked spells, defeating curses and winning against the Forces of Evil. Suzy grinned, and replied: 'Me too, I am your regular little Aussie battler!'

I continued to weave themes of 'valuing self' and 'increasing sense of safety' into our therapeutic conversation, that I believed would prove to be curse-breakers: How Suzy had chosen Georgio, a peaceable non-competitive man, to affirm for her that not all relationships with men need be violating. This might now be creating a problem, as both partners in a relationship require some assertion to mutually resolve problems. Perhaps Suzy also had chosen an overweight man, one who was not overtly sexual, to ease the pressures on her in this area? What would happen if Georgio decided to become fitter and lose weight? How would Suzy handle her husband's new image? We discussed ways in which Suzy might assert herself more effectively: how to examine what she wanted and ask for it? We discussed messages that Suzy could give to herself that would help boost her sense of worth. Suzy said that she had a love of animals because she felt she could give them adequate nourishment and protection. She and Georgio had decided to move into a larger house, and Suzy was fearful for the safety of her pet dog during the journey. We discussed a bit of magic, how some stones were worn as amulets to protect their bearers. Suzy purchased a garnet, the stone that traditionally shields travellers from evil spirits on the way, and fastened it to her dog's collar. The shift to the new house proceeded without mishap. A week later Suzy told me that she and Georgio had purchased their own 'lucky stones', and had surprised each other with their selection. Suzy had chosen a smooth agate pebble, which she loved to hold and fondle, whereas Georgio had purchased a lovely spray of rock-crystals, which he had displayed on the mantelpiece for viewing. Every now and then they would lend each other their special charms to share the luck around. We talked about the catastrophic expectations that survivors of violating families sometimes experience. Life for them often seemed to be a journey filled with unpredictable and disassembling moments, and markers along the way, like Suzy and Georgio's stones, helped maintain a sense of equilibrium and continuity.

At our next joint session, I wanted to build on the closeness that Georgio and Suzy were developing. Georgio's anger at Geoff's abuse of Suzy, his drawing of Cindy, and his sharing in the therapy appeared to have increased Suzy's trust in him. I encouraged them to go out to a restaurant and, during the meal, to occasionally feed each other. I asked them what sacrifices were they prepared to make to ensure each other's comfort, safety and fun? More and more, Suzy was allowing Georgio to plan leisure routines and activities around the house without preceding discussion . . . and more and more, Georgio was including Suzy in conversation about what they might do next. The tension between them certainly appeared to be easing. We discussed how Suzy might close the distance in her relationship with Lucy. They had drifted over the years. I asked Suzy to compose a conversation with her mother. How might they achieve a more comfortable intimacy? We talked about Suzy's and Georgio's favourite foods, and other special sensual pleasures – music, flowers, times when they had enjoyed sex. A couples massage course was considered.

Therapy lasted 29 weeks. By that time, Georgio had lost ten kilograms in weight, Suzy had arranged a luncheon appointment with her mother, and Suzy and Georgio were participating sexually every two to three weeks.

A year later, Lucy came to my surgery, furious and frightened. Her own mother had always wanted her to reconcile with Geoff, and now that he was out of jail, had told him where Suzy and Georgio lived. In response to this, Lucy, Len, Suzy and Georgio had all met to discuss ways in which they might protect themselves, legally if need be. I quietly congratulated Lucy that she and her family had managed to preserve safety against such an unpleasant threat. Lucy said that she was so pleased that she and Suzy were such amicable friends now, and we discussed how Lucy might approach her own mother in the future.

— · · · —

DISCUSSION

Defining the problem

Suzy's description: Suzy tells of her depression and despair that her marriage is breaking up.
Suzy's construction: Suzy blames Georgio for his withdrawal whenever she approaches him to tend to their problems.

Exploring the context

Therapist's deconstruction: After affirming Suzy's determination to achieve a fulfilling lifestyle against seemingly insurmountable odds, I suggest that her insecurities and lack of trust stem from the sexual abuse and discounting of Geoff. Suzy is asked to invite Georgio to a session of therapy, and to seek support from a friend, Marcy.

Joint session

Georgio's construction: Georgio blames Suzy as 'demanding, clinging, a burden'. Both Marcy and Georgio support Suzy when she tells them of Geoff's abuse. We discuss Georgio's and Suzy's different negotiating patterns: Suzy wants sudden answers to problems, Georgio prefers to search for solutions for a while. They are asked to discuss the possibilities of having children. Suzy is encouraged to trust Georgio in planning a spontaneous leisure activity, and ask Georgio to draw a picture of Suzy's deceased pet, Cindy, all the time endeavouring to facilitate closeness and trust between them. Suzy is asked to express her anger in a letter to Geoff.

Options for the future

Mutual reconstruction: The discussions relating to future children, Georgio's picnic for Suzy and picture of Cindy, and Suzy's letter to Geoff, appear to give Georgio and Suzy greater optimism, and Suzy's depression and asthma improve. Suzy and I continue to discuss ways of defeating Geoff's curse, his 'kiss of death', and increasing her safety and self-esteem. Suzy and Georgio move to new accommodation and overturn some wicked spells with magic stones. Suzy closes the distance with her mother. Georgio, Suzy and I discuss ways of increasing sensuality and a safer expression of physicality through food, music, massage. Georgio reduces in weight and the couple increase their sexual participation. Finally, when Suzy's grandmother breaks confidentiality and reveals Suzy's address to her father, recently released from custody, the family unite to increase their defences against Geoff's potential threats to Georgio and his daughter.

· · ·

CASE STUDY

Case 14C   An extraordinary script
Arlene, 46, a primary-school teacher, told me of the panic attacks that had plagued her for five years, and of her dissatisfaction and emotional emptiness in her 26-year marriage to Hector, 46, an internationally famous author. Arlene despaired that her life could ever be any different. To compound her unhappiness, she had come to a crisis with her lover of 18 months, Les, 49, a solicitor. Les had told Arlene at the commencement of their affair that he had wanted to leave his wife Elaine, 48, a general practitioner, but he had found the attempt to separate too painful and had wanted to continue with wife and mistress both. Neither Hector nor Elaine knew of their partners' relationship.

'I feel a bit like the old song', Arlene commented. 'Torn between two lovers, feeling like a fool. I do not know what to do . . . I feel a failure, ashamed, and very stupid!'

Born in Berlin just before the end of World War Two, Arlene's Jewish mother Hilde had escaped Nazi persecution by going into hiding. Her Catholic father Pierre was classified as 'Aryan', and so

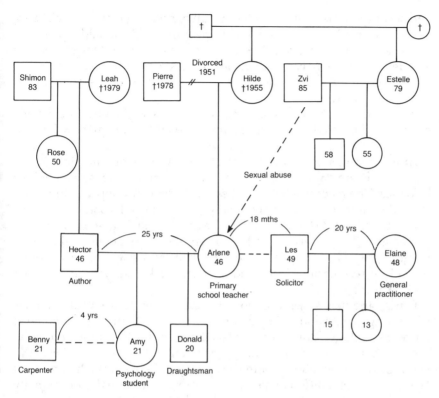

Fig. 14.4 Arlene commenced therapy in April 1991.

not at risk. Arlene was immediately sent to a convent, where she was raised and tutored during her first seven years. Hilde had left Pierre when Arlene was six, and a year later, mother and daughter had migrated to Australia. Arlene said that she had missed her young acquaintances from Germany. Hilde began to intergrate with the Melbourne Jewish community, and Arlene recalled her confusion in being taught at the convent that 'Jews were not really quite human', and discovering that she was one of them! Hilde died when Arlene was nine, and she went to live with her mother's sister, Estelle, her Uncle Zvi, and their two children. Arlene described her aunt as a witch who treated her like Cinderella. She could not remember ever sharing meals with the family, always being relegated to the kitchen to eat. Arlene had left to live with the family of a school friend when she was 15. Arlene had commenced studies for her Diploma of Education and, at 20 had married Hector, a cerebral, energetic, self-sufficient man, well on the way to his own success. The marriage had provided stability and security in the early years, with status, fulfilling careers, socializing and their involvement with children, Amy and Donald. With the passage of time, however, Arlene felt more and more that she had to accede to Hector's needs and wishes. He seemed to be happy with her as teacher, housewife, mother, but not to value her as companion, friend and lover.

'It sounds as though you became a character in one of Hector's scripts', I suggested. 'He authors your role and you somehow have to fit in.'

Arlene had met Les several years previously in an orienteering group. Hector was not a member of the society, abhorring such outdoor activities. The meetings between Les and Arlene developed into friendship, then to affection and eventually, a passionate liaison.

I commended Arlene on her courage in seeking a solution to her problems. Quite a large number of people remained in an impasse, caught between spouse and lover, for many years without ever trying to achieve resolution. We agreed to meet weekly to explore what her options were.

During the next several sessions I endeavoured to weave the themes of grieving, safety and intimacy into our conversation: Arlene had been raised as a refugee during dangerous times, and had lost her childhood friends, father and mother during her youth. It must have been difficult for Arlene to know where she belonged. Perhaps she had married Hector to script a different story for her, one that offered more stability and comfort? As she had grown within the relationship, she may have found Hector's script unchangeable and ultimately limiting. Arlene had always been shy of boys when young, had rarely dated, and had been a novice on her wedding night. Perhaps her affair might be regarded as an attempt to take time out and explore other elements of intimacy? It had been a long time since Arlene had felt cherished by Hector. What would have to happen for her to feel cherished again? How could she bring the knowledge that she had learnt within her affair into her marriage to give it sparkle? Arlene had definitely aroused Les's interest in her. Could she now intrigue Hector into a different and more rewarding kind of encounter? What were the pros and cons of remaining Les's lover? If Arlene's affair with Les had indeed ended, would she write him a letter of farewell? How might Arlene achieve mutuality and equity in her negotiations with Hector? Do brilliant authors' needs always supersede those of teachers, wives, mothers? Could Arlene visualize the final outcome if she ended the affair, the marriage, or even both? Having 'cheated on Hector', was Arlene grieving the loss of her self-image and integrity? How might she and Hector change so that the possibility of affairs would not be an issue in the future?

After about a dozen sessions, Arlene said: 'You know, I have never told anyone about this before, John, but when I went to live with my Aunt Estelle, when I was nine, my Uncle Zvi started to come into my bed at night two to three times each week, embracing me, kissing me and eventually having intercourse with me. He continued doing this until I left, at 15. I could never tell my Aunt Estelle about it. I could never tell anyone about it, my uncle was such a well-respected and public figure within the community. No-one would have believed me. I have not even told Hector about it. I found out later that Uncle Zvi's brother was doing it to his daughters also. Do you think that any of this has to do with my panic attacks?'

'So Les was not your first illicit relationship', I responded quietly. 'Your Uncle Zvi made you his lover.'

We discussed the 'extraordinary' script that Arlene's uncle had written for her, one which had denied her own needs for safety and nurturing and the ordinary fun of youth, and which instead had offered her an experience of shame, hurt, fear and disempowerment. Perhaps Arlene had reacted directly against her uncle's script in marrying the strong and intelligent Hector? This had proven partly successful. Arlene had found safety and protection in her marriage, but also a certain coercion to accommodate to Hector's image as 'famous author'. Perhaps Arlene had become involved in her affair to learn what she needed to know about emotional and physical intimacy within a script of her own choosing?

I suggested that many survivors of sexual abuse tried to live their lives pretending that such 'extraordinary' events had not happened. They tried to be 'ordinary people' but often felt plagued by 'extraordinary' feelings: alienated, disordered, poisoned, confused and panicky. However, many learnt to accept their feelings and live better with them once they acknowledged that their stories of surviving sexual abuse were extraordinary (though regrettably not uncommon!). Rather than continuing to search desperately for happiness, they chose to find contentment in discovering what their resources were: courage, determination, compassion, sensitivity, and frequently humour. Eventually, they became ordinary people through participating in ordinary activities.

I read Arlene a story, 'Painful Consequences' (Gunzburg, 1991), concerning a lover's dilemma, and contrasted it with her own situation: If Arlene left Les, might she and Hector co-author a new and fulfilling script? If she maintained the status quo, would her panic attacks remain? If Arlene divorced Hector and continued as Les's mistress, how would she feel, secreted away from other members of Les's family? Would Les perhaps acknowledge Arlene's presence to his family and give her an honoured place as special friend within it?

Hector came to our 15th session. He was a courteous, eloquent, scholarly man who appeared to tackle every interaction at the intellectual plane.

'You know, John', Hector assured me, 'all this talk of Arlene's about having a better quality marriage is women's stuff. We have a wonderful life. We go out with our friends, Arlene has her career, the kids are happy and she is free to do as she wishes.'

I felt patronized!

We discussed the theme of 'different languages': perhaps Hector and Arlene were speaking in different tongues. Hector appeared to prefer the analytical, concrete descriptive mode of communication, whereas Arlene seemed to know much about passion, rhythms and moods. I mentioned that recent scientific research indicated that our brains have subtle variations according to gender in the way we organize our sensory input. Men appear to be able to handle visuospatial information more effectively (e.g. they can assimilate details from road maps more easily), whereas women appear to be able to handle verbal skills more adequately (e.g. they can pick up on a wider range of nuances within conversation). I suggested that perhaps men and women needed to take more care in conversing with each other so that they could accommodate to each other's styles of relating to the world? Perhaps we had a great deal to understand about differences within our intimate partners? If Arlene and Hector did not eventually learn to tend to one other, would their marriage end?

'Oh, it is not that serious, really?', said Hector, sitting up suddenly in apparent genuine concern. 'We are not talking about separating, are we?'

I asked Arlene how Hector might respond so that she would know he was learning her language?

'If he would just spend some of the quieter moments with me', she replied. 'Hector is always so busy with his own work and interests. If he would occasionally sit with me, listen to music together, or walk the dog with me, or come for a coffee and a bit of cake in Acland Street, that would be lovely!'

Arlene and I continued to meet weekly. We discussed the theme of 'sham' in her life, relating to her uncle's abuse and how important it had become for Arlene to live a life of integrity. Perhaps 'sham' was a factor underlying her panic attacks? Arlene had found that she was living the sham of a happy marriage with Hector, had entered her affair with Les and found that this, too, involved sham. Perhaps it had all proven too scary and Arlene needed to make some decisions to discover a more authentic lifestyle? I asked Arlene to see the film *Sex, Lies and Videotape*, dealing with the dynamics and politics of 'sham'. Arlene was encouraged that, during our joint session, Hector had seemed concerned not to lose her. She felt valued. Hector was indeed starting to tend to her more, walking the dog regularly, and dining out together as a couple. After about six months of therapy, Arlene said goodbye to Les and her panic attacks disappeared. Amy, 21, a psychology student, attended for a few therapy sessions of her own. She was perturbed that her mother had changed and needed some help to accommodate to Arlene's increasing assertiveness. Amy had complained to Arlene that Hector's father, Shimon, 83, who lived with them, was giving her a hard time. Shimon blamed Amy for every little thing that went wrong in the household. Arlene spoke to Hector about it, and though he denied that he had mentioned a word to his father, the blaming behaviour ceased. Arlene also found Shimon's intrusiveness disconcerting. He would frequently enter her room, without knocking, while she was in bed. I linked Arlene's discomfort to memories of her uncle's abuse, and discussed the 'dripping water on stone' technique: gently asserting her needs to Shimon repeatedly until he received the message.

After a year's therapy, Arlene has had no contact with Les. Amy has moved out to live with her boyfriend, Benny, 21, a mechanic. Arlene says that she is pleasantly surprised that Hector is so supportive of her as she lets Amy go. Hector and Arlene continue their convivial moments together.

Recently, Arlene told me that she went to see the Al Pacino–Michelle Pfeiffer film *Frankie and Johnny*, with a group of friends. Hector had decided to stay home on the grounds that it was a 'girl's film'. On her return, Arlene had said to Hector: 'Make love to me like Al Pacino!', and they had enjoyed one of the best nights of their marriage. On the coming weekend, Hector commented to Arlene: 'I understand that Saturday night, you are going to your book club. I think that I will take myself out.' Arlene raised her eyebrows. Hector rarely sought entertainment on his own. 'Where are you going?', she asked. Hector replied: 'I think I will see that film, *Frankie and Johnny*!'

I asked Arlene what aspect of therapy had created the most impact for her. She replied: 'John, it was when you described my uncle's abuse as extraordinary. You believed that it happened and that it was wrong. After we had talked, I realized just how angry I was about it and I did not have to fight so hard to contain my anger after that. I have even been gaining in confidence about telling Hector. I think that he will believe my story also.'

· · ·

DISCUSSION

Defining the problem

Arlene's description: Arlene tells of her panic attacks, dissatisfaction with her marriage, crisis with her lover, and despair that her situation will ever improve.

Arlene's construction: Arlene calls herself a fool, a failure, ashamed and stupid.

Exploring the context

Therapist's deconstruction: Arlene's courage in entering therapy is affirmed, and our conversation focuses on the themes of 1) grief – the loss of homeland and parents; 2) safety – where does Arlene belong?; 3) intimacy – how Hector's strong character, initially supportive, has become stultifying, and how the affair with Les can be regarded as a way of examining a different intimacy. Arlene reveals her uncle's violation of her, and we discuss the various ways that she has been scripted, according to others' needs rather than her own, and how she is desperately trying to script her own story.

Joint session

Hector's construction: Hector regards Arlene's struggle as 'women's stuff' and tends to trivialize it. The idea that men and women communicate differently to one another is introduced, and Hector is alerted to the danger of Arlene leaving if she never manages to be heard. Arlene tells Hector some of her needs within the relationship. Arlene and I continue to discuss abandoning sham and achieving integrity.

Options for the future

Mutual reconstruction: Arlene becomes more assertive, ends the affair with Les, and her panic attacks vanish. Hector begins to share a closer intimacy with Arlene, supporting her in a struggle with his father. Amy leaves home. Arlene states that the most influential aspect of therapy for her was that I validated her story of childhood violation.

· · ·

CASE STUDY

Case 14D   Cleaning up his mess

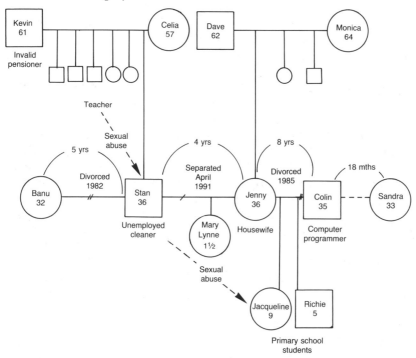

Fig. 14.5 Stan commenced therapy in May 1991.

I was expressing my confusion regarding Stan's story, during his first therapy session with me, to my supervision group that week. Stan, 36, an unemployed cleaner, had told me that he had separated a month previously from Jenny, 36, his wife of four years, their daughter Mary-Lynne, 18 months, and Jenny's two children, Jacqueline, 9, and Richie, 5, from her first marriage to Colin, 35, a computer programmer. Stan was now living temporarily at a friend's house. He was very dejected and upset. Jacqueline, he said, had never liked him from the start. She had been jealous of her own relationship with her mother, and had always tried to separate him from Jenny. He said that at the time of Mary-Lynne's birth, Jenny had become 'very distant' from him and he was worried about the state of their marriage. Stan told how Jacqueline had come up to him and ordered him: 'I want you to touch me the way you touch Mummy, and if you don't, I will tell Mummy that you did'. Stan had said that he was frightened that Jacqueline would tell Jenny and he would be asked to leave, so he had started to 'touch Jacqueline' regularly. After 18 months, Stan said, Jacqueline had told Jenny about the touching. Jenny had not believed her daughter. The next day Jacqueline told her teachers, who contacted Jenny and police action was sought. Stan said that he had admitted everything. Police charges of sexual abuse against Stan were now pending.

Stan's story left me reeling and I told my supervision group that I felt disoriented and distressed by it. I knew that daughters are sometimes antagonistic to their mother's new partner, but I had never heard such an account before.

'John', queried a member of my group firmly and gently, 'why aren't you treating this case as a classic example of sexual abuse?'

I then realized my situation: I had become part of the problem! I was indicating my reluctance, like Jenny, to believe Jacqueline's story, that an adult in the family was sexually abusing a minor! My colleagues referred me to Alan Jenkins' book *Invitations to Responsibility* (Jenkins, 1990) and afterwards, another member expressed her admiration that I had presented this case, with all my confusion, in front of a group that consisted of one man and six women very angry about the extent and mismanagement of sexual abuse within our community. Thus commenced my first therapeutic involvement with a sexual abuser!

During the next six sessions I focused on the theme of Stan's responsibility. He had admitted the sexual abuse immediately to the police, had left home to help ensure Jacqueline's safety, had entered therapy, and was looking to start his own cleaning business. These actions all showed elements of Stan's increasing responsibility. Every now and then Stan would say: 'But Jacqueline has always wanted me out of the way. She has always wanted to separate me from Jenny', and I would reply: 'Stan, can you take a challenge? It is not useful to think about your predicament like that. If there was no sexual abuse, I might have been able to see how you could all have been happier together as a 'remarried' family. At the moment, because of the sexual abuse, you are going to have to concentrate on your responsibility towards Jacqueline's safety'. Or Stan would say: 'Jacqueline was the one who started it. She asked me to touch her', and I would respond: 'Stan, can you bear to hear a different view? When you did touch Jacqueline, that was sexual abuse. Somehow you forgot the boundaries, you had your adult problems and struggles and you shifted responsibility for your adult problems on to Jacqueline. Many of us men would not touch young people's genitals because this is what we call sexual abuse. We would not want to make our children responsible for our adult problems. We would handle our adult problems differently, perhaps taking them to a therapist, as you are now doing.' As it happened, Stan had been given an excellent training in irresponsibility by other adults. His genitals had been fondled, along with a group of other boys', by a school teacher when he was nine. His father, Kevin, had sexually abused Stan's sister during her adolescence, and this had been kept a well guarded family secret. When Stan was a young adult, Kevin had taken him frequently to drinking houses and encouraged him to 'pick up a girl, lad, they're all waiting for you to screw!' Stan's first wife, Banu, had been 17 (just a girl!) when he had married her, he being 21. They had divorced five years later.

I emphasized to Stan that if the family were to heal, three factors were essential: 1) Jacqueline's safety was top priority: she had to feel secure; 2) Jenny had to be restored to a position where she felt she was able to give her children adequate protection; and 3) Stan would have to be accepted as a respected family member, having learnt to act responsibly and reliably.

I asked Stan to write a description of what responsibility meant to him, and how he could enable Jacqueline to grow away from his sexual abuse of her. Stan wrote:

> My definition of responsibility is that I have to be held accountable to myself for my actions, thoughts and anything that I have said or done whether in the past or present as well as in the future. There is an obligation to my wife and family that my actions and deeds show that morally I have to be held accountable from now on. My past deeds show that I did not hold myself morally accountable for them, as I was not showing any responsibility.
>
> I do accept that I was not acting responsibly in the past. I want to be held accountable and show that I have accepted my actions as irresponsible and that I was morally wrong in my deeds and actions. I know by showing that I am to be held accountable to myself, my wife and family, and by changing my ways of thought and actions, I am being responsible.
>
> I would like to see Jacqueline grow up into a responsible person, able to understand and respect her peers. I want her to be able to grow away from the abuse and also to know that it will not happen again, and that she will not ever be put in that position again. I hope that she will also find it in herself to be able to respect and understand where I went wrong in myself and that I have accepted responsibility for what I have done and how I have changed my attitude to what I have learnt over the years about adult–adult boundaries. I would like to see Jacqueline have a normal, family life.

Stan and I kept working at his description over the weeks, so that he clearly and unambiguously took responsibility for his sexual abuse of Jacqueline. Where he wrote: 'I am to be held accountable for my deeds', I encouraged him to write 'I hold myself responsible for sexually abusing Jacqueline'. Where Stan had said: 'I want Jacqueline to know it will not happen again', we changed the message to 'I want Jacqueline to know that I will not sexually abuse her again'. I asked Stan how he could relate to the family in the future so that Jacqueline would know that he had indeed changed: would he continue to live apart from the family to maintain Jacqueline's safety? What ordinary activities might he eventually participate in with the family to restore stability – attendance at mealtimes? doing gardening and other chores around the house, perhaps when Jacqueline was at school? participating in family outings? meeting Jenny to discuss the future? arranging not to be alone with Jacqueline in a situation in which she might feel threatened? I asked Stan to write a descritpion of how Jacqueline might be feeling about his sexual abuse of her. Stan wrote:

Jacqueline's feelings
Her feelings of mistrust and confusion are mixed as she was involved in adult activities: mistrust, in that she does not know what will happen when I have moved back in with the family, if it will happen again, how I will feel towards her; confusion, in that she is confused about the boundaries between being an adult and child, also confusion about what has happened to the family unit.

Again, I encouraged Stan to rewrite his description to indicate that he took more responsibility for his sexual abuse of Jacqueline. The final draft read: 'I believe that Jacqueline's feelings of mistrust and confusion would be mixed as I involved her in adult activities. She would mistrust me in that she does not know what will happen if I move back into the family. She does not know if I will abuse her again and how I will feel towards her. She would be confused because I confused the boundaries between adult and child for her, and I also confused the family unit for her'.

Stan started to express anger at his actions and sadness at the loss of his marriage, the break up of the family, and his lowered self-esteem. He talked of suicide. I suggested that he was grieving, and I encouraged Stan to image a different future, one in which he and the family had achieved a different understanding of each other.

Jenny attended a couple of joint sessions with Stan. She was grieving over her past. Jenny had left Colin because of his harsh, discounting treatment of her, and she had been attracted to Stan because of his kindness, sensitivity and generous nature. Now, this!. . . . Being a 'nice guy', it seemed, was not enough! Jenny felt extremely guilty that she had not believed Jacqueline immediately. I shared my experience that I had initially doubted Jacqueline's account also. I commented that some adults never verify the abused child's report. It was regrettable that Jenny had not protected or accepted Jacqueline in the first instance, but the important issue was that she was now learning how to guard her whole family, just as Stan was learning to be responsible for a non-abusive lifestyle. Jenny stated her ambivalence about continuing the relationship with Stan. I suggested that Jenny would have to ask herself continually: Were her children safe from any further abuse? Could she protect them? How was Stan behaving more responsibly? I believed that there was only one course for the future: that Stan, whether he and Jenny stayed together or not, maintained his commitment to non-abuse, and worked responsibly for the family's welfare. Jenny said that she was willing to continue the search for new solutions.

Therapy has lasted eight months. Our conversation has constantly emphasized the themes: How can Jacqueline's safety be maintained? How can Stan support Jenny in protecting her children? How can Stan be responsible and increase his respect within the family? Stan is facing 12 months' imprisonment when the court case is heard. He continues to work and build up his cleaning business, and visits the family home regularly when Jacqueline is at school to do repairs and renovations. Some six months into therapy, Jacqueline asked if the family could go on a picnic together. Stan had expressed his wish to be with the family for Christmas, and the family did arrange some time together over the holiday period. After eight months, Jenny and Jacqueline decided to come to a session together. I discussed with Jacqueline that Stan's actions had been absolutely wrong. He had introduced strange, confusing and adult sexual knowledge to her at a time when she should have been happy enjoying her 'kid stuff'. Jenny had not accepted Jacqueline's story, but had changed her mind after 24 hours. Jacqueline said that she was still angry that her Mum had only believed her after she had told her teachers about the abuse. I commented how common it is that parents do not believe their children when they reveal that other adults are sexually abusing them. I was pleased that Jenny had only taken one day to acknowledge her daughter's story. Some parents never believe their children, and actually blame them for provoking the sexual abuse. I asked Jacqueline if she believed that Stan could change? He had come along to therapy reliably and regularly, certainly appeared sorry about what he had done, and said that he wanted to learn to be responsible. Could he do it? What would have to happen for Jacqueline to feel safe? Could Jenny protect her? I suggested that she would not be able to go on as though the sexual abuse had never happened, but that she could let it become part of the past, and learn to have an ordinary and happy life ahead of her. Jacqueline replied: 'I think that Stan does want to be better. I don't want him to go to jail. I am willing to give him another chance, but he should not come back into our family too easily.' Jacqueline has now commenced her own dialogue with a female therapist.

I continue to see Stan weekly. He has moved into permanent separate accommodation. Jenny and Stan have agreed to live apart, and that it may be several years, when Jacqueline is 18, before they decide to live under the one roof again. I mentioned how frightened Jacqueline had been when discussing the sexual abuse, and how impressed I was that Stan, by choosing to live apart, was putting so much effort into ensuring her safety for the future. Many other men would have given up in this situation long ago.

Eighteen months after commencement of therapy, Stan was sentenced to serve six months of a custodial term. The judge expressed his admiration at Stan's admittance of guilt, his cooperation with the police, and his commitment to therapy and healing the breach of trust that he had caused. He felt that on the evidence given Stan was no longer a danger to Jacqueline, but also stated that a custodial sentence was the only appropriate outcome as the community had a right to express its condemnation of sexual abuse. Jenny had reported that Jacqueline had been asking for the family to reconcile sooner rather than later, perhaps in six months time, and that she now supported this. The judge had praised Jenny's courage in supporting her husband and children.

———————————— · · · ————————————

DISCUSSION

Defining the problem

Stan's description: Stan tells of his dejection following his separation from Jenny. He says he is upset that Jacqueline has accused him of 'touching' her and that there are police charges against him.
Stan's construction: Stan says that Jacqueline 'seduced' him and has been trying to separate him from Jenny since their marriage.

Exploring the context

Therapist's deconstruction: After sorting out, within my supervision group, my own initial disinclination to believe that sexual abuse has occurred in this family, I encourage Stan to strengthen his sense of responsibility. He is affirmed for his acknowledgement of the sexual abuse. His own sexual abuse, and other areas where he has been taught to disrespect women, is examined. The themes of safety, protection and respect are woven into our conversation, and Stan is encouraged to focus, through writing, on how Jacqueline is feeling, rather than on his own emotions. As Stan accepts his responsibility for his actions, he starts to grieve the loss of his family.

Options for the future

Mutual reconstruction: Stan has moved out of the family home, has settled into his own residence, and only visits to do renovations when Jacqueline is at school. During a joint session, Jenny admits both her ambivalence and her willingness to seek new solutions. Jacqueline asks for some joint family leisure activities. Jacqueline, Jenny and I discuss consequences of Stan's sexual abuse and ways of overcoming it. Jacqueline says that she is willing to give Stan a second chance, but not too soon. Jenny and Stan agree to long-term separation and ways to work for the family's welfare. Stan begins to serve a short custodial sentence, by which time the family have agreed to reconcile sooner rather than later.

SUMMARY

In Chapter 14, we considered:
Case 14A, 'Tomahawks and Scuds', in which Shoshana, silenced by her stepfather's sexual abuse, learns to speak out and negotiate some resolutions to the struggles within her relationships.
Case 14B, 'The kiss of death', in which Suzy overcomes the incestuous curse that her father has placed on her, and achieves increased security, protection and intimacy within her marriage.
Case 14C, 'An extraordinary script', in which Arlene becomes empowered, makes her needs known, and starts to have them tended to.
Case 14D, 'Cleaning up his mess', in which Stan, a sexual abuser, takes responsibility for ensuring his stepdaughter's safety, supporting his wife's parenting, and regaining self-respect.

POINTS FOR REFLECTION

1. How do you ensure the safety, autonomy and empowerment of your clients?
2. Describe some of your own case studies which involve sexual abuse, using the Affirmation and Deconstruction schemas.
3. Besides reading Jenkins' excellent book, study White and Epston, 1990.

REFERENCES

Gunzburg, J.C. (1991) *Family Counselling Casebook*, McGraw-Hill, Sydney, pp. 125, 212.
Jenkins, A. (1990) *Invitations to Responsibility*, Dulwich Centre Publications, Adelaide.
White, M. and Epston, D. (1990) *Narrative Means to Therapeutic Ends*, W.W. Norton, London.

PART FOUR
Options for the Future

*Every individual should be unmolested in his or her autonomy,
protected in her or his physical and spiritual integrity*
Jurgen Habermas, *Autonomy and Solidarity: Interviews*,
(Ed. P. Dews, Verso, London, 1986, p. 216)

In Part 4, a selection of stories, letters, anecdotes and poems is presented. These can be useful to share with clients towards the end of their therapy, when encouraging them to examine their options for the future.

Defining the problem and exploring the various contexts within which grief occurs usually involves hard and dedicated intellectual and emotional work on the parts of both therapist and client. It can be rewarding, during the closing stages of therapy, to highlight the collective wisdom which has been discovered earlier, in a clear, sensitive, and often humorous manner, using a story, poem or anecdote.

The cases in each chapter of Part 4 have been organized quite arbitrarily, according to themes which have not yet been dealt with, such as fostering/adoption and change of vocation. Readers may find this material useful to introduce into their own therapeutic conversations arranged as it as, or they may wish to play around with it, restructuring it according to those themes considered in Parts 1, 2 and 3, such as chemical abuse and incest. Or they may be stimulated to compose tales from their own experience, adding their own unique touch of creativity to generate a conversation that leaves the client unmolested in their autonomy, protected in their physical and spiritual integrity.

Affairs

15

...

CASE STUDY

Case 15A   Chemistry

Nigel, 31, an industrial chemist, was disconsolate following a series of what he called 'failed' relationships over the past several years. The first, with Alison, a teacher about his own age, commenced when Nigel was 25. Alison was beautiful, very much a socialite, but also very much an 'ice queen', intellectual and passionless. They both decided to conclude their friendship after four years, and Nigel immediately chose Tanya, a teacher ten years his junior, as an intimate partner. Tanya was adoring of Nigel, idolizing him, but also very clinging, always wanting to spend their every moment together. Nigel ended their liaison after 18 months, and went on a four-month holiday to the USA. In Los Angeles he shared a two-week whirlwind romance with Dayna, 36, a cosmetician, culminating in Dayna's decision to leave her photographer husband of ten years, Macon, 40, and emigrate to Australia. She wrote profusely to Nigel on his return, affirming her desire to join him, but during the past week had informed Nigel that she was choosing to remain in California with Macon.

I asked Nigel to compose a short essay describing his struggle within his relationships, and he wrote: 'I know what my problem is. I think that I need another person there to give me some sort of external fix when what I really need is inner strength and contentment. I am always afraid that other people will take me down. I never have been able to speak up for myself. I always feel that with a girlfriend there, I will get that external fix. I will always be someone important. She will give me a boost. But what I really need is some way to boost myself up from within.'

We discussed how each partner had given Nigel a lift: Alison because of her beauty and intelligence; Tanya's unswerving devotion; Dayna's lusty sensuality. I asked Nigel which relationship had influenced him the most.

'Alison was a great conversationalist, but it was a bit like living in the Arctic, brrrrr! very chilly! Tanya was nice but too dependent, too heavy. I could not carry her for long. Dayna was fantastic! We had chemistry. We were magic together. But do you want to know something funny? I was shocked when she told me it was all off, but I was so relieved too. I really hated the cheating and lying to Macon. It is the first time that I have ever been with a married person. I feel like a real shit for having done that. Never again!'

We talked about Nigel's family of origin. His parents, two sisters and brother, had migrated to Melbourne from London when Nigel was 16. Nigel remembered them as quiet, dedicated and loyal to one another, but without any colour, dialogue or praising of each other. He could not recall having ever had a conversation of any substance with his father, although he was sure that his Dad was proud of him having joined the Military Reserve Corps. His mother had been too preoccupied with housework to spend much time with them either. Nigel said that, at school, university, and in the army, he had been shy and a loner.

'So perhaps you are not really such a failure at your relationships?', I suggested. 'It seems that you did not have much discussion with your parents or peers to learn what your values were, what you believed in, what the world was about. It also sounds as though you did not feel very important growing up in your family. Perhaps your friendships have been explorations, short-term relationships that were never meant to last a great length of time. Your affair with Dayna certainly seems to have created impact for you. It may have been fun to be infatuated with each other for a while, but out of it, you seem to be approaching your relationships with more sensitivity and responsibility, acknowledging other peoples's needs as well as your own. Do you think that this could become the inner strength about which you write in your essay: your newfound sense of ethics, integrity, authenticity and self-worth, so that you will never need to involve yourself in another person's marriage again?

Nigel smiled from ear to ear, and his despondency lifted over the next two weekly sessions.

Nigel has set intimate relationships aside for the moment. He is exploring ways to live more comfortably as a lone person, and we are examining means whereby he can boost his self-esteem. Recently, Nigel asserted: 'It's good stuff, this therapy! I'm really enjoying all this talking. You are kind of like a different Dad to me.'

· · ·

—————————   · · ·   —————————

CASE STUDY

Case 15B   The boss's wife

Arlette, 41, a restaurateur, and partner with her husband Lawrence, 47, in their venture, Arlette's Bistro, said that she was beside herself with anxiety.

'I have fallen in love with Danny, 33, one of our waiters. Danny has just left his own wife Cheryl, 32, and I cannot stop thinking about him. I cannot believe it. I offered to meet with Danny anywhere, anytime, to become lovers if he so wished. He said no and I cannot let it rest. I am so obsessed, and depressed, with wanting him. I think that I am having a nervous breakdown.'

A professional ballet dancer, Arlette had married Lawrence 17 years ago after having conceived their first child. She had settled, she said, too easily into the role of 'cook, wife, and bottle-washer', accommodating her own needs to Lawrence's wishes for the family. They had three children, Antoinette, 17, Jasmine, 14, and Tommy, 3. Arlette had been on the point of leaving Lawrence when she had conceived Tommy unexpectedly.

I decided to weave the theme of 'revenge' into our conversation. I suggested that Arlette had been trapped (twice!) and compromised in her marriage to Lawrence, and that, underneath her depression and anxiety, she sounded furious about it. Was she contemplating an affair with Danny to demean her husband? How humiliating for the boss if he were to discover his underling underlying his wife! Would Arlette and Danny one day find that Lawrence, seeking his revenge, had skewered their giblets?

Arlette took a vacation in the Daylesford mountain ranges to contemplate her future. After a week of relaxing massages, tension-relieving saunas and refreshing mineral spas, Arlette told me at our next session that her lusting for Danny had disappeared, and that she had commenced negotiations with Lawrence about proceeding as gently as possible towards divorce.

—————————   · · ·   —————————

CASE STUDY

Case 15C   Searching

Austin, 22, a media student, had met his girlfriend Tess, 22, a graphic design trainee, while they were both members of a charismatic faith three years ago. The religion had provided purpose, fulfilment, direction and vision, but both had decided to leave when they discovered nepotism and corruption among the church's elders. Austin complained of his aimlessness, emptiness, and increasing arguments with Tess, who was currently seeking help from Anne, another family therapist. Anne had seen them together a couple of times and had referred Austin to me because she felt that he might benefit from therapy with a male practitioner. When life went well, Tess and Austin enjoyed socializing, dining out and cult cinema. Austin was also studying Italian.

As we met weekly, Austin described his emptiness. His family was one in which there were high expectations and pressures to perform. There appeared to have been no time made for the young Austin to fill himself up with warm, emotional experiences. Austin was quiet and serious in nature, with no concept of 'ordinary naughtiness' or fun, and we discussed how Indiana Jones always seemed to survive his scrapes unscathed. I asked Austin to do a sensory exercise: would he focus on ten different objects during the coming week and note what he particularly liked about each of them – shape, colour, size, texture, substance, consistency?

At our next session, Austin said that he had reached out to touch the world, fingering twigs and leaves, smelling flowers, even tasting a new exotic fruit, and that he was experiencing a great deal of sadness. He felt more open, vulnerable, and had been dreaming again of sexual encounters with men. Austin had been attracted to his own gender ever since adolescence. He wondered if he should go out to a local gay discotheque, and have a 'one-night stand' to sort himself out?

I told Austin that I admired his willingness to examine his world, spiritually through religion, emotionally with Tess, sensorily during the exercise, culturally via Italian, and now wanting to explore his sexuality. But what would happen if he carried out his one-night affair and found that he really liked the experience better than Tess, or that he was smitten with his lover? Would he be wracked with guilt over his betrayal of Tess? Did he deserve to put himself in a position where he faced Tess' outrage at his disloyalty? Might it not be more appropriate, fairer even, to negotiate with Tess an end to their monogamous contract and let her adapt to the changes necessary? Her disappointment might be easier to counter than her rage, and would Austin be left with a sense that he had acted with some integrity towards her? I asked Austin to list the pros and cons of a gay lifestyle.

Austin came to our next session visibly relieved. His sadness had gone and the arguments with Tess had ceased. I asked him what had created change. Austin said that being able to discuss his homosexual feelings without being blamed had been important, and somehow it had emphasized that he did have some options. He had thought about the advantages/disadvantages of a gay relationship, had decided that he was in fact bisexual, not gay, and in such a circumstance his life with Tess was proving reasonable. Were he eventually to be single at some future date, he might reconsider the issue of choice of intimate friend. Austin believed that he had been feeding into the arguments to form a pretext whereby he could have a covert affair with less guilt. Now that he had determined to stay with Tess, there was no need to continue the bickering.

· · ·

CASE STUDY

Case 15D   Betrayed!
Kemal, 27, a cabinet-maker, was expressing his sense of betrayal, anger, sadness and loss after his wife of four years, Aliye, 24, a delicatessen assistant, had informed him about a weekend affair that she had had with Tony, 31, a car mechanic. Kemal had left Aliye for a month after the news, then had decided to try reconciliation, and said that he now felt that his wife was always comparing his sexual prowess with Tony's. To make matters worse, Tony's garage was opposite Kemal's workplace, and Kemal was beset with murderous thoughts every time he saw his perceived rival.

During a series of joint fortnightly therapy sessions, Aliye said that she did not know why she had become involved with Tony. The sex had been poor and he had 'dumped' her, rejecting every contact after that weekend. Aliye had been left feeling confused and guilty. She described her marriage to Kemal as going downhill for perhaps two years. Not only were they both often fatigued in the evenings from the rigours of their employment, Aliye said that Kemal had been 'romantically' very demanding of her, and would sulk if he did not get his way. His need for sexual contact seemed to have increased severalfold after her affair.

'But Aliye is never very happy when we have sex', Kemal commented. 'I can feel it; she holds back. There is always something there between us.'

I affirmed this couple's struggle to achieve a more rewarding relationship. I praised Kemal's restraint. Many other men might have done injury to their wives for their betrayal, yet Kemal had chosen the difficult, and sometimes painful, path of therapy to help heal the wounds. I was admiring that Aliye had not given in to her guilt, and was wanting to learn a new way of partnering Kemal. I asked Kemal to write a letter to Tony (but not necessarily send it) expressing his feelings and sense of revenge. We worked for a while on negotiating. Aliye valued her independence, wanting to go out to lunches and theatre nights with her friends.

'But you see what happens when she does her own thing', said

Kemal. He was obviously grieving the loss of 'specialness' in the relationship, and had difficulty in trusting his wife during her leisure activities. I asked Aliye and Kemal to do a grieving task: to take out photos of their wedding, contemplate what their dreams had been at that time, and to imagine some new dreams for the future. I asked Kemal what Aliye would have to do to increase his trust whenever she went out: Tell him where she was going? With whom she was mingling? How long she would be? Leave a telephone contact? I asked Aliye how she could increase Kemal's sense of belonging within the marriage: Confide in him more? Plan activities with him as well as without him? Give him special, surprise treats?

Kemal and Aliye were starting to warm towards each other after six months, and we took a break. About ten months after their initial session, they both came back, with Kemal furious and Aliye forlorn. Aliye had been diagnosed as having herpes and all Kemal's anger had resurfaced again.

'I can understand that this is upsetting news', I said. 'I guess how you both handle it will be important. You could regard it as an unfortunate setback or a major catastrophe.'

I asked them to draw how they saw each other at this point in time (Figs 15.1, 15.2), and they brought their images to the next session.

'That is Kemal, alright', Aliye said. 'With a big dick, and always sulking!'

'And that is Aliye . . . all locked up!', snorted Kemal.

They both laughed.

'You have drawn a halo around his head', I commented, 'and you have noted a lot of good qualities like love, trust, sweetness, on his left arm.'

'Well, he is a lot better since we have been coming', said Aliye. 'It is only his moods since I got herpes that get to me.'

Kemal turned to his wife: 'But you still do not enjoy our love making; you hold back. I can feel it. There is a barrier there between us.'

Kemal and Aliye settled once more and commenced planning a vacation to their Turkish Cypriot homeland. At our last session, a week before they were due to leave, Aliye was distressed to have heard that her father had sexually abused a couple of her pre-adolescent cousins, and now wondered if he had abused her also.

'So perhaps that is the presence that Kemal experiences when you two make love', I suggested gently. 'The devil in the bed is Aliye's father.'

Learning of the father's violations appeared to have joined Aliye and Kemal in their anger against him. They were furious that his irresponsibility should have proven so influential within their marriage.

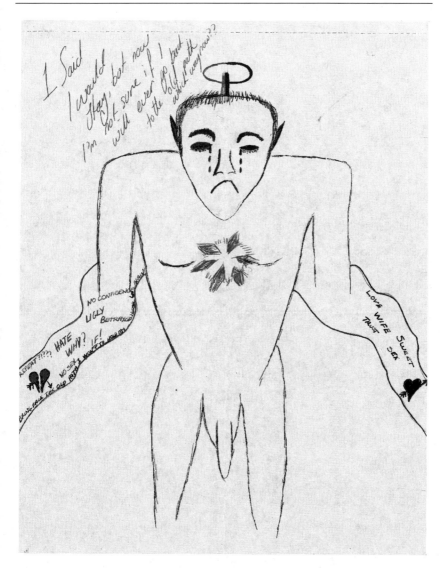

Fig. 15.1 Aliye's drawing of Kemal.

'Perhaps that is why Aliye let Tony con her', Kemal said. 'She was all mixed up by the past.'

I received the following postcard a month later:

Dear John,
Well, how are you? Kemal and myself are having a good time. We have seen a lot of sights, both in London and England. Now we

Fig. 15.2 Kemal's drawing of Aliye.

have just arrived in Cyprus. When we arrived at the airport, I got a big shock; the airport was so small! I was planning to write this in Istanbul Airport because we had a six hour stopover. But when we arrived, one of our suitcases got lost. I was so upset, I just wanted to come back home. But that's our luck for you. But we remembered what you said: 'It's just a minor setback!' Ha! Ha!,
Love,
Aliye and Kemal

--- . . . ---

CASE STUDY

Case 15E Like father, like son?
Felix, 39, a motor mechanic, and Stacy, 29, a part-time cleaner, were at the point of separation. Stacy said that she had had enough of Felix's flip attitude, his tendency to walk away from problems, and his seeming inability to be affectionate. She was still furious at a weekend extramarital affair in which Felix had participated several years earlier. Felix had walked out on Stacy in a huff after a quarrel, had stayed out all night, then next morning, had told Stacy about his dalliance with the 'dolly bird' at the disco because he felt guilty and did not want her to hear of it from a third party. Felix and Stacy had three children, Tamara, 9, Bentley, 7, and Susan, 2. Stacy was despairing that her relationship with Felix could ever be repaired, and that divorce was the inevitable outcome. Felix sat silently while Stacy told their tale. I asked them both to consider how their marriage might be different, and we agreed to meet weekly.

As our conversation continued, it became clear that Felix's father, Friderich, 65, was an 'ein, zwei, drei' patriarch who had given his son a dedicated training in 'disrespecting women'. He had constantly berated both his wife and daughter-in-law as 'hopeless, incompetent, stupid cattle'. Recently at a family barbecue, Friderich had approached Stacy, grabbed a handful of buttock and stated: 'What you need, my dear, is a good smack!' Stacy had slapped his face, Felix said that he had been stunned by his father's and wife's actions. It was the first time that he had noted his father might not be the 'good bloke' he always thought he was, but Felix still had not known how to respond. Stacy was furious that Felix had not spoken to his father in her defence. I turned to Stacy and suggested: 'What you need is a divorce, but not from Felix, from Friderich. Would you both write a bill of divorce for the next session?'

This seemed to create some impact. Stacy had immediately thought that I was suggesting divorce from Felix, as she had expected me to do.

When I focused on 'divorcing' Friderich as the villain, Stacy had started to compare father and son. They were both male-oriented, but Felix certainly had a sense of fairness which Friderich did not, and her husband did value their children. I asked Stacy and Felix to list ways that they made each other happy, what was not acceptable in their relationship, and what was negotiable.

Stacy decided that their marriage could survive and grow, and that perhaps Felix really did not have to change too much for both of them to get most of what they wanted. Therapy lasted seven sessions, and during our final meeting, I offered them one of my poems that I sometimes give to couples who are deepening their intimacy.

Sonnet
Friendship is the meeting of two hearts,
The interchange of feelings, redefining
Of how two intimates relate. Unlike the refining
Of precious metals, with removal of unwanted parts,
The dross in our friends is accepted. Our rough, rude
Corners are not smoothed over, sculpted away,
But loved and understood. That is a friend's way.
We cherish our friends and accept their change in mood.
In friends we find ourselves. We complete
Ourselves and are larger than before.
We accept ourselves. We become more
Tolerant. We learn how others feel
And think, their pains and joys, the real,
The dishonest, the bitter – and the sweet.

——————— · · · ———————

Death

16

— . . . —

CASE STUDY

Case 16A   Nightmares

Della, 33, an insurance agent, described her recurrent nightmares that had commenced when her brother Alex, younger by two years, had been killed in a head-on car collision 18 months previously. The drunken driver of the other vehicle had been charged with manslaughter and imprisoned.

'Alex wore his hair Afro style', Della said. 'I keep seeing the accident when I am asleep. Alex is burning; his hair is all alight. It is horrible!'

'I wonder if you could re-dream the scene and view Alex being killed instantaneously on impact. Then he would not be suffering the pain of the flames.'

Over two weekly therapy sessions, Della's nightmares ceased. I asked her to compose a letter, addressed to Alex, expressing her feelings about his death. Della wrote:

Dear Alex,

I hope you are peaceful wherever you are. Were you alive when the flames touched your hair? Was your car like a fiery tomb? Oh God, I hope not, you did not do anything to deserve that. I got the bastard who killed you, but anyway, you would know that.

I know that you had no choice but what a dowry you left me with. It is worse than it was when you were alive, because now you are dead. This has made a perfect excuse for everyone to drop their bundle. I know you want me to love and look after Mum, but by Christ, sometimes she is not look-afterable or lovable. I miss you because you are the only one who really understands the family history. I really need to talk to you; it is your turn to take over; I am getting tired and confused. Mum used to have her shit together and Dad was the bastard. Would you believe that Dad is really trying and Mum is playing games? If you were alive, and had children, the heat would be off. You do not have to come back, but if only I could have your opinion, your company, your understanding. I hate playing the martyr but I feel that there is no choice; come back and rescue me!

Mum really was affected by your going. Doesn't that sound admirable? It is such a game, a measure of how much she loved you. If she shows that she is more affected than others, it is obvious she loved you more than others. There may be some element of truth in this. Although she carried you for nine months, and lived through Dad's alcoholism with you, I reckon she really plays it up.

Right now, you are probably thinking: 'Della, you are a bitch, those are very significant things. Of course Mum will be grieving, she may never be the same and you will have to learn to understand that, and support her, no matter what!'.

But Alex, there are degrees! Mum always has a perfect alibi. She can do whatever she wants because she has a caseful of scapegoats: Aunty Sally's death, molestation as a child, written out of her mother's will, your death, an alcoholic bastard of a husband, hard work, the men in and out of my life. Mum never has to take responsibility for her actions (perhaps she should not have to!) but every time I want her to be positive or simply to 'have a go', she cries and says 'I can't . . .'

I almost feel pity. Only almost, because she has learned to play me off around these issues. I really do hate her for it sometimes. I feel like saying 'get some balls' and do something; see a psychiatrist, tell the whole world to get f---d, but DO SOMETHING. Mum wobbles like a pitiful mass of jelly on my plate. She used to have balls, guts, determination, a zest for life and that is why you loved her, but you should see her now. Maybe you would not see her the way that I do. That would be OK. You could side with her and I could go and do my own thing,

I love you, I miss you,

Della

It was obvious that Della was furious that she had been left to clear up the family mess. This appeared to have been Alex's role, and now it seemed to have passed on to her. We concentrated on how Della might lay down boundaries between herself and her mother, and mark out her own territory. Therapy lasted ten sessions, with Della eventually leaving for an extended holiday in Europe.

· · ·

——————————— · · · ———————————

CASE STUDY

Case 16B   The suicide

Liz, 22, a photographer's assistant, was deeply depressed since the suicide of her mother Nan, 46, a month earlier. Nan had been disabled due to congenital dislocated hips, and plagued by recurrent episodes of depression.

'Mum seemed so strong-willed, so tough', said Liz. 'I did not expect her to go like that.'

Liz's elder sister Jessica, 26, a singer, was 'totally overwhelmed' by the event and the younger sister Lesley, 21, a nurse and heroin addict, was 'angry as hell'. The three women were very close and were supporting each other in their grief.

I asked Liz to write a letter of farewell to Nan. Liz showed me her letter at our next meeting, a week later.

Dear Mama,

I love you so much and wish that I could have held your hand and said goodbye properly. I spoke to you briefly Wednesday night, never knowing that would be the last time I heard your voice. I miss you so much. I hope you are still with me and that you are happy at last and free to go where you wish – wherever that is, I love you forever, goodbye, Liz.

Liz said that her mood had changed after she had completed the letter, and she was experiencing Nan's death as a 'mellow sorrow, with many tears', rather than the heaviness of depression. We discussed how the three sisters might gather together in memoriam for their mother, and share their feelings. Liz said that she was now experiencing some anger that her mother had always appeared preoccupied with her own struggles, with little time left to acknowledge the youthful Liz's needs. It was as if Liz now bore a placard: 'Here stands Liz who might have been nice for Nan to know'. We talked about how Liz might reach out to some friends over the next few weeks to remind herself that others found her nice to know. Therapy lasted three sessions. I asked Liz how I might have been helpful to her. She replied: 'It was when you suggested that I write my farewell letter. I was able to say the things that I feel without cracking up'.

——————————— · · · ———————————

CASE STUDY

Case 16C   Breaking down the wall

Anton, 15, a secondary-school student, and his mother Irina, 42, a secondary-school English teacher, were referred to me because of

Anton's obsession with death. He stated repeatedly that on his 18th birthday, the age on which he would be permitted to own a gun, he was going to purchase a weapon and shoot himself. Anton had no friends and would lounge around the house in the evenings and at weekends, smoking cigars, and watching violent horror movies on the video. He would pronounce his intention frequently, apparently quite oblivious of Irina's obvious distress.

Anton's father had died of brain cancer when Anton was five, and Irina and her son had moved into her mother's house and had been living there since. The mother, Marina, 75, had proved to be a feisty tyrant who, Irina said, demanded complete fealty to her rules. Anton would vent his anger on Marina's cat, and torment it most cruelly.

As joint fortnightly therapy progressed, I found myself dealing with Irina and her efforts to break free from Marina's control. Anton largely sat silent, occasionally indicating his thoughts in brief, single sentences. Anton was furious at Irina's brother, Andrei, 48, a mathematics professor, who seemed to be a bit of a martinet and wanted greater influence over Anton's welfare.

'He's not my father', Anton asserted. 'He behaves like a bloody school ma'am!'

I asked Anton, who had artistic ability, if he would draw a picture of Andrei. Anton seemed pleased with his effort (Fig. 16.1). He had drawn the uncle's face over that of a glossy magazine female cover model. The picture appeared to be a good revenge for Andrei's attempts to control him.

We discussed what would happen if Anton did carry out his plans for suicide? Would Irina survive the distress? What would she miss about him? How would she build a new future? After many months, Irina and Anton moved into their own two-bedroom unit. Irina commented that, although she had sought help for Anton's struggles, she was finding our conversation enlightening in a way that she had not expected. Somehow she had found the strength to stand up to Marina and Andrei.

Many world events were happening during the course of our meetings. The Berlin wall had come down and the Soviet Union had started to disintegrate. It seemed distinctly possible that countries like Irina's Ukrainian homeland might achieve their independence. Irina and Anton appeared also to be enjoying their new-found freedom in their unit. I asked Anton: 'Are you still going to kill yourself when you are 18?'

'It is an option', Anton replied. I almost fell off my chair.

'But you were so certain for so long', I commented. 'What has made the change?'

'It was when the Berlin wall came down', Anton said. 'I never thought that such a thing could happen.'

Fig. 16.1 Anton's drawing of Andrei.

I turned to Irina and said: 'It is nice for me to have such competent co-therapists as the German diplomats helping me here in Australia!'

Therapy, which lasted two years, concluded with encouraging Anton's continued growth and independence from Irina, as she had grown away from her own mother and brother. We talked about some leisure routines and a future vocation, Egyptology. Anton told me that he was organizing a trip to Germany with an exchange student with whom he had become friendly. At our final meeting, I offered Anton one of my stories, which I said I had written during his therapy.

Cleaning up the pond

On the first day of the fortnight, Jessie the kangaroo came to a large pond to drink. Jessie liked the pond. The water was fresh and cool. Honeyeaters sucked nectar from the bright spring blossoms that grew around the edge. Small green frogs shone in the sunlight like jewels on the wet, grey rocks and fish darted back and forth in the crystal clear water. It felt good to be alive here!

On the second day of the fortnight, Jessie came to drink and found a tin, a straw and a plastic bag left on the banks of the pond. Some people had come to have lunch the previous day and had forgotten to take away their waste.

On the third day of the fortnight, Jessie and her friend Lester, the emu, came to drink and found that their favourite spot had been spoiled. Someone had come to picnic and had let a can of fuel leak into the pond. Large blobs of oil dotted the surface and the body of a dead fish floated towards them. Jessie and Lester had to walk a long way around the pond to find fresh water to drink.

On the fourth day of the fortnight, Jessie found that her favourite food bush had been burnt. Some campers had neglected their fire and it had spread. There were no leaves or berries for Jessie to chew and no seeds or fruits for Lester to peck. The animals did not eat that morning and had to search until sunset to find food.

On the fifth day of the fortnight, Jessie and Lester discovered that the special gumtree under which they liked to rest in the heat of the day was gone. Some loggers had cut it down to make woodchips for their paper factory.

On the sixth day of the fortnight, Jessie and Lester were frightened by a dreadful noise. Some people were starting to build a large factory. There were many big gumtrees growing at the pond and the people wanted to turn them all into small woodchips. The clatter of the machines and the smelly smoke were very disturbing to the creatures of the pond.

On the seventh day of the fortnight, Jessie and Lester found that great changes had happened at the pond. The honeyeaters had gone because the smoke from the factory had dirtied their air and poisoned their flowers. The fish were nowhere to be seen and the frogs had vanished. Their water was filled with grime from the factory. There was no drink, nothing to eat and no shade. Jessie and Lester felt thirsty, hungry, hot and lonely. They walked all around the pond and found no clean water, no food, nor shelter.

On the eighth day of the fortnight, some thoughtful and kind people came to the pond and were very sad to see what had come about. They wrote to the government of the country who instructed the owners of the factory to limit their logging, to grow more gumtrees whenever they cut down the big ones, and to stop spoiling the air and water with their smoke and poisons. The factory owners listened carefully. They had not realised at first how they were affecting the pond. Now that they knew, they decided to follow the instructions.

On the ninth day of the fortnight, a tiny flower sprouted from the soil and turned its petals towards the morning sun. Five days later, a small sprig of green inched upwards from between the rocks. It was the first of the new gumtrees. A new fortnight had commenced. But it took many fortnights before the trees grew to full height, before the honeyeaters returned and the fish splashed again in the pond. It took many more fortnights before Jessie and Lester could make this pond their very special place again, to rest and eat and drink. And after many, many, many fortnights had passed . . . just when everyone had thought that they had gone forever, one small green frog was heard croaking cheerily to another.

Two weeks after his 18th birthday, Anton came to say hello. He had passed his last year's examinations with distinction, and was pleased to tell me how his plans for his proposed trip to Germany were proceeding. No monosyllabic talk from Anton during this conversation!

_____ . . . _____

CASE STUDY

Case 16D   Come again
Ailsa, 32, an adolescent counsellor, was dejected over her current relationship of three years with Jeremy, 30, a bass guitarist in a heavy metal band. All her friends were advising her that Jeremy was a bit of a clown, unable to settle down, and that Ailsa, who wanted marriage and children, should leave him.

As we met weekly, Ailsa told me of her parents' high expectations of all their children, and that she never felt able to achieve them, as had her siblings. Life in Ailsa's family of origin was remembered as a lonely experience, and recently she had been dreaming of buildings with empty windows in them.

At our fourth therapy session, Ailsa mentioned her sadness over a termination of pregnancy, fathered by Jeremy, five years earlier. I asked Ailsa if she would think about writing a letter to 'the baby that might have been'. Ailsa brought her letter a week later:

> It is difficult to write to someone or something that I have been so strongly denying. I had visions of wanting to do this properly, of going to the grave-side of a baby and finding your forgiveness in silence, surrounded by the protective, shaded spots of ancient trees. That being the dream, this being the reality.
>
> I write to you with the radio on, a snatched moment in between cooking dinner and organising other things. Never the way I wanted to do it, but at last, achieved. And maybe that is why I do not have you with me, because it would never have been the way I want it. I was so scared back then, not settled within myself, not able to be the mother you deserved and I would want to give you.
>
> Slowly I am finding that confidence and stability. If you can wait, you could come again and we could venture together along the rocky road. I sometimes think of you, and add that extra year to year life, and watch you grow that little more. In my mind, you are a pretty little girl with pigtails now; a pretty child. So do not go, but wait for me. It will be worth the wait. I will be a great mother.
>
> To tell you about Jeremy and I, we are still together and I have my hands full with him. We hurt each other enough on our own. I dare not think of the pain that we would inflict on each other, and you, if you had been.
>
> Resolution is achievable. I feel more and more the role I play with Jeremy becomes impossible, and I will move on to find a new role, as mother, wife, lover . . . so please wait for me as I wait for you.

During our next final three meetings, Ailsa's sorrow dissipated. She said that she had realized that she was beating herself for not being strong enough to continue the pregnancy, and that her friends were also expecting her to end the relationship completely with Jeremy and move towards successful marriage, as had her family. Ailsa felt that she might focus more on enjoying her life as a single person. She was considering ending the intimacy with Jeremy while retaining him as a good friend. Ailsa said that she even saw herself having a child by a committed 'live-out' lover . . . and she was dreaming of buildings with windows, some of which had faces in them.

· · ·

--- · · · ---

CASE STUDY

Case 16E   Fire!

Frima, 54, had sought help after her husband, Mottel, 76, had died from bowel cancer. Mottel's passing had not been an easy one.

'Why are you still alive?', he had shouted at his wife during the last days of his decline. 'Don't you remember we promised to die together when we married?'

Over a few therapy sessions I helped Frima defuse the guilt aroused by Mottel's statement, by discussing his unkindness in reminding Frima of vows that they had made when they had first met. I suggested that young lovers often made unrealistic promises during their initial passion, and I felt that it was unfair of Mottel to renew the pledge, when Frima was vulnerable and sorrowing over his demise. Frima had responded, and, after Mottel's death, had continued to grieve quietly without too much anxiety, but now, a year later, she was in a terror!

'It is terrible, doctor', Frima said. 'I am so scared about starting fires. Everywhere I go, I search to see if I have dropped a tissue or handkerchief from my pocket or handbag. I think that it will burst into flame and that I will be responsible for a large fire and cause injury and death. I know that this is meshugah (crazy) but I cannot help myself.'

I listened to Frima for about 30 minutes, then said: 'Mrs. Bloom, I want you to do something which you might find rather strange, in fact you may think that I am a bit meshugah in suggesting it. Would you walk immediately to the hardware store closest to you, purchase a small fire extinguisher, and hang it in your kitchen?'

Frima came the next week. 'I went to three hardware stores, and even the third one said that they would have to order an extinguisher for me, but I do not think that I need it now. I am no longer bothered by fires inside my house. But I have another problem. Next weekend is my granddaughter's Bat Mitzvah, and I am worried that I am going to drop a tissue out of my pocket and set the reception hall on fire. So I have worked out what to do. On Friday I am going to walk in front of the hall, and drop a tissue outside the front gate. Then I am going to walk around the block. When I come to the front gate, if the tissue has not caught fire, I am going to leave it there on the footpath, and not put it into the rubbish bin as I would usually do. I will leave it there.'

'This is a terrific idea', I said enthusiastically, 'but make sure you do not get booked for littering.' Smiles from us both, and problem solved!

--- · · · ---

Fostering/adoption

17

--- ... ---

CASE STUDY

Case 17A Call me madam

Marika, 40, a mature-age student of English for 'University Entrance Examination', was distraught that her son Nathan, 28, whom she had adopted out, had contacted her. Raised in Queensland, Marika had conceived Nathan when she was 12 years old. Her mother had just left the family home and Marika's alcohol-abusing father had raped her in a bout of drunken fury. Marika had chosen to continue with the pregnancy, adopt the baby out, and get on with her own life. Now Nathan had appeared unexpectedly, and demanded to know who his real father was. Nathan would not reveal how he had obtained details concerning his biological parents, but it did not seem to have been through legal channels. Marika had given no permission to tell him. Marika had told Nathan that she did not wish to discuss the circumstances of his birth, and had requested that he did not contact her in future. Marika was extremely distressed about the whole incident.

'I thought that this was all behind me', she said. 'Now all the old manure has been stirred up and I am sinking into it!'

As we conversed weekly, we discussed the numerous violations within Marika's life: the father's rape, her marriage to Malcolm, a verbose, alcohol-abusing brothel owner, who had left his first wife and children well before he had met Marika. He had intimidated Marika into working for him as a prostitute. Marika and Malcolm had twin sons, Robert and Michael, but Malcolm had 'persuaded' Marika to undergo two terminations of pregnancy after this. Working for Malcolm, trying to raise their sons, dealing with the children from Malcom's first family, all proved too stressful for Marika. She felt that she 'was going mad', and eventually left the family home. She divorced Malcolm, who was awarded custody of Robert and Michael because of their mother's 'desertion'.

'I just would not have coped with custody of the boys', Marika asserted. 'It was as much as I could do to hold myself together. Malcolm is a bastard to women, but he has never abused any of his children and has shown concern and commitment to their welfare.'

Marika moved to Melbourne and spent some time organizing her own escort agency.

'I was a pretty good Madam in my time', she said. 'I ran one of the most successful agencies in Melbourne for several years.'

Marika, having set herself up financially, had sold the agency to commence studying, and had become involved with David, 42, an alcohol-abusing psychotherapist. She had kept in regular correspondence with her sons, and had visited them twice. Marika also kept good contact with her mother, brothers and sisters, and a few close friends, but the encounter with Nathan had really sucked her back into the swamp and she did not know how to clamber out again.

I mentioned that one of my clients, Miriam, a 42-year-old woman who had also been physically and sexually abused, was currently considering working as a prostitute, and I was concerned for her welfare that she might be exploited. Marika must have learnt a great deal of wisdom in her time as a Madam. Would she write an anonymous letter that I could give to Miriam to help guide her in her choices? Marika wrote:

So you want to be a prostitute? Why? There can be only two reasons. You know that? I do. I have been there. One is money, and yes, it is a lucrative business if, and only if, you are good at what you do and have the luck to attract wealthy clients. The latter must have another prerequisite; they must be of high social standing. It is safer for you that way.

The second reason might be the same as what brings your client to you; some-one to talk to, some-one to share with for a little while, but, it does not work. Why not, you ask? These men do not want emotional involvement, and empty sex is pretty bad for your ego, so in the long run, what you end up with is dollars and dollars of loneliness. You spend the dollars as fast as you make them in a futile effort to fill the emptiness inside. But, let me tell you some of my experiences.

I started in a parlour and quickly built up a clientele. These men would sit and wait for me even though other ladies were available. This created problems for me with the other girls and after putting up with this for a while, in the futile hope that things might get better, I set up on my own, in a telephone service; this service has since developed into today's escort service.

Well, things really started to happen then. There are dangers associated with being in this business. Terrifying situations, that are hard to get out of. One night, I was called to a plush hotel in the city and headed straight for the lift to get to my client's room. There to greet me was not only my client, but four of his mates. To say I was frightened is an understatement. I managed to talk my way out of this, could you? And what if the men you copped were not as nice as the blokes with whom this happened to me? I could have been raped. I could have been mutilated. I could have been murdered. No-one would have cared much except those who love me and they would have been very hurt by the revelation that their daughter, sister, aunt, mother, they loved was a prostitute. Would they understand? Would they forgive? Could I forgive myself? Could you, if you were ever found beaten and battered, perhaps mutilated beyond repair. I have seen it happen to others and I have had a few close calls. One night, a very wealthy visitor from overseas, who said that he was of noble birth, chased me round and round a room. He thought he got ownership for the money he paid and wanted to beat me to get his kicks. I managed to get into the bathroom, which thank goodness, had a lock, and wonder of wonders, a phone in it. I rang room service and when the waiter came up I calmly slipped by him and left. One time I was caught by the police (this one is very good for your self worth) and decided: no more! My children are starting to grow up. I do not want them to know this of their mother. I did not work again, but the humiliation to which I had subjected myself had left its mark. Others might have coerced me into this way of life, but I allowed it. I made many excuses to myself about why I had done this. The truth, which I never admitted, was that my sense of self worth was reduced to a big, fat zero. The shame of having allowed myself to be reduced to a commodity, and putting a price on myself like any other commodity, has been devastating and destructive.

It took a long time, and the love and support of a lot of people, to find myself again. My children are now nearly grown up and I am faced with telling them my past. If I do not, my former stepchildren will. Could you face that? I sure find it difficult.

My advice to you is: do not do it – the price is too high. The possible prizes are mutilation, rape, death, disease, and the newest and grandest prize of all, AIDS.

Value yourself and others will value you. That cannot be bought with dollars and cents. I am now a student and life for me is truly wonderful. My greatest friend and asset is myself. But, the road is long and, if you have been that far down, it is a hard road too. Now, do you really want to go down there?

I hope not.

Chelsea Williams (Marika's professional name)

Following this, Marika's mood lightened and we discussed future directions. Robert, now 14, moved to live with his Mum, after he decided that his Dad was a bit too verbally aggressive to handle. Marika ended the relationship with David, whom she had found too dependent, and moved back to Queensland, where eventually Michael also came to live with her. I heard a year later that Marika had passed her first-year psychology examinations with honours.

And Miriam? She read Chelsea William's letter, decided to dabble at escort work and left four weeks later, after one of her colleagues had been beaten to a pulp by two foreign diplomats. Miriam has now embarked on an extended tour of Europe and America.

· · ·

CASE STUDY

Case 17B   Something's happened!

Alice, 48, a secretary, was upset at the behaviour of her daughter Heather, 16, a secondary-school student, both of whom attended our first therapy session. Heather and her eldest brother Charlie, 22, an arts student, were always fighting, largely because Charlie teased Heather over her having been adopted by Alice's family.

'You are not really one of us', Charlie would say, 'not really the proper article.' Heather would react immediately, often pummelling Charlie with her fists. Her other brother Nick, 19, a psychology student, would be continually involved in assisting Alice to restore the peace. Alice's husband Tom, 50, a public servant, was often at work during the times of conflict.

As our conversation progressed over the next four weekly meetings, it became clear that Alice was the hub of family activity, bending over backwards for everyone else until her spine creaked. Alice said that quite recently she had contemplated leaving them all.

'Oh, she will never do it', cut in Heather brusquely. 'She's always complaining. Nothing ever happens in this family. Nothing ever changes. But what can you expect. She never has any time for me. I am adopted. You cannot expect her to love me like a real child. She would never pay attention to me as she would a real daughter. She is always on Charlie's side.'

I commented that the family appeared to be a very busy one, everyone being involved with studies or duties of some sort. I wondered if it was true what Heather had said: that there was no time for the family to get together to enjoy themselves? Perhaps that is why there was so much fighting all the time, to make sure that everyone was getting a fair share of the attention? Sometimes families are so busy with their routines that they miss the good times when they do happen. Would Alice and Heather take time out for coffee one evening and discuss what they wanted from each other? Would Alice list the happy times that she did remember spending with Heather? Would Heather plan a special treat for Alice, something really subtle, and see if her mother did detect it?

At our sixth meeting, Alice brought along a collection of photographs of those moments with Heather that she cherished, winning swimming trophies, and at the debutantes ball, and said that Heather was still being very rude to her.

'Oh, nothing's happening', retorted Heather. 'She is still the same as always.'

They had not planned any time together as yet, and we talked more about how this might happen: lunching? shopping? walking together in the bush? Heather said that she wanted to shop around for a dress on her own. She had never done this and all her friends were allowed by *their* mothers to do this. Alice, while expressing doubts that Heather would be able to spend within a budget effectively, agreed to let her try next Saturday morning. At the end of our meeting, Alice read out a poem that she had cut out of a magazine, and treasured, to both Heather and me:

The Adopting Mother's Poem
Not flesh of my flesh, nor bone of my bone,
But none-the-less, my very own;
Never forget, not for a minute,
You were born, not beneath my heart, but in it.

By our seventh session, Alice stated: 'Something's happened! After our last session, Heather threw her arms around me, and said: I do love you, Mum'. Heather smiled quietly, pleasantly. She had purchased a dress as planned and had not broken the bank. Afterwards, mother and daughter had met for lunch. The fighting at home had all stopped. I congratulated both of them on having achieved a major change in their relationship, and we discussed how this might be maintained in the future. We conversed on how scary it was to grow into adulthood with all the work and responsibility it entailed, and the importance of setting aside time for fun and refreshment. I asked Heather what part of our conversation had created the most impact for her, and she replied: 'It was when Mum brought the photos and read her poem. I felt then that she really made time and cared for me'. We decided to leave the date for our next meeting open, and I gave Heather the following story, which I said I had written for my own daughters when they had reached their teens.

A Wallaby's Tale

There once was a young wallaby, a girl, who had reached the age to go on a journey. One sunny summer's morning, she came to a beautiful forest. There were tall stately gumtrees, ferns in the undergrowth, white daisies, fragrant yellow wattles, salmon pink banksia blossoms and the occasional bottlebrush and melaleuca bush, with their crimson and mauve blooms. Also in the forest were many winding pathways that seemingly led to nowhere. During her childhood, the wallaby had gained no knowledge about forests. Her parents' view had been that children should learn about their world entirely by themselves, without guidance. Consequently, as the young wallaby commenced to explore one path, then another – stumbling down a gully here, falling over a rotting stump there – she ended her journey bruised, puzzled and a little lost. Another young wallaby, also a girl of similar age, had been given a map to the forest by her parents. They had told her that she should follow its direction, without question. During her travels, she missed out on seeing many aspects of the forest and was left feeling isolated from other forest dwellers. Yet a third wallaby came along, same age, carrying the same map. Her parents had told her that this map was the same one that they, and their parents and grand-parents had used. 'Study the map well', her parents had said, 'but do not accept it blindly. Go to the billabongs where other wallabies and their teachers, the wise wombats, discuss it, learning about it together, and finding different meanings in it.' This the wallaby did. She invited the first two wallabies, who were sitting at the edge of the forest weeping quietly, to join her. They travelled through the forest and met others of their kind who were also exploring the map. As their journey proceeded, they found that they experienced, and understood much about, the ways of the forest. They made other friends both amongst wallabies and other forest creatures, numbats and dunnarts, possums and gliders ('Who is clever?', the wise wombats had taught, 'she who learns from all animals'). As the years passed by, the wallabies continued to learn and grow, and eventually, chose to have families of their own. They felt very good about themselves, and were particularly pleased that they had developed rich and rewarding maps to pass on to their children.

Six months later, Alice telephoned me to say that the improvements had remained. Heather had decided that she would feel more comfor-table engaging in some personal 'women's talk' with a female therapist.

Alice said that Heather seemed to be gaining confidence in her own self-image through these conversations, and was entering into dialogue with her mother more and more. I told Alice that I was delighted that Heather was choosing to discuss issues concerning womanhood with her own gender. To me it was a great outcome, wallabies and wise wombats gathering at the billabongs together!

— — — · · · — — —

CASE STUDY

Case 17C   Reconnecting

Amelia, 15, a secondary-school student, told me of her confusion, disorientation and lack of direction since she had left her mother Sandra, 44, a secretary, three months previously. Sandra, an imbiber of alcohol, had been verbally abusive to her daughter for many years. Amelia had decided that she would take no more and had moved into the home of Jana, 15, a schoolfriend. Now, Jana and Amelia were fighting, with Jana bashing the less robust Amelia, and Jana's mother, Lainie, 44, apparently unable to control her daughter. Amelia did not know what to do.

Sandra's life had been filled with upheaval. She had divorced Amelia's father Colin, a storeman, when Amelia was six, and almost immediately had entered a relationship with Tim, an alcohol-abusing bricklayer, who physically violated Sandra, Amelia and sister Kate, three years Amelia's senior. Sandra and Tim's daughter Kelly, now 7, seemed to have been spared Tim's attacks. Kate had left the family when Amelia was 11, to live with her boyfriend, and about this time one of Tim's friends sexually abused Amelia. Sandra had commenced her own reliance on alcohol, separated from Tim when Amelia was 12, and a year later had migrated from New Zealand to Australia. As it happened, before she had married Colin, Sandra had divorced her first husband Jeff, who had fathered their daughter Mandy, 25. So Amelia had lots of family: sister Kate, stepsister Mandy, both of whom lived in New Zealand, Kelly, who lived with Sandra, and a father who lived in New Zealand, from all of whom Amelia was disconnected. Amelia said that she missed Kelly enormously.

I was concerned at Jana's beatings of Amelia and phoned Lainie, who came to a therapy session on her own. She described Jana as a difficult girl who, Lainie suspected, was heavily into drugs. Because of Jana's big build, her mother was frightened of being hit also. We discussed Jana's apparent jealousy of Amelia, and the possibility of transferring Amelia to emergency foster care. This was arranged within the next 48 hours, and Jana settled down during the subsequent few days.

During that week, Sandra had flown to the United Kingdom, taking Kelly with her, to start a new life for herself. There had been no message of farewell for Amelia from either of them. Amelia said that she was devastated. She surely felt apart from every member of her family, yet did not belong to her new foster family. I offered Amelia the following story that I had written for another young person in similar circumstances:

A Place to Belong

[Gail, 8, is a survivor of abuse by several male relatives and associates of her family. Recently, she has returned from her father's house to live at her mother's place. Gail and her mum are fighting constantly. Gail was telling me during a weekly therapy session about some of her pets. I said that I would like to write a story about Gail . . . would she draw a picture to go with the tale? Gail has given me permission to share the story and illustration (Fig. 17.1) with you.]

Gail sat underneath the willow tree at the bottom of her garden in the cool of a Melbourne summer's eve. She was a pretty eight-year-old girl with long blonde tresses of hair and eyes that matched the blue corn-flowers by the pool. Gail was very unhappy. She had recently come to live with her mother, brother, and four step-brothers. For two years, she had been living with her father in another country, but the father had sent Gail to her mother's house because he was no longer able to care for her. Mother's house seemed so new and nobody seemed to have much time to play with Gail. She felt so lonely and very sad that she did not have any place to belong.

Midnight, the cat, wandered out from behind the willow's trunk, rubbed himself against Gail's legs, and purred: 'What is the matter, Gail? Why are you crying?'

'I am so sad, Midnight', replied Gail. 'I do not feel that I really belong in this family and I do not know where else to go. Sometimes I feel so lonely that I get angry and make a fuss to get someone's attention, but it is always the wrong sort of attention . . . a yell or a smack . . . and I end up feeling even more sad.'

There was a rustle in the branches of the willow. Max, the cockatoo, had landed after his evening flight. In a cage nearby, Mischief and Mitzi, the two guineapigs who had been tussling over a piece of lettuce, paused and turned towards Gail.

'We felt just like you do when we first came here', said Mischief. 'We were a bit frightened to be in a strange and different place.'

Fig. 17.1 Gail's drawing.

'Then we decided to rearrange the furniture in our cage', Mitzi continued. 'We made sure that the food bowl and water jar were exactly where we wanted them. We put the straw in a special corner where we would be most warm.'

'Our cage became our very special place!', they both said.

Max the cockatoo cackled from the treetop: 'Whenever I am lonely, I fly. I soar up into the air and join my friends. For hours, I curl and swoop and curve with my mates, feeling as free as a bird.'

'Whenever I am sad, I stroke myself against someone's legs', purred Midnight knowingly. 'Then I get caresses and cuddles and lots of delicious food!'

Gail got up immediately and ran into her bedroom. She took one of her favourite pictures that had been stored in a box for years and hung it on the wall next to her door. She fetched Teddy Bear and gave his coat a good brush, and put him next to her pillow. Gail would remember to give him a big cuddle before going to sleep. Then she went and gave her mother a hug.

'It is nice that your are my Mum', said Gail.

Mother smiled and replied: 'You are a real sweetie when you are in a good mood. Would you like a piece of pie, and we could go and get a video to watch?'

Mother took Gail to hire *The Wizard of Oz*. Gail shared all the adventures of Dorothy, Lion, Tinman and Scarecrow, and by the end of the film, she felt that she had found some new imaginary friends with which to share her dreams. As she fell asleep, Gail wondered: would she one day find some new real friends, within her family or at school, with whom to share her dreams?

At our next session, Amelia said that she had decorated her new bedroom to a design of her own choosing, and the family had held a special welcoming dinner for her. As we continued to converse weekly, Amelia said that she was feeling more and more a part of that home, but it was difficult to trust anyone after her stepfather's abuse and her mother's rejection. We talked about ways that Amelia could get what she wanted within her foster family. We discussed assertiveness, and the use of 'I' messages to express feelings, e.g. I feel unheard, I feel intruded upon, I feel comforted by what you are saying. We considered sharing resources and taking risks, e.g. Amelia liked writing poetry. Would she compose a poem for the family about how she felt? Would the family respect expression of her feelings?

Three months later, Amelia came to therapy with brilliant green hair and a cheeky grin. She had joined the school's theatre company and had been chosen for the role of Puck in Shakespeare's *Midsummer Night's Dream*. I said to Amelia that I was glad. It was about time that she had some magical moments in her life! Amelia had initiated correspondence with her father Colin, and expected to spend next Christmas in New Zealand with him.

Change of vocation 18

CASE STUDY

Case 18A   The critic

Cathryn, 29, a hospital microbiologist, was saddened at the thought that her planned third child might never be. Married for six years to Timothy, 46, a university lecturer in comparative religion, their two children Peter, 5, and Anne, 3, were giving Cathryn much pleasure. Cathryn felt that a third child would be truly 'life-giving'. A major area of conflict, however, was that Timothy had commenced earning income late in life. A member of a religious order for 20 years, Timothy had decided to embark on a secular life, had married Cathryn, and believed that because of his delayed start as breadwinner, he could not afford financially to support a family of five. Timothy found that his two active youngsters were already a distraction for him, and together with the stresses of his work and Cathryn's part-time employment in a hospice, felt that another child would surely create an intolerable pressure. Cathryn was of a different opinion. She felt certain that they would both accommodate well to a third child, if only Timothy would take the risk.

'I feel so often attacked by Tim', said Cathryn, in tears. 'He bludgeons me intellectually into submission and frequently criticizes me for being an inadequate wife and mother. He says I am unable to keep the house tidy to his standard. I feel he is always using this argument against having another child.'

The couple rarely shared time together to enjoy themselves. Their main conversation appeared always to focus on: child, or no child?

'Another problem', said Cathryn, 'is that Tim wants me to take second place to his career. He does not seem to acknowledge my earning capacity as valid. Perhaps if he did, he would be more assured that we could afford an addition to our family.'

Timothy said that he was willing to attend therapy, but not until he had completed working on his thesis for a higher degree, which might take some months.

We discussed Cathryn's family of origin, and she described her mother Therese, 60, a nursing sister (retired), as a judgemental, guilt-provoking person who always expected high standards of her daughter. Cathryn's father Paul, 63, an accountant, seemed rather like Timothy, kind yet dogmatic. I suggested to Cathryn, who was very intuitive and psychologically aware, that perhaps something rather Freudian was happening here: Perhaps Cathryn had internalized the critical part of her mother Therese, and had married an authoritarian man rather like her father, and this was contributing to part of her conflict? Would Cathryn write a letter to her 'internal critic' and find out what it wanted of her? Cathryn wrote:

What is your name?
How do I access you, inner critic? How do I learn your name?
Maybe if I try to think of something good about myself . . . something I am proud of . . . or perhaps if I look in the mirror . . . examine my premenstrual skin . . . look at my hefty outline . . . or even step on the scales . . .
Why do you choose late at night to taunt me . . . to ruin my well-earned rest?
Why do you chosse the times I feel most content . . . most pleased with who I am . . . to jab a pin into my joyous balloon?
Who are you? What is your name?
You seem so familiar, yet you evade my direct glances. You never look me in the eyes . . . you lurk around the edges . . . leak out.
Your odour, your fragrance of disease surrounds you.
What do you gain from your spite . . . your self-righteous, judge-mental, moralistic taunts . . . what good do they achieve?
I set out to befriend you . . . and have lured you out of your bottle only to have you control me once more.
Why do I let you have power over me?
Are you afraid that I will have power over you if you tell me your name?
Are you afraid I will trick you back into your prison and seal off the lid?
Well, I must admit that you serve a useful purpose . . . you keep me honest most of the time . . . keep 'Integrity' as my breast plate . . . keep my feet on the sweet earth . . . help me to enjoy the simple pleasures of my life . . . swing my pendulum back from the triumphs and achievements that are only half of life.
What is your name, little one?
I see that you must be little, to slip into so small a sanctuary.

Why are you so fearful? So angry? So sad?

Why are you so separate? You are really a part of me.

'I have carved you in the palm of my hand . . . you are precious to me' . . . are you a child? left behind from years gone by?

Were you hurt as I struggled to be me? Were you rejected as I competed to be best . . . and failed?

You seem sad . . . head hanging low, shadowy figure . . . you have no power now . . . at this moment . . . and yet I give you such power . . . such disproportionate power . . .

Shadow . . . critic . . . self.

How can I appease you? How can I persuade you to be a little more gentle with me? I am keen to hear what you have to say, but could you be a little more civilised?

Give me credit for what good is in me. After all, I am created in my Father's image . . . His handiwork . . . even if flawed.

Perhaps that is blasphemy to think of myself as flawed?

The beauty in the potter's ware is in the uniqueness . . . the unevenness . . . the very characteristics that make it a handmade piece.

You help me to balance, proprioceptor-like, as I tilt to and fro, like a spirit level, you affect the spirit of my being.

Are you a victim as much as I? Are you empowered as I am too?

How can we live together . . . you and I?

For I am determined . . . determined to grow.

I will not allow you to hold me back,

Let us move ahead together.

Ah, you have tricked me again . . . I have lost sight of you . . . you nag like a mother . . . you twist your wire with barbs that sting.

You sound so reasonable at first . . . a simple suggestion . . . an uncomfortable feeling stirs . . .

No, I do not want to do it your way . . . I do not want to feel guilty for being independent . . . for meeting my own needs . . . for being more truly myself. I do not want to feel guilty for being a sexual, grown up being. I want to be free . . . to be a seductress when it fits . . . free to be a nurturer in the Spring . . . free to mourn and weep in the Autumn . . . free to change and challenge when the Summer breeze blows through . . .

Like an asthmatic spasm, you choke the life out of me.

I am so frustrated in your wake . . . I do not know who I am . . . who to listen to . . . who to discount . . .

For too long you have mirrored the Great External Matriarch.

Now, you seem to be outside myself . . . but I know you are not.

I have some control over you, as you have over me.

I will answer you back now, critic, and you will change from witch to wise old woman . . . or will you?

Following this, we discussed how Timothy's demands might be triggering off Cathryn's 'internal critic', and how she might separate her internalized discounting messages from Timothy's comments so that she might present her own needs more clearly. Whether they decided to have another child or not, the choice had to be reached in such a way that both Timothy and Cathryn felt that they had mutual influence on the outcome. Timothy, on completion of his thesis, attended some joint therapy sessions and our dialogue focused on clarifying communication and ways that they might nourish each other more. I asked Cathryn to script an argument against having another child, and Timothy to argue for it. They did not do this task. Cathryn found it too painful, Timothy too overwhelming. We discussed their differences in age, how each of them was wanting activities that could be regarded perhaps as age-appropriate: Cathryn, the younger person desired another child, Timothy wanted some of the comforts of middle age. I read them the story of 'The draftsman's contract' (Gunzburg, 1991), which deals with some of these issues. Finally, I offered Cathryn and Timothy a biblical tradition that is not often mentioned by our various patriarchal religious ministries to their congregations. Rather than considering Eve to have been created from Adam's rib, another understanding of Creation has it that humanity was initially formed by God with male and female joined together (Genesis 1:27), hermaphrodite, with faces on opposite sides of the head, and that God separated them at the level of the rib so that they could face each other and cooperate as equal partners with each other. From the root of the Hebrew word k'negdo (Genesis 2:18), we can learn out that the phrase 'Adam and Eve were created to cooperate with each other' can also be understood as 'Adam and Eve were created to challenge one another'. They were created with different perspectives of the world, to challenge each other respectfully, to achieve resolution of dilemmas, each speaking from their own unique experience of the world. Timothy, Cathryn and I chuckled. Here were two devout Catholics and their committed Jewish therapist discussing a fairly radical interpretation of scripture with the enthusiasm of fresh-faced students from a theological seminary!

Our conversation has continued for six months. Cathryn is starting to consider other experiences that she might find 'life-giving' in her vocation (having applied for another job), studies and social contacts. Timothy is more generous in his praise of Cathryn's input into household maintenance, and he is ceasing working at weekends so that the family can have more time together, and so that their marriage can be enriched. I commented that perhaps their relationship had become their third child?

— — — — — · · · — — — —

CASE STUDY

Case 18B   Broken?

Austin, 44, a stockbroker originally from Manchester, was downhearted that his marriage of 18 years to Sue, 36, a nurse, was in the process of breaking up. They had two children James, 16, and Martin, 13.

Over the last six months, Austin had become very fond of Irene, 30, a nurse, and single mother of Jessie, 3. Whereas Sue was pleasant, supportive, sensitive and kind, Irene was intellectual, sophisticated, social and exciting. Austin and Irene did not share a sexual intimacy, but Austin felt that he now had to make some choices about which woman to partner in the future.

There were several other areas of his life in which Austin felt broken. An asthmatic since infancy, and teased cruelly at school as a wimp because of this undeveloped physique, Austin was experiencing increasing wheeze and cough since he had met Irene. He had been hospitalized two months previously with severe asthma. Austin related how, as he lay on a bed in the Emergency section awaiting admittance, the presence of his deceased father, William, came to him and took him on a journey, out of his body, past his residence.

'That is where I live', Austin had said.

'No', William had replied. 'That is where you used to live.'

The father and son had encountered a beautiful, mellow, warming ball of light and Austin felt, at that moment, that he had to choose between going with William into the light or back to his body. He said farewell to his father and returned to the hospital.

'I have no doubt that you were very close to death at that moment', I said to Austin gently.

Austin told me that his memories of William were very powerful. He remembered his father as an alcohol-imbibing, autocratic hardware merchant, who had fought with British forces in France, Holland and Germany, and had been among those troops who had liberated Belsen concentration camp. William had physically abused Austin's mother, Clara, and had been involved for many years with a 'Mrs Beveredge', which had caused great scandal within their local community. I commented that William seemed indeed to have been influential in Austin's growth to adulthood. Would he compose a letter to his father now, expressing his feelings? Austin wrote:

Dear Dad,
I am sorry to disturb you after all this time but I need your help to help me understand some things from the past. This is because I am now in a great deal of trouble.

All my dreams are turning to dust. My finances are a disaster. My self-esteem and self-worth are at an all time low. I have never before ever been involved in so many arguments and litigations at the same time. Very few people like me . . . probably only Sue, James and Martin. I even seem to be arguing with friends, even Irene, whom you would like.

I felt your presence, the love of a father, yet I also felt the terror of a small defenceless child at the mercy of an adult. You seemed so close that I felt your breath on the side of my neck. I could smell you. It would have been so easy to have gone with you and died.

The question is: Did you, father, experience my situation? Is it some family trait that goes back generations that is destroying me now and stopping me doing justice to myself (I am worthwhile, I do have talents) and my family?

If it was not for my responsibility to my family (compare this with your own example), I would either have run away with Irene or ended it all. But why should I give in? I have still got a lot to give. I will not let the bastards grind me down. They can all get f———d!

I will understand, learn and try to lead a worthwhile life, even if only as an example to my family not to give in, and rise from the ashes like a Phoenix.

Why: – did you treat me so harshly as a child?
 – did you take no interest in my education? I produced one of the best ever geographical field studies.
 – did you find so much fault in Mum and argue so much and fight?
 – did you not love me?
 – did you not take control of your life?
 – did you behave like a sniffling, querullous, servile servant to upper class people, and not treat Mum with more respect, and bring shame on Mum and your family?
 – Dad, at this time of crisis, for whatever reason, I have relived some of these memories, these events from the past. Although there were good things in my childhood – our travels overseas, uncles and aunts, grandparents, Mum needing me – there were also events that have left permanent scars.
 – your Victorian attitudes that terrorised us as children.
 – hiding in my bedroom as a scared child.
 – your banging on the stairwell.
 – your punishment of my bed-wetting.
 – your smashing the window frame.
 – your affair with Mrs Beveredge, a source of argument for evermore.

– your inability to control yourself.
– your anger around the time of the birth of my sister.
– my asthma, spending time in hospital, giving away my cats.
– my calling the police to stop you and Mum fighting.
– your drinking.

Yet, given all this, your shop was always the best branch out of 112, the most profitable, with the highest turnover. You were devoted to your work, never to your family.

If your childhood and life were unhappy, why inflict the pain and guilt on me?

Remember me now,

Austin

Austin told me that writing this letter had unleashed a great deal of pent-up anger that he had carried for much of his life and that he had been thinking differently about his options. He felt that his attraction to Irene was largely because she represented the upper class. Austin has always wanted to be part of the British Establishment, and on the face of it, although he enjoyed Irene's company immensely, he did not feel that he could really make a go of it being her partner. Austin had decided that what he needed was a change of vocation, rather than spouse. He had started legal moves to sell his business, realize what assets he had, cover his debts, and commence anew in a consultancy.

Six months later, Austin says that he has ended his relationship with Irene, that he and Sue have considered some quite fresh and exciting pathways that their marriage could take, that his new venture is under way, and that he has had no further episodes of asthma.

--- . . . ---

CASE STUDY

Case 18C   The growth

Mara, 32, a psychologist and family therapist, asked me if I would see her aunt and uncle. They had been arguing incessantly for months and appeared to be on the point of separation. Mara was very fond of them, and wondered if I might be able to help them resolve their painful impasse.

The uncle and aunt, Tom, 49, a Roads Corporation inspector for many years, and Eileen, 52, a retired housemaid, had been married for 28 years, and were content in having raised daughter Nancy, 28, to adulthood, a career, and a family of her own. Tom, who had also followed a part-time vocation as a professional wrestler, wanted to make a change and was training to qualify as a sports masseur. They were tired of their quarrelling, felt that their marriage was dead, yet somehow could not agree on a time schedule for separation.

I asked them why they originally chose each other as partners? Could they remember any of the good times they enjoyed when they were courting?

'Oh, no, doctor', Eileen responded, 'that was a terrible time. Eight months before we married, Tom underwent a lobectomy for lung cancer. It really blew the wind out of our sails.'

I commented that Tom and Eileen must have really believed in each other to have continued their course into marriage with each other, and give life to Nancy, after such a rocky event, but that it must have been rough sailing for much of their time together. They would have never been quite easy with each other, never knowing if and when Tom's cancer was going to recur. I was very admiring of their endurance and commitment to each other over this time. But it must have taken a lot of time and energy learning the ropes when sailing such rough seas. Perhaps there had been little time for fun, or to care for each other, working under such duress? Perhaps some of their current emotions were grief? for lost moments, opportunities for intimacy, peace of mind, growth?

I said that I wanted them to participate in some experiments before next meeting. I wanted to see if they could uncover some information that might be helpful to them in coming to a decision about their future. Would Tom consider giving Eileen a massage, and Eileen give him feedback on his technique? Would they have a meal together and, every now and then, offer each other a spoonful of food from their own plate? Would they plan and spend an hour together each week 'not being nasty' to each other? Would they make a list of what was going right for them? Sometimes, when our lives have been rough sailing, we tend to miss what is going right for us. And would they go and see the Billy Crystal–Meg Ryan film *When Harry Met Sally*, dealing with the many facets of commencing and maintaining intimate relationships.

At our second and final meeting, a week later, Tom said: 'We did not do that feeding exercise, John. We both thought that it was a bit over the top. But everything else seems to be going all right now. We have had a really nice week. I gave Eileen a massage and what she told me about it was really helpful to my learning. We enjoyed the film you suggested. We do not need to see you again.'

Six months later, Mara passed on a message to me from her mother, who is Eileen's sister.

'Your friend John is a miracle worker. . . . Eileen and Tom are terrific now!'

I mused to myself: 'Mara's experise is in brief therapy, and it took two sessions to make some significant gains with Tom and Eileen. I wonder . . . had Mara been a psychoanalyst, would I have taken a little longer?'

———————— . . . ————————

REFERENCE

Gunzburg, J. (1991) *Family Counselling Casebook*, McGraw-Hill, Sydney, p. 258.

Past involvement in a war zone

19

CASE STUDY

Case 19A   Reflections in the dark

Zev, 73, a retired university lecturer in humanities, was depressed. He feared for the future that, with the union of the two Germanies and the fall of the Soviet Union, fascism would rear its ugly head, as in the 1930s and 1940s. Zev had spent two years hiding from the Nazis in a Dutch farmer's cellar, without even a candle light to give him solace. Zev was also mourning the compulsory retirement from his job at 65.

'It was ridiculous for me to have cease working at the university when I still had so much to give', he said.

'You have a remarkable skill', I responded. 'You survived in a dark place without light. It is the sort of skill that many of us would like to cultivate. Would you write an account describing how you did it?' Zev wrote:

When the Germans overran Holland in 1940, I served in the Dutch army. At that time, prominent Jews committed suicide. As my fellow soldiers reminded me later, I saw the future for our people as being rather bleak. After my dismissal from the army, I went back to my previous job as assistant manager of a large dye works, but I knew the bad days were still to come. Slowly the noose around the necks of the Jews was tightened. I was one of the last Jews to be sacked by the Germans who took over the factory of the Jewish owner. I then went to work with our friend, the wooden shoe maker. I was arrested by a local Nazi who accused me of having changed a V sign (Victory for the Germans) into a W (Wilhelmina, the Queen of Holland). I was six weeks in the local police cell. I was able to do some painting notwithstanding the danger for the police who allowed this. I had to appear before the S.S. Commandant who threatened to send me to a concentration camp. Suddenly I was on the street once more, and knowing that I could be arrested again, I fled to another part of Holland. I worked as a farmer's help but a local Nazi policeman recognised me and I had to return in a hurry to my parents' home.

Radio, cars, bicycles, etc. were all confiscated and Jews were not allowed to travel more than about one kilometre from their homes. In the meantime, my elder brother had already been killed. The message said that he 'died of pneumonia' within the concentration camp. My younger brother and I were ordered to go to a so-called work camp in the middle of Holland.

Most of us who worked there dug trenches. I, however, was the only one selected to look after the sick and feeble. All I could do was comfort the weak, old men; shoemakers, tailors and the like. One day, the S.S. surrounded the camp to transport everyone to an assembly centre further within Holland, and from there, to Auschwitz. Unfortunately many Jews were not aware that the trains were taking them, not to nice work camps, but to places of mass slaughter.

My brother and I fled. We crept through a gap in the barbed wire fence and ran across a paddock to hide in the neighbouring bushes. We hid for about half a year with fond friends. A Dutch Nazi nearly arrested us. We fled again, sleeping a few nights in the fields, then hid in the attic of an acquaintance's farmhouse. But that place was not safe. At night we made our way to another farmer, who had always been a good friend of our family, not far from my birthplace. The son of the farmer was not afraid but his elderly parents were very scared. The place assigned to us was an underground liquid cow dung reservoir (Fig. 19.1)

The cow-shed and also the reservoir were not in use any more and the cellar was full of water. The farmer's son would pump out the water and build a wall somewhere in the middle so that on one side the water which constantly seeped through the walls would be collected. In the meantime we hid in a neighbouring cow-shed in the comfort of the rather warm hay which was on our bed and dining-room floor. From there we went to our underground dwelling where we stayed for more than two years. We never could change clothes. All the time we were wearing, day and night, the same underwear and suit which were our dinner dress and pyjamas. The manhole inside the shed was just suited for us. A somewhat fatter person could never have gone through. A bucket was our toilet. The floor in our part of the dwelling was always wet. When we were on our feet we wore clogs as they are

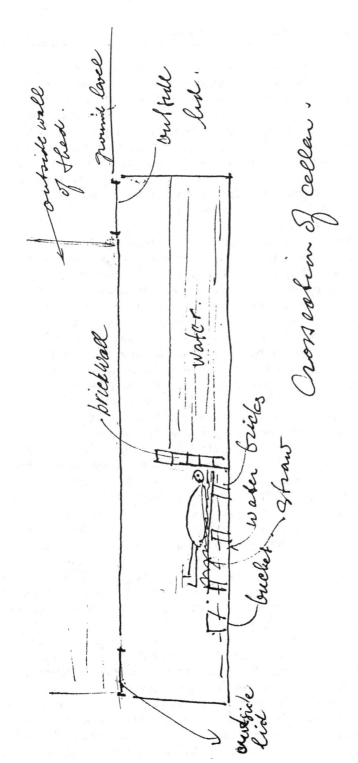

Fig. 19.1 Zev's drawing.

warm and comfortable. Our bed where we spent nearly twenty four hours of the day consisted of: some bricks on the floor, on top of which were some planks, and then straw. We had a few blankets which kept us pretty warm, moreso underground, especially in the winter, when the temperature is much higher than outside. Two times a day the farmer brought us food in a big pan with two spoons. Breakfast was oats with delicious fresh cow's milk, a luxury in that time, and towards evening a pot with potatoes in buttermilk, and sometimes a piece of wholemeal rye bread. A few times we had a small piece of veal, from a clandestinely slaughtered animal.

During our stay there one of us had to watch through a slit in the door of the cow-shed. If there was a suspected danger we immediately disappeared through the hole, attempting to cover the lid with pieces of straw. A few times the German soldiers were manoeuvering not more than twenty centimetres from the wall of the cow-shed. Our dinner place was always underground. It was dark. Only a bit of light came through the lid of the cellar from the outside reflecting on the water like a lake on which a faint light, in a far distance, is reflected. The water before the wall had to be scooped out regularly otherwise we would have been flooded.

Our favoured occupation at night was to listen to noisy rats upstairs and place traps so that we could care for the poor creatures as pets. Also a sow was our companion upstairs in a pen. Twice a year she got piglets. The little fellows made a hell of a noise fighting for their mother's teats. Mother pig was not so fussy about her diet. She gobbled up with gusto the afterbirth.

The last winter, 1944–45, was especially cold. The temperature was about ten degrees (C) below zero. At that time, the world did not yet have central heating and all the other modern comforts. We remembered our father washing himself with icy cold water from our house pump. We now followed his example, one of us always watching for danger, whilst the other undressed and washed his body with the cold water under the pump in the shed upstairs. But one time my brother became very sick. According to the farmer there was an epidemic of what we now call gastro-enteritis. We had to leave our underground hiding place and wait in the attic of the shed packed full with hay. This situation became very critical. I noticed that my brother had a constantly high temperature, diarrhoea, and was discharging blood.

The farmer became increasingly concerned. His main worry was, in case of death, how to dispose of the body. I prayed with all my might. My brother became very cold, then suddenly, like a wonder, he seemed to recover. As soon as he was sufficiently fit again, we went back to our safe underground home. Several times we had arguments. My brother wanted to leave the place and flee to the unoccupied zone in the south of France. The farmer warned us not to bring his life into danger in case we were caught. My thoughts were mainly religious ones: Trust in G-d and I felt His Presence constantly. The short times we were in the shed, we read a bit in a Dutch bible provided by a colleague from work. I thought of the prophecy of the great prophet Ezekiel who spoke about the time when we rose from the dead. We were told that our whole family was taken away by the Nazis on a Wednesday, and from that time on, we fasted on a Wednesday, sometimes even until the next day.

As an amateur artist, I had a lot of fantasies, saw pictures by day, or at night, dreamed about our past and present. In the day time, we would hear the farmer and his workers talking. We heard the ducks and poultry and sows. Night was often the most exciting time when hundreds of English and American bombers thundered over on their way to Germany. We were not far from the German border and, when it was safe, we went out and saw the mighty, German floodlights trying to catch the Tommies. There were heavy air battles and, with great sorrow, we sometimes saw a Spitfire come down. The farmer gave us pure silk boots from a pilot who was shot down not far from the farm house. Often heaven and earth were trembling from the cannon fire and bombardments.

In general, I felt a sense of well-being, tranquility and peace. The days and nights went rather quickly. My mind was mostly occupied with pleasant thoughts, and sometimes, with the disaster that the world was in. Most of the time we were staring at the water and the light in the distance, talking to each other about our lost family and the friends who had helped us.

It was with some reluctance that we left, after liberation, our dark world where I had felt safe. The doctors gave me about six weeks U.V. light treatment and high energy fools . . . and then, I started my new life.

Zev's depression lifted over the next four weekly meetings as we continued to discuss coping with boredom in retirement, the pleasures he got from his grandchildren, and working towards communal equity. I saw Zev some five months later, riding down the street on his bicycle, waving to me as chirpy as a young lark!

———————— · · · ————————

——————————————— . . . ———————————————

CASE STUDY

Case 19B   The immigrant
Toni, 17, a secondary-school student, and her mother Edith, 40, a housewife, both attended our first therapy session. Toni was telling me of her increasing fear of school examinations. Although she had had no troubles until the past few months, and had achieved pass results until now, Toni constantly dreaded the recurring tests during term. Toni said that she felt 'really stupid'.

Edith, who spoke only rudimentary English, added little to our conversation and Toni frequently translated our words to her mother in their native Hungarian.

Toni and her family had come to Melbourne from their homeland two years previously, at the end of 1988. Toni's eyes moistened as she remembered the friends whom she had left behind. She described the emigration as a confidential one. They had not been able to tell anyone of their intentions to leave for fear of being stopped by the authorities, and Toni had found the secrecy rather scary. En route, the family had spent seven days in an Austrian transition camp while their papers had been processed. During this time, one internee had battered another to death. When Toni arrived in Australia, she had been excited by the expanse of the place, the space and country-like atmosphere.

Toni had gone straight into state school, had encountered language problems, and after three weeks, had entered a language school for five months. She made lots of friends among the cosmopolitan community there, losing them again when she reentered state school. Toni said that now she numbered only two friends, a girl from Chile and another from Spain.

I commented on the many changes in Toni's life as an immigrant to Australia, and admired the family's pioneering spirit, coming to another country to make a new future for themselves. I said that I would try to help Toni overcome her fears. We agreed to meet a week later.

Between our first and second meetings, Toni spent three days in hospital with stomach ache. Appendicitis had been suspected, but her condition had settled and she was discharged without intervention.

Toni, who attended this time on her own, told me that besides her examination anxieties, she was experiencing great fears concerning death. She was bothered by all the turmoil in the world: the impending Gulf–UN conflict, the political changes in Germany and the Soviet Union, and was dreaming repeatedly about the murder in the Austrian transit camp.

'But', I interjected suddenly, 'it would be terrible if you were to grow to old age and die before achieving what you want out of life. You are young, and there have been so many upheavals in your life: leaving your homeland, the violence in the transit camp, losing your friends, learning a new language. It must be very difficult for you to find firm ground on which to keep your feet, so that you can make some choices about your life . . . and that seems to be your problem; how to make the choices in your life so that you are going to get what you want before you die. You are afraid of doing examinations. Passing examinations will help you to progress and get the things that you want in life. If you choose to sit for your examinations, you will have to face your fear of doing them . . . and if you choose not to sit for your examinations, you will have to face your fear of dying without having achieved the goals in life that you wish. I wonder if you would make a list of the things that you want to achieve in your life to see if they are worth facing the fear of sitting for your examinations?'

As we continued to meet weekly over the next month, the focus of our conversation shifted from Toni's fears of further loss to her hopes for the future. She wanted to become a travel agent. I asked her if she would acquire the information necessary to do this, and she brought me in all the details. Toni listed the things that she still missed from Hungary: her hometown friends, mountains, snow, and we discussed how she might find them here: Bright, in winter, strengthening the friendships that Toni was making at school with some Indonesian, Japanese and Chinese students who, like her, were new settlers. Finally, we discussed how Edith did not allow Toni to have her newfound friends visit, and sleep over, at their home, and how Toni might have to initiate a 'loving tussle' with her mother to achieve some adult rights.

-------- . . . --------

CASE STUDY

Case 19C   Farewell
Alison, 55, a Telecom personnel officer, had recently separated from Lachlan, 60, an alcohol-imbibing construction supervisor. I had seen the two of them weekly for three therapy sessions, which appeared to help them let go of each other emotionally. Initially, Alison had wanted to leave and Lachlan had asked for reconciliation. They said they were pleased to have raised two daughters, Sandra, 30, and Kirsten, 25, to successful adulthood. I admired their dedication and suggested that perhaps all their energy had gone into parenting? Would they take themselves out for a celebratory meal and discuss if there was 'life after the children'?

At our next weekly meeting, Lachlan and Alison said that they had gone out to a restaurant, that the food was awful, and that, when they did not talk about their daughters, they found that they had little to say to each other.

I then asked Alison to argue the case for reconciliation, and Lachlan to offer an argument for separation. After attempting to do this exercise, they had both agreed that there really was not much territory that they shared, and that they would do better to separate amicably. Lachlan moved north to Queensland to seek further employment. Alison attended a final session to say farewell.

'You know, Dr Gunzburg', Alison said, 'I was born in Glasgow. When I was a young girl, during World War Two, I was taken to the Scotland countryside away from the major areas of enemy bombing. I remember one night when the husband of the lady who was caring for me returned home. He was a soldier on leave and he had come home drunk. On finding his wife away, he thought that she must be having a good time with the American GIs who were stationed nearby, and he grabbed an axe and began smashing the house to pieces. I was so terrified that I hid in the wardrobe under the stairs for hours. I was very scared of being on my own after that, and when Lachlan proposed to me, I accepted immediately. Although I knew he loved his beer, he was gentle and not demanding. But it is funny, now that I am 55, I feel I am able to stand on my own two feet. I am no longer frightened. I am going to explore the world to see what it is like out there on my own.'

——————————— . . . ———————————

Catastrophic loss **20**

In this chapter clients identified their losses as 'catastrophic', and said that they were overwhelmed by a multitude of feelings related to them.

——————————— . . . ———————————

CASE STUDY

Case 20A   Retarded

Wendy, 35, a secondary-school drama teacher, felt that her life had come to an end. She had left her alcohol-abusing, physically violent husband Terry, 37, a panel beater, 12 months previously. I had actually seen Wendy and Terry as a couple during their struggles. He was very much a Ramboesque figure: brusque, male-oriented, quite insensitive to the needs of his wife and their daughter Terri, 3. Terry had left a previous girlfriend and daughter before he had met Wendy. Terry had claimed, during our conversations together, that he had no problems and that it was all right if Wendy came to talk to me and I could make her see some sense. Wendy and I had met for some weeks after that, discussing the dangers of remaining in this abusive family situation: the lack of safety and security, the limiting of her and Terri's autonomy, and the modelling to her daughter that men are permitted to assault their female partners.

Wendy had eventually left Terry during her second pregnancy. While she was in labour, the fetal heartbeat disappeared, and the baby, Josephine, was born severely brain damaged, due to cerebral hypoxia.

Wendy was stressed over a number of consequences regarding this tragedy. First, Terry denied paternity and refused to pay any maintenance. Wendy was pursuing this matter legally. Secondly, acquaintances kept saying: 'You never know, dear, she could always improve. You never know what is around the corner.' Their denial made it difficult for Wendy to come to terms with her situation. Lastly, Wendy's sister had been born mentally retarded, and even though her doctors had assured Wendy that Josephine's damage was due to mechanical causes (the umbilical cord having been twisted tightly around the baby's neck), Wendy was concerned about any hereditary trait being passed on eventually through Terri.

Our fortnightly meetings became very much a time during which Wendy was cradled in her grief. We discussed finding some nourishing social outlets and supports, ways to deal with community insensitivity and the sometimes intrusive and demanding nature of hospital staff, and eventually our conversation turned to the spiritual.

'I have been exploring various religions to find a meaning for Josephine's birth', Wendy said. 'Perhaps she was really evil in a previous life, and her karma has caught up with her, and this retardation is her punishment?'

'But she could not have been totally evil', I responded, 'because she has been given you, as a mother, to love her.' Wendy smiled.

A fortnight later, Wendy said: 'Terri hung herself'. I almost fell off my chair in shock. Three-year-old children do not suicide!?!

'Oh, she is all right now', Wendy continued. 'She was playing on school equipment and her bicycle safety helmet got caught in the bars of the climbing frame and she throttled herself. I was looking the other way, at some other kids playing, at that moment. If the headmaster had not seen her, she would have been dead for sure. I wonder if God is punishing me for some past misdeed?'

'But God saw fit to save Terri', I replied. 'Perhaps the message is to go ahead, just love your daughters and raise them as best you can, and God will help you through the tricky bits?' Another smile from Wendy . . . and so our banter continues, considering practical care where appropriate, illuminating shadows that might otherwise darken, with a brighter, Divine light.

   . . .

CASE STUDY

Case 20B   The exhibitionist
Valentino, 21, an invalid pensioner, had been in trouble, yet again, exposing his genitals to hospital staff. He did this two or three times weekly. Val had been involved in a motor vehicle accident when he was 17 years old. He had been intoxicated with alcohol, marijuana and amphetamines when the car he was driving ploughed into the front of a truck. Comatose for several months, and eventually requiring

neurosurgery which only partially controlled his disabling limb and head tremors and spasticity, Val was confined to a wheelchair, and required even the most basic tasks to be done for him. Besides his exposure, Val would offend by swearing continually at his mother, Maria, and caretaker, Ted, and he would frequently proposition nursing staff.

I decided to see Val weekly. We talked about his fantasies: he was going to walk out of his chair and cure the world of AIDS. His mother was worried because Val would share these hopes with all and sundry. I praised Val for his idealism and encouraged him to keep these ideas for discussion within our meetings. I felt that the general community would have great difficulty accommodating to his different way of thinking. I could well understand how after such a catastrophic accident he would hope for a major change in his life, but many others would not be able to understand his thoughts as an expression of that hope. They might consider him a little crazy, and so perhaps it was better to be cautious and not talk to everyone about it.

Val told me that he showed his genitals regularly to others, and loved playing with this area of his body, because it was the only part of him that worked one hundred percent! I said that I accepted one hundred percent that Val should be able enjoy his sexuality, and that sexual pleasuring was generally regarded as a private activity. Would he agree to enjoy himself in the privacy of his room? We discussed for a while movies that Val could watch on the video while he was enjoying himself. He said that his mother was against him watching sexy movies, but during our conversation Val showed considerable sensitivity in his selection of movies, spurning those which included violence or demeaning actions to women. I talked with Maria on Val's need for sexually explicit videos, and commended him to her that he did show a great deal of respect for women, and Maria agreed not to hassle Val about his hobby.

Some months later, I received a letter from Val's general practitioner, stating that his exposure in the last month had been zero.

I saw Val weekly for about eight months, then fortnightly, and now, 18 months later, we are meeting monthly. He has received his compensation payout and now lives in an extension built next to Maria's house. His disparagement of Maria has ceased, although Ted, his caretaker, says that Val still occasionally gives him a hard time, swearing at him and being uncooperative. Val still exposes, perhaps every three or four months, after which he appears genuinely remorseful. There is no doubt that the times of restraint between exposure are slowly increasing. As far as I know, Val enjoys himself immensely with his movies in private!

————————— · · · —————————

———————— · · · ————————

CASE STUDY

Case 20C   Robbery under arms
Damien, 26, a rigger, was in tears after having been caught and charged with armed robbery.

'It is not fair', he said. 'I got married to Karen (22) a year ago. She got pregnant, without my knowledge, and immediately shot through. Then the next thing I know is I get a letter from the Taxation Department telling me that they are going to take eighteen percent of my wages to pay maintenance for a son that I have not seen. I thought, bugger this! No one is giving a damn about me, why should I give a damn about anybody else. I will go and do a 'job' and get some quick cash to help pay the debt.'

Damien had disguised himself as an invalid in a wheelchair, taken himself to a post office, grabbed a money satchel from a female employee's hands, sprayed her in the face with a can of aerosol when she resisted him, and raced off down the street, firing a couple of shots into the air as he was being chased. The police had apprehended Damien and recovered the money that he had stolen 24 hours later.

We agreed to meet weekly and it became reasonably clear that Damien was genuinely remorseful. He had pleaded guilty, was prepared to serve a gaol term if necessary, and was currently involved in community works, doing voluntary repairs. I asked him to make a contract of non-abuse, and to write an account of the woman whom he had attacked and how she might now be feeling. Damien wrote:

> When I think about how the woman I robbed and assaulted would have felt, both at the time of the incident and after, I find it hard to continue contemplating the whole thing and not just switch off. I guess she would have felt a mixture of emotions. Her initial reaction would have been shock, then fear, outrage, anger, a sense of violation, and a lingering feeling of no longer being safe going about her daily business.
>
> I think her first reaction would have been shock. Obviously, she had not contemplated the thought of being robbed or she would not have carried such a large amount of money in such a casual manner. Because she performed the same task day in and day out for probably years on end she would have built up a feeling of complacency about the money. No longer was it thirty thousand dollars cash she was handling but only a calico bag with some colored paper in it. So when some one leapt from a wheelchair, and grabbed the bag, it was a shock.
>
> After the first feeling of surprise had passed and the realisation

that she was being robbed came home to her, her next feeling might have been fear. Right in her own workplace, she was being robbed . . . the feeling of unreality: 'this cannot be happening to me'.

This must have turned to outrage because she struggled with me over the money. After I sprayed her face she let go, fear from my assault overcoming her outrage. As I ran out of the building, she chased me calling for some one to stop me. Maybe she felt some feeling of fear for her job because she had lost so much of her employer's money. Perhaps she had been violating security procedures by moving the cash like that and now was concerned for her job.

Her face would have stung from the spray. Her eyes would have watered and she would have sneezed a lot. Anger might have overcome her; the audacity of somebody sitting in a wheelchair and robbing her in broad daylight; that she was going about her normal lawful job, and she was robbed.

After the other feelings had passed, the one that would, I think, last longest would be fear: the feeling of not being safe anywhere. When I was granted bail, she and her husband complained to the police. Apparently they felt I was a threat to their safety and would want some sort of revenge. Long after the event had passed, the fear would stick in her mind.

I continue to see Damien weekly, waiting for his court case to eventuate. I use Alan Jenkins's model (Jenkins, 1990) for violent men, focusing our conversation on the feelings of the survivors of violation, rather than those of the perpetrators, and praising Damien for his continued efforts in becoming a responsible man. (At his trial, Damien was sentenced to two and a half years imprisonment. We correspond regularly, and he reports that he has begun a tertiary degree in business studies and is learning another language in preparation for his future after release.)

——————————— · · · ———————————

CASE STUDY

Case 20D   Breathless
Deidre, 53, formerly a clerical manager for a brokers' firm but given early retirement 11 months previously due to increasing disability with emphysema, said that she had come to the end of her tether. Widowed 11 years earlier, she lived on the second story of a block of units and was finding herself becoming too breathless to climb the stairs. Her son Brett, 24, a gardener, and his wife Celia, 20, a secretary, lived

in a property in Brighton which Deidre owned. Deidre wanted to sell both the Brighton house that Brett and Celia rented from her and her own unit and move into residence into the country to spend her last few years peacefully. Brett and Celia had told Deidre that they would attempt to have her certified mentally incapable if she sold 'their' home. Deidre was both furious and despairing.

Another area in which Deidre wanted to change was her smoking. Previously a smoker of 30 to 40 cigarettes daily, she had all but given up this habit years ago. She now smoked only three to four cigarettes daily, yet felt she should let go of it altogether for her own good.

Over several weekly meetings, I encouraged Deidre to reflect on her life. A deeply spiritual Catholic, she was offended that she had done so much for Brett and that he was now so disrespectful towards her. Yet Deidre persisted in defending and protecting him. Deidre's daughter, Jenny, 18, a biology student, was also encouraging her mother to 'let go', sell the properties, and focus on her own needs.

'If you keep always making allowances for Brett', Jenny had said in a joint therapy session, 'he will never grow up. He will always want to lean on me after you have passed on. He has to learn how to fend for himself!'

Deidre said that she always had a hard time saying no to anyone, and I asked her to list those areas in which she would like to say no in 1992. Deidre's list read:

Things I would like to say no to –
The dishonesty of most people.
Giving in to my illness, emphysema.
Brett's dependence on me, both financially and emotionally.
Celia's insolence and disrespect.
Their apparent heartlessness.

Our conversation turned to ways that Deidre might assert herself towards Brett and Celia:

1. Normalizing their comments:
   Brett: How will we get on if you sell the house?
   Deidre: Yes, I know it is quite difficult for young people at the moment, but you are in a good job, and I can see you building up your assets over a few years.
2. Validating their feelings:
   Celia: I think that you are being totally unfair, not helping your son.
   Deidre: I can hear that you are upset about the future and you would like me to help you out.
3. Countering disrespect:
   Brett: I think that you are being an absolute bitch.
   Deidre: I am prepared to talk with you about your problems, Brett,

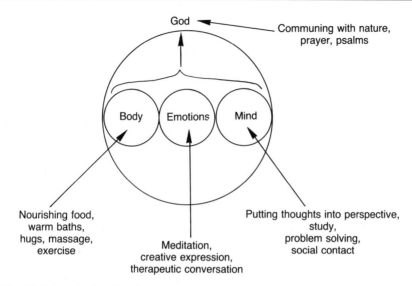

Fig. 20.1 John's drawing for Deidre.

but I will not be treated disrespectfully. So long for now (ending telephone call, or leaving).

We talked about ways in which Deidre might care for herself to nourish her spirit, and I drew for her an illustration (Fig. 20.1). I also asked Deidre if she would write out a contract of non-abuse. She shared it with me at our next session.

Contract of Non-abuse
I . . . (Deidre Simpson) . . . have made a very firm commitment to myself not to take abuse from any person, being male or female, adult or child, for the rest of my life. With the help of. . . . (Dr John, Jenny, and my dear friends). . . . I will get over any guilty feelings that I may have.
Signed: D. Simpson
Witnessed: J.C. Gunzburg

Deidre has given up smoking, commenced a course in philosophy, taken up swimming and started legal proceedings to sell the Brighton house. She has placed both her contract of non-abuse and my illustration on her kitchen wall.

When I read the contract of non-abuse, I commented: 'Brett certify you as mentally incapable? Your contract is just about the sanest thing that I have ever read!'

— . . . —

REFERENCE

Jenkins, A. (1990) *Invitations to Responsibility*, Dulwich Centre Publications, Adelaide.

Epilogue

It is March, 1992 . . . The Iraq – UN Gulf War concluded in February 1991, with an estimated 150 000 Iraquis, 30 000 Kuwaitis and several hundred United Nations forces slain. When a friend asked me, during the conflict, if I had any family in the war zone, I replied: 'Yes, Iraquis, Kuwaitis, Israelis, Americans, British, Egyptians, Saudis, Australians, Belgians, French, Italians, Canadians . . . they are all my family'.

Over the past year, the economic recession has worsened. A popular bumper sticker appearing in the USA reads: 'Saddam Hussein still has his job . . . do you?' Cyclones have ravaged Bangladesh, leaving approximately 100 000 individuals dead. The Soviet Union has crumbled and Muscovites are starving. Fighting in Yugoslavia and the Baltic states has claimed tens of thousands of casualties. Neo-fascist groups are fomenting nationalism, racism and antisemitism in Germany and Russia.

April, 1992 . . . unemployment in Australia has reached 11.6%. In Victoria, the body of a teenage schoolgirl missing for a year and presumed murdered by her kidnapper, 'Mr Cruel', has been found. A convicted rapist, released after four months' gaol, has sought revenge against the woman who brought him to trial, and violated her yet again. Buckingham Palace confirms the separation of the Duke and Duchess of York.

May, 1992 . . . Los Angeles is reeling after racial riots which have left some 50 persons dead, 3000 wounded, and half a billion dollars' worth of property damaged. Rival guerrilla factions are battling for the control of Kabul. A sharp rise in the incidence of HIV infections has alarmed the Japanese. The collapse of a makeshift football stadium in Corsica has killed ten spectators.

More loss, more grieving. . . .

There are great social and political deconstructions taking place all around us. Will we – the politicians, media magnates, union bosses and multinational corporations – underworld associations and central intelligence agencies – revolutionary councils and loyalist supporters – religious leaders, scientists, social thinkers, literati and academics – therapists and clients – affirm our brothers and sisters within the human family, so that we are left unmolested in our autonomy and protected in our physical and spiritual integrity? Will we mutually reconstruct a brighter and more hopeful future? Or will our 'new world order' be simply a different set of powerful institutions participating in the same old habitual patterns of violence and exploitation? 'Plus ça change, plus c'est la même chose . . . the more things change, the more they remain the same.'

STONE SOUP

A mediaevial European traveller at an inn overheard the cook's conversation with the innkeeper that she was having difficulty making soup for the evening meal. No matter how hard she tried, she did not seem to be able to create a wholesome flavour on this particular occasion.

The traveller, who was grateful that his hosts had found him a bed in their crowded premises on sudden notice, said to them: 'I have a recipe which has never failed me. It is called 'Stone Soup'. Would you like me to try it for you?'

The innkeeper and cook, fearing the anger of their hungry clients if they were not able to satisfy them, both readily agreed. The traveller heated up a large pot of water, took a beautiful silk scarf from his pocket, and unwrapped it to reveal a large, smooth pebble. He placed the pebble into the pot of boiling water, and then began to add various ingredients: onions, which he first simmered in some oil in a pan, carrots, potatoes, tomatoes, leeks, mushrooms and spices. All the time, the traveller stirred the pot with a large shank bone, making sure that the meaty end was always immersed in the bubbling mixture. After an hour, the traveller served the soup in the inn's finest crockery, and the clients all praised the innkeeper and cook for their most delicious fare. The traveller very carefully cleaned the pebble, and placed it, within its scarf, in his pocket once more.

The central theme – the stone – in this book, unchanging and per-sistent, is unresolved grief, yet there are a number of other themes that might be considered stones in their own right: safety, autonomy and choices; gender issues, and the struggle against patriarchy, inequity and abuse; affirmation, deconstruction and reconstruction; exploring and stimulating clients' creative resources. Our therapeutic frame-works: psychoanalytic, behavioural, systemic, feminist, narrative, etc., may also be considered as stones, adding a balance, stability and continuity to the therapeutic process. Whatever the central theme, whatever the stone used, it is, I believe, the mutual contribution of therapist and client, our essences and eccentricities and ethical awareness, that can be regarded as adding spice and variety to our therapeutic soup. It is our whole range of human qualities that we offer, personal, ethnic and cultural, that can make for a flavoursome and delicious experience.

And so, to an ending . . . not an easy thing to achieve after having been involved so intimately in this creative activity – conversing, writing, further conversations, and more writing – over such a lengthy period of time, and requiring some grieving of its own. Here is a poem which I composed during a walk in the Australian bush. I share it quite often with clients during our final meeting. They express fears of the journey ahead, about 'life after therapy', and I offer the lines as an equalizer, a means of incorporating them, me, us, within the human family.

THE JOURNEY

I had a vision that was not purely fancy;
Above the world I hovered as a spirit
Free from the binds of 'this all too solid flesh'
And from my vantage point was able to observe
A trail below me well-covered with brown dirt;
A winding path that wavered in its width,
Here large enough for a human form to pass,
There narrowed, stopping passage of all but smallest
Creatures. Rocks rough-hewn by winter's frosty
Morn lay strewn, grey granite cracked and worn;
Scattered stones and tufts of withered grass,
And shiny pieces of broken glass. Wasps
And mayflies flew there, gumtrees drooped, dried
Bushes scratched the naked legs of travellers
Passing along who paused to wince. The sun
Shone down and raised a sweat on necks and backs,
Moist patches spread on shorts and shirts. All sorts
Of hats were worn to cover aching heads from heat.
A motley of shapes and sizes trekked that track;
Young lads who wandered off into the scrub
Were called by snarling mothers: 'Andrew, don't you
Go too far!' The men came stumbling, bruising
Knees and cursing softly, hoping for a breeze
To cool them down; the women wilting, fumbling
With anxious fingers, fiddling in bags for tissues
To wipe the plump, wet cheeks of babes; the grizzle

Of a fallen toddler, and tousle-haired sisters singing
Gaily a nursery rhyme, hands held. And as this multitude
Proceeded on their journey, the bushland sounded
With their conversations of money and friendships and leisure,
With good-humoured chuckles, chatting and moans of ill-temper,
Young lover's snippets and dreary whistles of boredom.
Incessantly, inexorably, the flow of persons continued
Along this well-worked route that led to forests afar.
Sometimes they happened upon a stagnant pool
Where they would dip their feet and, with wet kerchief
On brow, would soothe their fevers. Occasionally running
Streams provided drink and, if their luck was fair,
Blackberries were there to eat. When there was shade
They took it, otherwise enduring harsh open spaces
With resignation and the chance of a better track ahead.
They progressed as best as they knew how with whatever
Skills they possessed; some faltered, halting on the way,
Then moving on, others determined to go no further,
But for all, there was no possibility of retreat,
No option for return;
For this was their only journey,
It was their life.

Appendix A Some useful questions to facilitate the therapy of unresolved grief

---

DEFINING THE PROBLEM

How did you get to hear of me?
How do you come to be here?
What is happening with you?
What is troubling you?
What are your struggles?
What are you stuck with?
Which area of stress most bothers you?
How might I be of help to you?
How could things be different for you?
Would you write a few lines (draw a picture, compose a poem or song) for the next session, describing what it is like for you at the moment?
Would your partner, family come to a future session of therapy with you?

EXPLORING THE CONTEXT

When did you first feel like this?
What was happening at the time?
Where did you learn to do that?
Where did that come from?
What do you think that means?
I note that today's date is close to that of your parent's death (your divorce, your redundancy, etc.) last year; could you be suffering anniversary blues?
What role do you think you played in the family in which you grew up?
What unreasonable expectation of your family of origin is most bothersome to you?
Who, of all those persons in your family of origin, was there to tend to your youthful needs adequately and appropriately?

How have you been able to cope with the demands and competition within your original family?

Where was the opportunity for privacy and adolescent reflection in your family of origin?

Would you write a conversation with your grieving self, who has missed out on many nourishing moments within your original family?

Is that why you are so scared, and vomiting? Is there so much sick feeling inside you, that once started, you may never stop?

Was this one of the reasons that one parent was so angry at the other? Did one parent slot the other into a subordinate role?

Have you internalized the critical part of one parent and partnered an authoritarian person very much like the other parent? Is this contributing to your inner conflict?

Do you think that your partner is inherently evil or is he following a well-learned patriarchal script?

Are your panic attacks and headaches and neck pains more to do with cementing your relationship to your partner, than with your work?

Would you read this story during a quiet moment with your parent and let me know your opinion of it?

Would you see the film of . . . ?

Would you write a letter to God to find out why He has said 'No!' to you so often?

Would you both draw some pictures of the monsters that are disturbing your peace?

Would you draw a 'rogues' gallery' of all the partners who have mistreated you in the past?

Will you write a letter to your 'internal critic' and find out what it wants of you?

WHEN PHYSICAL ABUSE IS INVOLVED

QUESTIONS TO THE ABUSER

Will you stop the physical abuse?

Will you make a commitment not to physically abuse your partner/child in the future?

What will life be like if you maintain your commitment not to physically abuse your partner/child?

Do you think that you are treating your partner similarly to the way one of your parents treated the other?

QUESTIONS TO THE ABUSED

Will you protect your child from physical abuse?

Can your parent protect you from further abuse?

Do you know the telephone number of a refuge where you and your child can go?

Is your partner's current behaviour consistent with wanting a more rewarding relationship?

Are you trying to preserve the ideal of an intact family at the risk of bodily injury?

Can you find safety in a life of your own, perhaps with the support of friends, rather than an abusive primary relationship?

Would you compose a letter to your abusive relative and tell him/her what you have just told to me?

Would you take some time out to draw your experiences of the rape?

Is some of your anger now inwardly channelled and contributing to your low spirits?

Would you make a commitment to contest any person who attempts to abuse you?

QUESTIONS TO COUPLES WHO HAVE MADE A COMMITMENT TO A NON-ABUSIVE RELATIONSHIP

Would you try together to identify some of the trigger points at which you start quarrelling?

Would you turn your words into praise for your partner's victories whenever he holds back from violence, rather than reminding your partner of those times he has lashed out?

Would you draw the demons that you see within each other and experience within yourselves when you are angry?

WHEN DIVORCE/SEPARATION IS INVOLVED

QUESTIONS TO THE CHILDREN

Is your family better or worse since the separation?

Do you see the parent who lives away regularly on access? Do you want to? Does the parent who lives away know that you want to see them?

Do you think that you drove Mum or Dad away? If you had behaved better, might they might have stayed together? Do you feel it is your fault that they have separated?

Do you think that some of the emotions that you feel because one parent blamed you for the other parent leaving have become stuck inside of you, and are not able to get out?

Do you believe that your custodial parent is committed to caring for you until adulthood?

QUESTIONS TO THE ADULTS

Did your parents, in parting when you were young, sensitize you to the risks and possible losses inherent in intimate relationships?

Was one parent overcome with grief when the separation occurred?

Perhaps this parent felt immobilized and needed your young strength to help him/her succeed?

Would things have been better/worse if your parents had parted during your infancy?

Do you think that you married your partner to gain some of the emotional nourishment that you had been denied earlier on?

Would you remember back to the time you were courting, and think about what you had hoped for at the beginning of your acquaintance?

Would you write the pros and cons of continuing a relationship with your partner?

How would you benefit from separation?

Over what aspects of the past relationship would you grieve?

What memories would you take with you to nourish your future?

Would you plan a time schedule and budget for separation?

How can you contest your partner's 'guilt-hooks' and vengeful remarks?

What 'unspeakable things' have you really done to drive your former partner away?

Is your former partner behaving with goodwill towards your family?

Is your former partner being respectful and sensitive to the needs of other family members?

Would you contact your former partner, who broke off your relationship unilaterally, and clarify the reasons as to why he/she acted in this way?

Would you make a specific list of ten curses to fall upon your former partner?

Would you compose a few lines for your Valentine's card to let your former partner know that she/he is indeed loved, without raising any false hopes for the future?

WHEN CHEMICAL ABUSE IS INVOLVED

Did your family, frustrated by your parent's alcohol abuse, agree to a secret agenda not to comment about it?

Is your parent/partner's behaviour (drinking, leaving), a response to your actions, or is he/she responsible for his/her own actions and choices?

Would you list the ways that you have tried to tackle your 'emptiness'?

Would you write a conversation with your rage: what is it doing for you? What would happen if you became less forceful? How can you and your rage strike a bargain so that you do not have to drink, either for comfort or to temper your anger?

WHEN PHYSICAL ILLNESS IS INVOLVED

What if your illness is not caused by your quarrels with your family? What if it is bad luck that you have now got this disease, and your anger at your family is getting in the way of any chance of reconciliation that you might have with them before you die?
What do you hope for in the time left to you?
Are you hopeful of something better?
Would you write a letter to the 'healthy person you were' saying goodbye?

WHEN REMARRIED/BLENDED FAMILIES ARE INVOLVED

QUESTIONS TO THE CHILDREN

Is there so much fighting all the time in the family, to make sure that everyone is getting a fair share of the attention?
What would your parents do if you pushed them just that bit too far?
Do you feel confident about reaching adulthood? Is it worthwhile to grow to adulthood, with all the struggles that you have already witnessed within your families? Is adulthood all hard work and sorrows, with little fun and rewards?
Would you do a sketch of the family as you see them?

QUESTIONS TO THE PARTNERS

What is it specifically that troubles you about your relationship with your partner?
Why did you originally choose each other as partners?
How can you assess your partner's ability to make commitment to an intimacy?
Do you interpret your partner's wishes for closeness as clinging?
Would you be prepared to experiment together as to just how you might achieve closeness and permanency within your relationship?
What shared experiences might continue to nourish you?
How can you intrigue your partner into a different and more rewarding kind of encounter?
How can you both find your own roots within your relationship?
Would you do some nice things for each other, and see if each of you notices what the other person does?
Would you both consider some ways to fire up your match?

What would happen if you reversed roles?

What sacrifices are you prepared to make for each other's comfort, safety and fun?

Would you continue to plan a direction that offers safety for you both?

How might you achieve mutuality and equity in your negotiations with your partner?

How can you learn to compete successfully with your partner?

How can you ask for what you want without feeling guilty?

Are your arguments involving you with each other or creating distance?

Is it easier to argue with your partner than to be sad?

Have you been working under such duress that there has been little time for fun?

Have all your energies gone into parenting?

Are some of your current emotions grief for lost moments, opportunities for intimacy, peace of mind growth?

Will you discuss the issue of whether you are to have children or not?

Would the two of you sit down, for a couple of hours each week, and talk about how one of you could support the other in the parenting of the other's children?

Is your relationship another child, to be nurtured into growth?

Would you write to your parent describing how you are experiencing your relationship with your partner differently to the one you had with your parent?

Would you write an essay describing the struggle within your relationships?

Would you both write a bill of divorce from your parents/in-laws for the next session?

Would you trust your partner enough to organize a spontaneous weekend entertainment without your partner knowing what it is beforehand?

Would you give each other a massage?

Would you plan an hour a week 'not being nasty' to each other?

Would you make a list of what is going right for you?

Would the two of you do a trade? Would you . . . ?

Would you take yourselves out for a meal to celebrate raising your offspring to adulthood and discuss if there is 'life after the children'?

Would you prepare yourself a special meal, a treat, and while eating it, occasionally feed one another a tasty morsel?

WHEN INCEST IS INVOLVED

QUESTIONS TO THE ABUSER

Will you stop the sexual abuse?

Will you make a commitment not to sexually abuse your child in the future?

What will life be like if you maintain your commitment not to sexually abuse your child?

Would you write a description of what responsibility means to you and how you can help the person you sexually abused grow away from your abuse of her?

Would you write a description of how the person you sexually abused feels?

Will you continue to live apart from the family to maintain the safety of the person you sexually abused?

What ordinary activities might you participate in with the family to restore stability?

QUESTIONS TO THE NON-ABUSING ADULT

Will you protect your child?

Do you know the telephone number of a refuge where you and your child could go?

QUESTIONS TO THE ABUSED CHILD

What has to happen so that you can now feel safe?

Do you think that your mother can now protect you?

Do you think that the person who sexually abused you can change?

Can this person become responsible? Do you know what this person is doing to learn responsibility?

WHEN AFFAIRS ARE INVOLVED

Do the triangular relationships within which you live prevent you from gaining the information you need to know before making a couples commitment?

Do you believe that you will ever maintain a monogamous relationship?

How can you make a permanent and enduring commitment to a partner?

Should you proceed with reconciliation with your former partner, or follow a future with your new friend?

If you were prepared to invite your former partner or your new friend to therapy, which one would attend?

Would you compose a list of qualities that you, your former partner, and your new friend have contributed to your relationships?

Should you be residing with your former partner, offering him/her false hope, if you have definitely decided to leave?

Did you have an affair to learn new information and bring this into your primary intimacy?

Was your affair a rebellion against your parents' values?

What would have happened if you had taken a lover of different faith to yours?

Do you expect Divine retribution for your adultery?

How does your client with whom you are professionally involved and having an affair feel? Will you stop this professional abuse?

Will you make a commitment not to professionally abuse your clients in the future? What will life be like if you maintain your commitment not to professionally abuse your clients? How will you redress your professional abuse of your clients?

What would happen if you carried out your one-night homosexual affair and found that you really liked the experience better than your current partner?

What will your partner have to do now, after his/her affair, to restore your trust?

How can your sense of 'belonging' in your relationship now be restored after her/his affair?

WHEN DEATH IS INVOLVED

How will you manage at your partner's funeral?

Do you need to let your child experience the privacy of his grief for his deceased parent?

What will happen if you do carry out your plans to suicide?

Does the presence of your parent's ghost now plague you with panicky feelings, headaches and muscle tensions?

Would you look at some photographs of your deceased partner, prepare a list of your memories, and choose those that you want to keep secret and those that you might reveal?

Would you bring some of your deceased parent's drawings to the next session?

Would you write yourself a letter from your deceased partner advising you on how to cope in this difficult situation?

Would you draw a picture in memory of your partner's beloved deceased pet?

Would you re-dream the scene of your relative's death and visualize a different ending?

Would you visit your relative's grave and say goodbye?

WHEN FOSTERING/ADOPTION IS INVOLVED

QUESTIONS TO FOSTERING/ADOPTING PARENTS

Would you and your adopted child go out for coffee one evening and discuss what you want from each other?

Would you list the happy times that you do remember spending with your adopted child?

Will you hold a special dinner to welcome your new foster-child?

QUESTIONS FOR FOSTERED/ADOPTED CHILDREN

Would you plan a special treat for your adopting parent, something really subtle, and see if your parent detects it?

Will you compose a poem for your foster family describing how you feel about them?

Will your foster family respect expression of your feelings?

Would you furnish your new bedroom to your own unique style?

WHEN EXAMINING OPTIONS FOR THE FUTURE

What will it be like for you when life is better?

What is happening now that life is better?

Was there ever a time when life was better?

Were there people in the past who helped life to be better?

Are they available to you now?

If, by magic, you woke up, and life was better, how would you know?

What character from a film, book, opera etc, would you most like to be like?

If you wanted to change your name, which one would you choose?

Does the way you present yourself frighten others a little?

What bridges are there to cross for you to succeed in your search for a fulfilling life?

When do you think that your wandering will come to an end and you will 'be at home'?

Will you imagine a different future?

Which chosen scenario will leave you a bitter old person?

Will you reach old age with your potential intact?

What messages of self-esteem will you give to yourself?

How will you take charge of your life?

How will you ask for what you want more effectively?

What will have to happen for you to feel cherished again?

How will you become the central character in a script of your own choosing?

What decisions do you need to discover a more authentic lifestyle?

Will you compose a self-advertisement for the next session?

Will you list ten ways to boost your confidence when feeling low?

Will you make a list of things that you want to achieve in your life?

Will you write a description of what it means to be an adequate parent?

Will you write a letter before your next access telling your parent just how the weekend could be made more fun if you spent better quality time together?

Will you gather the necessary information you need to know to pursue a career in . . . ?

Will you seek personal integration and fulfilment in the pursuit of social justice through action groups, such as MASA (Men against sexual assault) and TAGS (Towards a gentler society)?

Will you write a conversation with your developing self, who wishes to explore more rewarding directions for the future?

Will you talk to your partner about your future dreams together?

What aspect of therapy has been most helpful to you?

This list is by no means exhaustive! Readers are encouraged to explore and play with the list, exchanging questions from one category to another, adding and subtracting items according to their own preference.

Appendix B Some themes to weave into the therapeutic conversation

Entries in *italics* are case studies.

Index